Microsoft

Microsoft
SharePoint 2016
Step by Step

Olga Londer
Penelope Coventry

PUBLISHED BY
Microsoft Press
A division of Microsoft Corporation
One Microsoft Way
Redmond, Washington 98052-6399

Library of Congress Control Number: 2015938172
ISBN: 978-0-7356-9776-8

Printed and bound in the United States of America.

1   16

Microsoft Press books are available through booksellers and distributors worldwide. If you need support related to this book, email Microsoft Press Support at mspinput@microsoft.com. Please tell us what you think of this book at http://aka.ms/tellpress.

This book is provided "as-is" and expresses the author's views and opinions. The views, opinions, and information expressed in this book, including URL and other Internet website references, may change without notice.

Some examples depicted herein are provided for illustration only and are fictitious. No real association or connection is intended or should be inferred.

Microsoft and the trademarks listed at www.microsoft.com on the "Trademarks" webpage are trademarks of the Microsoft group of companies. All other marks are property of their respective owners.

Acquisitions and Developmental Editor: Rosemary Caperton
Editorial Production: Online Training Solutions, Inc. (OTSI)
Technical Reviewer: Chris Casingena
Copyeditor: Kathy Krause (OTSI)
Indexer: Susie Carr (OTSI)
Cover: Twist Creative • Seattle

Contents

Give us feedback
Tell us what you think of this book and help Microsoft improve our products for you. Thank you!
https://aka.ms/tellpress

Create and manage sites **273**

Work with wikis, blogs, and community sites **323**

Manage work tasks 365

Work with workflows 391

Give us feedback
Tell us what you think of this book and help Microsoft improve our products for you. Thank you!
https://aka.ms/tellpress

Introduction

Welcome! This *Step by Step* book has been designed so you can read it from the beginning to learn about SharePoint 2016 and then build your skills as you learn to perform increasingly specialized procedures. Or, if you prefer, you can jump in wherever you need ready guidance for performing tasks. The how-to steps are delivered crisply and concisely—just the facts. You'll also find informative, full-color graphics that support the instructional content.

Who this book is for

Microsoft SharePoint 2016 Step by Step is designed for use as a learning and reference resource by beginning-level and intermediate-level users who want to use Share-Point Server 2016 and/or SharePoint Online to create, modify, share, and manage sites, webpages, documents, and other content and capabilities; find information and people; and collaborate with others. *Microsoft SharePoint 2016 Step by Step* offers a comprehensive look at the capabilities and features of SharePoint Server 2016 and SharePoint Online that most people will use most frequently. The content of the book is designed to be useful for people who have previously used earlier versions of SharePoint and for people who are discovering SharePoint for the first time.

The *Step by Step* approach

The book's coverage is divided into 14 chapters representing skill set areas. Chapters 1 through 3 address foundation skills such as navigating a SharePoint site and working with documents and information in lists and libraries. Chapters 4 through 6 show you how to make lists and libraries work for you, how to work with search, and how to use My Site and Microsoft OneDrive for Business. Chapters 7 and 8 focus on working with webpages and creating and managing SharePoint sites. Chapter 9 considers the social capabilities of SharePoint 2016, such as community sites, blogs, and wikis. Chapters 10 and 11 show you how to use business process features such as tasks and workflows.

Chapters 12 and 13 cover using SharePoint with Microsoft Office applications and the power of business intelligence. Finally, Chapter 14 drills into content management and monitoring.

> ✅ **TIP** The first part of Chapter 1 contains introductory information that will primarily be of interest to readers who are new to SharePoint. If you have worked with SharePoint before, you might want to skip past that material.

Each chapter is divided into topics that group related skills. Each topic includes expository information followed by generic procedures. At the end of the chapter, you'll find a series of practice tasks you can complete on your own by using the skills taught in the chapter. The practice files for the practice tasks are available from this book's website.

Download the practice files

Before you can complete the practice tasks in this book, you need to download the book's practice files to your computer from *https://aka.ms/SP2016SBS/downloads*. Follow the instructions on the webpage to install the files on your computer in the default practice file folder structure.

> ⚠ **IMPORTANT** The SharePoint 2016 software is not available from the book's website. You must have access to a SharePoint Server 2016 deployment before performing the practice tasks in this book. Alternatively, you can use SharePoint Online for most practice tasks in this book.

Whenever possible, we start each set of practice tasks with a standard SharePoint 2016 team site, which occasionally must be a top-level team site. If you perform all the practice tasks in all the chapters, you might choose to start with a new team site for every chapter.

However, the practice tasks in Chapters 2 and 5 require additional settings for their practice sites. This is where the starter WSP files will come in handy. The starter WSP files contain lists, libraries, files, and pages that are needed for the practice tasks in the chapter. If you have sufficient rights, you can create a new practice site from the chapter's starter WSP file by following the detailed step-by-step installation instructions in the setup guide that is provided in the chapter's practice folder.

The following table lists the practice files supplied for this book.

Chapter	Folder	File
1: Introduction to SharePoint 2016	Ch01	None
2: Navigate SharePoint sites	Ch02	Chapter2_Setup.pdf Chapter2FacilitiesSubsite.wsp Chapter2TeamSite.wsp Chapter2TravelSubsite.wsp WideWorldTravelGuidelines.docx
3: Work with content in lists and libraries	Ch03	OakChest.docx OakDesk.docx OakEndTable.docx OakNightStand.docx WideWorldPurchaseOrder.docx
4: Make lists and libraries work for you	Ch04	Global Proposal.docx Invoice.docx Project.docx
5: Search for information and people	Ch05	Chapter5_Setup.pdf Chapter5.wsp
6: Work with My Site and OneDrive for Business	Ch06	WideWorldImportersExpenses.docx
7: Work with webpages	Ch07	pjcov.jpg Wildlife.wmv
8: Create and manage sites	Ch08	None
9: Work with wikis, blogs, and community sites	Ch09	Sales.jpg
10: Manage work tasks	Ch10	None
11: Work with workflows	Ch11	None
12: Collaborate with Office programs by using SharePoint	Ch12	Furniture_Price.xlsx Sales_Figures.xlsx
13: Work with business intelligence	Ch13	SalesData.xlsx
14: Manage and monitor content	Ch14	HolidayPlanner.xlsx WWI_Financials.xlsx WWI_HolidayPlanner.xlsx WWI_Presentation.pptx WWI_ProductSheet.docx

The practice tasks in this book cover features across SharePoint 2016 solutions deployed on-premises and SharePoint Online.

SharePoint Server 2016 solutions provide different sets of features and functionality depending on the client access licenses (CALs) activated in your organization. There are two SharePoint Server 2016 CALs, as follows:

- SharePoint Server 2016 Standard CAL
- SharePoint Server 2016 Enterprise CAL

SharePoint Online standalone subscription plans provide different sets of features and functionality depending on the plan you are subscribed to. There are two SharePoint Online plans, as follows:

- SharePoint Online subscription plan P1
- SharePoint Online subscription plan P2

To complete a practice task in this book, you need a SharePoint 2016 on-premises solution or SharePoint Online subscription plan that includes the SharePoint features used in that practice task.

> **SEE ALSO** For a list of the SharePoint 2016 solutions (Standard or Enterprise) and SharePoint Online plans (P1 or P2) you can use to complete each practice task, refer to Appendix B in the downloadable content. (The downloadable content for this book is available from the book's Microsoft Press website at *https://aka.ms/SP2016SBS/downloads*.)

All practice tasks will work in SharePoint Server 2016 Enterprise. All practice tasks that cover features included in SharePoint Server 2016 Standard will work in SharePoint Server 2016 Standard. If you are using SharePoint Server 2016 Standard and a feature is not available in it, you will not be able to complete practice tasks that cover that feature. For example, the business intelligence features are available only in Share-Point Server 2016 Enterprise; therefore, the practice tasks in Chapter 13, "Work with business intelligence," require SharePoint Server 2016 Enterprise.

All practice tasks that cover features included in SharePoint Online P2 will work in SharePoint Online P2. Equally, all practice tasks that cover features included in SharePoint Online P1 will work in SharePoint Online P1. If you are using SharePoint Online P1 and a feature is not available in it, you will not be able to complete practice tasks that cover that feature. For example, the business intelligence features are only available in SharePoint Online P2; therefore, the practice tasks in Chapter 13, "Work with business intelligence," require SharePoint Online P2.

> ⊙ **SEE ALSO** For SharePoint 2016 and SharePoint Online feature availability across solutions and subscription plans, refer to Appendix C in the downloadable content. (The downloadable content for this book is available from the book's Microsoft Press website at *https://aka.ms/SP2016SBS/downloads*.)

Ebook edition

If you're reading the ebook edition of this book, you can do the following:

- Search the full text
- Print
- Copy and paste

You can purchase and download the ebook edition from the Microsoft Press Store at *https://aka.ms/SP2016SBS/details*.

Get support and give feedback

This topic provides information about getting help with this book and contacting us to provide feedback or report errors.

Errata and support

We've made every effort to ensure the accuracy of this book and its companion content. If you discover an error, please submit it to us at *https://aka.ms/SP2016SBS /errata*.

If you need to contact the Microsoft Press Support team, please send an email message to *mspinput@microsoft.com*.

For help with Microsoft software and hardware, go to *https://support.microsoft.com*.

We want to hear from you

At Microsoft Press, your satisfaction is our top priority, and your feedback our most valuable asset. Please tell us what you think of this book at *https://aka.ms/tellpress*.

The survey is short, and we read every one of your comments and ideas. Thanks in advance for your input!

Stay in touch

Let's keep the conversation going! We're on Twitter at *https://twitter.com /MicrosoftPress*.

Introduction to SharePoint 2016

In the modern business environment, with its distributed workforce that assists customers at any time and in any location, team members need to be in closer contact than ever before. Effective collaboration is becoming increasingly important; however, it is often difficult to achieve. Microsoft SharePoint addresses this problem by incorporating a variety of collaboration and communication technologies into a single web-based environment that is closely integrated with productivity programs such as Microsoft Office. SharePoint empowers individuals, teams, and organizations to intelligently discover, share, and collaborate on content from anywhere and on any device.

SharePoint Server 2016 provides the flexibility to tailor deployments based on your unique business needs. SharePoint Server 2016 can be deployed on the infrastructure in your organization, whereas SharePoint Online is available as a cloud service. You can decide which product is right for you, and whether an on-premises deployment, a cloud model, or a hybrid environment is better suited to the needs of your organization.

This chapter guides you through procedures related to getting started with SharePoint, collaborating and sharing within teams, controlling access to SharePoint sites, using SharePoint integration with Office, and comparing SharePoint products.

In this chapter

- Get started with SharePoint
- Collaborate and share within teams
- Control access to SharePoint sites
- Use SharePoint integration with Office
- Compare SharePoint products

Practice files

No practice files are necessary to complete the practice tasks in this chapter.

Get started with SharePoint

SharePoint is a technology that organizations and business units of all sizes use to improve team productivity and to increase the efficiency of business processes. SharePoint capabilities are available in SharePoint Server 2016 and SharePoint Online.

SharePoint Server 2016 gives you a powerful toolset for organizing content, managing documents, sharing knowledge, providing robust collaboration environments, and finding information and people. You and your colleagues can use the social functionality in SharePoint Server 2016 to build communities, share thoughts and ideas, and discover resources and knowledge in your organization.

SharePoint Server 2016 helps teams stay connected and productive by providing an infrastructure and capabilities that allow easy access to people, documents, and information that they need. By using SharePoint 2016, teams can create websites to share information and foster collaboration with other users. You can access content stored within a SharePoint site from a web browser and through client programs and apps, such as Office, running on multiple devices.

> **SEE ALSO** For information about the hardware and software requirements for SharePoint Server 2016, go to *https://technet.microsoft.com/en-us/library/cc262485(v=office.16).aspx.*

In addition to SharePoint Server 2016, which resides on one or more servers in your organization (that is, *on-premises*), SharePoint capabilities are available as a web-based service called SharePoint Online that is hosted outside your organization in the cloud. "In the cloud" means that the IT infrastructure resides off your organization's property (that is, *off-premises*), and that the infrastructure is maintained by a third party. SharePoint Online is a cloud service that you can use to access information and interact with your team from nearly anywhere, on many types of devices.

SharePoint Online is a subscription-based service. Instead of installing SharePoint Server 2016 software in your organization, you can buy a subscription plan to use this software as a service. SharePoint Online is a part of Microsoft Office 365, which also includes Microsoft Exchange Online for web-hosted mail service and Skype for Business for web-based conferencing. There are a number of subscription plans available that provide different sets of features and capabilities, from basic to enterprise level, for a monthly fee. The SharePoint Online service is available as a part of multiple Office 365 subscription plans, or as a standalone subscription plan.

>
> **SEE ALSO** For more information about Office 365 and available plans and pricing, go to *office365.microsoft.com.*

You can integrate the productivity services in SharePoint Online with on-premises SharePoint Server 2016 by using a SharePoint Server 2016 hybrid environment. A SharePoint Server 2016 hybrid environment is based on trusted communications between SharePoint Online and SharePoint Server 2016. When you have established this trust framework, you can combine an on-premises SharePoint Server deployment with a SharePoint Online cloud solution and deliver a consistent user experience across a combined environment. For example, you can use the unified search capability to search across both parts of a hybrid solution (on-premises and online) by using a single search query.

Hybrid environments are helpful when it is not possible for an organization to fully migrate its SharePoint deployment to the cloud due to business, technical, or other reasons. For example, there might be a compliance or data sovereignty policy in your organization that requires data to be hosted in a particular location. By using the hybrid model, your organization can start to achieve the benefits associated with the use of a cloud solution while at the same time continuing to use an on-premises deployment that provides the data governance and customization flexibility you require. By using a hybrid solution, your organization can achieve a higher degree of flexibility than you would have achieved if you forced a choice between an on-premises model or a cloud model. For users, the hybrid model is mostly transparent.

> **SEE ALSO** For information about SharePoint Server 2016 hybrid configuration road-maps, go to *https://technet.microsoft.com/en-us/library/dn197168(v=office.16).aspx.*

When you open a SharePoint site, the home page of the site is displayed. Although the appearance of home pages may vary, any team site home page is likely to include links to a variety of information and the information-sharing tools provided by SharePoint.

Explore the home page of a SharePoint site

On the left side of the page, you might see links to the following: Home, Documents, and Recycle Bin. This collection of links to frequently used site resources is called a Quick Launch. You use the Quick Launch, as the name suggests, to navigate straight to the information and tools that you require. The panel that contains the Quick Launch is referred to as the *left navigation panel*.

The area at the top of the page is referred to as the *top navigation area*. This area contains a top link bar that appears at the top of each page. It consists of several tabs with links, such as the default tab on the left that points to the home page of the current site. It might also include other tabs with links to the subsites of the current site.

> ⚠️ **IMPORTANT** Your screen might not include links to all parts of the site because of the way security permissions on your server have been set up. SharePoint site users see only the parts of the site that they can actually access; if you don't have access to a part of the site, the link to it is not displayed. To obtain additional access, contact your SharePoint administrator.

In the upper right of the page, there is a Help button with a question mark; use this button to access SharePoint Help.

Get useful information from SharePoint Help

SharePoint Help opens in a separate window in which you can search for a help topic or browse the articles.

> 🔍 **SEE ALSO** For more information about site navigation and home pages, see Chapter 2, "Navigate SharePoint sites."

To open a SharePoint site

1. In your browser's address bar, enter the URL (the location) of your SharePoint site.

> ⚠️ **IMPORTANT** The examples in this book use a site located at the wideworldimporters server. Its URL is *http://wideworldimporters*. However, in your environment, you will be using a different site installed on a different server. You will need to refer to your site location, *http://<yourservername/path>*, when you see *http://wideworldimporters* in the book.

2. If prompted, enter your user name and password, and then do one of the following:

- In SharePoint Server 2016, select **OK**.

Sign in to SharePoint Server 2016

- In SharePoint Online, select **Sign In.**

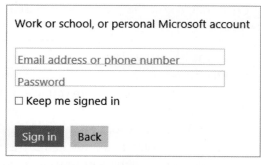

Sign in to SharePoint Online

After you've signed in, the site home page is displayed.

To open SharePoint Help

1. Go to the SharePoint site where you want to open Help.

2. In the upper right of the page, select the **Help** button (an icon with a question mark), and then select **Help** to launch SharePoint Help in a separate window.

Collaborate and share within teams

SharePoint sites provide places to capture and share ideas, information, communications, and documents. The sites facilitate team participation in communities, document collaboration, tracking tasks and issues, blogging and microblogging, building knowledge bases by using wikis, and more.

> **TIP** A *blog*, or *web log*, is an online diary. A blog site allows the diarists, called *bloggers*, to post articles, whereupon readers can comment on them. A *wiki* (pronounced *wee-kee*) is a web environment that allows users to quickly and easily add and edit text and links that appear on the webpage. A wiki site can be used, for example, to build a knowledge base, a community resource, or an online encyclopedia, such as Wikipedia. For more information about blogs and wikis, see Chapter 9, "Work with wikis, blogs, and community sites."

The document collaboration features allow for easy check-in and check-out of documents, document version control, and recovery of previous versions, in addition to document-level security. To facilitate document collaboration and sharing, a library called Documents is created automatically when you create a new SharePoint site.

> **TIP** The Documents library can be renamed after the site has been created. The library can also be removed from your site if you do not need it. For more information about working with libraries, see Chapter 3, "Work with content in lists and libraries," and Chapter 4, "Make lists and libraries work for you."

A SharePoint site can have many subsites, the hierarchy of which, on web servers, resembles the hierarchy of folders on file systems—it is a tree-like structure. Similar to storing your files in folders on file systems, you can store your files within SharePoint sites. However, SharePoint sites take file storage to a new level, providing communities for team collaboration and making it easy for users to work together on documents, tasks, contacts, events, calendars, wikis, and other items. This team collaboration environment can increase individual and team productivity greatly. For example, you can store your files and documents in OneDrive for Business, in your own professional library, where only you can see them, and at the same time you can share them with your coworkers and access them on multiple devices including PCs, tablets, and smartphones.

> **SEE ALSO** For more information about OneDrive for Business, see Chapter 6, "Work with My Sites and OneDrive for Business."

The collaborative tools provided by SharePoint are intuitive and easy to use, so you can share files and information and communicate with your coworkers more effectively. You can create and use SharePoint sites for any purpose. For example, you can build a site to serve as the primary website for a team, create a site to facilitate the organization of a meeting, create a wiki site to capture team knowledge, or create a community site to build a community for a particular project or subject area. A typical SharePoint site might include a variety of useful tools and information, such as document libraries, contacts, calendars, task lists, and other information-sharing and visualization tools. You can use SharePoint's social features, including newsfeeds, to view and post updates, use microblogging, and follow documents, sites, and people.

SharePoint site users can find and communicate with key contacts and experts by using email, instant messaging, or microblogging. Site content can be searched easily, and users can follow a site or a document and receive newsfeed notifications to tell them when existing documents and information have been changed or when new items have been added. Custom business processes can be attached to the documents. You can customize site content and layout to present targeted information to specific users on precise topics.

To open the Documents library

1. Go to a SharePoint site where you want to open the Documents library.

2. On the left side of the screen, on the Quick Launch, select **Documents**.

To post to a site newsfeed

1. Go to a SharePoint site where you want to post to the site newsfeed.

2. On the site home page, under **Newsfeed,** in the **Start a conversation** box, enter your message.

Post a message to a newsfeed

3. Click or tap the **Post** button to post your message to the site newsfeed.

Control access to SharePoint sites

In SharePoint 2016, access to sites is controlled through a role-based system that uses permission levels. Permission levels specify what permissions users have on a SharePoint site. These permissions determine the specific actions that users can perform on the site; in essence, each permission level is a collection of permissions.

SharePoint has a number of default permission levels, including the following:

- **Read** This permission level gives you read-only access to the website.

- **Contribute** In addition to all the permissions included in the Read permission level, the Contribute permission level allows you to create, edit, and delete items in existing lists and libraries.

- **Edit** In addition to all the permissions included in the Contribute permission level, the Edit permission level allows you to create, manage, and delete lists and libraries.

- **Design** In addition to all the permissions included in the Edit permission level, the Design permission level allows you to edit pages in the website.

- **Full Control** This permission level gives you full control.

- **Limited** The Limited permission level allows access to a shared resource within a site, such as a specific list, document library, folder, list item, or document, without giving access to the entire site.

> ⚠ **IMPORTANT** You will need Read or Contribute permission levels for most of the practice tasks in this book. We will instruct you to verify whether you have the sufficient permission level before we introduce practice tasks, particularly those in which a higher level of access, such as Full Control, is needed. If you are not sure what permissions are set on your SharePoint site, check with your SharePoint administrator. For more information about permission levels, see Chapter 8, "Create and manage sites." A full list of permissions and their associated permission levels is provided in Appendix A, "SharePoint 2016 user permissions and permission levels."

To share your site with other people and give them the Edit permission level

1. Go to the SharePoint site you want to share.

2. In the upper right of the page, select the **Share** icon.

Share your site

3. Enter the names or email addresses of the users you want to share the site with, and then select **Share**.

Share 'Team Site'	×
👥 Shared with lots of people	
Invite people / Shared with Enter names or email addresses…	

Enter the names of the users to share your site with

> ✅ **TIP** The users will be assigned the default permission level of Edit. For more information about sharing your sites and granting user permissions, see Chapter 8, "Create and manage sites."

> ⚠ **IMPORTANT** Depending on the site security settings, your request to share the site might need to be approved by the site owner who has Full Control permission level on the site.

Use SharePoint integration with Office

Office 2016 and SharePoint 2016 are designed to create an integrated productivity environment for users and teams across the server and client programs on multiple devices. They work together to provide you with a set of seamlessly integrated capabilities. In other words, many Office features and functionality, in addition to commands and menus, are integrated closely with SharePoint features and functionality. You can use SharePoint 2016 functionality not only from a browser, but also from within your Office programs.

The SharePoint 2016 capabilities you can access in the context of Office programs include document libraries, social capabilities, and SharePoint sites. For example, you can create a new SharePoint site and save your files to it without leaving your Office client program. A SharePoint site's collaborative content—including documents, lists, events, calendars, task assignments, blogs, and membership rosters—can be read and edited within Office programs. You can also share your documents and specify their SharePoint permissions without leaving the Office 2016 program.

In addition, rich business intelligence (BI) capabilities provided in SharePoint 2016 and Office Online Server integrate with the Microsoft Excel 2016 client program so that you can explore and visualize data.

> 🔍 **SEE ALSO** For more information about the BI capabilities provided by SharePoint 2016, see Chapter 13, "Work with Business Intelligence."

Making decisions faster and staying in contact are critical for maintaining your organization's effectiveness. The ability to access information on the go is now a workplace necessity. To this end, SharePoint 2016 provides close integration with Office Online apps. *Office Online apps* is a collective name for the online companions to Microsoft Word, Excel, PowerPoint, and OneNote, with which you can view and edit documents by using your browser.

> **TIP** For SharePoint Server 2016, your organization must have an Office Online Server (OOS) installed and activated in your on-premises environment to use the Office Online apps. For SharePoint Online, the Office Online apps are available by default. Office Online apps are also available for documents stored on your OneDrive and are accessible on multiple devices from virtually anywhere.

The Office Online apps give you a browser-based viewing and editing experience by providing a representation of the Office document in your browser. For example, when you click or tap a document stored in a SharePoint document library, the document opens directly in your browser. The document's appearance in the browser is similar to its appearance in the Office client program. Although most Office Online apps offer lighter editing functionality than their associated Office client programs, you can open the document for editing in the associated client program (if that program is installed on the client device) by using a link within the Office Online app page. On a SharePoint site where Office Online apps have been installed and configured, you can view and edit Office documents in the browser from anywhere on any device.

> **SEE ALSO** For more information about Office Online apps, go to *https://products.office.com/en-gb/office-online/documents-spreadsheets-presentations-office-online*.

You can also view and edit documents from anywhere on smartphones and tablets by using free Office mobile apps that you can download and install on your devices.

> **SEE ALSO** For more information about Office mobile apps, go to *https://products.office.com/en-gb/mobile/office*.

There are different levels of integration between various versions of Office and SharePoint. The Office 2016 family of products provides the most powerful, tight, native, rich, built-in integration with SharePoint 2016, followed by Office 2013 and Office 2010, which are also well integrated with SharePoint 2016. Office 2007 provides a contextual interoperability between SharePoint and Office client programs. The earlier versions of Office have file save integration with SharePoint. For example, you can open and save files stored on SharePoint sites from your Office programs and receive alerts in Microsoft Outlook. Later Office versions provide additional data integration, including interactive access to data stored on SharePoint sites. For example, you can export list data from SharePoint sites to Excel and view properties and metadata for files that are stored on SharePoint sites. Starting with Word 2007, you can create and post to a blog on your SharePoint blog site, and you can check documents in and out of a SharePoint library from within Word. Starting with Office 2010, you can work offline with SharePoint content and synchronize the changes when you are reconnected to your network. You can view, add, edit, and delete SharePoint library documents or list items while you are offline. While you are connected to the network, updates to data on your computer and on the network are automatic, providing bidirectional synchronization between your computer and the live SharePoint sites, libraries, and lists. In SharePoint 2016 and 2013, the working offline functionality is available through synchronizing a SharePoint library to your computer. The synced files on your computer can be viewed by using File Explorer, and the updates to the files sync to SharePoint whenever you're online. Both your OneDrive and a library on a team site can be synced to your computer to allow you to work offline.

> **SEE ALSO** For more information about working offline in SharePoint 2016, see Chapter 3, "Work with content in lists and libraries."

Although all Office 2016 client programs are well integrated with SharePoint, Outlook provides the closest, most feature-rich integration. Starting from Outlook 2007, you can create and manage sites for sharing documents and organizing meetings, and have read and write access from Outlook to SharePoint items such as calendars, tasks, contacts, and documents, in addition to offline capabilities.

> **SEE ALSO** For more information about integration between SharePoint 2016 and Office, see Chapter 12, "Collaborate with Office programs by using SharePoint."

> **TIP** This book—particularly Chapters 3, 4, and 12—guides you through detailed procedures based on the integration between SharePoint and different Office client programs and apps, such as Word, Outlook, and Excel. The following procedure provides a common example of one of many ways in which SharePoint integration with Office can be used.

To create a new Word document in the Documents library

1. Open the **Documents** library on the site in which you want to create the document.

2. Do one of the following:

   - In SharePoint Server 2016, select the **Files** tab at the top of the page to display the ribbon, and then in the **New** group, select **New Document**.

Create a new document in SharePoint Server 2016

   - In SharePoint Online, select the **+New** link, and then select **Word document**.

Create a new document in SharePoint Online

3. Do one of the following:

   - If a new document opens in Word Online in your browser, enter any text you want in the body of the document, and then return to the Documents library by using your browser's **Back** button.

   > ✓ **TIP** The new document is automatically saved in the Documents library.

   - If the new document opens in the Word client program, enter any text you want in the body of the document, and then select **Save** in the upper-left corner of the Word window to save the document to the Documents library on your SharePoint site.

   > ✓ **TIP** If a warning about allowing this website to open a program on your device appears, select Allow. If prompted, provide your user name and password for the SharePoint site. If a Read Only banner appears at the top of the document in Word, select Edit Document.

1

4. In the browser window, refresh the **Documents** library page to confirm that the new document with a default name has been created.

> **TIP** The default name for a document created in the Documents library is Document*N*, where *N* is a consecutive number used to create a unique file name, starting at 1. The first default name assigned to a new file in the Documents library is Document1. If the file with the name Document1 exists, the next default name is Document2, and so on.

> **SEE ALSO** For more information about creating documents, see Chapter 3, "Work with content in lists and libraries."

Compare SharePoint products

SharePoint Server 2016 is the latest version in the line of SharePoint products and technologies. Previous versions of products and technologies in the SharePoint family include the following:

- SharePoint Server versions 2013, 2010, 2007, and 2003
- Search Server 2010
- FAST Search Server for SharePoint
- SharePoint Portal Server 2001
- SharePoint Foundation versions 2013 and 2010
- Windows SharePoint Services versions 3.0 and 2.0
- SharePoint Team Services

SharePoint Server 2016 provides many new, enhanced, and updated features in comparison with its predecessors, with focus on the following areas:

- **Cloud-inspired infrastructure** Ever-changing business conditions require your organization to be agile, and that means that solutions need to provide reliability and choice. There are many infrastructure improvements and changes in SharePoint Server 2016 that you can use to build on-premises and hybrid deployments that are flexible and consistent with the cloud infrastructure.

■ **Modern user experience across devices** SharePoint Server 2016 makes file storage and document collaboration across devices easier than ever, with touch-based experiences and mobile access to content. When you use a mobile device to access the home page for a SharePoint Server 2016 team site, you can tap tiles or links on the screen to navigate the site. You can also switch from mobile view to PC view, which displays site pages as they are seen on a client computer. This view is also touch enabled.

■ **People-centric compliance** Data loss is non-negotiable, and overexposure to information can have legal and compliance implications. SharePoint Server 2016 provides a broad array of features and capabilities to help ensure that sensitive information remains safe and that the right people have access to the right information, at the right time.

> **SEE ALSO** For a full list of new features and updates to existing features in SharePoint Server 2016, go to *https://technet.microsoft.com/en-gb/library/mt346121(v=office.16).aspx*.

There are a number of features that have been deprecated or removed from SharePoint Server 2016 in comparison with SharePoint 2013 products. For example, previous releases of SharePoint Server included SharePoint Foundation, a free edition of SharePoint that included most of the core functionality and architecture provided by the commercial editions of SharePoint. SharePoint Foundation is no longer available in the SharePoint Server 2016 release.

Another notable example is Excel Services. Excel Services and its associated business intelligence capabilities are no longer hosted on SharePoint Server. Excel Services functionality is now part of Excel Online in Office Online Server, and SharePoint users can use the services from there.

Deprecated features are included in SharePoint 2016 for compatibility with previous product versions; however, these features will be removed in the next major release of SharePoint.

> **SEE ALSO** For a full list of deprecated and removed features in SharePoint 2016, go to *https://technet.microsoft.com/en-gb/library/mt346112(v=office.16).aspx*.

SharePoint Server 2016 is available in two editions that can be deployed on servers within your organizational infrastructure:

■ SharePoint Server 2016 Standard CAL

■ SharePoint Server 2016 Enterprise CAL

The editions provide different sets of features and functionality in on-premises deploy-ments depending on the client access license (CAL), Both SharePoint 2016 editions facilitate collaboration within an organization and with partners and customers. However, the capabilities and feature sets differ between the products. All capabili-ties of the Standard edition are available in the Enterprise edition. Additionally, the Enterprise edition provides enterprise-wide capabilities in a number of areas, including data compliance, enterprise search, and business intelligence. To decide whether you need an Enterprise or a Standard edition of SharePoint Server 2016, you need to assess how your requirements are met by the particular features and functionality of these products.

> **SEE ALSO** For a detailed comparison between the feature sets of the different editions of SharePoint 2016, go to *https://go.microsoft.com/fwlink/p/?LinkID=510822*.

SharePoint Online delivers SharePoint features in the cloud, without the associated overhead of managing the underlying infrastructure. SharePoint Online is available as a standalone offering or as part of an Office 365 suite, where you can also get access to other parts of Office 365, including Exchange, OneDrive for Business, Skype for Business, and the Office client programs.

> **TIP** All Office 365 plans include the SharePoint Online service, but not all plans support all SharePoint features. For detailed information about SharePoint Online feature availability in Office 365 plans, go to *https://technet.microsoft.com/en-us/library/sharepoint-online-service-description.aspx#bkmk_tableo365*. For a comparison of the feature sets in the SharePoint Online subscription plans, go to *https://products.office.com/en-us/SharePoint/compare-sharepoint-plans*. For a more detailed comparison of the features included in the SharePoint Online standalone subscription plans, go to *https://technet.microsoft.com/en-GB/library/jj819267.aspx#bkmk_tablespo*.

The features of SharePoint Server 2016 deployed on-premises are engineered to run in the same way as the features of SharePoint Online. When new features are added, they appear first on SharePoint Online and then become available for installation on SharePoint Server 2016 through updates.

> **SEE ALSO** For an up-to-date list of new features in SharePoint Online, go to *http://go.microsoft.com/fwlink/?LinkId=271744*.

At the time of writing, in several countries/regions, SharePoint Online has started an initial rollout of a new user experience known as the *modern user experience*, includ-ing modern SharePoint lists and libraries. The new experience provides additional phone and tablet features, improved performance, and a simplified user interface. At the same time, the original SharePoint user interface is also available. It is referred to as a *classic experience*, or *classic mode*. You can choose to revert to the classic experience in SharePoint Online at any time, and administrators can configure the classic experience as the default at the list, library, site, site collection, or tenant level.

> ⚠️ **IMPORTANT** At the time of writing, SharePoint Server 2016 is only available in the original, classic mode. To this end, this book focuses on the classic experience.

Although modern SharePoint lists and libraries support the themes, navigation, and custom buttons that were created in classic mode, the look and feel of the user interface have been changed. You can easily switch the interface back to classic for the lists, libraries, and Site Contents page on your site.

To switch to the classic SharePoint experience from a modern list or library

1. Go to the modern library or list that you want to switch to the classic experience.

Modern user experience

2. In the lower-left corner of the page, select **Return to classic SharePoint**.

Skills review

In this chapter, you learned how to:

- Get started with SharePoint

- Collaborate and share within teams

- Control access to SharePoint sites

- Use SharePoint integration with Office

- Compare SharePoint products

Practice tasks

No practice files are necessary to complete the practice tasks in this chapter.

> **IMPORTANT** You must have sufficient permissions to perform the operations involved in each practice task to complete that practice task. For more information, see Appendix A, "SharePoint 2016 user permissions and permission levels."

Get started with SharePoint

Open your browser, and then perform the following tasks:

1. Open your SharePoint site by entering its URL: **http://<yourservername/path>**.

    > **TIP** The *yourservername* portion of the URL is the name of the SharePoint server you will be using for the practice tasks in this book. The path portion might be empty or might include one or more levels in the site hierarchy on your SharePoint server. If in doubt about the location of your SharePoint site, check with your SharePoint administrator.

2. Explore the site home page and identify the Quick Launch and top navigation areas.

3. Open SharePoint Help.

4. Familiarize yourself with the Help contents, and then close the Help window.

Collaborate and share within teams

Continuing in your SharePoint team site, perform the following tasks:

1. Open the Documents library.

2. In the Quick Launch, select **Home** to return to the home page.

3. Post the following message to the site newsfeed: **Hello World from** *<your name>* **on** *<today's date>*!

4. Confirm that your message is displayed in the newsfeed on the site home page, below the text box.

Control access to SharePoint sites

Continuing in your SharePoint team site, perform the following task:

1. Share the site with a colleague, giving that colleague the Edit permission level.

Use SharePoint integration with Office

Continuing in your SharePoint team site, perform the following task:

1. Create a Word document in the Documents library.

Compare SharePoint products

Go to a SharePoint site where the modern user experience is in use, and perform the following tasks:

1. Open the Documents library.

2. Switch to the classic SharePoint experience.

Navigate SharePoint sites

A SharePoint website provides a structured environment built for a specific purpose. A typical SharePoint 2016 collaboration site provides structure and functionality for your team to communicate, share documents and data, and work together. There are several different types of SharePoint collaboration sites, each with a unique structure: team sites, project sites, community sites, and blog sites. A site's home page brings the site components together and provides capabilities for navigating them.

In addition to collaboration sites, SharePoint 2016 includes blueprints for enterprise sites and publishing sites. Enterprise sites provide setup for content and record management, search functionality, and business intelligence centers. Publishing sites provide infrastructure for quickly publishing webpages and for co-authoring content for sharing knowledge by using wikis.

> **SEE ALSO** For more information about SharePoint sites, see Chapter 8, "Create and manage sites."

This chapter guides you through procedures related to navigating home pages and SharePoint sites, understanding site structure, customizing site navigation, working with the ribbon, navigating lists and libraries, understanding web parts and app parts, and working with the Recycle Bin.

In this chapter

- Navigate home pages and SharePoint sites

- Understand site structure

- Customize site navigation

- Work with the ribbon

- Navigate lists and libraries

- Understand web parts and app parts

- Work with the Recycle Bin

Practice files

For this chapter, use the practice files from the SP2016SBS\Ch02 folder. For practice file download instructions, see the introduction.

Navigate home pages and SharePoint sites

A home page is the main page of a SharePoint website. A site's home page provides a navigational structure that links the site components together. The functionality of each site component is encapsulated in an app.

A SharePoint team site usually includes the following components:

- **Libraries**   Document, picture, form, and other libraries represent a collection of files that you share and work on with your team members. A typical team site includes a built-in document library called Documents that is displayed on the team site home page. You can create your own document, picture, form, and other libraries when needed.

- **Lists**   With SharePoint lists, you and your team members can work with structured, tabular data on the website. A typical team site includes several list apps that you can add to your site, including Announcements, Calendar, Links, and Tasks. You can also create custom lists by using the Custom list app. In addition, there are other list apps provided by SharePoint that you can add to your site if required.

- **Newsfeed**   A site newsfeed is the site's communication hub. It displays posts and replies from the users of the site. You and your team members can post comments and reply to each others' posts. The site newsfeed, or site feed, is implemented via a MicroFeed app and is displayed on the team site home page by default.

- **Surveys**   Surveys provide a way of polling team members. You can use a Survey app to create your own surveys.

- **Recycle Bin**   You can use the Recycle Bin to restore items that have been deleted from the site.

Typically, the home page of a SharePoint site has two main navigation areas: the left navigation area, which is a panel on the left side of the page, and the top navigation area, which is a strip at the top of the page. Cumulatively, these areas are referred to as the *site navigation*.

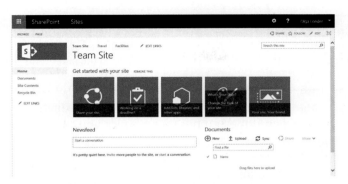

2

Navigate from the home page to the site components, subsites, site settings, and other components of a website

The left navigation panel contains a set of Quick Launch links. Typically, the Quick Launch contains the following links:

- **Home** This link points to the home page of the current site.

- **Documents** This link opens the built-in Documents library.

- **Recent** When a new list or library is created, its link is displayed in the Recent section on the Quick Launch. The five newest links are shown in this section.

- **Site Contents** This link opens the Site Contents page, which lists all of the libraries, lists, newsfeeds, surveys, and other apps on your site. The Site Contents page also provides links to the subsites.

- **Recycle Bin** This link opens the site Recycle Bin, from which you can restore the items deleted from the site to their original locations.

The Quick Launch can also contain links to the subsites of the current site and to the site components created by you and your team members, such as specific document libraries or lists.

The top navigation area contains the top link bar, located above the page title. It consists of the tabs displayed on all pages within the SharePoint site. The top link bar typically includes the following links:

- **Current Site Title** This is the link to the home page of the current site; it is usually displayed on the first tab at the left end of the top link bar.

- **Links to subsites** On a well-organized site, the top link bar contains tabs with links to the subsites of the current site—for example, the top link bar of a team site could display the team site as its home page, and a Travel site link and Facilities site link as its second and third tabs.

> ⚠️ **IMPORTANT** If a subsite is configured to use the top link bar of its parent site, the first tab link on the subsite points to the home page of the parent site. When the subsite inherits the top link bar from its parent site, the top link bar can be edited only in the parent site and not in the subsite.

In the upper-right corner of the page, to the left of the Help button, is the Settings icon (a gear image). Selecting this icon opens the Settings menu, which you can use to edit the current page, add a new page or an app, share the site, access the Site Contents page, change the settings for your site, and view the Getting Started links. The options displayed on the Settings menu depend on the permissions that you have on the site: only options applicable to you are displayed.

⚙️

Shared with...

Edit page

Add a page

Add an app

Site contents

Change the look

Site settings

Getting started

Use the Settings menu to add and edit pages, change settings, and more

The Site Contents link on the Settings menu is identical to the Site Contents link on the Quick Launch. This link takes you to the Site Contents page, which lists all of the libraries, lists, and other apps on your site, and the child sites if there are any. The Site Contents page also has a link to the site's Recycle Bin. The Site Contents page contains links to all of the major parts of the site's structure and is your main navigational aid for the site you are on.

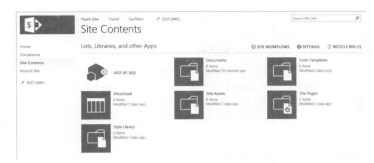

Use the Site Contents page as a main navigational aid for the site you are in

The Site Settings link on the Settings menu opens the Site Settings page, which enables you to administer and customize your site.

Use the links on the Site Settings page to administer and customize your site

In addition to site navigation, the home page of a typical SharePoint team site includes the Getting Started area with tile links, the site newsfeed, and a view of the Documents library. This view is presented within its own page component, called a web part, which allows you to work with the documents in the library without leaving the home page. On the upper-right side of the page is a search box that you can use to search the current site.

The bar at the very top of the page is referred to as the global navigation bar. On its left, in the upper-left corner of the screen, there is an icon that looks like a grid or a waffle; this is called the app launcher. The app launcher is a navigational aid that provides quick access to your apps via a menu of app and service links that is arranged as a grid of tiles. The grid appears when you click or tap the waffle icon. To go to an app or a service, you need to click or tap its tile.

In a hybrid environment, the app launcher might display different tiles depending on whether you are browsing the SharePoint on-premises site or the SharePoint Online site. The app launcher in the SharePoint on-premises environment includes the Newsfeed, One Drive for Business, and Sites tiles. For example, you might select OneDrive to go to your OneDrive for Business library.

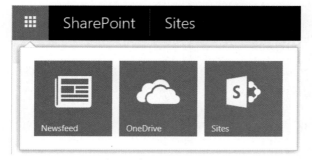

Use the app launcher for quick access to apps and services

⚠ **IMPORTANT** Your app launcher might contain more or fewer tiles, depending on how your environment is set up. The administrator of your SharePoint deployment can pin or unpin the tiles in the app launcher.

In SharePoint Online, the app launcher might include tiles for other services and apps, such as Office Online apps, the administration links for managing security and compliance, and other settings.

Use the app launcher in SharePoint Online

> ✓ **TIP** In SharePoint Online, the tiles that are displayed in the app launcher depend on your Office 365 subscription, the features that have been activated, and your access rights to the SharePoint Online deployment.

The app launcher contains links to your personal SharePoint social components such as your Newsfeed, your OneDrive for Business, and the sites that you are following. Although the site components are stored within the site that they are a part of and are shared between the site's users, your personal components are dedicated to you and are stored centrally in a secure, password-protected location on your organization's SharePoint servers, or in the cloud if yours is a hybrid deployment. The app launcher links to your Newsfeed, OneDrive, and the sites that you are following accompany you across all of the SharePoint sites you have access to. The following list describes these components in more detail:

- **Newsfeed** This is your own social hub, where updates from people, posts, documents, and sites you're following are displayed, in addition to the system alerts. Your posts to the site newsfeeds are also displayed, and you can post to a site newsfeed from your own newsfeed.

- **OneDrive for Business** This is your own personal library, in which you can store your private work documents. By using OneDrive, you can share your private files with your co-workers and give them permission to review or edit the content. You can also sync your work files to your local device to work on the documents offline.

- **Sites** This link in SharePoint 2016 on-premises, or the SharePoint link in SharePoint Online, gives you easy access to the sites you are interested in. All the sites that you are following are listed on your Sites page.

In hybrid deployments, you can seamlessly navigate between the content in on-premises SharePoint 2016 and that in SharePoint Online. The option listed in the global navigation bar to the left of the app launcher in the full-screen browser view indicates whether you are currently using content in SharePoint on-premises or in SharePoint Online; you can use it to distinguish between them, as follows:

- If the SharePoint link is displayed next to the app launcher, you are using content in SharePoint 2016 on-premises.

- If the Office 365 link is displayed next to the app launcher, you are using content in SharePoint Online.

> **TIP** The content indicators for SharePoint on-premises and SharePoint Online are best viewed in the maximized browser window. If the browser window is resized, the Office 365 link might not be visible, and the app launcher might change its position and appear to the right of the global navigation area.

On the global navigation bar for a SharePoint 2016 on-premises deployment, to the right of the SharePoint link, there is a Sites link. This link is the same as the Sites tile link on the app launcher. It provides you with access to the Sites page, which lists all sites that you are following. In a SharePoint Online deployment, you can see the sites you are following by using the SharePoint link to the right of the Office 365 link.

Underneath the global navigation bar, on the right side of the team site home page, are the following buttons:

- **Share** Use the Share button to share the current site with other users and assign them permissions for accessing the site.

- **Follow** Use the Follow button to follow this site and be notified of changes.

- **Sync** Use the Sync button to synchronize the Documents library—which is displayed in the lower-right portion of the page—with your local device, such as a PC, tablet, or phone, for working offline.

- **Edit** Use the Edit button to edit the current page.

- **Focus on Content** Use the Focus On Content button to switch between hiding the site navigation so that the page content is displayed in full page view, and displaying the site navigation.

To display the Site Settings page for a SharePoint site

1. On the site, select the **Settings** icon (gear) in the upper-right corner of the page to open the Settings menu.

2. Select **Site settings**.

To display the Site Contents page for a SharePoint site

1. On the site, do one of the following:

   - On the Quick Launch, select **Site Contents**.

   - Display the **Settings** menu, and then select **Site contents**.

To display your newsfeed

1. From any SharePoint site in your deployment, select the app launcher.

2. In the app launcher grid, select the **Newsfeed** tile.

To display your OneDrive for Business

1. From any SharePoint site in your deployment, select the app launcher.

2. In the app launcher grid, select the **OneDrive** tile.

To follow a site

1. On the site you want to follow, in the upper-right area of the page, select **Follow**.

   A message is displayed in the upper-right area of the page, confirming that you are now following this site.

To display the sites you are following

1. From any SharePoint site in your deployment, do one of the following:

   - For SharePoint 2016 on-premises, do one of the following:

     - In the global navigation bar, select the **Sites** link.

     - Open the app launcher, and select the **Sites** tile.

   - For SharePoint Online, do one of the following:

     - In the global navigation bar, select the **SharePoint** link.

     - Open the app launcher, and select the **SharePoint** tile.

To hide or display the page navigation

1. On a page, select **Focus on Content** in the upper-right of the page to switch between hiding page navigation (displaying the page in the full view) and displaying navigation.

Understand site structure

A typical SharePoint site contains the following components: webpages, document libraries, lists, a newsfeed, and other apps. These items are created and maintained by SharePoint and are linked together within the site structure. In graphical form, this site structure can be represented as a treelike diagram.

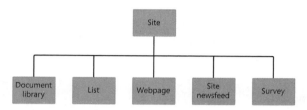

A SharePoint site structure

In addition to its own components, such as pages and document libraries, a SharePoint site can have many subsites, the hierarchy of which, on web servers, resembles the hierarchy of folders on file systems. Sites that do not have a parent site are referred to as top-level sites. Top-level sites can have multiple subsites, and these subsites can have multiple subsites, proceeding downward as many levels as you need. The entire hierarchical structure of a top-level site and all of its subsites is called a *site collection*.

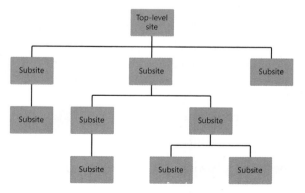

A SharePoint site collection

2

Because the subsites are contained within their parent site, the overall hierarchical structure of a SharePoint site has the site's own items—such as pages, libraries, lists, and other apps—in addition to the child sites. This overall structure can be represented as a site content tree.

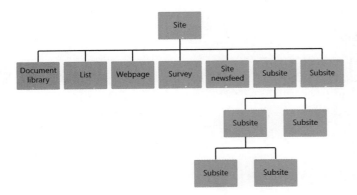

A site content tree

It can be useful to see the full structure of the site visually, in a graphical representation. SharePoint allows you to display the site content tree in the left navigation pane so that it can be used for navigation. The site tree can replace the Quick Launch, or it can be displayed together with the Quick Launch.

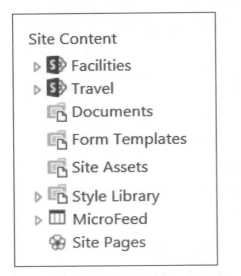

Use the site content tree in the left navigation pane

You can set the site content tree to be displayed in the left navigation pane by using the Tree View page that you can access via the link of the same name in the Look And Feel section on the Site Settings page. You can also use the Tree View page to hide or display the Quick Launch.

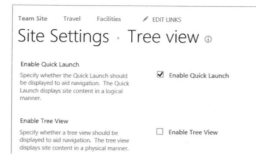

Display or hide the Quick Launch and the site content tree

To go to a subsite from its parent site

1. On the parent site, do one of the following:

   - Display the **Site Contents** page, and in the **Subsites** section, select the sub-site link.

   - If the subsite link is displayed in the top link bar of the parent site, select the link.

To hide or display the Quick Launch

1. On a site, display the **Site Settings** page.

2. In the **Look and Feel** section, select the **Tree View** link to display the **Tree View** page.

3. Do one of the following:

   - Clear the **Enable Quick Launch** check box to hide the Quick Launch.

   - Select the **Enable Quick Launch** check box to show the Quick Launch.

4. Select **OK** to confirm your settings and return to the Site Settings page.

To display or remove a site content tree

1. Go to a SharePoint site and display the **Site Settings** page.

2. In the **Look and Feel** section, select the **Tree View** link to display the Tree View page.

3. Do one of the following:

    - Select the **Enable Tree View** check box to display the site content tree in the left navigation panel.

    - Clear the **Enable Tree View** check box to remove the site content tree from the left navigation panel.

4. When you're done, select **OK** to confirm your settings and return to the Site Settings page.

Customize site navigation

On a SharePoint site, you can customize both the top and left navigation areas. There are many options available for navigation customization. You can add new links, edit and reposition existing links, and delete those links that you no longer require in both the top link bar and the Quick Launch by using in-page editing. You can switch into in-page edit mode by selecting the appropriate Edit Links option in the Quick Launch or on the top link bar.

Home	✖
Documents	✖
Site Contents	✖
Recycle Bin	
Drag and drop link here	
⊕ link	

Save   Cancel

The Quick Launch in edit mode

 TIP You cannot delete the Recycle Bin link from the Quick Launch.

To add new links in in-page edit mode, you can select the Link option and then provide the text and address for the link you want to add.

Add a link to the Quick Launch or the top link bar

In in-page edit mode, you can also drag items from the Site Contents page to create new links on the Quick Launch and the top link bar.

> ✓ **TIP** Links can be nested by dragging a link on top of an existing link.

In addition, you can do more advanced customization to modify the top link bar and the Quick Launch by using the Top Link Bar and Quick Launch pages. For example, you can group and sort links. You can display these pages by using the Top Link Bar and Quick Launch links in the Look And Feel section on the Site Settings page.

Team Site   Travel   Facilities   ✎ EDIT LINKS

Site Settings › Quick Launch ⓘ

New Navigation Link | New Heading | Change Order

Home

Documents

Site Contents

Customize the Quick Launch from the Quick Launch page

To customize the Quick Launch by using in-page editing

1. On the site where you want to customize the Quick Launch, in the Quick Launch, select **Edit Links**.

2. Do the following:

- To add a link, select **+link**, and in the **Add a link** dialog, enter the text to display and the address for your new link. Select **Try a link** to validate the address, and then select **OK**.

- To remove a link, click or tap the **X** to the right of a link.

- To rename a link, click or tap a link and then enter a new name. Then click or tap outside the link to commit the change.

- To edit both the link text and the address the link is pointing to, click or tap the link, select the hyperlink icon to display the Edit Link dialog, and then edit the name or address (or both) for the link.

Edit a link in the Quick Launch or top link bar

- To change the position of a link, click or tap a link and then drag it to a new position on the Quick Launch.

3. When you're done, select **Save**.

To customize the top link bar for a site by using in-page editing

1. On the site, on the top link bar, select **Edit Links**.

2. Do the following:

- To add a link, select **+link**, and in the **Add a link** dialog, provide the text to display and the address for your new link. Select **Try a link** to validate the address, and then select **OK**.

- To remove a link, click or tap the **X** to the right of the link.

- To rename a link, click or tap a link and then enter the new name. Then click or tap outside the link to commit the change.

- To edit both link text and the address the link is pointing to, click or tap a link, select the hyperlink icon to display the Edit Link dialog, and then edit the name or address (or both) for the link.

- To change the position of a link, click or tap the link and then drag it to a new position on the top link bar.

3. When you're done, select **Save**.

To add links to site navigation by dragging them from the Site Contents page

1. Go to a site and display the **Site Contents** page.

2. In the navigation area that you want to customize, select **Edit Links**.

3. In the **Site Contents** page, select the site component that you want to add, and drag it to the navigation area, where it says **Drag and drop link here**.

4. When you're done, select **Save** in the navigation area.

To customize the Quick Launch for a site by using the Quick Launch page

1. Go to the site, display the **Site Settings** page, and then in the **Look and Feel** section, select **Quick Launch**.

2. On the **Quick Launch** page, do any of the following:

   • If you want to create a new section heading, select **New Heading**, and then on the **New Heading** page, in the **URL** section, enter the web address and provide the text for the new heading. Select **OK** to create the section heading and return to the Quick Launch page.

   > **TIP** If you don't want the heading to be a link, enter # in the web address box.

   Create a new section heading on the Quick Launch

   • If you want to create a new link, select **New Navigation Link**, and then on the **New Navigation Link** page, in the **URL** section, enter the web address and provide the text for the new link. In the **Heading** section, select the heading under which you want the new link to appear on the Quick Launch, and then select **OK** to create the link and return to the Quick Launch page.

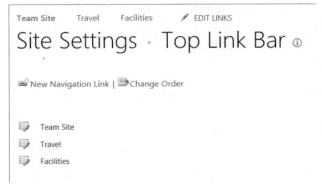

Create a new link on the Quick Launch

- If you want to change the order of the links, select **Change Order**, and then, on the **Change Order** page, modify the numbers that show the sequence in which the section headings appear. You can also change the order of the links within each section. When you're done, select **OK** to apply the changes and return to the Quick Launch page.

Change the order of the links on the Quick Launch

To customize the top link bar for a site by using the Top Link Bar page

1. Go to the site, display the **Site Settings** page, and then in the **Look and Feel** section, select **Top link bar**.

Customize the top link bar

2. On the **Top Link Bar** page, do any of the following:

    *   If you want to create a new link, select **New Navigation Link**, and then on the **New Navigation Link** page, in the **URL** section, enter the web address and provide the text for the new link. Select **OK** to create the link and return to the Top Link Bar page.

    *   If you want to change the order of the links, select **Change Order**, and then, on the **Change Order** page, modify the numbers that show the sequence in which the links appear. When you're done, select **OK** to apply the changes and return to the Top Link Bar page.

Work with the ribbon

In SharePoint 2016, the ribbon provides a consistent interface for accessing the commands and tools you require for the tasks you want to accomplish, like the ribbon in other Office programs such as Microsoft Word and Excel. On a SharePoint site, the ribbon appears across the top of a webpage and is designed to help you quickly locate the most commonly used commands and tools for performing actions on pages, documents, and lists.

Commands on the ribbon are organized on tabs, and further organized into groups on those tabs. Each ribbon tab relates to a type of SharePoint site component you are working with, such as a document library or a webpage. Tabs, groups, and commands on the ribbon are contextual: the ribbon commands available to you change depending on what you are doing and where you are on the SharePoint site. The tabs are displayed at the top of webpages on your site. To use the ribbon commands, you select the tab that corresponds to the kind of task you want to perform. The currently selected tab is highlighted. Each tab provides a specific set of commands, depending on the actions that you can perform.

The Browse tab, as the name suggests, is used to browse the current page. It is selected when you open a page, providing you with the ability to view the page in your browser. The top link bar is displayed on the Browse tab. This tab does not have ribbon-based tools associated with it.

Depending on the page you are viewing, other tabs might be available. For example, the home page of a team site provides a Page tab that contains commands you can use to modify the page and its settings.

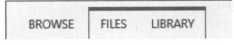

The Browse and Page tabs on a webpage

On a list page, SharePoint provides two ribbon tabs: Items and List. The Items tab provides a set of commands for working with the individual list items. The List tab provides the commands for working with the list as a whole.

BROWSE | ITEMS | LIST

The Browse, Item, and List tabs on a list page

Similarly, a library page provides two tabs—Files and Library—for working with individual files and configuring a library, respectively.

BROWSE | FILES | LIBRARY

The Browse, Files, and Library tabs on a library page

Commands on the ribbon are represented as buttons, drop-down lists, and other controls. To make it easier for you to locate the commands you need, they are grouped together by common functionality into several sections on each tab. The names of the groups are shown at the bottom of the tab. For example, on the Page tab, the Edit group contains commands you can use to edit the page, and the Manage group contains commands you can use to manage the page.

The number and types of commands that are available to you on each tab on the ribbon depend not only on where you are and what you are doing, but also on your permission level and the configuration of your site. Some commands on the ribbon might be unavailable because you do not have sufficient permissions to use them, or because they have not been enabled for your site. In other cases, to enable a command, you might need to select an object. In a document library, for example, you must first select a document in the library to enable the ribbon commands for working with the document.

When the ribbon is displayed, the top links bar is not visible. On all pages that show the ribbon, you can use the following navigation aids for moving to other pages within the site and the site collection:

- The Browse tab, which displays the top link bar

- The Site Contents link on the Settings menu, which takes you to the Site Contents page

- The Sites link (for SharePoint on-premises) or SharePoint link (for SharePoint Online) which allows you to navigate to a page that lists the sites that you are following

In addition, on the pages that show the ribbon and on which the left navigation pane is available, you can use the Quick Launch, including the Site Contents link.

To display the ribbon on a page

1. In the upper-left corner of the page, underneath the global navigation bar, select the ribbon tab that you want to display. For example:

    - On a webpage, select the **Page** tab.

    - On a list page, select the **Items** or **List** tab.

    - On a library page, select the **Files** or **Library** tab.

To hide the ribbon on a page

1. In the upper-left corner of the page, under the global navigation bar, select **Browse** to hide the ribbon and display the top link bar.

Navigate lists and libraries

SharePoint lists and libraries provide rich capabilities for working with the list items and files they contain. Lists have many built-in features that provide a robust way to store, share, and work with structured data. Libraries provide a location to store files where you and your co-workers can work on them together and access them from any device.

There are several ways to access the commands and tools for performing tasks for list items and library files.

> **SEE ALSO** For more information about working with content in lists and libraries, see Chapter 3, "Work with content in lists and libraries." For more information about configuring lists and libraries, see Chapter 4, "Make lists and libraries work for you."

The commands that apply to a list as a whole are on the List tab of the ribbon. The commands that apply to individual list items within a list are on the Items tab of the ribbon. For the commands on the Items tab to be available, one or more list items must be selected in the list. You select a list item by clicking or tapping in its leftmost column. Clicking or tapping the list item itself opens its properties form on a separate page. In addition, you can display the commands for an individual list item by selecting the ellipsis to the right of the item.

The commands that apply to a library as a whole are on the Library tab of the ribbon. The commands that apply to individual files in the library are on the Files tab of the ribbon. For the commands on the Files tab to be available, one or more files in the library must be selected. For example, to rename a file in a library, you first need to select the file, and then select the Edit Properties command on the Files tab to open the file's properties page and modify its name. You select a file in a library by clicking or tapping in its leftmost column. Clicking or tapping a file name opens the file in the associated program—for example, Word or Word Online.

Select a file by clicking or tapping in its leftmost column

Right-clicking a file name will open the shortcut menu, which provides links to frequently used commands. You can also display the shortcut menu by selecting a file and pressing Alt+M on the keyboard. On touch devices, you can open the shortcut menu by pressing and holding the document name.

Docum	Olga Londer

Open in Word

Open in Word Online

Download

Share

Rename

Delete

Copy

Version History

Properties

Advanced ▶

Shared With

Compliance Details

Check Out

Follow

Workflows

Right-click a file name to display its shortcut menu

In addition, the commands for the file are available in the file callout that can be displayed by selecting the ellipsis to the right of the file name. The callout shows the file preview, the link to the file, and the commands menu at the bottom of the callout. An additional commands menu, similar to the shortcut menu, is displayed by selecting the ellipsis at the bottom of the callout box.

Document.docx ✕

Wide World Importers

PAGE 1 OF 1

Changed by you on 6/11/2016 5:26 PM

Shared with lots of people

ents/Document.docx?d=w34b41c3f4e6240af95017672471617 ✕

Document ····

OPEN   SHARE   FOLLOW   ····

Select the ellipsis to display a file's callout

2

If durable links are enabled in the site collection where your site is located, the file link that is provided in the callout persists even if the file is renamed or moved within the site collection. With durable links, if you share a link to a file, and then change the file name or location in the site collection, the link still stays valid.

A durable link includes a resource identifier that is assigned to an individual document. The identifier is stored in the content database and is related to the document. When a user selects a durable link to a specific document, SharePoint Server looks up the file by the resource identifier and opens it in Office Online Server.

> ⚠ **IMPORTANT** For durable links to be available in your deployment, you must have Office Online Server deployed and activated and the Document ID feature enabled in your site collection.

The resource identifier is appended at the end of the file URL as a query string, after the question mark. For example, the URL *http://wideworldimporters/Shared%20Documents/Document.docx?d= w34b41c3f4e6240af95017672471617a8* points to a file named Document.docx with the resource identifier w34b41c3f4e6240af95017672471617a8.

> ⚠ **IMPORTANT** For a durable link, you must use the URL that includes the resource identifier.

The durable link for a file relies on the resource identifier and will work if the file name has changed or if the file has been moved from its original location, as long as it stays within the same site collection.

> ✓ **TIP** The durable links capability is based on the Web Application Open Platform Interface Protocol (WOPI).

The file callout also provides a QR (Quick Response) code for the file link, so that any device with a QR scanner, such as a smartphone or a tablet, can access the file directly. The QR code is a two-dimensional barcode represented as a square image made up of two colors: white as a background color and black as the foreground color. The image represents a bitmap and contains the file URL. Most smartphones have QR scanners. To access the QR code that stores the file link, you select the phone icon to the right of the link box in the file callout.

Scan this QR code with your phone or tablet to open
http://wideworldimporters/Shared%20Documents/Document.docx?
d=w34b41c3f4e6240af95017672471617a8

Use the QR code for direct access from mobile devices

You can obtain a file's durable link and its QR code by using the file callout or by using the Get Link command in the Share dialog for the file.

 TIP At the time of writing, the Get Link command is available in SharePoint Online.

SEE ALSO For more information about the Get Link command in the Share dialog, see Chapter 4, "Make lists and libraries work for you."

To select list items in a SharePoint list

1. In the list, do one of the following:

   - To select a single item, click or tap in its leftmost column.

   - To select multiple items, click or tap in the items' leftmost columns.

To select files in a SharePoint library

1. In the library, do one of the following:

   - To select a single file, click or tap in its leftmost column.

   - To select multiple files, click or tap in the files' leftmost columns.

To open a file's shortcut menu

1. Go to the library that contains the file.

2. Right-click the file, or, on a touch device, press and hold the file.

To display a file's callout

1. In the library that contains the file, select the ellipsis to the right of the file name to display the file callout.

To obtain a file's durable link by using the file's callout

1. On the file's callout, select the file link and copy it.

2. Paste the link into a document or other location where you want to store the link, and save it. You can then share a link—for example, via an email.

To obtain a file's QR code by using the file's callout

1. On the file's callout, to the right of the file link, select the phone icon to open the QR code page.

2. On the QR code page, copy the QR code bitmap image.

3. Save the image.

To rename a file in a library

1. In the library that contains the file, do one of the following:

   - Display the file shortcut menu and select **Rename**.

   - Display the file callout, select the ellipsis to display the menu, and select **Rename**.

   - Select the file you want to rename, select the **Files** tab of the ribbon, and then, in the **Manage** group, select **Edit Properties**. On the file's properties page, in the **Name** field, modify the file name, and then select **Save** to save the changes and return to the library page.

Understand web parts and app parts

A webpage on a SharePoint site can contain, in addition to text, images, and links, one or more web parts. A web part is an independent component that can be reused, shared, and personalized by all users who have permission to access it. Web parts are the basic building blocks of a page; each web part occupies its own rectangular area within the page.

Apps for SharePoint provide the functionality of site components such as lists and libraries. For example, a library is implemented as a library app that you can add to your site. Each list is implemented by using a list-specific app—for example, a tasks list is implemented by using a Task app. Apps are self-contained functional components. In addition to the apps provided by SharePoint, you can download apps that extend the SharePoint functionality from your organization's internal App Catalog and from a public SharePoint Store.

An app part is a type of web part that you can use to expose the content of a SharePoint app such as a list or library in a web part. For example, the home page of a newly created team site contains a web part that displays the content of the Documents library app.

Webpages can contain several web parts that can be connected together if necessary. SharePoint provides built-in app parts for all lists and libraries on the current site that you can insert in a webpage. By using web parts, you can organize disparate information and consolidate data (such as lists and charts) and web content (such as text, links, and images) into a single webpage.

> **SEE ALSO** For more information about webpages, web parts, and app parts, see Chapter 7, "Work with webpages."

You can view and edit the web parts and app parts in a webpage by using the Edit Page command on the Settings menu. Selecting this command displays the ribbon. The web parts on the page are displayed within rectangular areas that show the position of each web part on the page.

View and edit the web parts on a webpage

2

When you display a webpage in edit mode, two additional tabs appear on the ribbon: the Format Text tab and the Insert tab. The Format Text tab provides controls that you can use to change and format the text on the page, in addition to its markup. The Insert tab provides controls for inserting video, audio, graphics, and web parts onto the page.

In addition, when you select a web part on the page, the Web Part tab becomes available. The Web Part tab provides commands for working with the web parts. If the selected web part is an app part that exposes a list or a library, the relevant ribbon tabs also become available. For example, when you select the Documents library app part, the Files tab and the Library tab become available on the ribbon.

To display web parts on a webpage

1. On the webpage, do one of the following:

   - On the **Settings** menu, select the **Edit page** option.
   - Select the **Page** tab to display the ribbon, and then in the **Edit** group, select **Edit**.

   > ✓ **TIP** You might want to display the page in full view to better see the page.

To stop displaying web parts on a webpage

1. On the webpage, select the **Page** tab or the **Format Text** tab.

2. In the **Edit** group, select **Save** to close the ribbon and return to the Browse view of the page.

Work with the Recycle Bin

The Recycle Bin in SharePoint provides two-stage protection against accidental deletions. When you delete a document or other item from a SharePoint site, it is deleted from the site and moved to the site's Recycle Bin, from which it can be restored to its original location, if needed. If you then delete this item from the site's Recycle Bin, it is moved to the second-stage Recycle Bin of the site collection. From there, the document can be either restored to its original location or deleted.

Restore items from the Recycle Bin

> ⚠️ **IMPORTANT** By default, the site's Recycle Bin in SharePoint on-premises holds items for 30 days. Your SharePoint administrator can modify this setting. The site's Recycle Bin in SharePoint Online holds items for 93 days.

> ✓ **TIP** Site users can only restore the content that they themselves have deleted, whereas a site collection administrator can restore any content deleted by the site users.

If an item is deleted accidentally from a site's Recycle Bin, it can be restored from the second-stage Recycle Bin of the site collection.

To open a site's Recycle Bin

1. Go to the site, and do one of the following:

   - On the Quick Launch, select **Recycle Bin**.

   - Display the **Site Contents** page, and then select **Recycle Bin** in the upper-right corner of the page.

To restore an item from a site's Recycle Bin

1. Open the site's Recycle Bin, and select the item you want to restore by clicking or tapping in its leftmost column. You can select multiple items.

2. At the top of the deleted items list, select **Restore Selection** to restore the item to its original location, and then select **OK** in the confirmation box to confirm your action.

To remove an item from a site's Recycle Bin

1. Open the site's Recycle Bin, and select the item you want to remove by clicking or tapping in its leftmost column. You can select multiple items.

2. At the top of the deleted items list, select **Delete Selection** to remove the items from the site's Recycle Bin, and then select **OK** in the confirmation box to confirm your action.

To open the second-stage Recycle Bin

> ⚠ **IMPORTANT** You need to be a site collection administrator to be able to view, delete, and restore items from the second-stage Recycle Bin.

1. Open the Recycle Bin for a site in the site collection.

2. At the bottom of the list of items, select **second-stage recycle bin**.

☑	📄	Document.docx	/wideworldimporters/Shared Documents	☐	Olga Londer

Can't find what you're looking for? Check the second-stage recycle bin.

Open the second-stage Recycle Bin

To restore an item from the second-stage Recycle Bin

1. Open the second-stage Recycle Bin, and select the item you want to restore. You can select multiple items.

2. At the top of the deleted items list, select **Restore Selection** to restore the items to their original location, and then select **OK** in the confirmation box to confirm your action.

Skills review

In this chapter, you learned how to:

- Navigate home pages and SharePoint sites
- Understand site structure
- Customize site navigation
- Work with the ribbon
- Navigate lists and libraries
- Understand web parts and app parts
- Work with the Recycle Bin

Chapter 2

Practice tasks

The practice files for these tasks are located in the SP2016SBS\Ch02 folder.

To set up your environment to perform the practice tasks in this chapter, follow the instructions in the Chapter2_Setup file in the practice file folder.

> ⚠ **IMPORTANT** You must have sufficient permissions to perform the operations involved in each practice task to complete that practice task. For more information, see Appendix A, "SharePoint 2016 user permissions and permission levels."

Navigate home pages and SharePoint sites

Go to the SharePoint Team Site and sign in if prompted. Then perform the following tasks:

1. Display the **Site Contents** page. Explore the page and locate the links for the site components, such as apps for lists and libraries, subsites, and the site Recycle Bin.

2. Select the **Team Announcements** list to go to the list page.

3. On the **Team Announcements** page, select **Travel** on the top link bar to go to the Travel subsite.

4. On the **Travel** site home page, in the site newsfeed, enter **Hi Everyone!** and select the **Post** button to post to the site newsfeed.

5. On the **Travel** site home page, display your personal **Newsfeed** page by using the app launcher. Enter your credentials if prompted.

6. On your **Newsfeed** page, in the box at the top of the page, enter **Hello World!** and then select **Post** to post to your newsfeed.

7. Return to the **Travel** site by selecting the browser's **Back** button, and then return to the **Team Site** home page by entering its URL in the browser address bar.

8. On the **Team Site** home page, display your personal **Newsfeed** page and verify that this is the same page that you were taken to from the **Travel** site. Return to the **Team Site** home page by selecting the browser's **Back** button.

9. Display your **OneDrive** personal library. Explore the page and then return to the **Team Site** home page by selecting the browser's **Back** button.

10. Set up following for the **Team Site**. Display the page for the sites you are following, and confirm that the **Team Site** is listed there. Return to the **Team Site** home page by selecting the browser's **Back** button.

Understand site structure

Continuing on your SharePoint Team Site, perform the following tasks:

1. On the **Travel** subsite, notice that the top link bar of the **Travel** subsite is different from the top link bar of the parent team site, and then return to the **Team Site** home page by selecting the browser's **Back** button.

2. Go to the **Facilities** subsite.

3. Notice that the top link bar of the **Facilities** subsite is the same as the top link bar of the parent team site, and then return to the **Team Site** home page by selecting the first link, **Team Site,** on the top link bar.

4. On the **Team Site**, hide the Quick Launch and display the site content tree in the left navigation pane.

5. Restore the original navigation setup by displaying the Quick Launch and removing the site content tree from the left navigation pane.

Customize site navigation

Continuing on your SharePoint Team Site, perform the following tasks:

1. Go to the **Travel** site, and customize the top link bar by using in-page editing, as follows:

   - Add a link to the parent team site with the following parameters:

Text to Display	Home
Address	The URL of the team site

   - Change the position of the new link on the top link bar so that it is the first from the left.

2. Display the **Site Contents** page.

3. Customize the Quick Launch by using in-page editing, as follows:

- Rename the **Home** link to Travel, so that this link is not confused with the link to the parent team site on the top link bar that you created in step 1.

- Add a permanent link to the **Travel Calendar** list by dragging it to the Quick Launch.

- Remove the temporary link to the **Travel Calendar** from the **Recent** section on the Quick Launch.

4. Customize the Quick Launch by using the **Quick Launch** page, as follows:

- Create a new section heading with the following parameters:

  Address   #

  Description   SharePoint Resources

- Create a new navigation link with the following parameters:

  Web address   http://sharepoint.microsoft.com

  Description   SharePoint products

  Heading   SharePoint Resources

5. Return to the home page of the **Travel** site.

Work with the ribbon

Continuing on your Travel site, perform the following tasks:

1. On the home page, select the **Page** tab to display the ribbon. Explore the ribbon commands, and then hide the ribbon.

2. Open the **Documents** library from the Quick Launch.

3. Select the **Files** tab to display the ribbon. Notice that only the **New** group commands are available, whereas the others are dimmed.

4. Select a document by clicking or tapping in its leftmost column. Notice that the commands on the **Files** tab that were dimmed are now available.

5. Select the **Library** tab. Explore the commands, and then hide the ribbon.

6. Open the **Travel Announcements** list from the Quick Launch.

7. Select the **Items** tab to display the ribbon. Notice that only the **New** group commands are available, whereas the others are dimmed.

8. Select a list item by clicking or tapping in its leftmost column. Notice that the commands on the **Items** tab become available.

9. Select the **List** tab. Explore the commands, and then hide the ribbon.

10. Return to the Travel site home page.

Navigate lists and libraries

Continuing on your Travel site, perform the following tasks:

1. Open the **Documents** library.

2. Display a callout for the **WideWorldTravelGuidelines** document.

3. Obtain the document link by using its callout. Then either save it in a file on your device or email it to yourself.

4. Obtain the document QR code by using its callout. Then either save it in a file on your device or email it to yourself, and return to the **Documents** library.

5. Rename the **WideWorldTravelGuidelines** document to TravelGuidelines.

6. Confirm that the document link you obtained in step 3 is a durable link by checking that it has the resource identifier appended at the end of the URL, after the path to the **WideWorldTravelGuidelines** document. Copy the link in your browser address bar and open the document. Confirm that the link works even though the file has been renamed.

> **TIP** If durable links are not available on your site, step 6 will not work.

Understand web parts and app parts

Continuing on your Travel site, perform the following tasks:

1. On the home page of the **Travel** site, display the web parts. Notice that the Format Text and Insert tabs become available on the ribbon.

2. Click or tap in the **Newsfeed** web part and notice that the **Web Part** tab becomes available.

3. Click or tap in the **Documents** web part and notice that the Files and the Library tabs become available.

4. Stop displaying the web parts on the home page of the **Travel** site.

Work with the Recycle Bin

Continuing on your Travel site, perform the following tasks:

1. Go to the **Documents** library and select the **TravelGuidelines** document.

2. Display the document shortcut menu and select **Delete**. Then select **OK** in the confirmation message that appears to confirm that you want to move this document to the Recycle Bin.

3. Restore the document from the site Recycle Bin.

4. Return to the **Documents** library and confirm that the document has been restored.

5. Delete the document from the **Documents** library again, and this time remove it from the site Recycle Bin.

6. Restore the document from the second-stage Recycle Bin.

7. Return to the **Documents** library in the **Travel** site, and confirm that the document has been restored to its original location.

Work with content in lists and libraries

Microsoft SharePoint lists and libraries provide information management and collaboration capabilities. You can think of SharePoint 2016 lists as spreadsheets that you and your coworkers can simultaneously use. SharePoint lists represent editable, web-based tables that facilitate concurrent, multi-user interactions against a common, centralized, extensible set of columns and rows. All of the webpages you need to create, review, update, delete, and manage lists and their data are automatically and dynamically generated by SharePoint.

One of the most compelling features that SharePoint 2016 provides is libraries. A library can be thought of as a list of files. Just as lists provide an effective way to work with all types of data they contain, SharePoint libraries function similarly for documents and files, such as Microsoft Word documents. By using SharePoint document libraries, you can filter and group documents and view metadata for documents stored in the library.

This chapter guides you through procedures related to discovering lists and libraries in a site, creating and populating lists and libraries, checking files out and working with versions, organizing lists and libraries, deleting and restoring list items and documents, staying up to date with content changes, and working offline.

In this chapter

- Discover lists and libraries in a site
- Create and populate lists
- Create and populate libraries
- Check files out and work with versions
- Organize lists and libraries
- Delete and restore list items and documents
- Stay up to date with content changes
- Work offline

Practice files

For this chapter, use the practice files from the SP2016SBS\Ch03 folder. For practice file download instructions, see the introduction.

Discover lists and libraries in a site

SharePoint 2016 includes several templates that you can use to create the default types of lists and libraries. In SharePoint, each list and library is implemented as an app. You can choose a template app from the list and library apps available in the Your Apps page to generate a new list or library with a specific predefined function-ality and set of columns. Each list or library app has a specific purpose, and its tile visually indicates the type of list or library the app will create. Later in this chapter, the "Organize lists and libraries" topic explores how to add, alter, and delete columns in lists and libraries; most default columns can be altered or deleted, even after data has been entered into them.

There are 20 list apps and 10 library apps provided by SharePoint 2016; these are described in the following table.

> ✅ **TIP** Your site might provide a different number of default list and library apps, depend-
> ing on your SharePoint 2016 edition, the enabled features, or the Microsoft Office 365
> plan that your organization subscribes to.

List apps

Tile	List app	Description
📢	Announcements	Create an announcements list when you want a place to share news, status, and other short bits of information.
📅	Calendar	Create a calendar list when you want a calendar-based view of upcoming meetings, deadlines, and other important events. You can share information between your Calendar list and Microsoft Outlook.
▦	Circulations	Create a circulations list when you want publications to be sent to specific recipients. This list contains many unique capabilities for distributing information to these selected users.
📇	Contacts	Create a contacts list when you want to manage information about people your team works with, such as customers or partners. You can share information between your contacts list and Outlook.
▦	Custom List	Create a custom list when you want to specify your own columns. The list opens as a webpage on which you can add or edit items one at a time.

List apps

Tile	List app	Description
	Custom List In Datasheet View	Create a custom list in Datasheet view when you want to specify your own columns. The list opens in a spreadsheet-like environment for convenient data entry, editing, and formatting.
	Discussion Board	Create a discussion board when you want to provide a place for newsgroup-style discussion. Discussion boards provide features for managing discussion threads and ensuring that only approved posts appear.
	External List	Create an external list to work with data that is stored outside of SharePoint, but that you can read and write within SharePoint. The data source for an External List is called an External content type. Unlike a native SharePoint list, an External List uses Business Connectivity Services to access data directly from an external system.
	Import Spreadsheet	Import a spreadsheet when you want to create a list that has the same columns and contents as an existing spreadsheet. Importing a spreadsheet requires Microsoft Excel.
	Issue Tracking	Create an issue tracking list when you want to manage a set of issues or problems. You can assign, prioritize, and follow the progress of issues from start to finish.
	KPI List	Create a KPI list to track key performance indicators (KPIs) and to display the status of each indicator on a dashboard page. You can set up KPI lists to track performance by using one of four data sources: manually entered data, data in a SharePoint list, data in an Excel workbook, or data from Microsoft SQL Server Analysis Services (SSAS).
	Languages And Translators	Create a languages and translators list to use with a Translation Management workflow. The workflow uses the list to assign translation tasks to the translator specified in the list for each language.
	Links	Create a links list when you have links to webpages or other resources that you want to share.
	Microsoft IME Dictionary List	Create a Microsoft IME dictionary list (IME stands for Input Method Editor) when you want to use data in the list as a Microsoft IME dictionary.

3

List apps

Tile	List app	Description
	PerformancePoint Content List	Create a PerformancePoint content list to store dashboard items, such as scorecards, reports, filters, dashboard pages, and other dashboard items that you create by using PerformancePoint Dashboard Designer.
	Project Tasks	Create a Project Tasks list when you want a graphical view (a Gantt chart) of a group of work items that you or your team needs to complete. You can share information between your Project Tasks list and Outlook.
	Promoted Links	Create a Project Tasks list when you want a graphical view (a Gantt chart) of a group of work items that you or your team needs to complete. You can share information between your Project Tasks list and Outlook.
	Status list	Create a status list to display and track the goals of your project. The list includes a set of colored icons to communicate the degree to which goals are met.
	Survey	Create a survey when you want to poll other users of the website. Surveys provide features that you can use to quickly create questions and define how users specify their answers.
	Tasks	Create a tasks list when you want to track a group of work items that you or your team must complete.

Library apps

Tile	Library app	Description
	Asset Library	Create an asset library to share and manage digital media assets, such as image, audio, and video files. An asset library provides content types, with properties and views such as thumbnails and metadata keywords for managing and browsing media assets.
	Dashboards Library	Create a dashboards library to contain PerformancePoint-deployed dashboards.

Library apps

Tile	Library app	Description
	Data Connection Library	Create a data connection library to simplify the maintenance and management of data connections. A data connection library is a centralized place to store Office Data Connection (ODC) files. Each of these files (which have an .odc extension) contains information about how to locate, log on to, query, and access an external data source.
	Document Library	Create a document library when you have a collection of documents or other files that you want to share. Document libraries support features such as folders, versioning, and checking out.
	Form Library	Create a form library when you have XML-based business forms, such as status reports or purchase orders, that you want to manage. These libraries require an XML editor, such as Microsoft InfoPath.
	Picture Library	Create a picture library when you have pictures you want to share. Picture libraries provide special features for managing and displaying pictures.
	Record Library	Create a record library to keep a central repository for storing and managing your organization's records or important business documents. You can set policies that determine what records to store, how to route and manage the documents, and how long these records must be retained.
	Report Library	Create a report library to simplify the creation, management, and delivery of webpages, documents, and KPIs of metrics and goals. The report library is a central place where you can create and save reports and dashboards.
	Process Diagram Library	Create a process diagram library to store and share process diagram documents, such as those created with Microsoft Visio.
	Wiki Page Library	Create a wiki page library when you want to have an interconnected collection of wiki pages that multiple people can use to gather information in a format that is easy to create and modify. Wiki page libraries support pictures, tables, hyperlinks, and internal wiki linking.

3

To display all apps available on your site

1. Go to the Your Apps page by doing any of the following:

    - On the **Settings** menu, select **Add an app**.

    - On the Quick Launch, select **Site Contents**, and then on the **Site Contents** page, select the **add an app** tile.

    - On the **Get started with your site** page, select the **Add lists, libraries, and other apps** tile.

To display the list apps available on your site

1. Display the **Your Apps** page.

2. In the search box at the top of the page, enter list.

3. Press **Enter** on the keyboard or select the **Search** icon.

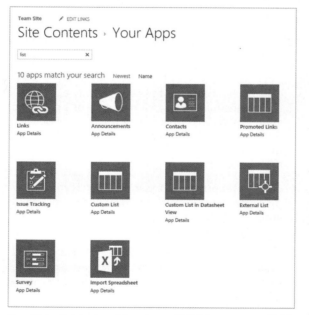

Your SharePoint setup determines which list apps are available on your site

To display the library apps available on your site

1. Display the **Your Apps** page.

2. In the search box at the top of the page, enter library.

3. Press **Enter** on the keyboard or select the **Search** button to start the search.

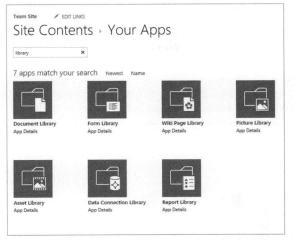

Your SharePoint setup determines which library apps are available on your site

Create and populate lists

SharePoint lists empower you to provision your own repositories of structured information in which list items behave like rows consisting of self-labeled columns. After you've provisioned a list, you can create and edit list items in several ways, either one by one by using a form on a separate page, or within the list page in a grid that is similar to a spreadsheet.

Create lists

The first step in creating a new list is to ask yourself, "What kind of information do I want to gather (or display)?" The answer to this question will help you determine which list app to choose. Perhaps you want to start with a list that is close to your end goal and then add, delete, and alter the default columns to provide the solution you are trying to achieve. For example, if you are planning to collect information such as names and addresses, you can choose the Contacts list app to create your initial list, and then modify it. Or perhaps you want to start with a bare-bones list and build it entirely from scratch. In that case, you would likely choose the Custom List app to create your initial list.

> **TIP** If the list items in the list you want to create always contain files, consider using a document library instead of a list.

When you create a list, a new tile for the list is added to the Site Contents page, with a green "new" icon to the right of the tile. A link to the new list is shown on the Quick Launch, in the Recent section.

> **TIP** The link to the new list in the Recent section on the Quick Launch is displayed temporarily. When more lists and libraries are created, their links take precedence over the older ones in the Recent section. The Recent section displays five of the newest links.

The Site Contents page with a new tile for the new BuyerTasks list and a new BuyerTasks link in the Recent section on the Quick Launch

When you initially create a list in SharePoint, you are establishing two name values: the display name, usually labeled *Name* or *Title*; and the URL name, also known as the internal name. The display name is used to populate both names. However, only the display name can be changed after the list is created.

After the list has been created, it is often useful to modify a list's display name so that it is more descriptive than the initial name that is used in the URL. The revisions to the list name only affect the display name and not the URL name. For example, if the list was named *BuyerTasks* without a space between *Buyer* and *Tasks*, it would be useful to change the display name so that it has a space in it.

> **TIP** Best practices to follow when initially naming a list in SharePoint include the following: The initial name should be descriptive, intuitive, and easy to remember. It should be concise and should not contain spaces (a space gets converted to *%20* in the URL). The initial name should be consistently used throughout the site. Your organization might also have specific naming conventions that you will want to follow.

To create a list

1. Display the **Your Apps** page.

2. Select the tile for the type of list you want to create, such as Tasks or Contacts. The Adding dialog box opens.

3. In the **Name** box, enter a display name for the new list. This box also supplies the value that SharePoint uses for the new list's URL.

3

Adding Tasks ✕

Pick a name
You can add this app multiple times to your site. Give it a unique name.

Name:
BuyerTasks

Advanced Options   Create   Cancel

Creating a new Tasks list

4. Select **Create**.

> ✓ **TIP** Selecting Advanced Options allows you to provide both a name and a description for your new list at the time of creation. You can change the list name and description after the list has been created.

To change the display name of a list

1. On the Settings menu, select **Site Contents** to go to the Site Contents page.
2. Locate the tile for the list whose display name you want to change, and select the tile to go to the default list view page for the list.
3. In the upper-left of the page, select the **List** tab, and then at the right end of the **List** tab, in the **Settings** group, select **List Settings**.

Select List to display the List tab

4. On the **Settings** page, in the **General Settings** area, select **List name, description and navigation**.

General Settings

- List name, description and navigation
- Versioning settings
- Advanced settings
- Validation settings
- Audience targeting settings
- Rating settings
- Form settings

Selecting List Name, Description And Navigation in the General Settings area in the Settings page for a list

5. On the **General Settings** page, in the **Name** box, replace the initial list name by entering a new display name.

The General Settings page, with Common Buyer Tasks entered in the Name box

> ✓ **TIP** On the General Settings page, you can enter the list description and choose to permanently display the list link on the Quick Launch.

6. Select **Save** to save the change.

> ✓ **TIP** Notice that the list name on the top of the page and the link on the Quick Launch now reflect the modified display name. However, if you navigate to the list default page, you can see that the browser's address bar still reflects the initial name (internal name) given to the list when it was created.

Add and edit list items

Creating a SharePoint list automatically generates the pages you need to view the list as a whole, view a list item, add a new list item, and edit an existing list item.

A *view* defines how the information in a list or library is displayed to the users. Although some lists only have a single view when they are created, SharePoint generates multiple list views for others. For example, when a new Tasks list is created, the following seven list views are generated: All Tasks (the default), Calendar, Completed, Gantt Chart, Late Tasks, My Tasks, and Upcoming. You can navigate to a list default view page from other locations by selecting the list name on the Quick Launch. When you display a list, several links for the views available for that list are shown at the top of the list. You can display more links to list views by selecting the ellipsis to the right of the displayed view links.

You can create and edit list items individually by using a form on a separate page, or you can create and edit items within the list page, in a grid that is similar to working in Excel. The grid is referred to as a datasheet view, also known as a Quick Edit view or just a Quick Edit. It is handy when you need to add or edit multiple list items.

> ✓ **TIP** When you use Quick Edit, you can only enter values for columns featured in the view you are currently using. When you use list item forms, you can enter values into all available columns.

After you have created a list item, the new item is displayed on the list default view page with a green icon to its right.

⊕ **new task** or edit this list

All Tasks   Calendar   Completed   ••• | Find an item   🔎 |

✓	☑		Task Name		Due Date	Assigned To
	☐		Create vendor SharePoint list ❄ •••			

A new list item on a Task list page

Occasionally, you might want to attach one or more documents to a list item. You can do so by using the Attach File command on the Items tab. By default, all lists in SharePoint allow attachments. However, if every list item always has one and only one document, reconsider the use of a list and opt for a document library instead.

To add a list item

1.   Go to the list's default view page and do one of the following:

   •   In the body of the page, at the top of the list, select the **plus sign**.

   •   In the body of the page, at the top of the list, select **new item**. (In a Tasks list, the new item link is displayed as *New Task*.)

   ⊕ **new task** or edit this list

   The New Task link

   •   On the **Items** tab of the ribbon, select **New Item**. (In a Tasks list, the Items tab is named *Tasks*.)

2. On the list item page, provide the list item details. For example, if you are creating a new task, in the **Task Name** box, enter the new task name.

Task Name *	Create vendor SharePoint list
Start Date	
Due Date	
Assigned To	Enter names or email addresses...

Creating a new task

3. Select **Save** to save the new item and return to the list default view page.

To add list items in a Quick Edit view

1. Open the list default view page.

2. In the body of the page, select **edit** to the right of the **new item** (or **new task**) link to display the list as a grid in the Quick Edit view (also known as the datasheet view), with a new empty row at the bottom.

3. Fill in the details of the new list item in the empty row. For example, for a new task, enter a name in the **Task Name** column and a date for when the task is due in the **Due Date** column.

Stop editing this list

		Task Name		Due Date	Assigned To	+
	☐	Create vendor SharePoint list ✳	...			
	☐	Ensure vendor access ✳	...	September 9		

All Tasks   Calendar   Completed   ...   Find an item

Shortcuts ⓘ

Creating a list item in the Quick Edit view

> ✅ **TIP** In Quick Edit, you can enter values only for columns featured in the view you are using. In list item forms, you can enter values into all available columns.

You can use the empty row at the bottom of the grid to add more list items if you want to.

4. When you have finished adding items, select **Stop** at the top of the list to return to the default view.

To edit a list item

1. On the list default view page, select the list item you want to edit by clicking or tapping in its leftmost column.

  Create vendor SharePoint list ≠ •••

Selecting a list item

2. Select *Items* at the top of the page to display the ribbon. (The actual name of the *Items* tab depends on the type of list you are working with—for example, it could be called *Tasks* or *Contacts*.)

The Tasks tab

3. In the **Manage** group, select **Edit Item** to open the list item page in edit mode.

4. Make the changes you want. For example, in a **Tasks** list, for a completed task, you can enter **100** in the **% Complete** box to mark the task as completed.

Task Name *	Create vendor SharePoint list
Start Date	
Due Date	
Assigned To	Enter names or email addresses...
% Complete	100 %

Editing a list item

5. When you have finished making your edits, select **Save** to return to the list default page.

To attach a document to a list item

1. Open the list default view page.

2. In the body of the page, select the list item you want to attach a document to by clicking or tapping in its leftmost column.

3. On the *Items* tab, in the **Action** group, select **Attach File** to open the Attach File dialog box.

Attach File	×
Name:	Browse...

Attaching a file

4. Select **Browse** to open the Choose File To Upload dialog box.

5. Navigate to the file you want to attach to the list item, and select **Open** to return to the Attach File dialog box. The location of the selected document is displayed in the Name box.

> ⚠ **IMPORTANT** At this point, the document is only associated with the list item in memory. Closing the browser abandons the attachment. You must select OK to save the attachment's association with this task.

6. Select **OK** to upload the document and attach it to the list item.

Create and populate libraries

A library is a location in a site where you can create, collect, update, and manage documents and other files with other team members. Each library displays a list of files and key information about the files, which helps people use the files to work together. In the business world, being able to work with documents quickly and effectively is of paramount importance.

You can use libraries to store your documents and other files on a SharePoint site rather than on your local computer's hard drive, so that coworkers can find and work with them more easily. Libraries are used to store files, whereas lists are used to store other types of content. Like lists, libraries contain metadata stored in columns that you can use to filter, sort, and group the items.

After you have created a library, you can populate it with files. For example, you can upload existing documents into a document library, or you can create new documents from within the library based on the default document template for the library. After documents are placed in the library, you can search and filter them to make it easier to find what you are looking for, and you can collaborate with others to help develop the final version of a document. You can edit documents in a SharePoint library by using an Office client program such as Word or an Office Online program such as Word Online.

Create libraries

When you create a new SharePoint team site, a generic document library called *Documents* is created. Because this library lacks a descriptive name, a best practice is to create a new library for a particular business category or subject instead of just using the Documents library for your documents. Make sure that the names of your document libraries are descriptive and that each library has a specific topic, to make it easier to find documents. Storing all documents together in the default Documents library—or any one document library—defeats the purpose of using SharePoint sites to make information easier to locate.

When a library is created, a new tile for this library is added to the Site Contents page with a green "new" icon to the right of the tile. A link to the new library is shown on the Quick Launch, in the Recent section.

Team Site   ✎ EDIT LINKS

Site Contents

Home
Notebook
Documents
Recent
    Furniture
    Common Buyer Tasks

Lists, Libraries, and other Apps

add an app

Common Buyer Tasks
new!
2 items
Modified 41 minutes ago

The Site Contents page with a new tile for the newly created Furniture library and a new link to the library in the Recent section on the Quick Launch

The procedure in this section also applies to creating types of libraries other than document libraries.

To create a library

1. Display the **Your Apps** page.
2. Select the tile for the type of library you want to create, such as **Document Library**. The Adding Library dialog opens.
3. In the **Name** box, enter a name for the new library, such as *Furniture*.

Adding Document Library   ×

Pick a name   Name:
You can add this app multiple times to your site. Give it a   Furniture
unique name.

Advanced Options   Create   Cancel

Creating a new library

4. Select **Create**.

Upload existing files

There are several ways to add existing files to a library, including the following:

- You can use your browser to upload files to the library via the SharePoint interface.

- You can use File Explorer to copy or move files into the library, such as by dragging them from your desktop or any other location to SharePoint.

- You can use sync to upload files that are stored offline.

This section focuses on the first two methods: using your browser and using File Explorer. The "Work offline" topic later in this chapter covers using sync to add a file to a library.

To add a file to a library by using a browser

1. Go to a library you want to add a file to.

2. Do one of the following to open the Add A Document dialog:

   - In the library, in the body of the page, select **Upload**.

   - On the keyboard, press **Alt+U**.

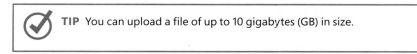

Uploading a file to a library

3. Select **Browse** to open the Open dialog, browse to the file you want to upload, select the file, and then select **Open**.

> ✓ **TIP** You can upload a file of up to 10 gigabytes (GB) in size.

4. In the **Add a document** dialog, select **OK** to confirm the upload and return to the library.

> ✓ **TIP** You can add one file at a time by using this method. To upload multiple files at the same time, use the dragging method or the copy-and-paste methods covered in the next two procedures.

3

To add files to a library by dragging

1. In a library you want to add files to, open File Explorer, and navigate to the folder where the files you want to add are located.

2. Position the File Explorer window next to the browser window displaying the library so that you can drag files from File Explorer to the browser.

3. In File Explorer, select the files to upload by doing one of the following:

    - To add one file, select the file.

    - To add multiple files, press and hold down the **Ctrl** key when you select the files.

4. Drag the files to the library in the browser window, to where it says **Drag files here to upload**.

Drag files to where it says "Drag files here to upload"

> **TIP** When you drag files into a browser window, the Drop Here box appears, identifying the broader area on the page where you can drop the files.

5. After the upload, select **Dismiss** at the top of the documents list to dismiss the confirmation message that an upload has been completed.

To add files to a library by using copy and paste

1. In a library you want to add a file or files to, on the **Library** tab, in the **Connect and Export** group, select **Open with Explorer**.

The Library tab

The library content is displayed in File Explorer. Displaying the SharePoint library content in File Explorer is referred to as an Explorer View.

> **TIP** The Open With Explorer button is typically disabled for an unsupported browser or unsupported operating system. If the button is unavailable, your browser might not be compatible with SharePoint.

2. Open another instance of File Explorer, navigate to the folder where the files you want to add are located, and select the files.

3. Copy the files by doing one of the following:

   - In File Explorer, from the shortcut menu, select **Copy**.
   - Press **Ctrl+C** on the keyboard.

> **TIP** When you cut and paste, you are moving the file. When you copy and paste, or drag from File Explorer to a SharePoint library, you are copying the file.

4. Go to the File Explorer window that is displaying the library files, and do one of the following to add the files to the library:

   - From the document's shortcut menu, select **Paste**.
   - Press **Ctrl+V** on the keyboard.

> **TIP** In the browser where the library is displayed, refresh the page to verify that the files are listed in the library.

Create documents from a library

You can create new Office documents directly from a SharePoint library. A new document will be based on a default template for the library.

You can create a new document in the Office client program, such as Word, if it is installed on your device. You can also create it in your browser, by using an Office Online program such as Word Online.

To create a document from a library by using an Office Online program such as Word Online

1. Go to a library in which you want to create a document.

2. Do one of the following:

   - In the document library, in the body of the page, select **New**.
   - On the keyboard, press **Alt+N**.

3. Select the type of document you want to create.

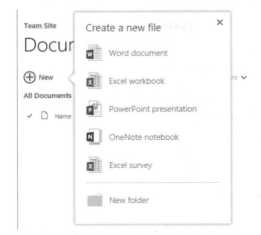

Types of Office documents that can be created from a library

A new document opens in the Office Online program you selected. For example, selecting Word Document opens Word Online.

> ⚠ **IMPORTANT** At the time of writing, selecting a type of document is available in SharePoint Online. In SharePoint on-premises, selecting the New link displays the Add A Document dialog that you can use to upload a file, as discussed in the previous section, rather than create a new document.

A new document in Word Online

> ✓ **TIP** Depending on your server settings, the new document will open either in your browser in Word Online or in the Word client program, if it is installed on your device. If the new document opens in the Word client, go the next procedure. Otherwise, continue to the next step.

4. The new document is automatically saved in the library with the default name that is shown in the title bar, such as *Document*. To rename the document, select its name in the title bar, enter the new name, and then press **Enter**.

5. Add the content you want to the new document.

> **TIP** If you require access to features that are available only in the full Office program, you can switch to the full Office client program. For example, in Word Online, select Open In Word to continue working on the document in Word.

6. When you're done, return to the library where the file is saved by doing one of the following:

    • Select the site link in the title bar, to the left of the file name.

    • Select the **Back** button in your browser.

7. On the library page, select **Refresh** to confirm that your new document is now listed in the library.

Office Online programs

The Office Online programs, or apps, are part of Office 365 and are available if you are using SharePoint Online. If you are using SharePoint 2016 on-premises, the Office Online Server (OOS) in your organization must be installed and activated before you can create or edit documents in the Office Online programs such as Word Online, Excel Online, PowerPoint Online, and OneNote Online. If OOS is installed and activated, you can view and, depending on your organization's license terms, edit Office documents by using a supported web browser on computers and on various mobile devices and tablets, such as Windows Phones, iPhones, iPads, and Android tablets and phones. The Office Online programs can be used from any device where a browser is available; however, they have less functionality in comparison with Office client programs such as Word, Excel, PowerPoint, and OneNote.

To create a document from a library by using Word

1. Go to a library in which you want to create a document.

2. On the **Files** tab, in the **New** group, select **New Document**.

The New group on the Files tab

> ✓ **TIP** Depending on your server settings, the new document will open either in the Word client program or in Word Online. If the new document opens in Word Online, select Edit In Word on the title bar.

3. A new document opens in the Word client program. If a warning about allowing this website to open a program on your device appears, select **Allow**.

> ✓ **TIP** New Word documents created from SharePoint are based on the default template for the SharePoint library, which is called *template.dotx*. If a warning about this template appears, select Yes to confirm that you want to proceed with opening a file.

4. If prompted, provide your user name and password for the SharePoint site.

5. If a **Read-Only** banner appears at the top of the document, select **Edit Document**.

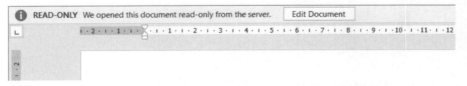

The Read-Only banner that appears when a SharePoint document is opened in Word

6. Add the content you want to the new document.

7. When you're done, go to the **File** tab and select **Save** to save the document to the document library.

8. To name the file, under **Current Folder**, select the library to open the Save As dialog box. Note that the location points to the document library.

9. Enter the name of the new document, and then select **Save**.

10. In the browser, refresh the library page to confirm that your new document is listed in the library.

Edit documents

In SharePoint, you can edit documents in Office client programs such as Word and Excel or in your browser by using Office Online apps that provide online companion web apps to Office client programs, such as Word Online or Excel Online. (For more information, see the "Office Online programs" sidebar earlier in this topic.)

When you're on the move, it is often very useful to be able to edit your documents within a browser, without the need for the client program to be installed on the device you're using.

To edit a document in an Office client program from a library

1. Go to the library that contains the document you want to edit.

2. Open the document for editing in the Office client program by doing one of the following:

    -   Select the ellipsis to the right of the document's name, and in the callout that opens, do one of the following:

        -   Select **Open**.

        -   Select the ellipsis, and then select **Open in Word.**

Opening a Word document for editing in the Word client

- Display the document's shortcut menu, and then select **Open in Word**.

- Select the document by clicking or tapping in its leftmost column, go to the **Files** tab, and then select **Edit Document**.

The Edit Document button on the Files tab

> **TIP** Depending on your server settings, you might be able to just click or tap the document you want to edit to open it. The document will open in either the Office Online app in your browser, or in the Office client program, if it is installed on your device. If the document opens in Office Online in your browser, in the title bar, select Edit Document. If the document opens in Office Online for viewing, open the Edit Document menu and select Edit In Word. In either case, you can then continue to the next step.

3. The document opens in the Office client program such as Word. Do the following:

   - If a warning about allowing this website to open a program on your computer appears, select **Allow**.

   - If a warning about the document appears, select **Yes** to confirm that you want to proceed with opening a file.

   - If prompted, provide your user name and password for the SharePoint site.

   - If a **Read-Only** banner appears at the top of the document, select **Edit Document**.

4. In Word, edit the document.

5. On the **File** tab, select **Save** to save the document to the document library.

> **TIP** You can configure whether your device opens a document within your browser or in the document's native Office client program. The default option is to open in a browser by using Office Online apps, such as Word Online, so that users can use their browsers to view their documents online. For on-premises deployments, this capability depends on Office Online programs being installed and activated on the server in your organization. For more details, see Chapter 4, "Make lists and libraries work for you."

To edit a document in Office Online from a library

1. Go to the library that contains the document you want to edit.

2. Open the document in its corresponding Office Online app by doing one of the following:

   - Display the document's shortcut menu by right-clicking the document name, or on touch devices by pressing and holding the document name, and select **Open in** *Office App* **Online** (for example, Open In Word Online).

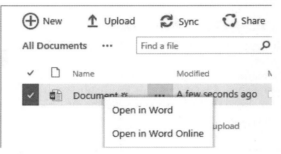

   Opening a document in Word Online

   - Select the ellipsis to the right of the document's name, and in the callout that opens, select the ellipsis, and then select **Open in** *Office App* **Online** (for example, Open In Word Online).

   - Click or tap the document you want to edit.

3. The document opens in Office Online. If the document opens for viewing, select **Edit Document** and then select **Edit in** *Office App* **Online** (for example, Edit In Word Online).

   When you make your edits, the document is saved automatically.

4. When you're done, return to the library where the file is saved by doing one of the following:

   - Select the site link in the title bar, to the left of the file name.

   - Select the **Back** button in your browser.

5. In the library, select **Refresh** and confirm that the document has been saved to the library by checking its timestamp.

> ✓ **TIP** If you open a document in Office Online and the Edit Document option is unavailable, it means that Office Online programs have not been activated for editing in your environment.

To rename a file in a library

1. In the library that contains the file you want to rename, display the file's short-cut menu, and select **Rename**.

2. On the file page, enter a new name in the **Name** box, and select **Save**.

Name *	Document	×	.docx
Title			

Renaming a document

Check files out and work with versions

SharePoint 2016 provides several content management capabilities, including checking files in and out and version control.

Check files in and out

Checking out and checking in documents and other files lets others know what documents you are working on so that they don't work on them at the same time.

When you check out a file, you lock the file for editing to prevent other users from editing the file at the same time. When you are done editing the file, you check the file back in, allowing other users to edit the file. When you check in a document, you can also enter comments about what you've changed so that others can see them.

When you want to check out and edit a document, whether you plan to edit it online or download it to the client program, the following sequence is recommended:

1. Check out the document.

2. Download the document and open it in the client program, or open the document in an Office Online app.

3. Edit the document.

4. Upload the document, if necessary. (If you used Office Online, your edits are automatically saved.)

5. Check in the document.

When a document has been checked out, the file icon changes to include a green, downward-pointing arrow, indicating that the document is now checked out. No one else can change this document, and no one else can see your changes while you have it checked out.

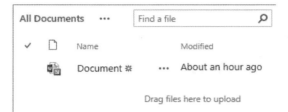

A checked-out document

> ✅ **TIP** Point to the file icon to display the name of the person that the file is checked out to.

When a document is checked out to you, only you can do anything with the file. However, checking out a document is only the first step. You still need to open the file, download it, or edit it online. Finally, after you have finished your edits and saved the document back to the library, you need to check it back in.

> ✅ **TIP** If you check out a file and don't make changes to it, or if you make changes that you don't want to keep, you can discard the checkout, rather than saving and checking in the file.

To check a file out from a library

1. Go to a library where you want to check out a file.

2. Do either of the following:

   - Select the file or files that you want to check out by clicking or tapping in the column to the left of each file. Then, at the top of the page, select the **Files** tab, and in the **Open & Check Out** group, select **Check Out**.

   - Right-click (or on touch devices press and hold) the file that you want to check out, and on the shortcut menu, select **Advanced**, and then select **Check Out**.

Advanced	▸	Shared With
		Compliance Details
		Check Out
		Follow
		Workflows

Display the Advanced shortcut menu by right-clicking or pressing and holding the file name and then selecting Advanced

To check a file in to a library

1. Go to the library where you want to check in a file.

2. Do either of the following:

    • Select the file that you want to check in by clicking or tapping in its leftmost column, go to the **Files** tab, and then in the **Open & Check Out** group, select **Check In**.

    • On the shortcut menu for the file you want to check in, select **Advanced**, and then select **Check In**.

3. In the **Check in** dialog, in the **Retain Check Out** area, select **Yes** if you want to do an interim check-in so you can continue working on the file. Otherwise, leave the default option **No** selected.

Check in   ×

Retain Check Out
Other users will not see your   Retain your check out after checking in?
changes until you check in. If you   ○ Yes ● No
wish to continue editing, you can
retain your check out after
checking in.

Comments
Type comments describing what   Comments:
has changed in this version.

The Check In dialog

4. In the **Comments** box, enter a comment that describes the changes you made. Although this is optional, it is recommended as a best practice.

5. Select **OK**. The file is checked back in and the green arrow disappears from the file icon.

To discard a checkout

1. Go to the library where you want to discard a checkout.

2. Do either of the following:

   - Select the file for which you want to discard the checkout by clicking or tapping in its leftmost column, go to the **Files** tab, and then in the **Open & Check Out** group, select **Discard Check Out**.

   - On the shortcut menu for the file that you want to check in, select **Advanced**, and then select **Discard Check Out**.

3. In the message box that appears, select **OK**.

Work with version history

When versioning is enabled in your list or library, SharePoint 2016 creates a separate copy of the list item or document each time it is edited. With versioning, you can store, track, and restore items in a list and files in a library whenever they change. Although this takes up extra space on the server, it also makes it easy to revert to an older version of the list item or document if necessary.

A library can be configured to keep only major versions or both major and minor versions. Major versions are indicated with whole numbers, such as 1, 2, 3, and so on. Minor versions are indicated with decimals, such as 1.1, 1.2, 1.3, and so on. A major version number is associated with a version that has been published. A minor version number is associated with a version that is in progress but that has not yet been published.

Major versions are available for lists, but minor versions are not. Each version of a list item is numbered with a whole number.

When you view a document's version history, SharePoint displays a list of the occasions when this document was edited and saved, and the author's comments on those changes. From this list you can restore an older version of the document. The restored version becomes the new current version.

To view the version history of a file

1. Go to the library that contains the file.

2. Do either of the following:

   - Select the file by clicking or tapping in its leftmost column and then, on the **Files** tab, in the **Manage** group, select **Version History**.

   - Display the shortcut menu for the file, and then select **Version History**.

To view an earlier version of a file without overwriting your current version

1. Display the version history of the file.

2. In the **Version History** dialog, do either of the following for the file version you want to view:

    *   Select the date/time stamp of the file version.

    *   Point to the date/time stamp of the file version, select the arrow that appears, and select **View** from the menu.

The Version History dialog

Then select the document name in the **Version History** form.

The Version History form for a document that is checked out

Depending on the settings in the library, the document opens for viewing in Word Online or as a read-only document in the Word client program, if it is installed on your device.

To restore an earlier version of a file

1. Display the version history of the file.

2. In the **Version History** dialog, point to the date/time stamp of the file version, select the arrow that appears, and then select **Restore** from the menu.

3. In the confirmation dialog box, select **OK** to replace the current version with the selected version.

> ✅ **TIP** There will now be a new version shown in the Version History dialog that is a copy of the earlier version that you have restored. If major versioning is enabled, this is the latest version that is published on the site. If minor versioning is enabled, the restored version is shown as an additional, unpublished version. SharePoint 2016 actually copies the version you want to restore and makes it the newest minor version. If you want to publish this version, you need to do so manually by using the Publish button on the ribbon.

4. Close the **Version History** dialog box to return to the library.

Organize lists and libraries

When a list or a library grows to large number of items, you often need to organize the content so that you and other users can quickly find information.

You can organize your content into folders. In SharePoint 2016, you can create folders in libraries and lists.

You can also use columns in lists or libraries to group, categorize, sort, and filter information. You can create, change, hide, and delete the list and library columns. These columns can be of multiple types, such as a single line of text, a drop-down list of options, a number that is calculated from other columns, and many others. You can create custom views to save the column and filter setup.

Create folders in a list or a library

Using folders is a common way to organize documents efficiently. SharePoint 2016 provides other mechanisms for organization of your documents, including views and filters. However, many people are most familiar with folders and thus find it easier to create a folder structure.

To create a new folder

1. Go to a library where you want to create a folder.

2. Do one of the following:

    *   On the **Files** tab, in the **New** group, select **New Folder**.
    *   In the body of the page, select **New**, and then select **New Folder.**

    > ✓ **TIP** You can create a new folder in most lists in the same way, by selecting New Folder in the New group on the Items tab. The list must be set up to allow creation of folders. The ability to create folders is a default setting for several lists, such as the Links list.

3. In the **Create a folder** dialog that opens, in the **Name** box, enter the name for the new folder, and then select **Create**.

Create a folder   ×

Name *

[   ]

👥 INVITE PEOPLE

The Create A Folder dialog

Add, edit, and remove list and library columns

The list and library apps in SharePoint 2016 provide an easy way to generate a list or a library with very little effort. And if you need to customize the list and library views, you can easily add, edit, and remove list and library columns in addition to creating additional custom columns by using the Settings page for the list or library. In addition, for a list, you can use Quick Edit view to add new columns, without leaving the list page.

There are many types of columns that can be added to a list or a library, including columns for a single line of text, currency values, date and time, a Yes/No check box, and a drop-down list of options. You can hide a column from being displayed in a list or a library view, and most columns in a list or library can be deleted. However, there are some columns that you cannot delete. All lists have at least one column that cannot be deleted. For instance, the Title column can be renamed but not deleted. Some lists also prevent the deletion of certain columns, so that the list can be displayed properly or integrate with Office programs properly. For example, the Assigned To, Status, and Category columns of any list based on the Issues list app cannot be deleted, and none of the default columns in any list based on the Calendar list app can be deleted.

There are five columns that are automatically created and populated for each list item or file in a library that cannot be changed: ID, Created, Created By, Modified, and Modified By. The ID column ensures that the list or library item is unique in the list or library. It contains a sequential number beginning with 1 and increments by 1 for each new list or library item. SharePoint automatically captures when the list or library item was created, who it was created by, when it was last modified, and who it was last modified by. Initially, the Created and Modified columns are equal, as are the Created By and Modified By columns.

You can choose which columns are displayed in a list or library. This can be done both with custom and default columns. You can also change the order in which columns are displayed in a list or a library. When you remove a column from the view, it hides the column but does not delete it or the data it contains. If you want to delete a column and the data within the column (versus just hiding the column from the view), you can permanently delete the column from a list or a library.

To create a new column in a list or a library

1. Go to the list or library where you want to create a new column.

2. On the **List** or **Library** tab, in the **Manage Views** group, select **Create Column** to open the Create Column page.

3. In the **Name and Type** section, in the **Column name** box, enter the name that you want for the column.

The Create Column page

4. Under **The type of information in this column is**, select the type of information that the new column will contain.

5. In the **Additional Column Settings** section, in the **Description** box, provide a description (this is optional).

> **TIP** Depending on the type of column you select, more options might appear in the Additional Column Settings section. Select additional settings as needed.

6. If the data in the column must be validated, select **Column Validation** to expand the Column Validation section.

> **TIP** If the Column Validation section is not available, the selected type of column does not allow validation.

```
□ Column Validation

Specify the formula that you want to use
to validate the data in this column when      Formula:
new items are saved to this list. The
formula must evaluate to TRUE for
validation to pass.

Example: If your column is called
"Company Name" a valid formula would
be [Company Name]="My Company".

Learn more about proper syntax for
formulas.

Type descriptive text that explains what is
needed for this column's value to be          User message:
considered valid.
```

The Column Validation section of the Create Column page

7. Provide the formula that you want to use to validate the data, and the user message that you want to display to the users to help them provide the valid data.

8. Select **OK** to create the new column and return to the list or library page.

To create a new column in the Quick Edit view

1. Go to a list or a library where you want to create a new column.

2. To switch to the Quick Edit view and display the list in a grid, do either of the following:

   - For a list, do one of the following:

     - At the top of the list, select **edit**.

     - Select **List** to open the ribbon, and then on the **List** tab, in the **View Format** group, select **Quick Edit**.

   - For a library, select **Library** to open the ribbon, and then on the **Library** tab, in the **View Format** group, select **Quick Edit**.

3. In the list or library header row, at the top of the rightmost column (which is empty), select the plus sign (+) to display the menu of column types.

4. Select the type of information that the new column will contain.

+

Text

Number

Date and Time

Person or Group

More Column Types...

The menu of column types in the Quick Edit view

The new column is created and is named after its type (for example, *Number*). The name is displayed highlighted and boxed, showing that you can rename the column.

5. If you want, position your cursor within the box and enter a new name for the column.

> **TIP** You can rename a column in Quick Edit at any time by selecting its name and then selecting Rename Column from the menu that appears.

To modify how the list and library columns are displayed

1. Go to a list or a library where you want to change columns.

2. On the **List** tab or **Library** tab, in the **Manage Views** group, select **Modify View** to go to the **Edit View** page.

3. In the **Columns** section, do either of the following:

   - To change whether a column is displayed in a list or a library page or hidden from view, under the **Display** heading to the left of the name of the column you want to change, select or clear the check box.

Display	Column Name	Position from Left
☑	Type (icon linked to document)	1
☑	Name (linked to document with edit menu)	2
☑	Modified	3
☑	Modified By	4
☐	App Created By	5
☐	App Modified By	6
☐	Check In Comment	7
☐	Checked Out To	8
☐	Content Type	9
☐	Copy Source	10
☐	Created	11
☐	Created By	12
☐	Edit (link to edit item)	13
☐	File Size	14
☐	Folder Child Count	15
☐	ID	16
☐	Item Child Count	17
☐	Name (for use in forms)	18
☐	Name (linked to document)	19
☐	Shared With	20
☐	Shared With Details	21
☐	Title	22
☐	Version	23

The Columns section of the Edit View page

- To change the order that a column appears on the list or library page, under the **Position from Left** heading for the column you want to change select the arrow to open the position number list, and then select the number that would show the new position of this column on the list or library page, counted from the left.

4. Repeat step 3 for all columns you want to modify, and then select **OK** to save your changes and return to the list or library page.

To permanently delete a column and its data from a list or a library

1. On the **List Settings** or **Library Settings** page for the list or library, display the **Columns** section.

2. Select the name of the column that you want to delete.

3. Scroll to the bottom of the **Change Column** page, and select **Delete**.

4. In the confirmation box, select **OK**.

> **TIP** Some columns in lists and libraries are required by SharePoint and can't be deleted, such as Title or Name. If the column can't be deleted, the Delete button is not available. If you can't delete a column, but you don't want the column to be displayed, you can hide it from view.

Sort and filter lists and libraries

As a list or library grows, it eventually becomes difficult to see the entire list or library on a single page. To this end, SharePoint provides built-in sorting and filtering capabilities. On any standard list and library view page, individual column headings can be used to alphabetically sort the entire list in ascending or descending order.

 TIP Selecting another column heading abandons the sort on the current column. You must use Quick Edit view to sort on more than one column.

Filtering on list and library pages works much like an Excel AutoFilter works. Each column has a filtering arrow in its upper-right corner, which appears when you point to the column heading. When you select the arrow, a unique list of the values for each column is generated and presented as a drop-down list above that column.

 TIP In Quick Edit view, sorting and filtering are available by using the arrow also located in the upper-right corner of every column.

A list or library view is a selection of columns on a page that displays items in a list or library, and often defines a specific sort order, filter, grouping, and custom layout. Filters are cumulative but temporal; the next time a list view is chosen, its settings, including filters, will be applied to the list regardless of what was previously chosen. You can save the view that you have created by sorting and filtering a list or a library so that you can keep the sorting orders and filters and come back to it again.

To sort a list or a library

1. In a list or a library in which you want to sort the items, do one of the following:

   - Select the column name. If the column has not had a sorting order applied, selecting its name will sort it in ascending order. To change the sort order, select the column name again.
   - Point to the name of the column by which you want to sort, select the arrow to the right of the column name, and select the sort order.

Name	▾
A↓ Ascending	
Z↓ Descending	

   The Sorting menu

A thin arrow appears to the right of the column name, indicating that the list is sorted by this column. The arrow points up for ascending order, and down for descending order.

To filter a list or a library

1. In a list or a library in which you want to filter the items, point to the name of the column that contains the data you want to filter, select the arrow next to the name, and then, from the list of the values, select the items you want to display.

Due Date ▼ ▾
A↓ Ascending
Z↓ Descending
▼ Clear Filters from Due Date
☐ (Empty)
☑ 9/9/2016
☐ 9/16/2016
☐ 9/20/2016
☐ 9/22/2016

Filtering a column

2. When you are done, select **Close**.

> **TIP** To save your sort order and filters, you can create a list or a library view by using the Save This View option that appears in the upper-right corner of a list that has sorting or filtering applied. For more information about creating views, see Chapter 4, "Make lists and libraries work for you."

To remove a filter from a list or library

1. Go to the list or library that you want to remove filtering from.

2. Locate the filtered column that you want to remove a filter from, point to the column heading, select the arrow at the right to display the filtering menu, and then select **Clear Filters from** *Column Name*.

Delete and restore list items and documents

When documents, list items, folders, or even entire lists are deleted, they are simply flagged as removed so that they no longer appear in the site from which they were deleted. By default, all sites in SharePoint 2016 are configured to display deleted items in the site's Recycle Bin for 30 days. The Recycle Bin provides a safety net when you are deleting documents, document sets, list items, lists, folders, and files. If the user hasn't restored the deleted item in that time period, it is then permanently expunged from the database. If the user empties the Recycle Bin before the 30 days have elapsed, the deleted item is still available to a site collection administrator from the site collection's Recycle Bin.

However, the total size of the deleted items must remain below a specified percentage (50 percent by default) of the total size that a site is allowed to consume (the site quota). If a newly deleted item causes the total to exceed the configured size allowed by the SharePoint central administrator, the items that were deleted first are purged even if 30 days have not elapsed, to make room for the newly deleted item. In this way, SharePoint administrators can make disaster recovery plans based on the Recycle Bin's allowable total maximum size. Of course, a SharePoint administrator can configure the number of days that the Recycle Bin retains deleted items, ranging from the default 30 days in SharePoint 2016 to a specific setting for a number of days, or to "never retain deleted items" or "never remove deleted items."

To delete a list or library item

1. Go to the list or library in which you want to delete an item.
2. Select the item you want to delete. You can select multiple items.
3. Do one of the following:
   - For a list item, do either of the following:
     - On the **Items** tab of the ribbon, in the **Manage** group, select **Delete Items**.
     - Select the ellipsis to the left of the item's name, and in the callout that opens, select the ellipsis again, and then select **Delete Item**.
   - For a document, do either of the following:
     - On the **Files** tab of the ribbon, in the **Manage** group, select **Delete Document**.
     - Display the shortcut menu for the selected document, and select **Delete**.
4. In the confirmation dialog, select **OK**.

To restore a list or library item

1. Go to the site that the list or library item was deleted from.

2. On the **Quick Launch**, select **Recycle Bin** to display the site Recycle Bin page.

3. Select the list item or document by selecting the check boxes at their left. You can select multiple list items and documents.

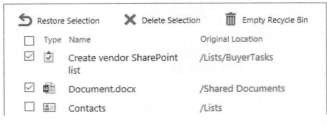

The Recycle Bin selection

4. At the top of the deleted items list, select **Restore Selection** to restore the selected items.

5. Select **OK** to confirm.

> ✓ **TIP** After you've restored the selection from the Recycle Bin, you might want to navigate to the original list or library to confirm that the list item or document has been restored to its original location.

Stay up to date with content changes

In SharePoint 2016, you can stay up to date with content changes by using features such as the following:

- You can set up alerts to receive notifications via email or SMS when changes are made to the content of a site.

- You can follow documents to track updates to those documents in your newsfeed.

Set up alerts

SharePoint 2016 includes a handy feature that sends an email notification or text message whenever changes are made to content in a site, including changes made to list items in a list. The setup for this notification is called an alert. You can set up an alert for a list, library, folder, file, or list item. No alerts are set up automatically, so you must subscribe to the alerts that you want. Alerts can be set up for different types of changes so that you can learn about the changes you are most interested in.

Alerts are quite easy to set up. Every list and library in a SharePoint 2016 site has an Alert Me button in the Share & Track group on the ribbon. You use the button on the List tab of the ribbon to subscribe to an alert on a list level, and the one on the Library tab to subscribe to an alert on a library level. To subscribe to an alert for an item or file, you select the item in a list or the file in a library, and then select the Alert Me button on the Items or Files tab, respectively.

> **TIP** For email alerts to be available, the SharePoint central administrator must configure the outgoing email settings for your server. Similarly, for text alerts to be available, the SharePoint Farm administrator must configure the SMS/MMS service settings. Both settings can be configured in SharePoint Central Administration. If these settings are not configured, the Alert Me button on the ribbon and the Alert Me option in the callout menu will not be available.

Alerts specify to whom the alert will be sent and the kind of changes and frequency for which the alert will be sent. By default, the alert is sent to the email address of the user who sets up the alert. If no email address has been established for the authenticated user, an email prompt is generated in the Send Alerts To area. After it has been provided, the address will be remembered for subsequent subscriptions.

When you set up an alert, you choose the type of change for which the alert should be initiated. For example, list-level alerts have subscriptions for All Changes To Any List Item, New Items Are Added Only, Existing Items Are Modified Only, or Items Are Deleted Only. If you want to see added and changed items but not deleted items, you need to set up two alerts. List item–level alerts, however, are only sent when the item changes, because you can only set up this alert after the list item already exists, and a deletion is considered a change to the list item.

You must specify when to send alerts; the default is when anything changes. Different lists and libraries have different options available. For example, a document library provides the following change alert options for a document:

- Anything Changes
- Someone Else Changes A Document
- Someone Else Changes A Document Created By Me
- Someone Else Changes A Document Last Modified By Me

You must also specify the alert frequency. There are three choices for any type of alert.

- Send Notification Immediately
- Send A Daily Summary
- Send A Weekly Summary

Choosing to receive an alert immediately actually queues the notice to be sent as soon as the next job runs after the alert is triggered. By default, the alert job runs every 5 minutes but could be configured by your administrator to wait as long as 59 minutes. The daily and weekly summaries store all changes made to the list or list item and send a summary at the end of the period. By default, daily summary alerts are generated at midnight each night, and weekly summary alerts are generated at midnight every Sunday night.

To set up an alert for a list item or a document

1. Go to a list or a library that contains an item that you want to set up an alert for.

2. Select the item or document for which you want to set up an alert.

3. Do one of the following to open the New Alert dialog box:

   - For a list item, do either of the following:

     - On the **Items** tab of the ribbon, in the **Manage** group, select **Alert Me**, and then select **Set alert on this item**.

     - Select the ellipsis to the left of the item's name, in the callout that opens, select the ellipsis again, select **Advanced**, and then select **Alert me**.

- For a document, on the **Files** tab, in the **Share & Track** group, select **Alert Me**, and then select **Set alert on this document**.

Setting up an alert on a document

4. In the **New Alert** dialog, provide the alert title, who the alerts should be sent to, and the delivery method. Select the criteria for the new alert and the alert frequency, and select **OK**.

Follow documents

In SharePoint 2016, you can follow documents to track updates to them in your newsfeed. Following a document is different from receiving alerts about the changes to the document; setting an alert for the document keeps you notified of specific changes at the predefined frequency, via an email or SMS, whereas following a document adds a link to this document in your newsfeed and provides notifications of all document changes via your newsfeed. In addition, people who are following you will get a newsfeed notification that you're following this document, if they have appropriate permissions to access it. All documents that you follow are shown in one place in your newsfeed, in the list of followed documents.

3

To follow a document

1. Go to a library that contains the document you want to follow.

2. Do one of the following:

   - Display the shortcut menu for the document, select **Advanced**, and then select **Follow**.

   - Select the ellipsis to the left of the document's name, and in the callout that opens, select **Follow**.

   Notice the confirmation that is displayed for a short time in the upper-right corner of the page.

OakDesk.docx
Now following this document

Confirmation that you are following the document

> **TIP** After you've set up document following, you might want to navigate to your newsfeed to confirm that the document has been added to the list of documents that you are following.

Work offline

If you are a mobile device user, you know that it's not always possible or convenient to connect to SharePoint every time you want to read or modify a document. In SharePoint 2016, you can work with your documents offline. You can synchronize, or sync, a SharePoint library to your device. This process creates a copy of the library on your device in the SharePoint folder, under the name that combines the name of the source SharePoint site with the name of the source library, with a hyphen in between—for example, *Team Site-Documents*. You can modify the location to one of your choosing. You can then work with files in the library by using File Explorer. When working offline, you can view and modify the content in the same way you can when working in SharePoint. Updates to the files synchronize back to SharePoint when you are back online. For example, if you create a new document in a library folder on your device, it will be synced back into the source library when you are online.

> **TIP** There are limits on the number and size of files you can sync. You can sync up to 5,000 items in a library, including folders and files. You can download files up to 10 GB.

> ⚠ **IMPORTANT** To use sync, you must have Office 2016 or Office 2013 installed on your device or have an Office 365 subscription that includes Office programs.

To sync a library to your device

1. In SharePoint, go to a library that you want to sync to your device.

2. In the body of the page, above the list of documents, select **Sync**.

3. Confirm that you want to sync the library by selecting **Sync now** in the confirmation dialog.

Sync this library to your device for easy access.

⌕ Sync now

Sync confirmation

4. If the browser security dialog box appears, select **Allow**.

5. In the message box that appears, select **Sync Now** to confirm the root location and start the sync.

6. A message appears confirming that the sync has started. The full path to the location is shown, including the root, the SharePoint folder, and the subfolder that is named after the site and the library, with a hyphen in between; for example, *C:\Sharepoint\Team Site-Documents*.

   If you want to see the files as they come in, select **Show my files**.

Skills review

In this chapter, you learned how to:

- Discover lists and libraries in a site
- Create and populate lists
- Create and populate libraries
- Check files out and work with versions
- Organize lists and libraries
- Delete and restore list items and documents
- Stay up to date with content changes
- Work offline

Practice tasks

The practice files for these tasks are located in the SP2016SBS\Ch03 folder.

> ⚠️ **IMPORTANT** You must have sufficient permissions to perform the operations involved in each practice task to complete that practice task. For more information, see Appendix A, "SharePoint 2016 user permissions and permission levels."

Discover lists and libraries in a site

Go to your SharePoint site and sign in if prompted. Then perform the following tasks:

1. Go to the **Your Apps** page.
2. Using Search, filter the page to display only the list apps available on your site.
3. Using Search, filter the page to display only the library apps available on your site.

Create and populate lists

Continuing on your SharePoint site, perform the following tasks:

1. From the **Your Apps** page, create a Tasks list and name it **BuyerTasks**.
2. Change the display name of the **BuyerTasks** list to **Common Buyer Tasks**.
3. Go to the **Common Buyer Tasks** default list view page, and confirm the following:
   - The page title shows the modified list name.
   - The browser's address bar reflects the original list name.
4. In the **Common Buyer Tasks** list, create a task named **Create vendor SharePoint list**.
5. Switch to the Quick Edit view of the list, and add the following tasks:

Task name	Due date
Ensure vendor access	Any date of your choosing
Identify products to purchase	Any date of your choosing
Generate purchase order	A date after the previous date
Notify Receiving about purchase	A date after the previous date

6. Return to the default list view page of the **Common Buyer Tasks** list.

7. Edit the **Create vendor SharePoint list** task to mark it as complete. Confirm that the completed task is now checked and crossed out.

8. Add the **WideWorldPurchaseOrder** document from the practice file folder to the **Generate purchase order** task, and then return to the default list view page.

9. To confirm that the document has been successfully attached, display the **Generate purchase order** list item's page. Verify that **WideWorldPurchaseOrder. docx** is shown in the **Attachments** field at the bottom of the list item page, and then return to the list.

Create and populate libraries

Continuing on your SharePoint site, perform the following tasks:

1. Create a library named Furniture.

2. Go to the **Furniture** library and do the following to upload documents from the practice file folder to the library:

   - From your browser, launch the **Add a Document** dialog and upload the **OakDesk** document from the practice file folder to the library.

   - Drag the **OakChest** document from the practice file folder to the library page in your browser.

   - Copy the **OakNightStand** and **OakEndTable** documents from the practice folder and paste them into the Explorer View of the library.

3. Refresh the library page in your browser and verify that the library contains the uploaded documents.

4. From within the library, create a new Word document, either in the Word client program or in Word Online. Enter the text Oak Mirror in the document, and then save the document back to the library with the name OakMirror.

5. Refresh the page and verify that the library contains the new document.

6. Open the **OakMirror** document for editing. Format the document text as bold and centered, and then save the document back to the library.

7. Refresh the library page in the browser and verify that the changes to the **OakMirror** document were saved by checking its timestamp.

8. Close the program you used to edit the **OakMirror** document if it's still open, either the Word client program or Word Online.

Check files out and work with versions

Continuing on your SharePoint site, perform the following tasks:

1. Go to the **Furniture** library.

2. Check out the **OakChest** document. Verify that the file icon indicates that the document has been checked out.

3. Check in the **OakChest** document, entering the comment **This is the final version of the document** in the **Check in** dialog box. Verify that the file icon indicates that the document is no longer checked out.

4. Display the **Version History** dialog for the **OakChest** document.

> **TIP** If the Version History option is unavailable, versioning is disabled for this document library. To enable versioning, on the Library tab of the ribbon, select Library Settings, and then on the Settings page, under General Settings, select Versioning Settings. On the Versioning Settings page, in the Document Version History section, select Create Major Versions, and then select OK. To continue with this set of tasks, go back to the Furniture library, check out the OakChest document, and then check it in to create a second version.

5. In the **Version History** dialog, review the versions saved for the **OakChest** document.

6. Restore the first version of the document, and then return to the library.

Organize lists and libraries

Continuing on your SharePoint site, perform the following tasks:

1. Go to the **Furniture** library.

2. In the library, create a folder named **In Progress**.

3. Modify the default list view of the **Furniture** library as follows:
   - Remove the **Modified By** column.
   - Display the **Version** column.

4. Save your changes and return to the library page. Confirm that the library columns are displayed as expected.

5. Sort the **Furniture** library documents in ascending alphabetical order by **Name**, and then reverse the sort order.

6. Go to the **Common Buyer Tasks** list, and switch to the Quick Edit view.

7. To the right of the existing columns, add a column of the type **Number**.

8. Rename the **Number** column to **Sequence**.

9. In the **Sequence** column, enter the following numbers to identify the preferred order of tasks in the list:

Title	Sequence
Create SharePoint list	2
Ensure vendor access	3
Identify products to purchase	1
Generate purchase order	5
Notify Receiving about purchase	4

10. Modify the default list view of the **Common Buyer Tasks** list as follows:
    - Hide the **Assigned To** and **Due Date** columns.
    - Display the **%Complete** column.
    - Change the position of the **Priority** column to **3** so that it appears immediately to the left of the **Task Name** column in the list view page.

11. Save your changes and return to the list page. Confirm that the list columns are displayed as expected.

12. Sort the **Common Buyer Tasks** list in ascending numerical order by **Sequence**, and then reverse the sort order.

13. Switch to the Quick Edit view of the list. Change the **Priority** of the **Ensure Vendor Access** and **Generate Purchase Order** list items to **(1) High**, and then return to the default list view.

Changing priority of tasks

14. In the default list view, filter the list to display only the items that have a **Priority** of **(1) High**. Then remove the filter from the **Priority** column to display a full list.

Delete and restore list items and documents

Continuing on your SharePoint site, perform the following tasks:

1. Go to the **Common Buyer Tasks** list if it is not already open.
2. Delete the **Create Vendor SharePoint list** item.
3. Go to the **Furniture** library.

4. Delete the **OakChest** document.

5. Go to the site **Recycle Bin** and restore the **Create vendor SharePoint list** item and the **OakChest** document.

6. Go to the **Common Buyer Tasks** list and verify that the list item has been restored.

7. Go to the **Furniture** library and verify that the **OakChest** document has been restored.

Stay up to date with content changes

Continuing on your SharePoint site, perform the following tasks:

1. Go to the **Common Buyer Tasks** list.

2. Set an alert on the **Generate purchase orders** task. Accept the default options.

3. Switch to the Quick Edit view of the list.

4. Change the **Priority** for the **Generate purchase orders** task to **(2) Normal**, and then switch back to the default list view.

5. Open your email program, and confirm that you have received an email alert notifying you of a change in priority in this list item.

6. Go to the **Furniture** library.

7. Select the **Follow** option for the **OakDesk** document.

8. On the top left of the page, select your **Newsfeed** page and verify that the **OakDesk** document is listed under **Docs I'm following**.

Work offline

Continuing on your SharePoint site, perform the following tasks:

1. Go to the **Furniture** library.

2. Start the library sync to your local device.

3. In File Explorer on your local device, go to the **C:\SharePoint \Team Site-Furniture** folder to confirm that the library has been synced.

 TIP Depending on your connection and the data volume, there might be a small delay before all the files are synced to your device and appear in the SharePoint folder.

Make lists and libraries work for you

4

Chapter 3, "Work with content in lists and libraries," discussed how to create and use the SharePoint lists and libraries, how to add and remove content, how to work with documents, how to add columns, and how to sort and filter lists and libraries. Now that you have a good grasp of SharePoint lists and libraries, this chapter explores the settings available for managing and configuring the features and functionality of SharePoint 2016 lists and libraries to make them work for you.

This chapter guides you through procedures related to using list and library settings, managing users and permissions, sharing content in lists and libraries, configuring versioning, working with advanced settings, working with content types and creating views, setting up validation settings and ratings, and deleting and restoring lists and libraries.

In this chapter

- Use list and library settings
- Manage list and library users and permissions
- Share content in lists and libraries
- Configure versioning
- Work with advanced settings
- Work with content types and create views
- Set up validation settings and ratings
- Delete and restore lists and libraries

Practice files

For this chapter, use the practice files from the SP2016SBS\Ch04 folder. For practice file download instructions, see the introduction.

Use list and library settings

SharePoint 2016 provides multiple configuration settings that you can use to manage the lists and the libraries on your site, including the basic settings for a list or library such as its name and description, and more advanced settings such as the navigation options.

Configure lists and libraries

Because a library is a list of files, most of the list settings and library settings are very similar. You use list and library settings to configure the options for a list or library, including the list's or library's name, navigation, content types, versioning, and validation, in addition to permissions for the users who might require access to the list or library.

There are also configuration settings that apply only to lists or only to libraries. For lists, these settings include list item-level access and the ability to add attachments to the list. For libraries, these settings include the default behavior for opening documents, the option to manage library templates, and the option to configure the Site Assets library.

The configuration options are available on the Settings page for a list or library. You can access the Settings page for a list from the list page by selecting the List Settings button in the Settings group on the List tab.

Use the List Settings page to configure a list

You can access the Settings page for a library from the library page by selecting the Library Settings button in the Settings group on the Library tab.

Team Site   ✏ EDIT LINKS

Documents › Settings

List Information

Name: Documents
Web Address: https://wideworldimporters.sharepoint.com/Shared Documents/Forms/AllItems.aspx
Description:

General Settings	Permissions and Management	Communications
▫ List name, description and navigation	▫ Delete this document library	▫ RSS settings
▫ Versioning settings	▫ Save document library as template	
▫ Advanced settings	▫ Permissions for this document library	
▫ Validation settings	▫ Manage files which have no checked in version	
▫ Column default value settings	▫ Workflow Settings	
▫ Audience targeting settings	▫ Generate file plan report	
▫ Rating settings	▫ Enterprise Metadata and Keywords Settings	
▫ Form settings	▫ Information management policy settings	

Use the Library Settings page to configure a library

The Settings page groups configuration settings in six sections, as follows: General Settings, Permissions And Management, Communications, Content Types, Columns, and Views. By using the links in the General Settings section, for example, you can change the name of a list or a library, its description and navigation, and the settings for versioning, validation, ratings, audience targeting, and the advanced and form settings. For a document library, this section also includes options for setting up the default values for columns.

> ✅ **TIP** If the Content Types section is not available on the Settings page, this means that the content types have not been enabled for the list or library. You can enable management of content types for a list or library by using the Content Types options in the Advanced Settings section on the Settings page for the list or library. For more information, see the "Work with content types and create views" topic later in this chapter.

To display the Settings page for a list

1. On the list page, display the **List** tab.

2. In the **Settings** group on the right end of the tab, select **List Settings**.

To display a list's Settings page, select List Settings on the List tab

To display the Settings page for a library

1. On the library page, display the **Library** tab.

2. In the **Settings** group on the right end of the tab, select **Library Settings**.

To display a library's Settings page, select Library Settings on the Library tab

Set up names, descriptions, and navigation for lists and libraries

As discussed in Chapter 3, "Work with content in lists and libraries," it is important to give the Name, Description, and Navigation settings some thought when you create a list or library. The default names of lists and libraries are descriptive, but making them more specific could be useful for an organization. Consider a Contacts list as an example: if the list contains only contact information for employees, *Employees* or *Staff* might be a better name for it.

> ✓ **TIP** To make navigation to a list or library easier, avoid using spaces within its name when it is created. A space in the name appears as *%20* within the URL. For more information, see the "Naming a URL" sidebar in Chapter 8, "Create and manage sites." You can also rename a list or library after setting up its URL. For more information, see Chapter 3, "Work with content in lists and libraries."

Team Site   ✏ EDIT LINKS

Settings ▸ General Settings

Name and Description

Type a new name as you want it to appear in headings and links throughout the site. Type descriptive text that will help site visitors use this document library.

Name:

Documents

Description:

Navigation

Specify whether a link to this document library appears in the Quick Launch. Note: it only appears if Quick Launch is used for navigation on your site.

☐ Display this document library on the Quick Launch?

● Yes ○ No

Set up the name, description, and navigation for a list or library

For list and library navigation, you might need to display a link to your new list or library on the Quick Launch. When you create a new list or library, its link is displayed in the Recent section on the Quick Launch. However, this link is temporary, because the Recent section only displays links to the five newest apps. After another five lists or libraries have been created on the site, the link to your new list or library will no longer be available in the Recent section on the Quick Launch. To address this, you can create a permanent Quick Launch link from the Settings page.

 TIP If you have added a list or library to a page on your site, you might find it unnecessary to also have a link to it on the Quick Launch.

 TIP You can also create a permanent Quick Launch link for a list or library by dragging its tile onto the Quick Launch in edit mode. For more information, see Chapter 2, "Navigate SharePoint sites."

To set up the name, description, and navigation for a list or library

1. On the **Settings** page for the list or library, in the **General Settings** area, select **List name, description and navigation**.

2. Do the following:

   - To set up a name as you want it to appear in headings and links throughout the site, enter the new name in the **Name** box.

   - To set up a description for your list or library, enter descriptive text in the **Description** box.

      TIP The description is displayed as an (i) icon to the right of the list or library name on its home page. To see the description, point to the icon, and then click or tap it.

   - To configure whether a link to this list or library appears on the Quick Launch, in the **Navigation** section, under **Display this list on the Quick Launch?** or **Display this document library on the Quick Launch?**, select **Yes** or **No**.

3. Select **Save** to save your settings and return to the Settings page.

Manage list and library users and permissions

Organizations are made up of people in many different roles. Therefore, different levels of permissions are required to be set up on lists and libraries to secure access to the information that those lists and libraries contain.

Information in SharePoint is secured at one of four levels: site level, list or library level, folder level, and list item or document level. By default, all lists and libraries inherit the permissions of the site that contains them, all folders inherit the permissions of the list or library that contains them, and all list items or documents inherit the permissions of the folder that contains them.

A list or library can inherit its permissions from the site where the list or library is located, or it can have its own unique permissions. If permissions are inherited, they will be managed either by the site in which the list or library resides or by a parent of the site. Permission inheritance within a list or a library can be turned off, and unique permissions can be managed for a folder or a document within a library, or for a list item in a list. When you break permissions inheritance between a site, folder, list, library, list item, or document and its parent, you can restore inheritance at any time. Restoring inheritance removes any unique permissions you set.

SharePoint includes 12 list and library permissions that determine the specific actions that users can perform in the list or library, as described in the following table.

Permission	Description
Manage Lists	Create and delete lists and libraries, add or remove columns in a list or a library, and add or remove public views of a list or a library.
Override List Behaviors	Discard and check in a document that is checked out to another user, and change or override settings that allow users to read or edit only their own items.
Add Items	Add items to lists and add documents to document libraries.
Edit Items	Edit items in lists, edit documents in document libraries, and customize web part pages in document libraries.
Delete Items	Delete items from a list and documents from a document library.

Permission	Description
View Items	View items in lists and documents in document libraries.
Approve Items	Approve a minor version of a list item or document.
Open Items	View the source of documents with server-side file handlers.
View Versions	View past versions of list items or documents.
Delete Versions	Delete past versions of list items or documents.
Create Alerts	Create alerts.
View Application Pages	View forms, views, and application pages, and enumerate lists.

The list and library permissions can be assigned to permission levels. Each permission level is a named collection of permissions that can be assigned to SharePoint users and groups.

There are several default permission levels in SharePoint 2016, as follows:

- **Read** The user can view site content, including downloading it as read-only content.

- **Contribute** The user can view, add, update, and delete site content.

- **Edit** The user can add, edit, and delete lists and can view, add, update, and delete list items and documents.

- **Design** The user can view, add, update, delete, approve, and customize site content.

- **Moderate** The user can view, add, update, delete, and moderate list items and documents.

- **Approve** The user can edit and approve pages, list items, and documents.

- **Manage Hierarchy** The user can create sites and edit pages, list items, and documents.

- **Restricted Read** The user can view pages and documents, but not historical versions or user permissions.

- **Full Control** The user has full control over site content.

- **Limited Access** The user has no permissions to the site in its entirety, but only to specific lists, document libraries, folders, list items, or documents when given explicit permission.

- **View Only** The user can view pages, list items, and documents. Document types with server-side file handlers can be viewed in the browser but not downloaded.

You can use the default permission levels or create your own.

The following table shows the mapping between permissions for lists and libraries and the permission levels they are included in by default.

List/Library Permission	Full Control	Design	Edit	Contribute	Read	Limited Access	Moderate	Approve	Manage Hierarchy	Restricted Read	View Only
Manage Lists	x	x	x				x		x		
Override List Behaviors	x	x					x	x	x		
Add Items	x	x	x	x			x	x	x		
Edit Items	x	x	x	x			x	x	x		
Delete Items	x	x	x	x			x	x	x		
View Items	x	x	x	x	x		x	x	x	x	x
Approve Items	x	x						x			
Open Items	x	x	x	x	x		x	x	x	x	
View Versions	x	x	x	x	x		x	x	x		
Delete Versions	x	x	x	x			x	x	x		
Create Alerts	x	x	x	x	x		x	x	x		x
View Application Pages	x	x	x	x	x	x	x	x	x		x

SEE ALSO For more information about permissions and permission levels, see Appendix A, "SharePoint 2016 user permissions and permission levels."

You can manage list and library users and their permissions from the Permissions page for the list or library, which is accessed from the Permissions And Management section of the Settings page.

When lists and libraries are created, they automatically inherit their permissions from the site in which they reside. This means, for example, that users who have Contribute permissions to the site will also have Contribute permissions to the list. When a list or library inherits its permissions from its parent, the Permissions page displays a yellow status bar below the ribbon indicating that permissions are inherited.

A permissions page for a library that has inherited permissions

You can stop inheriting permissions and create unique permissions for your list or library from the Permissions page, by using the Stop Inheriting Permissions option. When the inheritance is broken, the yellow status bar below the ribbon states that this list or library has unique permissions, and there are additional commands on the Permissions tab that allow you to manage unique permissions.

You can use permission settings to manage unique permissions when inheritance is turned off

You might want to grant more privileges to certain people or restrict their privileges. More often than not, you might want to give some people more access rights to a particular list or library. You can add users to the list or library, and you can also change and remove privileges for existing users. You grant permission levels to people and groups by using the Share dialog. Before granting permissions to specific users, you can check which permissions those users already have.

> **SEE ALSO** For more information about sharing documents and folders, see the "Share files and folders in a library" section later in this chapter.

To display the Permissions page for a list or library

1. On the **Settings** page for the list or library, in the **Permissions and Management** section, do one of the following:

   - For a list, select **Permissions for this list**.

   - For a library, select **Permissions for this library**.

To enable unique permissions for a list or library

1. On the **Permissions** page for the list or library, on the **Permissions** tab, select **Stop Inheriting Permissions**.

2. In the message that appears, asking you to confirm that you want to create unique permissions, select **OK**.

To restore permissions inheritance for a list or library

1. On the **Permissions** page for the list or library, on the **Permissions** tab, select **Delete Unique Permissions**.

2. In the message that appears, asking you to confirm that you want to inherit permissions, select **OK**.

To check user permissions for a list or library

1. On the **Permissions** page for the list or library, on the **Permissions** tab, select **Check Permissions**.

2. In the **Check Permissions** dialog, enter the name of the user you want to check permissions for, and select **Check Now**.

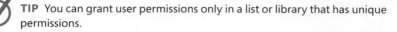

Documents: Check Permissions	✕

Check Permissions
To check permissions for a user or group, enter their name or e-mail address.

User/Group:

Olga Londer x

Check Now   Close

Permission levels given to Olga Londer

Full Control   Given through the "Team Site Owners" group.

Edit   Given through the "Team Site Members" group.

Checking user permissions

> ✓ **TIP** All permission levels assigned to the user are listed, including both individual permissions and permissions given through group memberships. Permissions are cumulative.

3. Check the permission levels for the user listed at the bottom of the box, and then select **Close**.

To grant user permissions for a list or library

1. On the **Permissions** page for the list or library, on the **Permissions** tab, select **Grant Permissions**.

> ✓ **TIP** You can grant user permissions only in a list or library that has unique permissions.

2. In the **Share** dialog, make sure that **Invite people** is selected, and then in the **Enter names or email addresses…** box, enter the names or email addresses of the people or groups in your organization to whom you want to grant access for this list or library.

Share 'Documents' and its contents   ×

   👥   Shared with lots of people

Invite people

Shared with

> Enter names or email addresses...

> Include a personal message with this invitation (Optional).

☑   Share everything in this folder, even items with unique permissions.

HIDE OPTIONS

☑   Send an email invitation

Select a permission level

Edit   ▾

Share   Cancel

Grant permissions to a list or library

3. To grant or restrict access to items with unique permissions in this list or library, select or clear the **Share everything in this folder, even items with unique permissions** check box.

 TIP At the time of writing, the option to share everything, even items with unique permissions, is available in SharePoint Online. In SharePoint 2016, this check box is not displayed in the Share dialog.

4. To configure the permission level to be granted to people and groups defined in step 2, select **Show options** and then select the permission level in the **Select a permission level** list.

TIP The default permission level to be granted is Edit.

5. Do one of the following:

   - In the **Include a personal message** box, add text for an optional email message that will be sent to everyone in the **Invite people** box.

   - If you don't want to send an email, under **Show options**, clear the **Send an email invitation** check box.

6. Select **Share** to confirm your settings and return to the **Permissions** page.

To change user permissions for a list or library

1. On the **Permissions** page for the list or library, in the **Name** list, select the check box next to the name of the user or group for whom you want to change the permission level. You can select multiple users and groups.

2. On the **Permissions** tab, select **Edit User Permissions**.

3. On the **Edit Permissions** page for this user or group, under **Permissions,** select the check boxes for the permissions you want these users or groups to have.

Team Site   ✎ EDIT LINKS
Permissions › Edit Permissions

Users or Groups
The permissions of these users or groups will be modified.

Users:
Olga Londer

Choose Permissions
Choose the permissions you want these users or groups to have.

Permissions:
☑ Full Control - Has full control.
☐ Design - Can view, add, update, delete, approve, and customize.
☐ Edit - Can add, edit and delete lists; can view, add, update and delete list items and documents.
☐ Contribute - Can view, add, update, and delete list items and documents.
☐ Read - Can view pages and list items and download documents.
☐ Create new subsites - Can create new subsites
☐ View Only - Can view pages, list items, and documents. Document types with server-side file handlers can be viewed in the browser but not downloaded.

Change permissions for users or groups

4. Select **OK** to return to the Permissions page.

To remove user permissions for a list or library

1. On the **Permissions** page for the list or library, in the **Name** list, select the check box next to the name of the user or group from whom you want to remove permissions. You can select multiple users and groups.

2. On the **Permissions** tab, select **Remove User Permissions**, and then select **OK** in the message box to confirm that you want to remove permissions from this user or group.

Share content in lists and libraries

Often you need to share content such as a document or folder in a library on your site for review and collaboration with other people inside or outside your organization. These people might not have access to the library or any other content on your internal site. You also often need to grant individual granular permissions to a list item or file.

Share files and folders in a library

You can give other people access to a document by using the Share command on the document shortcut menu or by using the Alt+S keyboard shortcut. You can also share a folder in a library in the same way. You can share the document or the folder with users who do not have any access to the library where the document is located or to the site where the library resides.

> **TIP** To share content outside your organization in SharePoint Online, external sharing needs to be turned on for the site collection where this content resides. You can also share access to the entire site. For more information, see Chapter 8 "Create and manage sites."

When you share a document, you can assign different access to the document to different people from the Invite People page of the Share dialog. There are two access options: View and Edit. When you share the document with the View option, users will be able to open the document but not modify it. The Edit option allows users to modify the document. The permission level assigned to those users is Contribute. If email has been turned on for your SharePoint deployment, you also have the option of sending a message to let people know that they have access to a document or a folder on your site.

Share documents and folders with others

You can share a link to a document that others can also share by using the Get A Link page of the Share dialog.

> **IMPORTANT** At the time of writing, the Get Link command is available in SharePoint Online.

Get A link is available only for individual files. Get A Link provides a durable link and is the quick and easy way to share documents with everyone in your organization or to share with people externally. When access to the document is no longer required, you can remove it.

When you share a link, you set up security for accessing the link. You assign View or Edit access to the users, and you can set up whether they are required to sign in to your site or whether they can access the link anonymously as guests. The latter is referred to as a guest link. You can set the expiration period for the guest link, for example, to a day or 30 days, or you can use the default setting so that the link never expires. Links that require an account on your site don't expire; there's no option to set an expiration for those links.

4

Share a link to a document or a folder

The security options for sharing a link are as follows:

- **Restricted link** Only people with appropriate permissions for a document can open the link

- **Edit link – account required** People in your organization can edit, copy, or download the document. Sign-in to SharePoint is required, so the user must have an account on your site.

- **View link – account required** People in your organization can view, copy, or download the document. Sign-in to SharePoint is required, so the user must have an account on your site.

- **Edit link – no sign-in required** People outside your organization can edit, copy, and download the document anonymously as guests, without signing in.

- **View link – no sign-in required** People outside your organization can view, copy, and download the document anonymously as guests, without signing in.

 TIP If you share documents outside your organization by using anonymous guest links, it is possible for the invitation recipients to share those guest links with others, who could use them to view content. If you want to limit access to the document only to invitation recipients, consider requiring external users to always sign in.

Selecting Shared With in the Share dialog displays a list of people who have access to a document or a folder. This is useful when you need to see who has access to specific content on your site.

To open the Share dialog for a file or folder

1. In the library that contains the file or folder you want to share, do one of the following:

   - On the shortcut menu for the file or folder, select **Share**.

   - Select the file or folder by clicking or tapping in its leftmost column, and then press **Alt+S** on the keyboard.

   - Select the ellipsis to the right of the file or folder name, and then select **Share** from the callout menu.

To share a file or folder with others

1. In the **Share** dialog for the file or folder, make sure **Invite people** is selected. In the **Enter names or email addresses...** box, enter the names or email addresses of the people or groups in your organization with whom you want to share this file.

2. Set up the access level to be granted to the people and groups defined in step 1 by selecting **Can edit** or **Can view**.

   TIP The default access level is Can Edit.

3. Do one of the following:

   - In the **Include a personal message** box, add text for an optional email message that will be sent to everyone in the **Invite people** box.

   - If you don't want to send an email, under **Show options**, clear the **Send an email invitation** check box.

4. Select **Share** to confirm your settings and return to the library page.

To share a file or folder via a link

1. In the **Share** dialog for the file or folder, select **Get a link**.

2. Choose the security option for the link you want to create.

> ✓ **TIP** If only "account required" options are available, it means that the guest access is turned off .

3. If you choose a No Sign-in Required link and you want to set the link to expire, select **Set expiration**, and then choose the expiration setting, such as 30 days.

4. Select **Copy** to copy the link to the clipboard. If a confirmation message box appears, confirm access to the clipboard by selecting **Allow Access**. Send the link to the people you want to share with—for example, by pasting it into an email.

5. Select **Close** to return to the library.

To remove access to a file or folder provided via a link

1. In the **Share** dialog for the file or folder, select **Get a link.**

2. Select **Remove**. In the confirmation message box that appears, confirm the link's removal by selecting **Disable link,** and then select **Close** to return to the library.

To see who has access to a file or folder

1. In the **Share** dialog for the file or folder, select **Shared With**.

2. Review the list of users and groups who have access, and then select **Close** to return to the library.

To stop sharing a document or folder

1. In the **Share** dialog for the file or folder, select **Shared With** and then select **Stop Sharing**.

2. In the confirmation message box that appears, select **Stop sharing** to confirm that you want to disable guest links and remove all users from the file except you and any other owners, and then select **Close** to return to the library.

Grant item-level permissions

You can grant unique permissions to list items or folders contained within lists, or to files or folders contained within libraries. List items and folders in the root of a list inherit permissions from the list, whereas files and folders in the root of a library inherit permissions from the library. In other words, the same inheritance rules that apply to lists and libraries also apply to the list items and files that they contain. A list item or file in a subfolder that is stored within a folder inherits permissions from the parent folder. Permission inheritance can be stopped for any list item, file, or folder at any level.

The ribbon commands for managing users and permissions for a list item or a file are the same as the commands for managing users and permissions for lists and libraries that were discussed in the "Manage list and library users and permissions" topic earlier in this chapter.

To display the Permissions page for a list item or file

1. In the list or library that contains the list item or file, do one of the following:

    *   Open the **Share** dialog for the list item or file, select **Shared With**, and then select **Advanced**.

    *   Select the list item or file by clicking or tapping in its leftmost column, and then do one of the following:

        *   For a list item, on the **Items** tab of the ribbon, select **Item Permissions**.

        *   For a file, on the **Files** tab of the ribbon, select **Shared With**, and then select **Advanced**.

Set up file permissions

To configure permissions inheritance for a list item or file

1. On the **Permissions** page for the list item or file, do one of the following:

   - To enable unique permissions for the list item or file, select **Stop Inheriting Permissions**, and then select **OK** in the message that appears, to confirm that you want to create unique permissions.

   - To restore permissions inheritance for the list item or file, select **Delete Unique Permissions**, and then select **OK** in the message that appears, to confirm that you want to inherit permissions.

To set up unique permissions for a list item or file

1. On the **Permissions** page for the list item or file, do one of the following:

   - To grant permissions for a list item or file to users and groups, select **Grant Permissions**, specify the settings you want in the **Share** dialog, and then select **Share** to return to the Permissions page.

   - To change permissions for a list item or file, select the user or group for whom you want to change the permissions, and select **Edit User Permissions**. On the **Edit Permissions** page, choose the permissions you want this user or group to have, and then select **OK** to return to the Permissions page.

   - To remove permissions for a list item or file, select a user or a group from whom you want to remove the permissions, select **Remove User Permissions**, and then select **OK** in the message box to confirm that you want to remove permissions from this user or group.

4

Configure versioning

Versioning is managed by using the Versioning Settings page, which provides a number of configuration settings for lists and libraries. Although there are similarities between versioning for lists and libraries, there are also differences in how versioning can be configured. For example, in SharePoint lists you can use major versions only, whereas in libraries you can use major and minor versions.

Configure versioning and content approval for lists

The Versioning page for lists provides Content Approval, Item Version History, and Draft Item Security options. Turning on content approval allows a list item to be created as a draft item that is not displayed to other users until the item has been approved. This means that you can work on the item in draft mode and then submit the item for approval when you are ready to do so. An approver (a user with Approve permission) can then approve the item, which allows the list item to be displayed for all users who have Read permission. The same options are available for libraries. By default, content approval is turned off; the default option is No.

Set up content approval for a list

When content approval is turned on, the Approval Status column is displayed on the list page. All existing list items are set to Approved. Any new list items will require approval.

> **TIP** When a list item is submitted for approval, there is no notification that is automatically sent to the approver. The approver should go to the list periodically to see if list items are waiting for approval. Alternative options are to set up an Approval Workflow or to configure alerts for the list. For more information, see Chapter 11, "Work with workflows."

You can use Item Version History settings to track the editing history of a list item. If versioning is turned on, a new version of the list item will be stored every time you edit the list item. This allows you to view the history and to restore a previous version so that it becomes the latest version of the list item. You can specify how many versions and how many approved versions to keep in the history. The version history is only available if versioning is turned on. By default, list versioning is turned off; the default option is No.

Item Version History

Specify whether a version is created each time you edit an item in this list. Learn about versions.

Create a version each time you edit an item in this list?
○ Yes ● No

Optionally limit the number of versions to retain:
☐ Keep the following number of versions:

☐ Keep drafts for the following number of approved versions:

Set up Item Version History for a list

4

Draft Item Security is an option that is specific to draft items. It provides additional user permissions to the Permission settings for list items. By using the Draft Item Security settings, you can choose who is allowed to view an item in draft. The default setting is Any User Who Can Read Items, but you can also choose Only Users Who Can Edit Items or Only Users Who Can Approve Items. Users with Contribute permissions or higher will see draft versions, whereas users with less than Contribute permissions will see the most recent approved item but not a more recent draft item. Therefore, users with different permissions are likely to see different list items and different versions of those list items. Draft Item Security settings become available when content approval is turned on. The same settings are available for libraries and define the permissions for viewing the draft documents in a library.

Draft Item Security

Drafts are minor versions or items which have not been approved. Specify which users should be able to view drafts in this list. Learn about specifying who can view and edit drafts.

Who should see draft items in this list?
● Any user who can read items
○ Only users who can edit items
○ Only users who can approve items (and the author of the item)

Set up Draft Item Security

To configure versioning for a list

1. On the **Settings** page for the list, select **Versioning settings**.

2. On the **Versioning Settings** page, in the **Version History** section, do one of the following:

   - To turn on versioning, under **Create a version each time you edit an item in this list**, select **Yes**. Optionally, set the number of versions and the number of approved version drafts you want to keep if content approval is turned on. Then select **OK** to return to the Settings page.

   - To turn off versioning, under **Create a version each time you edit an item in this list**, select **No**, and then select **OK** to return to the Settings page.

To set up content approval for a list

1. On the **Settings** page for the list, select **Versioning settings**.

2. On the **Versioning Settings** page, in the **Content Approval** section, under **Require Content Approval for Submitted Items**, select **Yes**.

3. In the **Draft Item Security** section, under **Who can see draft items in this list**, select the security option you require for access to the list item drafts.

> **TIP** After content approval has been turned on, the selected option in the Draft Item Security section changes from its default setting of Any User Who Can Read Items to Only Users Who Can Approve Items (And The Author Of The Item).

4. Select **OK** to return to the Settings page.

To approve or reject a list item

1. On the list page for the list that contains the item you want to approve, do one of the following:

   - Select the ellipsis to the right of the list item (which should have a Pending approval status), and then select **Approve/Reject** from the menu that appears.

   - Select the list item and then, on the **Items** tab of the ribbon, in the **Workflow** group, select **Approve/Reject**.

2. In the **Approve/Reject** dialog, do the following:

   a. In the **Approval status** section, select **Approved**, **Rejected**, or **Pending**.

   b. In the **Comment** section, enter a comment (optional).

   c. Select **OK** to close the dialog and return to the list page.

Configure versioning and required checkout for libraries

The versioning settings for libraries include options to configure content approval and draft item security, which are identical to those options in the list versioning settings. However, there are additional options available for libraries under the Versioning settings. Library versioning supports major and minor versions, and there is also a configuration setting for libraries to enforce document check out.

4

As with list items, you can turn on or off versioning for documents stored in a library via Versioning settings. When library versioning is turned on, SharePoint records changes in the edited version of a document each time the document is changed. This provides you with multiple versions of the same document so that you can easily see what the document contained before the modifications and can revert to any previous version if necessary.

When library versioning is turned on, you can select between two types of versioning: major versions only, or major and minor versions. Major versions provide full-text copies of each document version. The latest version is always published, meaning that those with access to the document library can view the most recent version of the document. By default, in SharePoint 2016 library versioning is turned on, with major versions turned on.

Set up Document Version History

You can use major and minor versioning to publish major versions of a document while creating modified, minor versions of the same document that only a subset of users with access to the library can view and edit. You can control who views a minor version by using the Draft Item Security configuration setting. Using major and minor versions is useful when you need to perform multiple modifications of a document prior to its publication or before submitting it for approval. When major and minor versioning is selected, you can control how many versions of each document are retained in the document library. You can think of this as "version pruning." As mentioned previously, only SharePoint libraries use both major and minor document versions. You cannot use major and minor versions with lists. By default, minor versions are turned off.

You can also use library versioning settings to configure mandatory checkout. The ability to check documents out of a library is invaluable when several people might be making changes to the same document at the same time. Chapter 3, "Work with content in lists and libraries," covered how to check documents out and in. You can enforce the check-out of a document before a user can edit it by setting up the Require Check Out option. The default for this option is No, meaning that users are not required to check out a document before it can be edited. Many organizations have a policy that requires all documents to be checked out for editing. To meet this requirement, a SharePoint library can be configured to require checkout before its documents can be edited.

Set up required checkout for a library

> **TIP** If a library contains Office documents that are required to be edited at the same time by multiple users (referred to as *co-authoring*), do not configure the library to require checkout. The users should just open the documents and edit them without checking them out. With co-authoring, it is a best practice to turn on versioning for the library, just in case someone makes a mistake and you need to restore an earlier version of the document.

To configure library versioning

1. On the **Settings** page for the library for which you want to configure versioning, select **Versioning settings**.

2. On the **Versioning Settings** page, in the **Document Version History** section, do one of the following:

    *   To turn on versioning, under **Create a version each time you edit a file in this document library**, do one of the following:

        *   To create only major versions, select **Create major versions**.

        *   To create both major and minor versions, select **Create major and minor (draft) versions**.

        Optionally, you can set up the number of major versions and the number of approved major version drafts you want to keep.

    *   To turn off versioning, under **Create a version each time you edit a file in this document library**, select **No versioning**.

3. Select **OK** to return to the Settings page.

To enforce file checkout in a library

1. On the **Settings** page for the library in which you want to enforce checkout, select **Versioning settings**.

2. On the **Versioning Settings** page, in the **Require Check Out** section, under **Require documents to be checked out before they can be edited?**, do one of the following:

   - To enforce checkout, select **Yes**.

   - To disable required checkout, select **No**.

3. Select **OK** to return to the Settings page.

To publish a document draft as a major version

1. In the library in which you want to publish a document draft (minor version), do one of the following:

   - In the document callout, select the ellipsis to display the menu, select **Advanced**, and then select **Publish a Major Version**.

   - Select the document draft, and then on the **Items** tab of the ribbon, in the **Workflow** group, select **Publish**.

2. In the **Publish Major Version** dialog, provide a comment if you want, and then select **OK** to publish the major version of the document.

Work with advanced settings

Advanced settings for lists and libraries include options for content types, folders, inclusion in search results, reindexing, offline client availability, and dialogs. There are also additional options that are available only for lists or only for libraries.

Advanced settings options that are available only for lists include Item-Level Permissions and Attachment options.

Advanced settings options that are available only for libraries include options for setting up document templates, configuring whether documents open in the client or a browser, setting up custom Send To destinations, and making a library a site assets library.

Work with advanced list settings

This section covers the list configuration options that are available on a list's Settings page, under Advanced Settings, with exception of content types settings. Content Types configuration is addressed later in this chapter, in the "Work with content types and create views" topic.

You can use the Item-Level Permissions option to refine default permission levels such as Read, Contribute, Design, or Full Control for a list item. This option is available for lists only; it is not applicable to libraries. For example, you can use this option to set what the creator of a list item is allowed to do. You can set it so that people with Read access can read all items or only those that they created. The default is Read All Items. You can also set whether users with Create And Edit access can edit all items or just those that they created, and you can prevent them from creating and editing any list item by selecting None. The default is Create And Edit All Items. By selecting the None option, you effectively make all users with Contribute permission readers for the list. However, users with rights to manage the list are able to read and edit all items.

Configure item-level permissions

You can use the Attachments option to allow or disallow attachments to list items. This option is available for lists only; it is not applicable to libraries. By default, the ability to add attachments to list items is turned on.

Turn list attachments on or off

> **SEE ALSO** For more information about attaching documents to list items, see Chapter 3, "Work with content in lists and libraries."

> **TIP** You might want to turn off list attachments if you prefer users to store documents within document libraries.

The Folders option is used to disable the New Folder command for a list. This command is enabled by default. The same setting is available for libraries.

An alternative to using folders is using custom columns. Since the introduction of SharePoint, users have been taking advantage of custom columns to organize their content. Through the use of custom columns, you can organize content into views by using filters rather than folders. If you prefer this method to using folders within lists, you can turn off the use of folders so that users do not become confused as to which approach they should use. If you do use folders, you should consider carefully training your users to use them effectively.

Folders	
Specify whether the "New Folder" command is available. Changing this setting does not affect existing folders.	Make "New Folder" command available? ○ Yes ● No

Turn the New Folder command on or off

> **TIP** In SharePoint, the recommended number of items within a view or a folder is limited to 5,000. This limitation is related to the time it takes to display items in a view or folder. Therefore, if you have 6,000 list items in a list, it would be better to create views or folders to display 5,000 or fewer list items, to allow for future growth.

> **SEE ALSO** For more information about managing lists and libraries with a large number of items, and recommended limits for lists and libraries, see the article at *https://support.office.com/en-us/article/Manage-lists-and-libraries-in-SharePoint-2013 -and-SharePoint-2016-b8588dae-9387-48c2-9248-c24122f07c59*.

By using the Search option, you can exclude the list from search results. Searching content in SharePoint returns search results from any list or library by default. All of the items that the current user has permission to view will display within the results, and no user will see content that he or she does not have permission to view. You can exclude an entire list from displaying within search results by selecting No for Allow Items From This List To Appear In Search Results. The same setting is available for libraries.

Search

Specify whether this list should
be visible in search results. Users
who do not have permission to
see these items will not see them
in search results, no matter what
this setting is.

Allow items from this list to appear in search results?

◉ Yes ○ No

Set up search result inclusion or exclusion

SEE ALSO For more information about searching in SharePoint, see Chapter 5, "Search for information and people."

You can use the Reindex List button to mark a list for full reindexing when the next scheduled content crawl occurs. If the list is not marked for full reindexing, the content will be indexed incrementally by default. A similar setting, Reindex Library, is available for libraries.

Reindex List

Click the Reindex List button to
reindex all of the content in this
document library during the next
scheduled crawl.

[Reindex List]

Mark a list for full reindexing

The Offline Client Availability setting defines whether a list is available for offline viewing in client programs that allow you to synchronize data for offline use, so that you have access to the SharePoint content while in a disconnected environment. The Microsoft Outlook client program can be used for offline access to list content. The default setting is to allow items to be downloaded to offline clients. If a list contains sensitive information, you can switch off offline availability to ensure that it is only available in an online environment.

The same setting is available for libraries. Turning it off will prevent library content from being synchronized to user devices for offline use.

Offline Client Availability

Specify whether this list should
be available for offline clients.

Allow items from this list to be downloaded to offline clients?

◉ Yes ○ No

Turn offline content availability on or off

The Quick Edit setting defines whether editing a list within its page by using the Quick Edit view is allowed. It is turned on by default. The Quick Edit view of a list provides a spreadsheet-type view of the list content, in which you can enter data more quickly and use operations such as filling down. Updates are provided in bulk, which is convenient for making modifications quickly. However, bulk updates can result in accidentally overwriting content, and it is difficult to undo a mistake that has been made in bulk. Therefore, you can choose not to allow the editing of a list by using Quick Edit. If Quick Edit is turned off, the inline edit option is not displayed, and the Quick Edit button on the List tab of the ribbon is unavailable.

The same option is available for the libraries. Turning Quick Edit off for a library makes the Quick Edit button on the Library tab unavailable; it is available by default.

4

Quick Edit

Specify whether Quick Edit can be used on this list to bulk edit data.

Allow items in this list to be edited using Quick Edit?

◉ Yes ○ No

Turn Quick Edit on or off

> **TIP** Some lists and libraries, such as External Lists and Picture Libraries, do not allow the use of Quick Edit.

You can use the Dialogs setting on the Advanced Settings page to switch between using dialogs and full pages for displaying list forms, such as new, edit, and display forms. When dialogs are turned on, SharePoint provides the forms within a dialog when you access a list item. The dialog is displayed within the webpage, and the rest of the webpage appears dimmed. The dialogs are implemented by using Microsoft Silverlight. If your work environment has computers or devices that do not have Silverlight installed, you might consider either installing Silverlight or not using this option. The default is No. The same option is available for libraries.

Dialogs

If dialogs are available, specify whether to launch the new, edit, and display forms in a dialog. Selecting "No" will cause these actions to navigate to the full page.

Note: Dialogs may not be available on all forms.

Launch forms in a dialog?

○ Yes ◉ No

Switch between dialogs and full pages for forms

To display the Advanced Settings page for a list or library

1. On the **Settings** page for the list or library, select **Advanced settings**.

To configure item-level permissions for a list

1. On the **Advanced Settings** page for the list, in the **Item-Level Permissions** section, do any of the following:

   - Under **Read access**, choose whether to allow people with Read access to read all items or only those that they created.

   - Under **Create and edit access**, choose whether to allow people with Create and Edit access to create and edit all items, only those that they created, or none.

2. Select **OK** to save your changes and return to the Settings page.

To configure attachments for a list

1. On the **Advanced Settings** page for the list, in the **Attachments** section, under **Attachments to list items are**, do one of the following:

   - To enable attachments, select **Enabled**.

   - To disable attachments, select **Disabled**.

2. Select **OK** to save your changes and return to the Settings page.

To configure folder availability for a list or library

1. On the **Advanced Settings** page for the list or library for which you want to configure the availability of the New Folder command, in the **Folders** section, under **Make 'New Folder' command available?**, do one of the following:

   - To make the New Folder command available, select **Yes**.

   - To make the New Folder command unavailable, select **No**.

2. Select **OK** to save your changes and return to the Settings page.

To include or exclude a list or library from search results

1. On the **Advanced Settings** page for the list or library, in the **Search** section, under **Allow items from this list to appear in the search results?**, do one of the following:

   - To allow the content to appear in the search results, select **Yes**.

   - To prevent the content from appearing in the search results, select **No**.

2. Select **OK** to save your changes and return to the Settings page.

To mark a list or library for full reindexing

1. On the **Advanced Settings** page for the list or library, in the **Reindex List** section, select **Reindex List**.

2. Select **OK** to save your changes and return to the Settings page.

To configure offline client availability for a list or library

1. On the **Advanced Settings** page for the list or library that contains the content for which you want to enable or disable offline use, in the **Offline Client Availability** section, under **Allow items from this list to be downloaded to the offline clients?**, do one of the following:

   - To allow the content to be downloaded, select **Yes**.

   - To prevent the content from being downloaded, select **No**.

2. Select **OK** to save your changes and return to the Settings page.

To configure Quick Edit availability for a list or library

1. On the **Advanced Settings** page for the list or library, in the **Quick Edit** section, under **Allow items from this list to be edited using Quick Edit?**, do one of the following:

   - To turn on Quick Edit and make the Quick Edit button available on the ribbon, select **Yes**.

   - To turn off Quick Edit and make the Quick Edit button unavailable on the ribbon, select **No**.

2. Select **OK** to save your changes and return to the Settings page.

To configure dialogs for a list or library

1. On the **Advanced Settings** page for the list or library, in the **Dialogs** section, under **Launch forms in a dialog?**, do one of the following:

   - To launch forms in dialogs, select **Yes**.

   - To launch forms in pages, select **No**.

2. Select **OK** to save your changes and return to the Settings page.

Work with advanced library settings

The advanced settings for libraries include options to configure content types, folders, inclusion in search results, library reindexing, offline client availability, and dialogs; these are the same as the respective list settings. However, there are also additional options available for libraries on the Advanced Settings page. These additional settings include options for setting up a document template, configuring whether documents open in the client or a browser, setting up custom Send To destinations, and making this library a site assets library.

You can use the Document Template option to set up a template for new documents created in a library. When you create a document library, you can choose the document template for the library. Then, when you select the New Document command on the Documents tab of the ribbon, the document template determines which Office client program, or which Office web app, is opened. The document template is then used as the basis for the new document. For example, the Documents library on a team site by default uses a blank Microsoft Word document as its document template. By using the Document Template option, you can change the template for the library. For example, you might prefer a blank Microsoft Excel workbook, or a Word template that contains headers, such as your corporate logo. By default, the template document resides in a hidden folder named Forms, within the library. You can edit the existing template, or you can provide another URL for an alternative template.

Document Template

Type the address of a template to use as the basis for all new files created in this document library. When multiple content types are enabled, this setting is managed on a per content type basis. Learn how to set up a template for a library.

Template URL:

Shared Documents/Forms/template.dotx

(Edit Template)

Set up a document template for a library

The Opening Documents In The Browser option is used to define the default open behavior for documents in a library. You can use it to choose whether to open a document within your browser or display it in its native Office client program, such as Word. The default option is to open the document in a browser by using Office Online programs such as Word Online, so that users can use their browsers to view the documents online. For on-premises deployments, this feature depends on Office Online Server being installed and activated on-premises. The benefit of opening Microsoft

Word, Excel, PowerPoint, and OneNote documents in a browser is that you can view and edit them by using Office Online from any device that has a browser. Although the functionality of Word Online, for example, is lighter in comparison with the Word client program, there are many everyday editing tasks that Word Online supports, and this is very handy for making changes to documents when you are on the go. You can configure the default open behavior to always open documents in the client program (or application), always open documents in the browser, or use the server default, which is to open in a browser.

4

Opening Documents in the Browser

Specify whether browser-enabled documents should be opened in the client or browser by default when a user clicks on them. If the client application is unavailable, the document will always be opened in the browser.

Default open behavior for browser-enabled documents:

◉ Open in the client application
◯ Open in the browser
◯ Use the server default (Open in the browser)

Configure how to open documents in a library

You can use the Custom Send To Destination option to enter a name and URL for a document library other than the document repository that your administrators might have set at the SharePoint Server farm level, to which users can automatically send their documents after they are finished and ready for a wider audience's consumption. This is a handy feature if you want to ensure that all documents under development are written in one document library, whereas those available for public consumption are hosted in a different document library (with different permissions) on the same site. Alternatively, you can set up (for example) an archive location so that you can send the documents from the current library to the archive. After you've set up a name and URL for the custom Send To destination, this name will be listed in the drop-down menu when the user selects the Send To button in the Copies group on the Files tab of the ribbon, on the library page.

Custom Send To Destination

Type the name and URL for a custom Send To destination that you want to appear as an option for this list. It is recommended that you choose a short name for the destination.

Destination name: (For example, Team Library)

URL:

Set up a custom Send To destination

You use the Site Assets Library option to specify a library to store site assets such as images. When you create a team site, the Site Assets library is created by default. Site assets are usually images and other files that are uploaded for use within a wiki page. When you upload a file to a site via the Insert tab when editing a wiki page, instead of being prompted for a location to save your files, the Site Assets library is used as the default location. This makes it easier to find site assets for wiki pages. However, you do not have to use the Site Assets library as the default location. By using this option, you can change the default Site Assets library to the current one. You can choose any document library as the default location for your site's assets.

Site Assets Library

Specify whether this library
should be presented as the
default location for storing
images or other files that users
upload to their wiki pages.

Should this document library be a site assets library?

○ Yes ● No

Set up a Site Assets library

To set up the document template for a library

1. On the **Advanced Settings** page for the library, in the **Document Template** section, under **Template URL**, enter the URL for the document template you want to use.

2. Select **OK** to save your changes and return to the Settings page.

To edit the document template for a library

1. On the **Advanced Settings** page for the library, in the **Document Template** section, under **Template URL,** select **Edit Template.**

2. Make your edits to the template in the Office Online app or the Office client program, and then save the template back to its original location in the document library.

To modify the default open behavior for documents in a library

1. On the **Advanced Settings** page for the library, in the **Open the Document in the Browser** section, under **Default open behavior for browser-enabled documents**, do one of the following:

   - To open files in the Office client program, such as Word, select **Open in the client application**.

- To open files in Office Online app, such as Word Online, select **Open in the browser**.

- To use the server default, which is to open in the browser, select **Use the server default (Open in the browser)**.

2. Select **OK** to save your changes and return to the Settings page.

To set up a custom Send To destination for a library

1. On the **Advanced Settings** page for the library, in the **Custom Send to Destination** section, enter the destination name and URL.

2. Select **OK** to save your changes and return to the Settings page.

To configure a Site Assets setting for a library

1. On the **Advanced Settings** page for the library, in the **Site Assets Library** section, under **Should this library be a site assets library?**, do one of the following:

- To make this library a site assets library, select **Yes**.

- To prevent this library from being a site assets library, select **No**.

2. Select **OK** to save your changes and return to the Settings page.

Work with content types and create views

A SharePoint content type combines an item and information about the item, or metadata. For example, an item can be a type of file, such as a document or an Excel workbook. A content type associates the item with key metadata and other information, such as a template or a retention policy. SharePoint includes many content types. Every piece of content in SharePoint is created from a content type. Content types are defined for a site and apply to that site and its subsites. You can use the predefined content types, such as Blank Document for a library or Announcement for an announcements list, or you can create custom content types.

You can also create views, which are used to display specific items in a list or library in a predefined way. For example, you can create a view of the files in a list or a library that includes specific columns, or a view that filters content by a specific content type.

Work with content types

SharePoint users often need to redesign a list or library and to add a new column. You would add a new column to a list or library if you needed to collect more information from the user than what is there by default within the list or library template. For example, consider a sales team site that allows salespeople to create price quotes, proposals, and invoices. You might want to create a new column to store the type of document, and provide choices such as Quote, Proposal, and Invoice.

Collecting the type of the document can be useful for creating a view and filtering by type, and also if you decide to roll up the documents by using an aggregation web part. You would then want to ensure that all document libraries have the option of using this new column, but it would be tedious to add the new column to every library. You could get around this by using a custom template. However, what would happen if the choices for a type of document changed? You might want to add another column to the type of document to provide additional information—for example, the value of a proposal. That is where site columns and content types become very useful.

A site column could also be described as a shared column. You create a site column once, and it resides in a gallery at the level of a site or site collection. It is inherited by all sites in the collection that are beneath the site in which it was created.

A content type is made up of the site columns and other configurations such as templates or workflows. You can use a content type to reuse a group of site columns and perhaps have a workflow associated with the content type, which you would then add to an existing list or library. Each content type has a predefined, specific set of columns, workflows, and metadata. Lists and libraries can use more than one content type. In the earlier example of the sales team site, the three document types (Quote, Proposal, and Invoice) could be created within the same document library, each one containing its own template.

Site content types can inherit from the site collection content types. All existing site content types are grouped in categories. When you create a new content type, you choose a category to become the parent group of your new content type. The new content type can belong to an existing category, or you can create a new category. When you create a new content type, you specify a parent content type that it is based on. In turn, new content types can be based on the content type you have created.

By default, content types for a list or library are turned off. You can turn on management of content types for a list or library by using the Content Types options on the Advanced Settings page for the list or library.

Content Types

Specify whether to allow the
management of content types on
this document library. Each
content type will appear on the
new button and can have a
unique set of columns, workflows
and other behaviors.

Allow management of content types?

○ Yes ● No

Manage content types

When you add a content type to a list or library, you enable that list or library to
contain items of that type. Users can use the New command to create an item of that
type. A single list or library can contain multiple content types, and each content type
can have unique metadata and policies.

To turn content types on or off for a list or library

1. On the **Advanced Settings** page for the list or library, in the **Content Types**
    section, under **Allow management of content types?**, do one of the following:

    -   To turn on content types for this list or library, select **Yes**.

    -   To turn off content types for this list or library, select **No**.

2. Select **OK** to save your changes and return to the Settings page.

To create a custom content type

1. On the site where you want to create a custom content type, select the gear
    icon in the upper-right corner and then select **Site settings** to go to the Site
    Settings page.

2. On the **Site Settings** page, under **Web Designer Galleries**, select **Site content
    types** to display the Site Content Types page.

Team Site   ✎ EDIT LINKS

Site Settings › Site Content Types ⓘ

📑 Create

The Create option for a new site content type

3. Select **Create** to display the New Site Content Type page.

4. In the **New Site Content Type** page, do the following:

    -   Provide a name and description for the new content type.

- In the **Parent Content Type** section, select the name of the parent group and then choose the **Parent Content Type**.

- In the **Group** section, either put the new content type in an existing group, or create a new group.

Set up a new content type

5. Select **OK** to create the new site content type. When SharePoint creates the new content type, it opens the Site Content Type page for it, where you can customize it further.

To add an existing site column to a content type

1. Display the **Site Content Type** page for a content type you want to add a column to, if it is not already displayed, by doing the following:

   a. On a site where you want to add a column to the content type, go to the **Site Settings** page.

   b. On the **Site Settings** page, under **Web Designer Galleries**, select **Site content types** to display the Site Content Types page, and select the name of the content type to which you want to add a column.

2. On the **Site Content Types** page, under **Columns**, select **Add from existing site columns**.

3. On the **Add Columns** page, do the following:

   a. In the **Select Columns** section, under **Select columns from**, choose the parent group for the column.

b. Under **Available columns**, select the name of the column that you want to add, and then select **Add**.

c. In the **Update List and Site Content Types** section, choose whether to update all content types that inherit from this site content type by selecting **Yes** or **No**, and then select **OK**.

4

Team Site   ✏ EDIT LINKS

Site Content Type › Add Columns ⓘ

Select Columns

Select from the list of available site columns to add them to this content type.

Select columns from:

All Groups

Available columns:

% Complete
Active
Actual Work
Address
Aliases
Anniversary
Append-Only Comments
Assigned To
Assistant's Name
Assistant's Phone

Add >

< Remove

Columns to add:

Column Description:
None

Group: Core Task and Issue Columns

Update List and Site Content Types

Specify whether all child site and list content types using this type should be updated with the settings on this page. This operation can take a long time, and any customizations made to these values on the child site and list content types will be lost.

Update all content types inheriting from this type?

◉ Yes
○ No

Add an existing site column to a content type

To add a new site column to a content type

1. On the **Site Content Types** page for the content type, under **Columns**, select **Add from new site column** to open the Create Column page.

2. On the **Create Column** page, in the **Name and Type** section, do the following:

   a. In the **Column name** box, enter the name of the new column.

   b. Under **The type of information in this column is**, select the type of information that you want to appear in the column.

Name and Type

Type a name for this column, and select the type of information you want to store in the column.

Column name:

The type of information in this column is:

◉ Single line of text
○ Multiple lines of text
○ Choice (menu to choose from)
○ Number (1, 1.0, 100)
○ Currency ($, ¥, €)
○ Date and Time
○ Lookup (information already on this site)
○ Yes/No (check box)
○ Person or Group
○ Hyperlink or Picture
○ Calculated (calculation based on other columns)
○ Task Outcome
○ External Data
○ Managed Metadata

Define a name and a type of column

3. In the **Additional Column Settings** section, in the **Description** box, enter a description to help people understand the purpose of the column and what data it should contain. This description is optional.

    Depending on the type of column you selected, more options might appear in the Additional Column Settings section—for example, options for whether the column must contain data or for the limit on how many characters the column can contain. Select the additional settings that you want.

Define additional settings for a column

4. In the **Update List and Site Content Types** section, choose whether to update all content types that inherit from this site content type by selecting **Yes** or **No**.

5. If you want the data in the column to be validated, expand the **Column Validation** section, and then enter the formula you want to use to validate the data and a user message that explains what is needed for the column's value to be valid. (The Column Validation section is not available for some types of columns.)

Set up validation for a column

6. Select **OK** to save your changes and return to the Site Content Type page.

To associate a document template with a content type

1. On the **Site Content Type** page for the content type, under **Settings**, select **Advanced settings** to display the Advanced Settings page.

2. In the **Document Template** section, do one of the following:

   - If the template is stored on your site, under **Enter the URL of an existing document template,** enter the URL for the template that you want to use.

   - If the template is stored on your local device, select **Upload a new document template**, and then select **Browse**. In the **Choose File** dialog box, locate the file that you want to use, select it, and then select **Open**.

Team Site   ✏ EDIT LINKS

Site Content Type › Advanced Settings ⓘ

Document Template
Specify the document template for this content type.

◉ Enter the URL of an existing document template:

◯ Upload a new document template:

Browse...

Specify the location of the document template for a content type

3. Under **Update all content types inheriting from this type**, choose whether to update all content types that inherit from this site content type by selecting **Yes** or **No**.

4. Select **OK** to save your configuration and return to the Site Content Type page.

To add a content type to a list or library

1. On the **Settings** page for the list or library, in the **Content Types** section, select **Add from existing site content types**.

2. On the **Add Content Types** page, display the **Select site content types from** list, and choose the group of site content types you want to select from.

Team Site   ✏ EDIT LINKS

Settings › Add Content Types ⓘ

Select Content Types
Select from the list of available site content types to add them to this list.

Select site content types from:
All Groups

Available Site Content Types:
Allow any content type *
Audio
Basic Page
Document Set
Dublin Core Columns
Form
Image
JavaScript Display Template
Link to a Document

Add »

« Remove

Content types to add:

Description:
Create a new basic page.

Group: Document Content Types

Add content types to a list or library

3. In the **Available Site Content Types** list, select the name of the content type that you want, and then select **Add** to move the selected content type to the Content Types To Add list.

4. Select **OK** to add the content type to your list or library and return to the Settings page.

Create views

Creating a view in a list or library is a beneficial way of organizing content within the list or library. A view can be created by using filters based on the columns, making it an easy way to find documents. If a library contains custom metadata, you might want to create your view with a filter on that custom column. Custom views work very well with content types, which were described in the previous section. For example, if you want to display all proposal documents in their own view to keep them separate from invoices, you could create a filter on each view based upon the content type column.

You can create personal views that are available only to you, or you can create public views that are available for other users of your list or library.

When you create a view, you first choose whether you want to base the view on the following:

- A predefined view type, such as calendar view or Gantt view
- An existing view, such as All Documents for a library or All Items for a list

You can also base your new view on the forms and reports created by using Microsoft Access.

Select the type of view to base your new view on

> ⚠️ **IMPORTANT** All predefined view types are not available for all types of lists and libraries.

The option that you choose determines the requirements for the data in the list or library and how the information will be displayed. The maximum number of items in a view is 5,000. You can create additional views of the same data, but you cannot alter the type of a view after it has been created—for example, you can't change a view from a calendar view to a Gantt view.

Views have many settings to help make it easier for you to quickly find the information that you need in a list or library. Not all view settings are available for all types of views. For example, the options for a calendar view differ from options for other types of views. You might find that, more often than not, you base your new views on the Standard view type.

4

> **SEE ALSO** For more information about view types and settings, see the article at
> *https://support.office.com/en-US/article/Create-change-or-delete-a-view-of-a-list-or*
> *-library-Admin-27ae65b8-bc5b-4949-b29b-4ee87144a9c9.*

To create a custom view for a list or library

1. To start creating the new view, do one of the following:

    *   On the list or library page, select the ellipsis at the top of the content, to the right of the horizontal list of views, and select **Create View**.

Create a new view from a library page

    *   Display the **Settings** page for the list or library, and in the **Views** section, select **Create view**.

    *   Display the **List** tab of the ribbon for the list, or the **Library** tab for the library, in the **Manage Views** group, select **Create View**.

2. On the **View Type** page, select the view on which you want to base your new view—for example, the Standard view type.

3. On the **Create View** page, in the **View Name** box, enter the name for your view. Select **Make this the default view** if you want to make this the default view for the list or library. (Only a public view can be set as the default view for a list or library.)

Team Site ✎ EDIT LINKS

Settings › Create View ⊕

OK   Cancel

Name

Type a name for this view of the document library. Make the name descriptive, such as "Sorted by Author", so that site visitors will know what to expect when they click this link.

View Name:

☐ Make this the default view
(Applies to public views only)

Audience

Select the option that represents the intended audience for this view.

View Audience:

○ Create a Personal View
Personal views are intended for your use only.

◉ Create a Public View
Public views can be visited by anyone using the site.

Set up a view's name and audience

4. In the **Audience** section, under **View Audience**, select **Create a Personal view** or **Create a Public view**.

> **TIP** If Create A Public View is unavailable, you don't have the permissions to create a public view for this list or library.

5. In the **Columns** section, under **Display**, select the columns that you want to appear in the view and clear the columns that you don't want to appear. Then, under **Position from Left,** set up the order in which you want the columns to appear in the view.

6. Configure the other settings for your view, such as **Sort** and **Filter**.

⊟ Sort

Select up to two columns to determine the order in which the items in the view are displayed. Learn about sorting items.

First sort by the column:
None

◉ Show items in ascending order
(A, B, C, or 1, 2, 3)

○ Show items in descending order
(C, B, A, or 3, 2, 1)

Then sort by the column:
None

◉ Show items in ascending order
(A, B, C, or 1, 2, 3)

○ Show items in descending order
(C, B, A, or 3, 2, 1)

☐ Sort only by specified criteria (folders may not appear before items).

⊟ Filter

Show all of the items in this view, or display a subset of the items by using filters. To filter on a column based on the current date or the current user of the site, type [Today] or [Me] as the column value. Use indexed columns in the first clause in order to speed up your view. Filters are particularly important for lists containing 5,000 or more items because they allow you to work with large lists more efficiently. Learn about filtering items.

○ Show all items in this view

◉ Show items only when the following is true:

Show the items when column
None
is equal to

○ And ◉ Or
When column
None
is equal to

Set up sorting and filtering for a view

> **TIP** You can use the Folders settings for the view to hide the folders in your list or library, so that items are displayed without folders. You can also define whether to display this view in the existing folders. For example, you can use the Folders options to create two views for the same library content so that one set of users can use folders and others can use columns.

7. Select **OK** to save the view and return to the list or library page.

4

Set up validation settings and ratings

This section looks at setting up validation and ratings for lists and libraries. You can configure validation requirements against which user entries are checked when a user enters data in a list or library. You can also set up ratings for a list or library so that users can rate the content to express what they like or don't like, or they can assign star ratings to the content.

Use validation settings

You can use the list and library validation settings to validate the entries that users provide for each column in a list or library. When a user enters a value that does not meet the requirements that you have defined, a custom message is displayed, prompting the user to correct the value.

> **TIP** Validation requirements are defined by using a formula that must evaluate to TRUE for the entries to be saved to the list or library.

Team Site   ✎ EDIT LINKS

Settings ▸ Validation Settings

Formula

Specify the formula you want to use to validate data when new items are saved to this list. To pass validation, the formula must evaluate to TRUE. For more information, see Formulas in Help.

Example: =[Discount]<[Cost] will only pass validation if column Discount is less than column Cost.

Learn more about proper syntax for formulas.

Formula:

Insert Column:

Created
Expires
Modified
Title

Add to formula

User Message

Type descriptive text that will help site visitors understand what is needed for a valid list item. This description will be shown if the validation expression fails.

User Message:

Configure validation settings

> ✓ **TIP** Validation of user entries can be configured in two places. You can configure validation by using validation settings on a list or library level, and you can also configure validation at the column level when you create or modify the column properties. The difference is that using column properties does not provide the ability to compare two columns in the same list, whereas the list settings validation option does. The column properties validation settings are useful when you want to compare a column's value with a static value.

> ✓ **TIP** You can also set up validation for site columns, as described in the "To add a new site column to a content type" procedure earlier in this chapter.

To configure validation settings for a list or library

1. On the **Settings** page for the list or library, select **Validation Settings**.

2. On the **Validation Settings** page, do the following:

   a. In the **Formula** section, enter the formula to validate the data when new items are saved to the list or library.

   b. In the **User Message** section, enter the message that explains what is needed for the list or library item to be valid.

   c. Select **Save** to save the validation settings and return to the Settings page.

Set up ratings

The Rating settings are used to add a rating control to a list or library, so that users can rate the content in the list or library. When rating is turned on, you can configure whether users rate content by using Likes (Like or Don't Like) or a star rating (from zero stars to five stars).

When the voting/rating experience is set to Likes, a new Number Of Likes column is created on the list or library page, so that users can select the Like links for the items they want to vote for.

When the voting/rating experience is set to Star Ratings, a new Ratings (0-5) column is created on the list or library page, so that users can select the number of stars to rate the content. The column displays the five stars that users can select from to rate the list items. The column also counts how many users have voted and shows the number of voters to the right of the star rating for each list item or file, displaying the average number of stars between all votes.

The default setting is that rating is turned off.

Set up ratings

To configure ratings for a list or library

1. On the **Settings** page for the list or library, select **Rating Settings**.

2. On the **Rating Settings** page, do one of the following:

   - To turn ratings on, under **Allow items in this list to be rated?**, select **Yes**. Then, under **Which voting/rating experience you would like to enable for this list?**, choose either **Likes** or **Star Ratings**.

   - To turn ratings off, under **Allow items in this list to be rated?**, select **No**.

3. Select **OK** to save the rating settings and return to the Settings page.

Delete and restore lists and libraries

When a SharePoint list or library is no longer required, you might want to delete it. Deleting a list will also delete all of the list items (content) within that list, and deleting a library will delete all files within the library, so this should be used with caution. It might reassure you to note that sufficient permissions are required to delete a list or library. For example, users with a Contribute permission level for a site (or a list or library) will not be able to delete the list or library. If a list or a library is accidentally deleted, as with list items and documents, it will be in the site Recycle Bin for 30 days (by default) in SharePoint 2016, or 93 days in SharePoint Online, and can be restored.

To delete a list or library

1. On the **Settings** page for the list or library, in the **Permissions and Management** section, do one of the following:

   - For a list, select **Delete this list**.

   - For a library, select **Delete this library**.

2. Confirm that you want to send the list or library to the Recycle Bin by selecting **OK** in the confirmation box that appears.

To restore a list or library

1. In the site **Recycle Bin**, select the list or library by clicking or tapping in its left-most column. You can select multiple lists and libraries.

2. In the upper-left, at the top of the list of deleted items, select **Restore Selection**.

3. Confirm that you want to restore the selected items by selecting **OK** in the con-firmation box that appears.

Skills review

In this chapter, you learned how to:

- Use list and library settings
- Manage list and library users and permissions
- Share content in lists and libraries
- Configure versioning
- Work with advanced settings
- Work with content types and create views
- Set up validation settings and ratings
- Delete and restore lists and libraries

Practice tasks

The practice files for these tasks are located in the SP2016SBS\Ch04 folder.

To set up your environment to perform the practice tasks in this chapter, do the following:

1. Go to your SharePoint site and sign in if prompted.

2. From the **Your Apps** page, create an Announcements list named Announcements.

3. In the Announcements list, create a new item called New Product Announcement.

4. Go to the **Documents** library and upload the **Project.docx** and **Invoice.docx** files from the practice file folder to the library.

> ⚠ **IMPORTANT** You must have sufficient permissions to perform the operations involved in each practice task to complete that practice task. For more information, see Appendix A, "SharePoint 2016 user permissions and permission levels."

Use list and library settings

Go to your SharePoint site and sign in if prompted. Then perform the following tasks:

1. Go to the **Announcements** list and display its **Settings** page.

2. Change the list name to Team Announcements and set a link to this list to appear on the Quick Launch.

Manage list and library users and permissions

Continuing on your SharePoint site, perform the following tasks:

1. Display the **Permissions** page for the **Documents** library.

2. Check the permissions for this library for your user name.

3. Enable unique permissions for the **Documents** library.

4. Grant the **Full Control** permission level for the **Documents** library to a user in your environment.

5. Check the permissions for this user to confirm that the user has **Full Control** permissions for the **Document** library.

6. Change the permission level for this user to **Contribute**.

7. Check permissions for this user again to confirm that they have **Contribute** level permissions for the **Documents** library.

8. Remove permissions from this user to the library, and then check permissions for this user again to confirm that the permissions have been removed.

Share content in lists and libraries

Continuing on your SharePoint site, perform the following tasks:

1. Go to the **Documents** library.

2. Share the **Project.docx** file with a user in your environment, using the **Can edit** access level and without sending an invitation via email.

3. Share the **Invoice.docx** file via a guest link, using the **Can view** access level. Email the link to yourself, and access the link by using a browser to confirm that this link provides view access to the file.

   If guest links are not available in your environment, move to step 5.

4. Remove the guest link access from the **Invoice.docx** file. Access the link in a browser, to confirm that the link no longer provides access to the file.

5. Display the **Permissions** page for the **Project.docx** file.

6. Remove the permissions for this file from the user you shared the file with in step 2.

7. Go to the **Team Announcements** list.

8. Display the **Permissions** page for the **New Product Announcement** list item.

9. Configure permission inheritance for this list item to enable unique permissions.

10. Grant yourself the **Full Control** permission level for this list item, and then check the permissions to confirm that you now have individual permissions for this list item.

Configure versioning

Continuing on your SharePoint site, perform the following tasks:

1. Turn on versioning and content approval for the **Team Announcements** list.

2. Go to the **Team Announcements** list page, and confirm that the approval status for the **New Product Announcement** is **Approved**.

3. Create a new list item, **Party on Thursday**. Notice that its approval status is **Pending**.

4. Approve the **Party on Thursday** list item.

5. Confirm that the approval status for **Party on Thursday** is **Approved**.

6. Go to the **Document** library.

7. Turn on versioning with major and minor versions, and enforce checkout for the **Documents** library.

8. In the **Documents** library, create a new Word document called **Report.docx**. Make sure it is saved back to the library, and notice that it is checked out to you.

9. Check in **Report.docx**, leave the selected option **0.1 Minor version (draft)**, and in the **Comments** box, enter **Wide World Report Changes**.

10. Display the version history for the **Report.docx** file, and confirm that version 0.1 is listed.

11. Publish the **Report.docx** file as a major version.

12. Display the version history for **Report.docx** again, and notice that its current version is the major version 1.0.

13. Set versioning for the **Documents** library to major versions.

Work with advanced settings

Continuing on your SharePoint site, perform the following tasks:

1. Go to the **Team Announcements** list.

2. Turn off attachments for the **Team Announcements** list.

3. Go to the **Documents** library, and set up the default open behavior so that documents open in the client program.

4. Edit the library's default template so that it has **Wide World Imports** at the top of the page, centered and in bold, and then save the template back to the **Documents** library.

5. Create a new document in the **Documents** library, and confirm that it is based on the new template. Name the document **Quote.docx**.

Work with content types and create views

Continuing on your SharePoint site, perform the following tasks:

1. Create a new content type named **Global Proposal** in the **Document Content Types** group, with the parent content type of **Document**.

2. Associate the **Global Proposal** content type with the **GlobalProposal** document template **GlobalProposal.docx** in the practice file folder for this chapter.

3. Add a new site column to the **Global Proposal** content type, using the following properties.

Name	Customer Name
Type	Single line of text

4. Add another site column to the **Global Proposal** content type, using the following properties.

Name	Value
Type	Currency
Minimum value	50
Maximum value	10000

5. Go to the **Documents** library and turn on content type management for the library.

6. Add the **Global Proposal** content type to the **Documents** library.

7. In the **Documents** library, on the **Files** tab, in the **New** command list, select the **Global Proposal** content type. In Word, enter the following in the header of the new document.

Title	My Company Proposal
Customer Name	My Company
Value	1000

8. Save the document back to the library as My Proposal.docx.

9. In the browser, display the callout for **My Proposal.docx**, select the ellipsis in the callout, and then select **View Properties**. Confirm that the document metadata that you created is displayed in the **My Proposal** properties dialog.

10. In the **Documents** library, create a new view based on the **Standard** view, and name the view Global Proposal.

11. In the **Columns** section, do the following:

    - Display the **Customer Name** column, and set its position from the left to 5.

    - Display the **Value** column, and set its position from the left to 6.

12. In the **Sort** section, in the **First sort by the column** list, select **Customer Name**.

13. In the **Filter** section, select **Show items only when the following is true**, and set the filter to Content Type is equal to Global Proposal.

14. In the **Total** section, for the **Value** column, set the **Total** to **Average**.

15. Back on the **Documents** library page, confirm that the new view is displayed as you expected, and then change to the default **All Documents** view.

Set up validation settings and ratings

Continuing on your SharePoint site, perform the following tasks:

1. In the **Team Announcements** list, create a new announcement named Past Announcement with the date in the **Expires** field set in the past, prior to today.

2. To ensure that only future dates are added to the **Expires** column, set up validation settings for the **Team Announcement** list, with the following parameters:

   Formula   =[Expires]>=[Created]

   Comment   Expiration date must be in the future

3. To test the validation, in the **Team Announcements** list, create a new announcement named Validated Announcement, again selecting a date in the **Expires** field that is in the past, and select **Save**. Check that the error message that you set up is displayed at the bottom of the page, indicating that the date is invalid.

4. Enter a future date in the **Expires** field, and select **Save**. The new Validated Announcement is created.

5. Turn on ratings for the **Team Announcement** list, selecting **Likes** as the voting/rating experience.

6. Go to the **Team Announcements** list, and in the new **Number of Likes** column, select the **Like** links for the items you want to vote for.

7. Turn on ratings for the **Documents** library, selecting **Star Ratings** as the voting/rating experience.

8. Go to the **Documents** library, and in the new **Ratings (0-5)** column, select the number of stars to rate the content.

Delete and restore lists and libraries

Continuing on your SharePoint site, perform the following tasks:

1. Delete the **Team Announcement** list from your site.

2. Delete the **Documents** library from your site.

3. Restore the **Team Announcement** list and the **Documents** library to their original locations.

4. Confirm that you can access the **Team Announcement** list and the **Documents** library on your site as before.

Search for information and people

In today's workplace, increasingly large volumes of different types of content are produced every day. Information workers need to quickly find people and content to get answers to their questions and to complete their everyday tasks. That's where the SharePoint 2016 search capabilities can help you: you can use them to surface the right information you need, when you need it. By using search in SharePoint, you can find relevant information quickly and easily.

The site search box appears in the upper right of most pages on a site. It can be used to search the current site and any subsites below it. In addition to the site search box, lists and libraries also have a search box at the top of the content list that you can use to search for content in that list or library. You can also search across the sites in your SharePoint deployment by using a Search Center.

This chapter guides you through procedures related to searching SharePoint sites, targeting search queries, creating and managing terms, influencing relevance rankings, configuring search behavior, customizing search results pages, defining visibility and indexing for sites, and searching for people.

In this chapter

- Search SharePoint sites
- Target search queries
- Create and manage terms
- Influence relevance rankings
- Configure search behavior
- Customize search results pages
- Define visibility and indexing for sites
- Search for people

Practice files

For this chapter, use the practice files from the SP2016SBS\Ch05 folder. For practice file download instructions, see the introduction.

Search SharePoint sites

Searching is the process of entering one or more search words in the search box to form a search query that is executed against an aggregated database of the content, known as the *search index*. The search index contains information from documents and pages on your site. You can think of the search index as similar to the index at the end of this book.

SharePoint builds the search index by crawling the content on your SharePoint server farm (for on-premises deployments) or your SharePoint Online tenant (for cloud deployments). The search index is updated periodically. By default, the content is crawled incrementally once every 20 minutes, but the frequency can be changed by your SharePoint administrator.

A search query is processed by the search application, which returns a set of search results that match your query. These search results contain links to the webpages, documents, list items, lists, libraries, or sites that you want to find.

When you create new data in your SharePoint site, such as a new document, it might not appear immediately in your result set. It needs to be crawled and added to the search index before it will appear in the search results. Similarly, if you delete a document from a document library, it still might appear in the result set, but when you select the link for the document, an error message saying that the webpage cannot be found is displayed. In this case, the link to the document in the result set is called a broken link.

In hybrid deployments, you can use hybrid search to search for content across SharePoint Server 2016 and SharePoint Online at the same time. There are two types of hybrid search:

- **Cloud hybrid search** With the cloud hybrid search solution, all content— including SharePoint Server 2016 on-premises content and SharePoint Online content—is aggregated in the search index in SharePoint Online. All search queries are executed against this aggregated SharePoint Online search index. Users get search results for both on-premises and online content in a single search results list.

- **Hybrid federated search** With the hybrid federated search solution, both the search index in SharePoint Server 2016 and the search index in SharePoint Online are used. Both SharePoint Server 2016 and SharePoint Online search services can query the search index in the other environment and return federated results. Users get search results from the SharePoint Online search index and from the SharePoint Server 2016 search index in two search results lists, both of which are displayed on the search results page.

The heart of the SharePoint search engine is its ability to get the search results users are looking for. Search results can differ based on who you are, your context and permissions, and also your previous searches. SharePoint search uses relevancy algorithms combined with an analysis engine to provide a search experience that is flexible, intuitive, tailored to user needs, and easy to use.

Site search results

The search results page displays the results of your search. It is made up of three main areas, as follows:

- The search box that displays your query

- The search results list shown below the search box, which contains items that match your query, including documents and webpages

- The search refiners pane displayed at the left of the page, which provides additional filters so that you can narrow the search results to help you find what you are looking for

The search results page functionality is provided by three interconnected web parts: the Search Box web part, the Search Results web part, and the Refiners web part.

In addition to viewing the search results, you can see their content and act without opening them by using the callout. When you point to a search result, the callout, also known as a *hover panel*, appears to the right of the result and shows you a preview of the search result content. For example, for a document, the callout provides a live preview of a document, including a deep dive into that document that takes you to the right part of the document by using deep links. You can also act on that result in the callout by using contextual actions based on the result itself. For a document, the menu of actions includes options to edit the document, follow the document, send its link to other people, and to open the library where the document resides. For a webpage, the actions include options to open the page or send its link to other people.

> **TIP** To display a live preview of Office documents in search results callouts in a SharePoint 2016 on-premises deployment, you must have Office Online Server installed and activated in your environment. SharePoint Online provides a live preview of Office documents by default.

> **IMPORTANT** Search results are security-trimmed so that only the content and actions that a user has rights to are displayed.

If more than one page of content items matches your query, the total number of pages in the search results appears at the bottom of the search results list, with each page number representing a link to that page of the overall result set. The search words are emphasized in the title and URL for each search result. The search words are also emphasized in the text of the information snippet, if any. The snippet might display the text at the beginning of the result document, the text at the beginning of the body of the result webpage, or the description metadata.

Depending on the type of search result, it might be displayed with additional indicators. For example, Microsoft Office files such as Word documents or Excel spreadsheets are displayed with the program icon in front of the title of the search result, whereas newsfeed conversations are displayed with the number of replies and the number of likes to the right.

In addition to using a search box on your site, you can also use an enterprise Search Center to enter search queries and view the search results. An enterprise Search Center is a site in on-premises deployments that you can use to search your entire enterprise, including all SharePoint sites, file shares, Microsoft Exchange folders, and other content sources that are set up by your SharePoint administrator. Similarly, in SharePoint Online, a tenant-wide search is provided by a Search Center site that is automatically available at *<host_name>*/search.

Search Center results page

A Search Center provides several pages known as search verticals. Search verticals are search pages that are targeted for searching specific content sources, including Everything for a search across all content, People for specific people searches, Conversations for searching newsfeed conversations, and Videos for searching different types of videos. The list of search verticals is located under the search box on the Search Center page. Search verticals provide different search experiences and display search results that are filtered and formatted for content that is specific to the selected vertical.

The links that users can use to move quickly between the search verticals are displayed by the Search Navigation web part. By default, the Search Navigation web part is set up to show links to the Everything, People, Conversations, and Videos search verticals. The Search Navigation web part changes the display of search results in the Search Results web part. When users select a link for a search vertical, the search results are displayed according to the search vertical configuration.

If you want to be notified of search results changes, you can set up a search alert on a search results page so that you receive an email or an SMS text message when results change for that search query. You can set up alerts on any site search results page or on the Search Center results page, by selecting the Alert Me link at the bottom of the results list, which displays the New Alert page.

Set up search alerts

You can choose the type of changes for which you want to be notified, such as new items in the search results, changes to existing items, or all changes. You can also set up the frequency of alerts; the choices are daily or weekly.

To search a SharePoint site

1. Go to a site you want to search.

2. Enter your query in the search box located in the upper right of the page.

3. Click or tap the magnifying glass icon at the right end of the search box, or press **Enter**.

To search your SharePoint deployment

1. Go to a Search Center site in your SharePoint deployment.

   > **TIP** The Search Center site location is configured by the SharePoint administrator. In a SharePoint Online deployment, the default Search Center site URL is *<host_name>*/search/. For more information on how to configure the Search Center site URL, see the "Configure search behavior" topic later in this chapter.

2. On the **Search** page, enter your query in the search box located in the middle of the page.

3. Click or tap the magnifying glass search icon, or press **Enter**.

To display vertical search results in the Search Center

1. Search your SharePoint deployment.

2. On the search results page, underneath the search box, select the link for the search vertical you want to display.

To filter search results by using a refiner

1. Search your site, or search your SharePoint deployment.

2. On the search results page, in the refiners pane on the left side of the screen, select the refiner you want to filter the search results by.

To remove search refiners from the search results page

1. On a search results page that is filtered by one or more refiners, in the refiners pane on the left side of the screen, for each selected refiner, select **All** in the refiner's group.

To set up a search alert

1. Run the search for which you want to set up an alert.

2. On the search results page, at the bottom of the results list, select **Alert Me**.

3. On the **New Alert** page, do the following:

    - Enter the title of the alert, or keep the default.

    - Select the delivery method.

    - Select the changes you want to be alerted to.

    - Select the frequency of alerts.

4. When you're done, select **OK**.

Target search queries

A search query contains one or more terms that represent the content that you are trying to find. When executing a query, SharePoint returns a set of content items that form a result set. To find information, you might need to enter more than one query term. The more query terms you enter, the more specific and precise your query becomes, thereby producing a more focused result set.

A search query can include the following:

- A single word
- Multiple words
- A single phrase in quotes
- Multiple phrases in quotes

SharePoint does an implicit AND logical operation when you search for multiple words or multiple phrases. For example, when you search for the separate words "oak" and "furniture," the search result set contains only those content items where both words occur. Those words do not have to be side by side, but they both need to be in the content item somewhere. If a document contains the words "oak" and "chest" but not "oak" and "furniture," that document will not appear in the result set. When you search for the complete phrase "oak furniture" the result set contains only those content items where the two words "oak furniture" appear together.

When you use two words or two phrases in your search query and separate them by the OR logical operator, when either word or phrase appears in a document, that document appears in the result set. You can create more complex search queries, such as *(chest OR furniture) AND oak*. This will return content items that contain the words "oak" and "chest" or the words "oak" and "furniture," but will not return content items that contain the word "chest" and "furniture."

In Chapter 3, "Work with content in lists and libraries," you used columns in lists and libraries to save list item and document property values, also known as *metadata*. Metadata can be defined as data about data. You can use the metadata properties to help you create powerful search queries, thereby creating a more focused result set. For those metadata properties that store text, in the search box, use the *property:value* syntax, where *value* is a word or phrase.

For example, you can use the following default metadata properties for more targeted searches:

- **Author** Use this to find all content items authored by a particular person or persons, such as *author:peter*.
- **Filename** Use this to find all documents with a particular file name, such as *filename:proposal*.
- **Filetype** Use this to find specific file types, such as *filetype:docx*.

- **Title** Use this to find content items based on the value entered in the title column, such as *title:"oak chest"*.

- **Description** Use this to find content items based on the value entered in the description column, such as *description:oak*.

- **Contenttype** Use this to find content items of a particular type; for example, *contenttype:document, contenttype:announcement, contenttype:task*.

- **Size** Use this to find files according to their size. For example, *size>45000* will find all files larger than 45,000 bytes.

You can build more precisely targeted search queries by using a Keyword Query Language (KQL). KQL queries consist of free-text keywords and property filters. You can combine query elements with the available operators. Keyword queries have a maximum length of 2,048 characters.

> **SEE ALSO** For more information about KQL syntax, go to *https://msdn.microsoft.com/en-us/library/ee558911(v=office.15).aspx*.

If you get no results when you're searching for information, you can widen the search query to include more results, as follows:

- Use fewer query terms. For example, search for "report" instead of "performance report."

- Use more general query terms. For example, search for "hard cheese" instead of "parmesan."

- Use the wildcard character * at the end of any term in your query. For example, searching for "micro*" returns content that contains "Microsoft" or "microchip."

> **TIP** If you search to locate information that you know exists and it doesn't appear in your result set, check the spelling of your search query, wait at least 30 minutes, and repeat the search query. If that doesn't help, check with the SharePoint administrator to make sure that the content hasn't been excluded from search, and that you have appropriate permissions to view it.

If you're getting far too many search results, even after using refiners to filter the results, you can use advanced search to make a more specific query. On the Advanced Search page in the Search Center, SharePoint provides a form you can use to construct targeted search queries. In the Advanced Search form, you can include or exclude words and phrases in the query, filter results by language, narrow results by document format, and filter results by content properties.

Find documents that have...

All of these words:
The exact phrase:
Any of these words:
None of these words:
Only the language(s): ☐ English
                       ☐ French
                       ☐ German
                       ☐ Japanese
                       ☐ Simplified Chinese
                       ☐ Spanish
                       ☐ Traditional Chinese
Result type: All Results ▾

Add property restrictions...

Where the Property... (Pick Property) ▾ Contains ▾   And ▾ ✛

Search

Use Advanced Search to target your queries

To search by using targeted queries

1. Do one of the following:

    *   Go to a site you want to search.

    *   To search your SharePoint deployment, go to a Search Center.

2. Enter your targeted query in the search box.

    > ✓ **TIP** You can build your targeted query by using logical operators, metadata, or more precise Keyword Query Language constructs.

3. Click or tap the magnifying glass icon on the right of the search box, or press **Enter**.

To create and run a search query by using Advanced Search

1. Go to the Search Center and run a search.

2. On the search results page, at the bottom of the search results list, select **Advanced Search**.

3. On the **Advanced Search** page, create a search query by doing the following:

   - To include words and phrases in the query, do any of the following:

     - In the **All of these words** box, enter the words you want to search for.

     - In the **The exact phrase** box, enter the exact phrase you want to search for.

     - In the **Any of these words** box, enter the words you want the search results to contain at least one of.

   - To exclude words from the query, enter them in the **None of these words** box.

   - Select the languages of the search results.

   - In the **Result type** list, select the format of the search results.

   - In the **Add Property restrictions** section, select the properties and their values that you want to search for.

   > **TIP** To add a property restriction to a search query, select the plus sign to the right of the last displayed rule.

4. When you're done, select **Search** to run your query.

Create and manage terms

SharePoint Server 2016 supports managed metadata, which is a hierarchical collection of centrally managed terms that you can define and then use as attributes, or properties, for content items. Consistent use of metadata across sites in your organization helps with content findability in searches. By using a metadata property as a search refiner, users can filter search results.

> **TIP** When you enable managed metadata, the managed metadata service application is automatically created to make it possible to use and share content types across the SharePoint sites in your deployment.

SharePoint metadata is arranged in managed taxonomies and user-driven folksonomies, as follows:

- A *taxonomy* is a formal classification system. A taxonomy groups the terms, and then arranges the groups into a hierarchy.

- A *folksonomy* is an informal classification system. It evolves gradually as the SharePoint site users collaborate on a site and add keywords to content items.

You can implement taxonomies through managed terms and term sets. A term is a specific word or phrase that is associated with an item on a SharePoint site. A term can have many synonyms implemented by using the text labels. On a multilingual site, a term can have labels in different languages. After a term has been created, you can use it for content tagging and searching. Terms can also be used as search refiners.

 TIP To get the content and metadata from the documents into the search index, SharePoint maps the crawled properties to managed properties.

Related terms can be grouped together into a term set. Terms sets can have different scopes, depending on where the term set has been created, as follows:

- *Local term sets* are created within the context of a site collection and are available only to users of that site collection.
- *Global term sets* are shared across site collections and web applications and are available for use across all sites that use the same managed metadata service application.

There are two types of terms, as follows:

- Managed terms are terms that are predefined and set up by people who have appropriate permissions to manage the taxonomies. Managed terms are grouped into a hierarchical term set within a taxonomy.
- Enterprise keywords are words or phrases that a site user adds to content items on a SharePoint site. SharePoint groups the enterprise keywords into a single, non-hierarchical term set that forms a folksonomy. To enable users to add keywords, you can add a special enterprise keywords column to a list or library. Then, to add words or phrases as keywords to a content item, users select the item and enter the keywords in the item properties.

A term set can be closed or open. In a closed term set, users can't add new terms unless they have appropriate permissions. In an open term set, users can add new terms in a column that is mapped to the term set.

SharePoint maintains terms and term sets in a term store. You can create and manage terms and term sets by using the Term Store Management Tool that is available from the Site Settings page.

 TIP You must have a Term Store Administrator, Term Store Group Manager, or Term Store Contributor role to create and manage terms. These roles are assigned by the SharePoint farm administrator.

Manage terms in the Term Store

The Term Store Management Tool displays the global term sets and local term sets available for the site collection from which you access the tool.

To open the Term Store Management Tool

1. Go to a site in the site collection for which you want to open the Term Store Management Tool.

2. On the **Site Settings** page, in the **Site Administration** group, select **Term store management**.

To view a term in a taxonomy in the Term Store

1. Open the **Term Store Management Tool**.

2. In the left pane, in the taxonomy in which you want to view a term, expand the group's hierarchy to find the term set in which the term you want to view is located.

3. Select the term to view its properties.

To view a Keywords folksonomy in the Term Store

1. Open the **Term Store Management Tool**.

2. In the left pane, expand **System**.

3. Under **System**, expand **Keywords**.

To create a term in a term set

1. Open the **Term Store Management Tool**.

2. In the left pane, expand the groups to display the term set to which you want to add a term.

3. Point to the term set where you want to add a term, select the arrow that appears, and then select **Create Term**.

   > **TIP** If the arrow does not appear, you don't have the appropriate permissions to create and manage terms.

4. Enter the name for the term that you want to use as the default label for the newly created term.

5. In the properties pane, configure the following settings for the new term:

   - Select the **Available for tagging** check box to make this term available for content tagging.

   - Select the language for this label for the term.

   - In the **Description** box, enter an optional description for the term.

   - In the **Default Label** box, enter the name that you want to use as the label for the term in this language.

   - In the **Other Labels** box, enter the optional synonyms for this term in this language. To add multiple synonyms, enter the first synonym and then press **Enter** to add more lines.

Set up properties for a term

6. When you're done, select **Save**.

To copy a term

1. Open the **Term Store Management Tool**.

2. In the left pane, expand the groups to display the term you want to copy.

3. Point to the term you want to copy, select the arrow that appears, and then select **Copy Term**. A new term named Copy Of *<Original Term Name>* is created.

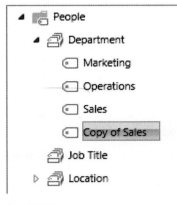

Copy a term

4. With the copy of the term selected, enter a name for it in the **Default Label** box in the properties pane. Configure the other properties you want for the new term, and then select **Save**.

To delete a term

1. Open the **Term Store Management Tool**.

2. In the left pane, expand the groups to display the term you want to delete.

3. Point to the term you want to delete, select the arrow that appears, and then select **Delete Term**. Confirm your action by selecting **OK** in the message box that is displayed.

To add an enterprise keywords column to a list or library

1. Go to the library or list where you want to add a keywords column.

2. On the **Library** or **List** tab, select **Library Settings** or **List Settings**.

3. On the **Settings** page, in the **Permissions and Management** section, select **Enterprise Metadata and Keywords Settings**.

4. On the **Enterprise Metadata and Keywords Settings** page, select the check box for **Add an Enterprise Keywords column to this list and enable Keyword synchronization**, and then select **OK** to return to the Settings page.

Team Site   ✎ EDIT LINKS

Enterprise Metadata and Keywords Settings

Add Enterprise Keywords

An enterprise keywords column allows users to enter one or more text values that will be shared with other users and applications to allow for ease of search and filtering, as well as metadata consistency and reuse.

Adding an Enterprise Keywords column also provides synchronization between existing legacy keyword fields and the managed metadata infrastructure. (Document tags will be copied into the Enterprise Keywords on upload.)

Enterprise Keywords

☑ Add an Enterprise Keywords column to this list and enable Keyword synchronization

Add an enterprise keywords column to a library or list

To add keywords to a file in a document library

1. Go to the library where you want to add keywords to a file.

2. Select the file you want to add keywords to by clicking or tapping in its leftmost column.

3. On the **Files** tab of the ribbon, in the **Manage** group, select **Edit Properties**.

4. On the properties page for the file, enter the keywords in the **Enterprise Keywords** box, separated by semicolons.

Name *	Oak desk	.docx
Title		
Enterprise Keywords		

Enterprise Keywords are shared with other users and applications to allow for ease of search and filtering, as well as metadata consistency and reuse

Created at 7/20/2016 4:56 PM by ☐ Olga Londer
Last modified at 7/21/2016 4:10 PM by ☐ Olga Londer   Save   Cancel

Enter keywords for a content item

5. When you're done, select **Save** to return to the library page.

Influence relevance rankings

When the results of a search are displayed, the search engine calculates the order in which the search results are listed. This order is referred to as the relevance rank. SharePoint search uses several ranking models, which are based on predefined algorithms that calculate the ranking score of a particular item in the search results. By default, search results are sorted in descending order based on their ranking score. The Item with the top score gets the top position in search results.

The ranking models combine weighted scores for several different criteria, including content, metadata, file type, and interaction. For example, depending on your business environment, some file types might be more important from a ranking perspective than others, and therefore their scores would be higher. Typically, Microsoft Word and PowerPoint search results have higher scores than Excel results, and therefore they are displayed higher in the search results page. Another example is an interaction score, which is based on the number of times a search result is clicked, and also on the queries that led to a result being clicked. For the final ranking score of a search result, all ranking criteria in the ranking model are combined.

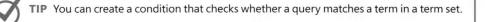 **TIP** The search system automatically uses the appropriate ranking models for the default search verticals Everything, People, Conversations, and Videos.

In SharePoint, you can influence the ranking of search results by using query rules. A query rule consists of a *query rule condition* and a *query rule action*. When a query matches a query rule condition, the query rule action is triggered.

TIP You can create a condition that checks whether a query matches a term in a term set.

By using a query rule, you can show a search result above all ranked results. This result is called a promoted result. You can also group several results in a result block, and then promote the group in the same way.

A query rule can specify the following types of actions:

- Add promoted results that appear above ranked results.
- Add one or more result blocks. As with individual results, you can promote a result block or rank it with other search results.
- Change the ranking of results.

For example, you can promote a specific content item to be displayed at the top of the search results if a user searches for particular topics.

Query rules can include the result sources for the query. A result source specifies a search location to get the search results from, including the search index. A query rule will be triggered if a user query is performed on these result sources.

You can also specify the time period during which the query rule is active. For example, you can promote a specific page that contains important information for site visitors to be aware of so that a link to this page appears at the top of all search results for a limited period of time, such as for a day.

You can create query rules for a site collection or for a site. When you create query rules for a site collection, the rules can be used on all sites in the site collection. When you create query rules for the site, the rules can be used only on that site.

> **IMPORTANT** Query rules for a site can be created by the members of the Owners group for the site. Query rules for a site collection can be created only by the site collection administrators.

> **TIP** In addition to creating rules for a site or a site collection, you can also create query rules that span multiple site collections. In SharePoint Server 2016, you can do this by creating a query rule for a Search application. The query rule can be used in all site collections that use this Search application. Likewise, in SharePoint Online, you can create query rules for the tenant. The query rule can be used in all site collections within this tenant.

To create a query rule

1. Go to a site where you want to create a query rule.

2. On the **Site Settings** page, in the **Search** section, select **Query Rules**.

> **TIP** To create a query rule for a site collection, go to the top-level site in the site collection, and on the Site Settings page, in the Site Collection Administration section, select Search Query Rules. You must be a site collection administrator to create a site collection query rule.

3. On the **Manage Query Rules** page, in the **Select a Result Source** list, select a result source for the new query rule. For example, the Local SharePoint Results (System) is a prebuilt result source that includes an index for all SharePoint sites in the current farm, with the exception of people.

Select a result source for a query rule

4. Select **New Query Rule**.

5. On the **Add Query Rule** page, in the **General Information** section, in the **Rule name** box, enter a name for the query rule.

Enter a name for the new query rule

6. Expand the **Context** section.

    ◢ Context

    You can restrict this rule to queries performed on a particular result source,
    from a particular category of topic page, or by a user matching a particular
    user segment. For instance, restrict a rule to the Local Video Results source
    so that it only fires in Video search.

    Query is performed on these sources
    ○ All sources
    ◉ One of these sources
        Local SharePoint Results remove
    Add Source

    Query is performed from these categories
    ◉ All categories
    ○ One of these categories
    Add Category

    Query is performed by these user segments
    ◉ All user segments
    ○ One of these user segments
    Add User Segment

    Configure the result sources, content categories, and user segments for your new query rule

7. In the **Context** section, do the following:

    - To configure the result sources, under **Query is performed on these sources**, do one of the following:

        - To apply the query rule to all result sources, select **All sources**.

        - To apply the query rule to one or more specific sources, select **One of these sources**. The source that you specified in step 3 is selected by default. To add a source, select **Add Source**, then in the **Add Source** dialog box, select an additional result source, and then select **Save** to save your settings and return to the Add Query Rule page.

    - To configure the categories, under **Query is performed from these categories**, do one of the following:

        - To apply the query rule when queries are performed from all categories, leave the default setting, **All categories**, selected.

        - To restrict the query rule to specific categories—for example, to specify that a query rule should be triggered only when a term from a term set is included in the query—under **Query is performed from these categories**, select **Add category**. In the **Import from term store** dialog, select a term that will cause the query rule to be triggered when it is included in a query, and then select **Save** to save your settings and return to the Add Query Rule page.

Select a term that will trigger the query rule when it is included in the query

- To configure the user segments, under **Query is performed by these user segments**, do one of the following:

    - To apply the query rule to queries from all user segments, leave the default setting, **All user segments**, selected.

    - To restrict the query rule to a particular user segment, select **Add User Segment**. In the **Add User Segment** dialog box, in the **Title** box, enter the title for this rule, and then select **Add user segment term**. In the **Import from term store** dialog, select a term that represents a user segment that will cause the query rule to be triggered when it appears in a query, and then select **Save** to save your settings and return to the **Add User Segment** dialog. Repeat for more terms if required, then select **Save** to save your settings and return to the Add Query Rule page.

8. In the **Query Conditions** section, do one of the following:

    - Select one of the conditions from the list of available conditions.

Select a query condition

> **TIP** Select Add Alternate Condition in the Query Conditions section of the Add Query Rules page to add more conditions. You can specify multiple conditions of different types.

- Select **Remove Condition** to configure this query rule to be triggered for every query that users enter.

9. In the **Actions** section, select one of the following to set up the action to take when the query rule is triggered:

- To promote individual results so that they appear at the top of the search results list, select **Add Promoted Result**. In the **Add Promoted Result** dialog, in the **Title** box, enter the name that you want to give to this promoted result. In the **URL** box, enter the URL of the result that should be promoted, and then select **Save** to save your settings and return to the Add Query Rule page.

Add Promoted Result   ✕

Title

URL

☐ Render the URL as a banner instead of as a hyperlink

Description

Save   Cancel

Configure a promoted result

TIP You can add several individual promoted results. When there is more than one promoted result, you can specify the relative ranking.

- To promote a group of search results, select **Add Result Block**. In the **Add Result Block** dialog, configure the query and settings for the block, and then select **OK** to save your configuration and return to the Add Query Rule page.

- To change ranked search results, select **Change ranked results by changing the query**. In the **Build Your Query** dialog, specify and test the modified query, and then select **OK** to save your settings and return to the Add Query Rule page.

10. To make the query rule active during a particular time period, expand the **Publishing** section, and then specify the period.

> ◢ Publishing
>
> These settings control when the rule can fire. If the rule is not active, it never fires. The start date is when you want it to start firing. The end date is when you want it to stop firing. The review date is when you want the contact to review the rule.
>
> ☑ Is Active
>
> Start Date
>
> [   ] 📅
>
> End Date
>
> [   ] 📅

Set up a time period when the query rule is active

> **TIP** In the Publishing section, you can also define the review date and the contact. The review date is when you want the contact to review the rule.

11. When you're done, select **Save** to save your settings and return to the Manage Query Rules page.

Configure search behavior

Search functionality is flexible and configurable, and you can tailor the search experience for your site. You can do so by using the Search settings on the Site Settings page. The search box and the search results page on your site will use these settings.

> **TIP** The Search settings you configure on the site collection level will be inherited by all sites within that site collection, unless you configure other settings for the site that would override the inheritance.

Site Settings › Search Settings

Use this page to configure how Search behaves on this site. The shared Search Box at the top of most pages will use these settings. Note: A change to these settings may take up to 30 minutes to take effect. Change search behavior for this site collection and all sites within it.

Enter a Search Center URL

When you've specified a search center, the search system displays a message to all users offering them the ability to try their search again from that Search Center.

Search Center URL:

Example: /SearchCenter/Pages or http://server/sites/SearchCenter/Pages

Which search results page should queries be sent to?

Custom results page URLs can be relative or absolute.

URLs can also include special tokens, such as {SearchCenterURL}. This token will be replaced by the value in the "Search Center URL" property. If the value in this property ever changes, any URL using the token will update automatically.

Example:
{SearchCenterURL}/results.aspx

☑ Use the same results page settings as my parent.
○ Send queries to a custom results page URL.
Results page URL:

Example: /SearchCenter/Pages/results.aspx or http://server/sites/SearchCenter/Pages/results.aspx

◉ Turn on the drop-down menu inside the search box, and use the first Search Navigation node as the destination results page.

Configure Search Navigation

Search Navigation allows users to move quickly between search experiences listed in the Navigation. Navigation is displayed in the Quick Launch control on search pages, and can also be shown as a drop-down menu from the search box.

↑ Move Up   ↓ Move Down   ✎ Edit...   ✕ Delete   ⊕ Add Link...

No items found.

Selected Item

No item currently selected.

Configure the Search settings for your site

By using the Search settings, you can add a link to a Search Center where users can search everything in your company. When you do so, the search verticals will be shown in the Search Navigation web part on search results pages on your site. In addition, the search box on your site can include the drop-down menu with search verticals from the Search Center. Users will be able to choose whether to search your site only or choose the verticals to search across all sites and other content sources by using the Search Center. The default setting for the search box is to search the site where it is located. If you configure the same settings for a site collection, search verticals will be shown on search results pages on all sites in the site collection, and the search boxes on all sites in the site collection will show the drop-down menu with the search verticals from the Search Center.

Search Everything	▾ 🔍
Everything	
People	
Conversations	
Video	

Show the search verticals in a site search box

You can also change which search results page queries are sent to. By default, queries are sent to the same search results page as the parent, but you can override this for a site collection or a site.

Additionally, for a site, you can edit the search verticals links and add a search vertical by using a search navigation configuration. The new link to the search vertical will be shown in the Search Navigation web part on search results pages and can also be shown in a drop-down menu in the search box.

To open the Search Settings page for a site or site collection

1. Do one of the following:

   - To open the **Search Settings** page for a site, go to the **Site Settings** page for the site, and then, in the **Search** group, select **Search Settings**.

   - To open the **Search Settings** page for a site collection, go to the **Site**

Settings page for the top-level site in the site collection and then, in the Site Collection Administration group, select Search Settings.

To set up a Search Center URL for a site or site collection

1. Open the Search Settings page for the site or site collection.

2. In the Search Center URL box, enter the URL of the Search Center site in your deployment where the user search queries would go.

> **TIP** For SharePoint 2016, enter the URL for an enterprise Search Center site. In SharePoint Online, if you do not enter a Search Center URL, searches will go to the default Search Center site at <host_name>/search/.

3. Select OK to return to the Site Settings page.

To change a search results page for a site or site collection

1. Open the Search Settings page for the site or site collection.

2. In the Which search results page should queries be sent to? section, clear the Use the same results page settings as my parent check box.

3. Select one of the following:

   - To send user queries to a custom search results page, select Send queries to a custom results page URL, and then enter the URL for the custom search page you want the queries to be sent to.

   - To turn on the drop-down menu inside the search box on the site so that the users can choose a search vertical in the search box when they enter a query, select Turn on the drop-down menu inside the search box, and use the first Search Navigation node as the destination results page.

4. Select OK to return to the Site Settings page.

To configure search navigation for a site

1. Go to the Search Settings page for the site and scroll down to the Configure Search Navigation section.

5

Configure search navigation for your site

2. Do any of the following:

    - To add a search vertical, select **Add link**. In the **Navigation Link** dialog, specify the title, the URL, and the optional description for the search vertical page, and then select **OK**.

> Navigation Link   ✕
>
> ⊞ Edit the title, URL, and description of the navigation item.
>
> Title: [   ]
>
> URL: [http://   ] [Browse...]

Set up a new search vertical link

    - To change the title, URL, and description of a search vertical, select the search vertical, and then select **Edit**. In the **Navigation link** dialog, make the edits you want, and then select **OK**.

    - To change the order of the search vertical links, select the link, and then select **Move Up** or **Move Down** as required.

    - To delete a search vertical link, select **Delete**.

3. When you're done, select **OK** to return to the Site Settings page.

Customize search results pages

On the Search Center site, the default search results page provides the search box and several search verticals. Search verticals are the search results pages targeted for searching specific content. By default, the web parts on different search vertical pages are the same. However, the query in the Search Results web part is executed against a particular result source that is configured differently for each search vertical page. For example, for the Everything vertical, the query is executed against the result source called Local SharePoint Results, which is a default result source that covers all content in your SharePoint installation, with the exception of people. For the People vertical, the search runs against a result source called Local People Results. It is the result source that defines the search results in the vertical page.

Several web part pages provide the search experience in the Search Center site, including the following:

- **Default.aspx** The Search Center home page where users enter their queries
- **Results.aspx** The default search results page for the Search Center, which is also the search results page for the Everything search vertical
- **Peopleresults.aspx** The search results page for the People search vertical
- **Conversationresults.aspx** The search results page for the Conversations search vertical
- **Videoresults.aspx** The search results page for the Videos search vertical
- **Advanced.aspx** The page that provides an Advanced Search form

All these pages are located in the Pages library on the Search Center site. You can navigate to each of them directly by entering its URL in the address bar of your browser. The URL format is *<Search Center>*/Pages/*<page>*. For example, you can go to the People search vertical page by using *<Search Center>*/Pages/ peopleresults.aspx.

The search results pages contain the following search web parts:

- **Search Box** This is the web part that provides the search box functionality. The Search Box web part is used on the home page for the Search Center and all default search vertical pages. It is displayed in the middle of the home page and at the top of the search vertical pages.
- **Search Results** This is the web part that provides the search results in the body of the search results page. The Search Results web part displays the search results for the query that was entered in a Search Box web part. The Search Results web part is used on all default search vertical pages. Depending on the vertical, this web part might display search results that are filtered and formatted for a specific type of content. The Search Results web part also sends the search results to the Refinement web part and to the Search Navigation web part.

- **Refinement** This is the web part that provides the refiners, or filters, in the left part of the search results pages. Users select the refiners to narrow search results to find what they're looking for. The Refinement web part is used on all default search vertical pages.

- **Search Navigation** This is the web part that provides the search verticals navigation links located beneath the search box. By default, the Search Navigation web part is set up to show links to the Everything, People, Conversations, and Videos search verticals. The Search Navigation web part uses search results from the Search Results web part so that when users select a search vertical link, the search results are filtered and displayed according to how the search vertical is set up.

You can customize web parts within the search results pages and configure the different web part settings to modify the page behavior. The Pages library is configured to require checkout, so you must check in and publish your changes to search results pages before other users can see them.

To customize a search results page

1. Go to the search results page you want to customize by doing one of the following:

   - Browse to the page you want to customize:

     - For a Search Center home page, go to the Search Center site.

     - For the search results page for a vertical, perform a Search Center search with any search word, and then select the search vertical link.

   - Navigate directly to the page you want to customize by entering its URL in the address bar of your browser, as follows:

     - *Search Center*/**Pages/default.aspx** for the Search Center home page

     - *Search Center*/**Pages/results.aspx** for the default search results page that is also the Everything search vertical page

     - *Search Center*/**Pages/peopleresults.aspx** for the People search vertical page

     - *Search Center*/**Pages/conversationresults.aspx** for the Conversations search vertical page

     - *Search Center*/**Pages/videoresults.aspx** for the Videos search vertical page

2. On the **Settings** menu, select **Edit Page**. The search results page is displayed in edit mode.

Customize a search results page

3. Do the following, as required:

    - Add and remove web parts.

    - Change the position of web parts on the page.

    > **SEE ALSO** For more information about working with web parts, see Chapter 7, "Work with webpages."

4. Configure the properties of the search web parts by doing the following:

    a. Point to the title of the search web part you want to configure, and select the arrow that appears in the upper-right corner of the web part to display the web part menu. Select **Edit Web Part**.

b. In the web part tool pane that appears, configure the properties for the web part as required. When you're done, select **OK**.

Configuring properties for a Refinement web part in a search results page

5. To check in the page, do one of the following:

   - On the **Page** tab, select **Check In**.

   - In the message bar at the top of the page, select **Check it in**.

6. Select **Continue** in the dialog that appears to check in the page and return to the search results page.

7. On the search results page, in the message bar that appears at the top of the page, select **Publish this draft** to publish the page and make it available to users.

> ⚠️ **Recent draft not published** Visitors can't see recent changes. Publish this draft.

> Search...   🔍
>
> Everything   People   Conversations   Videos

Publish the search results page to make it available to users

Define visibility and indexing for sites

By default, all local sites are included in the results of a search at a Search Center. The local sites are crawled and their content is indexed and included in the default result source Local SharePoint Results. Sometimes, you might need to exclude a site from the search results, even though the users in your organization have access rights to it. For example, when you are redesigning or updating a site, you might want to temporarily exclude the site from showing in the search results.

The Search And Offline Availability page provides an option to define whether the site is indexed and thus visible in the search results. When you exclude your site from indexing, you also exclude all of its subsites. When you exclude the top-level site, the whole site collection is excluded.

Indexing Site Content

Specify whether this site should be visible in search results. If a site is not visible to search, then content from that site and all of its subsites will not appear in search results.

Allow this site to appear in search results?
◉ Yes   ○ No

Define your site's visibility in search results

You can also force reindexing of your site from the Search And Offline Availability page. If you force reindexing, the site will be fully reindexed at the next scheduled crawl. Otherwise, a default incremental crawl will run that picks up the site changes since the last crawl.

Reindex site

Marking this site for reindexing will enable this site to be picked up during the next scheduled search crawl.

Reindex site

Force site reindexing

To configure site visibility in search results

1. Go the site that you want to include in or exclude from search results.

2. On the **Site Settings** page, in the **Search** section, select **Search and Offline Availability**.

3. In the **Indexing Site Content** section, do one of the following:

   - To include the site in search results, under **Allow this site to appear in search results?**, select **Yes**.

   - To exclude the site from the search results, under **Allow this site to appear in search results?**, select **No**.

4. When you're done, select **OK**.

To force site reindexing

1. Go the site that you want to reindex.

2. On the **Site Settings** page, in the **Search** section, select **Search and Offline Availability**.

3. In the **Reindex site** section, select **Reindex site**, and then select **OK**.

Search for people

You can use the People vertical to search for people in your organization against the default result source called Local People Results, which is dedicated to people information. The profile store and personal sites are major sources of information for the people search. The profile store is a repository of user profiles.

A user profile is a collection of properties that describes a single user, and also the settings associated with each property. User profiles are composed of properties that are imported from directory services and other systems, and also properties that are provided by users. Properties in a user profile usually include basic information about the user, including the user name, email address, phone numbers, manager, job title, and office location. User profiles can also contain more specific information about a user, such as the products the user works on, the user's areas of expertise, and the user's place in the organization's structure. User profiles help identify connections between users in an organization, such as their common managers, workgroups, group membership, and other connections.

> **TIP** User profiles are different from SharePoint user accounts and have their own dedicated data store. User accounts are used to provide security in SharePoint, including authentication and access control, whereas user profiles are used to organize information about users and about the relationships among users. Updating a user profile does not affect the user account.

The profile store is crawled on a regular basis much like other SharePoint sites and repositories are crawled, and the content is added to a people-specific index that the search queries in the People vertical are executed against. Conceptually, a user profile is treated as a document about that person with the user's name as the title.

At a basic level, the more search query terms appear in the person's profile, the more relevant the result. People search ranking models differ from information search ranking models. In the People search ranking models, the relevance rank is assigned to search results that are related to people; therefore, there are specific relevance criteria that include social distance and expertise.

Social distance is computed based on colleague relationships. For example, people who you work with on the same team will be close to you with respect to the social distance. You might also follow other people and content, and other people might follow you. You might participate in conversations with them, and they might provide regular comments on your newsfeed. You might also be a member of mailing lists and discussion groups, so you would be considered closer to the members of the same groups than to those who are not members, because your visibility to other people in these groups is higher. The search engine takes this data into consideration when calculating social distance.

Basic *expertise* information is collected from the user profile—in particular, the "Ask me about" and "Skills" fields in the user profile. The data from these fields is indexed for expertise searches and contributes to the expertise relevance ranking. In addition, other fields are taken into account, including "Past projects," "Interests," and also, more importantly, the documents that users worked on that are relevant to the search query.

> **TIP** To get the best results from a people search, people in your organization should add as much information as they can to their user profiles in the profile store and to their personal sites.

To search for people

1. Go to the **Search Center** in your deployment and do one of the following:

    *   Perform a search, and then select the **People** vertical to display the People search vertical page.

    *   Navigate to the People vertical page directly by entering its URL, *Search Center*/**Pages/peopleresults.aspx**, in the browser address bar, and then perform the search.

    > ✅ **TIP** If the drop-down menu inside your site search box is turned on to display the search verticals in your deployment, you can also enter the search query in your site search box and then select the People vertical from the menu.

To add information to your user profile

1. To access your user profile, select **Newsfeed** in the app launcher, then on the **Newsfeed** page, select **About Me** on the Quick Launch. Select **edit** to open your profile for editing.

2. In the **Edit Details** page, on the **Basic Information** tab, notice that some information has already been populated, such as your name. Provide any of the following data:

    *   **About me** Enter a personal description that contains what you want others to know about you.

    *   **Photo** Upload your photo to help others recognize you. Your photo will be displayed in the search results in the People vertical.

    *   **Ask me about** Enter text to describe your responsibilities or areas of expertise.

Provide information in your user profile

3. Select the **Contact Information** tab and fill in the details for any of the following fields: **Mobile phone**, **Fax**, **Home phone**, **Office location**, and **Assistant**.

Provide contact information

4. In the **Who can see this?** column, for the **Fax**, **Home phone**, and **Office Location** fields, select **Everyone** to make the information available for everyone to see, or select **Only Me** to keep the data private. The default setting is **Everyone**.

5. Select the **Details** tab, and fill in any of the following fields: **Past projects**, **Skills**, **Schools**, **Birthday**, and **Interests**.

		Who can see this?
Past projects		Everyone ▾
	Provide information on previous projects, teams or groups.	
Skills		Everyone ▾
	Include skills used to perform your job or previous projects. (e.g. C++, Public Speaking, Design)	
Schools		Everyone ▾
	List the schools you have attended.	
Birthday		Everyone ▾
	Enter the date in the following format: July 22	
Interests		Everyone ▾
	Share personal and business related interests.	

Provide more detailed information about you

6. In the **Who can see this?** column, select **Everyone** or **Only Me** for each field.

> **TIP** The data on the Details tab is used not only for relevance ranking but also for expertise searches (based on the Past Projects, Skills, and Interests fields) and as input for computing social distance (based on the Schools, Past Projects, and Interests fields).

7. Select the ellipsis to the right of the **Details** tab to display additional tabs such as Newsfeed Settings and Languages And Regions. Fill in as much information as you can.

> **TIP** The Newsfeed Settings page provides information that is used in computing social distance.

8. When you're done, at the bottom of the **Edit Details** page, select **Save all and close**. In the **Profile Changes** dialog that warns you that the user profile information might not be available right away, select **OK**.

> **TIP** Depending on the content crawler frequency, it can take some time before your profile is indexed and the data appears in the search results.

Skills review

In this chapter, you learned how to:

- Search SharePoint sites
- Target search queries
- Create and manage terms
- Influence relevance rankings
- Configure search behavior
- Customize search results pages
- Define visibility and indexing for sites
- Search for people

5

Practice tasks

The practice files for these tasks are located in the SP2016SBS\Ch05 folder.

To set up your environment so that you can perform the practice tasks in this chapter, follow the instructions in the Chapter5_Setup PDF file in the practice file folder.

> ✓ **TIP** Depending on the crawl frequency in your environment, you might need to wait at least 30 minutes after the site has been set up for the content to be indexed and appear in the search results.

> ⚠ **IMPORTANT** You must have sufficient permissions to perform the operations involved in each practice task to complete that practice task. For more information, see Appendix A, "SharePoint 2016 user permissions and permission levels."

Search SharePoint sites

Go to your SharePoint site, and perform the following tasks:

1. Search your site by using the query word **oak**.

2. Use the **Word** refiner to filter the search results to display only Word documents.

3. Point to the **Oak Chest** document to display its callout panel. Notice that the callout lists information about the document, such as when it was last modified.

4. Use the **Bill Malone** refiner to narrow the search results further to display only documents authored by Bill Malone.

5. Remove the **Word** and **Bill Malone** refiners from the search results page.

6. Use a **Web Page** refiner to filter the search results to display only webpages.

7. Point to the **Oak Furniture Buyer Tasks** to display its callout and view the live page in the callout.

8. Remove the **Web Page** refiner from the search page.

9. Go to a Search Center in your deployment and run a search with the query word **oak**.

10. Select the **Videos** vertical and validate that there is no video content that satisfies the query. Select the **Everything** vertical to return to the search results page.

11. Set up a search alert for the oak search query with the following settings:

    - Enter the query name or keep the default, which is the query itself.

    - Define the delivery method as **E-mail**.

    - In the **Change Type** section, select **All Changes**.

    - In the **When to Send Alerts** section, select **Send a daily summary**.

Target search queries

Go to your SharePoint site, and perform the following tasks:

1. Display all content items on your site authored by Todd Rowe by using the search query **Author:"Todd Rowe"**.

2. Display all files on your site with the file extension .docx by using the search query **Filetype:docx**.

3. Display the content items on your site that contain both "oak chairs" and "oak furniture" by using a search query **"oak chairs" AND "oak furniture"**.

4. Display the content items on your site that contain either "oak chairs" or "oak furniture" by using a search query **"oak chairs" OR "oak furniture"**.

5. Go to the Search Center in your deployment.

6. Create a search query by using Advanced Search. Use the following settings:

    - **All of these words** Enter oak table.

    - **Only the languages** Select **English**.

    - **Result type** Select **Word Document**.

    - **Add property restrictions**:

        - **Property** Select **Author**.

        - **Logical operator** Select **Contains**.

        - **Property value** Enter Bill Malone.

7. Run the search query and validate that only one document, Oak Night Stand, satisfies the search criteria in your query.

Create and manage terms

Go to your SharePoint site, and perform the following tasks:

1. Run a search with the search query **oak furniture**. Validate that the **Price list** file is not listed in the search results.

2. Add an enterprise keywords column to the Oak Furniture library.

3. Add keywords **Oak furniture** to the **Price list** file in the **Oak Furniture** library.

4. View the **Keywords** folksonomy in the Term Store and locate your new keywords **Oak furniture**.

5. Return to the home page of your site by selecting its link in the top link bar.

6. Repeat a search with the search query **oak furniture**. Validate that the **Price list** file is now listed in the search results.

> ✓ **TIP** Depending on the crawl frequency in your environment, you might need to wait at least 30 minutes for the content to be indexed and appear in the search results.

Influence relevance rankings

Continuing on your SharePoint site, perform the following tasks:

1. Create a query rule to promote the Oak Furniture library when a user searches for "oak" or "furniture". Use the following settings:

    a. On the **Manage Query Rules** page, use the result source **Local SharePoint Results (System)**.

    b. On the **Add Query Rule** page, configure your new query rule with the following settings:

    - Name the query rule **MyQueryRule**.

    - Expand the **Context** section. Under **Query Conditions**, select **Query Matches Keyword Exactly**, and then in the **Query exactly matches one of these phrases (semi-colon separated)** box, enter **oak; furniture**.

    - In the **Actions** section, select **Add Promoted Result**. In the **Add Promoted Result** dialog, in the **Title** box, enter the display name for the **Wide World Importers Oak Furniture** promoted result. In the URL field, enter the

URL for the *yoursite*/**Furniture/AllItems.aspx** promoted result (for example, http://wideworldimporters/Furniture/AllItems.aspx), and then select **Save** to return to the **Add Query Rule** page.

- Validate that your new promoted result is listed under **Promoted results** in the **Actions** section in the **Add New Query** page, and then select **Save** to return to the **Manage Query Rules** page.

2. On the **Manage Query Rules** page, validate that the **MyQueryRule** query rule is listed in the **Defined for this site** section.

3. To test your new query rule, navigate to the site home page and run the search with the query oak. On the search results page, validate that the **Wide World Importers Oak Furniture** link is displayed at the top of the results set.

4. Create a query rule to promote a webpage unconditionally for all queries for a limited period of time from today to the end of tomorrow. Use the following settings:

   a. On the **Manage Query Rules** page, select the result source to **Local SharePoint Results (System)**.

   b. On the **Add Query Rule** page, configure your new query rule with the following settings:

      - Name the query rule TodayQueryRule.

      - In the **Context** section, under **Query Conditions**, select **Remove Condition**, so that the query rule is triggered unconditionally by any search query.

      - In the **Actions** section, select **Add Promoted Result**. In the **Add Promoted Result** dialog, in the **Title** box, enter the display name for the Hello World! promoted result. In the URL field, enter the URL for the *yoursite*/**SitePages/HelloWorld.aspx** result webpage (for example, http://wideworldimporters/SitePages/HelloWorld.aspx), and then select **Save** to return to the **Add Query Rule** page. Validate that your new promoted result is listed under **Promoted results** in the **Actions** section in the **Add New Query** page.

      - In the **Publishing** section, set up the schedule for when the rule will be active. In the **Start Date** box, enter today's date, and in the **End Date** box, enter tomorrow's date. Then select **Save** to return to the **Manage Query Rules** page.

5. On the **Manage Query Rules** page, validate that the new **TodayQueryRule** query rule is listed in the **Defined for this site** section.

6. To test your new query rule, navigate to the site home page and run the search with any query—for example, chair. In the search results page, validate that the **Hello World!** link is displayed at the top of the results set.

Configure search behavior

Continuing on your SharePoint site, perform the following tasks:

1. On the **Search Settings** page for a site or site collection, do the following:

   a. In the **Search Center URL** box, enter the URL of the Search Center site in your deployment where user search queries would go.

   b. In the **Which search results page should queries be sent to?** section, do the following:

      - Clear the **Use the same results page settings as my parent** check box.

      - Select **Turn on the drop-down menu inside the search box, and use the first Search Navigation node as the destination results page**, if it is not already selected.

   c. Select **OK** to confirm your changes.

2. To test the search behavior you set up, go the site home page by selecting its link on the Quick Launch. In the search box on your site, select the arrow that opens the drop-down menu of search verticals, and then select **Everything** to search all content by using the Search Center.

> ✓ **TIP** Depending on the crawl frequency in your environment, you might need to wait at least 30 minutes for the new search settings to take effect.

Customize search results pages

Go to the Search Center site in your deployment, and perform the following tasks:

1. Customize a refiners pane in the default search results page *Search Center/ Pages/results.aspx* to remove a refiner that shows when the content was last modified and to display the content author refiners at the top of the pane, by doing the following:

   a. Go to the page and switch to edit mode.

   b. In the **Refinement** web part, display the web part menu and select **Edit Web Part.**

2. In the web part tool pane, do the following:

   a. In the **Properties for Search Refinement** section, verify that **Choose Refiners in this Web Part** is selected, and then select **Choose Refiners.**

   b. In the **Refinement configuration** dialog, in the **Selected refiners** list on the right, select **LastModifiedTime**, and then select **Remove** to remove the refiner that shows when the content item was last modified.

Configure the refiners

> ✓ **TIP** When you remove a refiner from the Selected Refiners list, the refiner is moved to the Available Refiners list.

c. To change the order in which the refiners are displayed in the page, in the **Selected refiners** list, move the **DisplayAuthor** refiner to the top of the **Selected refiners** list by clicking or tapping the **Move Up** button.

d. Select **OK** at the bottom of **Refinement configuration** dialog, and then in the web part tool pane on the right, select **Apply**. Verify that your modifications are shown in the **Refinement** web part, and then select **OK** in the web part tool pane to close it.

3. Check in the page, and then publish the draft to make the page available for users. The search results page is redisplayed.

4. To test your customizations of the search results page, run a search with any query—for example, **furniture**. Validate that the **Author** refiner group is displayed at the top of the refiners pane, and that there is no refiner that shows when the content was modified.

Define visibility and indexing for sites

Go to your SharePoint site, and perform the following tasks:

1. Exclude your site from search results.

 TIP Depending on the crawl frequency in your environment, you might need to wait at least 30 minutes for the changes to take effect.

2. Run a search by using the Search Center to validate that your site has been excluded from the search results.

3. Change the setting back to allow your site to appear in the search results.

Search for people

Continuing on your SharePoint site, perform the following tasks:

1. Add as much information as you can to your user profile, including your skills.

2. Search for people by using one of the skills in your profile as a search query, and validate that you are listed in the People vertical search results page.

 TIP If you do not see yourself in the People search results page, you might need to wait at least 30 minutes for your user profile data to be crawled and indexed.

Work with My Site and OneDrive for Business

My Site is a personal site that provides a central location to manage and store content, including personal information, that other people in your organization can use to find out about your skills and interests. It incorporates the Newsfeed, which includes functions like those you might have seen on Twitter and Facebook, such as the ability to write short messages. It also contains a library that you can sync across all devices where you have installed the OneDrive for Business sync client or app.

This chapter guides you through procedures related to using your My Site to engage in conversations and to monitor what you are following and who is following you; and using OneDrive for Business to store, sync, and share your work files.

> ⚠ **IMPORTANT** Not all personal and social features are enabled by default; therefore, your organization might have customized or not enabled the features described, so you might not be able to complete all the procedures described in this chapter.

In this chapter

- Understand your My Site
- Converse and monitor by using the Newsfeed page
- Work with OneDrive for Business

Practice files

For this chapter, use the practice file from the SP2016SBS\Ch06 folder. For practice file download instructions, see the introduction.

Understand your My Site

Your My Site website is an integral component of social networking and document management in SharePoint Server 2016 and Microsoft Office 365. The My Site website is the top-level site of your personal site collection and contains the following pages:

- **About Me** This is also known as your profile page. It includes personal information such as your name, job title, work address, and phone number. The content on your profile page is used to display information about you so other users can read about your skills, the projects you have worked on, ways to contact you, and what you are doing within SharePoint. You can view other users' profile pages; for example, as a result of a people search or by selecting a person's name in the Created By column of a list or library.

> **TIP** To get the best results from a people search, you should add as much information as you can to your user profile.

- **Newsfeed** This is where you can converse with other users and monitor content you are following.

> ⚠ **IMPORTANT** Your organization might have replaced the SharePoint newsfeed with Yammer or some other social-computing program. This book does not cover Yammer.

- **Sites** In Office 365, this page is labeled *SharePoint*. It displays a list of sites categorized as promoted sites, sites you are following, and suggested sites. Promoted sites are displayed as tiles and are configured by your SharePoint server administrator. You will not be able to modify which site tiles you see; however, you can pin sites so that they appear first in the list of sites you are following.

- **OneDrive** This page displays the contents of the Documents library, where you can store and share personal work files. You can view, and in some cases also sync, the contents of this library on your computers, tablets, and smartphones, by using a program or app named OneDrive for Business; therefore, on SharePoint, the Documents library is also known as your OneDrive for Business library, or just OneDrive for Business.

Your My Site can be pre-created by your IT department or, if self-site creation is enabled, your My Site will be created when you first select About Me, Newsfeed, Sites, or OneDrive, in which case the We're Almost Ready page is displayed and you will have to wait for your My Site to be created before the page you selected is displayed.

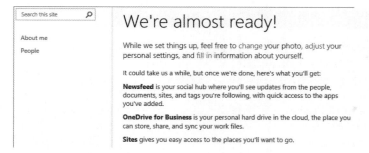

You might have to wait for your My Site to be created

> ✓ **TIP** You can find links to the Newsfeed, OneDrive for Business, and Sites on the app launcher as described in the "Navigate home pages and SharePoint Sites" topic in Chapter 2, "Navigate SharePoint sites."

When you select the Settings menu from the OneDrive or Sites pages, you will be directed to the Site Settings page of the top-level site of your My Site site collection; you are not only the site owner of the site, you are also the site collection administrator of the site collection. You can configure your site and site collection just as you can other sites and site collections. For example, you can turn on auditing by going to the Site Collection Audit Settings page from the Site Settings page.

On the Quick Launch of either the Newsfeed or About Me page, you can select Blog, which uses the Blog site template to create your personal blog site as a subsite.

> 🔍 **SEE ALSO** For information about blogs, see Chapter 9, "Work with wikis, blogs, and community sites."

To display your About Me page

1. Do one of the following:
   - Select your name in the navigation bar, and then select **About me**.
   - In the app launcher, select **Newsfeed**, and then on the Quick Launch, select **About Me**, or if the Newsfeed page displays any of your activities, select your name in one of those activities.

Use your About Me page, also known as your profile page, so that others can find and connect to you

To modify your user profile properties

1. Go to your **About Me** page.

2. Select **edit** to the left of the **your profile** text to display the **Edit Details** page, make your changes, and then select **Save all and close**.

> **SEE ALSO** For more information about modifying your user profile, see the "To add information to your user profile" procedure in the "Search for people" topic in Chapter 5, "Search for information and people."

To hide or delete an activity on your profile page

1. Go to your **About Me** page.

2. Point to the activity so that an x appears to the right of the activity, and then select the x.

3. Depending on the activity and whether you created it, you will then be able to either delete the activity or hide the activity from everyone.

To see sites you are following

1. Do one of the following to display the Sites page:

   - In the app launcher, select **Sites**.

   - In the app launcher, select **Newsfeed**, and then in the **I'm following** web part, select the number above **sites**.

To stop following a site

1. Do one of the following:

   - Go to your **Sites** page, select the ellipsis to the right of the site you want to stop following, and then select **Stop Following**.

The Sites page displays tiles of promoted sites, sites you are following, and suggested sites to follow

- If you have created a microblog for a site you are following, go to your Newsfeed page and then on any microblog for that site, select the ellipsis, and then select **Stop following this site**.

> **SEE ALSO** For information about displaying your Newsfeed page, see "The Newsfeed page" in the following topic, "Converse and monitor by using the Newsfeed."

To pin or unpin sites on your Sites page

1. Go to your **Sites** page, select the ellipsis to the right of the site you want to pin or unpin, and then select **Pin to top** or **Unpin**.

To go to the site contents page on your My Site

1. Do one of the following:

   - On your **About Me** or **Newsfeed** page, in the Quick Launch, select **Apps**.
   - On your **About Me**, **Newsfeed**, or **Sites** page or on your OneDrive, from the **Settings** menu, select **Site Contents**.

Hybrid OneDrive and hybrid sites

A hybrid SharePoint deployment takes advantage of both SharePoint Server 2016 and Office 365 SharePoint Online. There are a number of SharePoint hybrid solutions that your organization can choose to implement. Currently they include hybrid search, hybrid Business Connectivity Services, hybrid OneDrive, and hybrid sites features. This sidebar details hybrid OneDrive and hybrid sites features.

Your organization can choose to implement hybrid OneDrive or hybrid OneDrive and hybrid sites; that is, your organization cannot implement hybrid sites without implementing hybrid OneDrive.

Depending on which of these two hybrid solutions your organization has chosen, you could be redirected to an Office 365 page, and not a SharePoint 2016 page.

Hybrid OneDrive

In a hybrid OneDrive environment, both OneDrive and user profiles are redirected. Your About Me page will be hosted in Office 365, which is powered by Delve. You will be redirected to OneDrive in Office 365, also known as *OneDrive for Business redirection*. Your OneDrive storage is limited by Microsoft, and not by your IT department.

When hybrid OneDrive is configured, there is no link between OneDrive in SharePoint 2016 and OneDrive in Office 365. Files in your SharePoint 2016 OneDrive library or those files listed in your SharePoint 2016 Shared With Me list are not automatically moved to Office 365.

SEE ALSO For information about planning for hybrid OneDrive, go to *https://support.office.com/en-gb/article/Plan-hybrid-OneDrive-for-Business-b140bc4c-f54d-4b5a-9409-a3bece4a9cf9*.

Also, using OneDrive in Office 365 might implement the modern document library experience. SharePoint 2016 only supports classic mode on lists and libraries; therefore, your OneDrive in Office 365 might look different than you have previously experienced.

TIP Some features are currently only available in classic mode. If your OneDrive library is using the modern experience and you want to temporarily switch to classic mode, see the "Compare SharePoint products" topic in Chapter 1, "Introduction to SharePoint 2016."

SEE ALSO For information about the new experience in Office 365 libraries, go to *https://support.office.com/en-US/article /What-is-a-document-library-3b5976dd-65cf-4c9e-bf5a-713c10ca2872*.

6

Hybrid sites features

When the hybrid sites features are enabled by your SharePoint server administrator, a suite of site integration features is set up in addition to hybrid OneDrive. The site integration features include:

- **Hybrid site following** In the app launcher, when you select Sites from SharePoint 2016 or SharePoint from Office 365, you are redirected to the Office 365 sites list, where you will see both SharePoint 2016 sites you are following and Office 365 sites you are following.

- **Hybrid extensible app launcher** In SharePoint 2016, only three tiles are displayed on the app launcher, whereas in Office 365 a larger number of tiles are displayed, depending on your Office 365 subscription, your access permissions, and the services that are enabled. In a hybrid extensible app launcher, Office 365 services such as the Delve and Video apps are displayed, along with any custom apps you have pinned to the Office 365 app launcher.

Converse and monitor by using the Newsfeed page

In Chapter 2, "Navigate SharePoint sites," you were introduced to the Newsfeed page, which is the primary landing page for social activities; thus, it is also referred to as the *social hub*.

The Newsfeed page

The Newsfeed page is hosted in your My Site and provides quick access to the lists of people, documents, sites, and tags that you are following. It is also where users can create posts or start "conversations" with you by using the microblog feature.

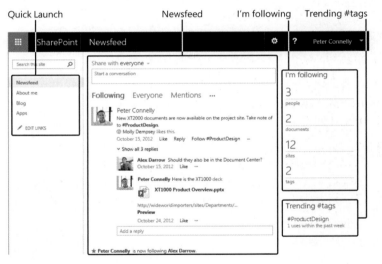

Use the Newsfeed page to quickly find what you are following and posts you have created

The Quick Launch contains the following links:

- **About Me** This displays your profile.

- **Blog site** This displays your personal blog site, which will be created the first time you select Blog in the Quick Launch. For more information about blog sites, see Chapter 9, "Work with wikis, blogs, and community sites."

- **Apps** This displays the Site Contents page, where you can add apps or subsites to your My Site. The Site Contents page of your My Site also contains links to the MicroFeed list and the Social List, which contain the two views used on the Sites page and OneDrive for Business.

> 🔍 **SEE ALSO** For information about adding apps to a site, see Chapter 3, "Work with content in lists and libraries."

The Newsfeed page is a web part page that contains four web part zones and the following web parts:

- **Newsfeed** This MicroFeed web part consists of the microblogging text box labeled *Share With Everyone* and a consolidated view of microblogs organized in conversations and displayed in modified time sort order, so that the most recent content is displayed at the top of the list.

  Each microblog displays the microblog author's name and a thumbnail image, if that user added one to his or her profile. When you select the name or thumbnail of the user, that user's profile page is displayed.

  The following filters can be used to organize the microblogs conversations:

  - **Following** Displays activities you are following
  - **Everyone** Displays conversations available to everyone in your organization
  - **Mentions** Displays conversations where you are mentioned
  - **Activities** Displays social activities you have completed, such as sites or people you are following, documents you have rated or tagged, and any microblogs you have created or replies you have made to other users' microblogs
  - **Likes** Displays conversations you have liked

  > ✅ **TIP** You might not see the last two filters; you might need to select the ellipsis to the right of Mentions to display them.

- **I'm following** This web part displays the number of people, files, sites, and tags you are following. By selecting one of the numbers, you can see details of the content you are following. You will automatically follow sites you create and users who are part of your organization's structure.

  > ✅ **TIP** Before you can follow documents or sites, the Following Content site feature must be activated.

6

■ **Trending #tags** This web part displays #tags (hashtags) that are currently popular. A tag is a keyword or topic preceded by a hash character (#). For example, if you want to find microblogs about marketing news and resources, you might follow *#marketing*. You can follow #tags and, if your newsfeed privacy settings allow it, people who follow you will get notifications in their newsfeed when you start following a tag.

> **SEE ALSO** For information about web parts, see Chapter 7, "Work with webpages."

You can modify the newsfeed settings. For example, you can decide whether to receive emails notifying you of events, such as when you have started following another user; you can determine whether others can see the list of people you are following or your list of followers; and you can choose which activities you want to share with other users. You can also configure whether you (Only Me) or other users (Everyone) can see the hashtags that you follow.

To display your newsfeed

1. In the app launcher, select **Newsfeed**.

To modify the newsfeed settings

1. Go to your **About Me** page, and then select **edit** to the left of **your profile** to display the Edit Details page.

2. Select the ellipsis to the right of **Details**, and then select **Newsfeed Settings**.

3. Select or clear the check boxes as needed, and then at the bottom of the **Edit Details** page, select **Save all and close**.

4. In the **Profile Changes** dialog box warning you that the user profile information might not be available right away, select **OK**.

To see people you are following

1. Go to your newsfeed, and then in the **I'm following** web part, select the number above **people** to display the People I'm Following page.

> **TIP** The People I'm Following page lists the people you are following, people who are following you and, under Suggest People, people you might want to follow.

To stop following a person

1. Display the **People I'm following** page.

2. Select the ellipsis to the right of the person, and select **Stop Following** in the callout.

To see documents you are following

1. Do one of the following to display the Docs I'm Following page:

   - Go to your newsfeed, and then in the **I'm following** web part, select the number above **documents**.

   - Go to OneDrive, and in the Quick Launch, select **Followed**.

Use this page to unfollow or follow suggested documents

To stop following a document

1. Display the **Docs I'm following** page.

2. Select **Stop following** below the document you want to stop following.

To see #tags you are following

1. Go to your newsfeed, and then in the **I'm following** web part, select the number above **tags** to display the #tags I'm Following page.

To find out more about a #tag

1. In any conversation, or in the **Trending #tags** section of the **Newsfeed** page or the **#tags I'm following** page, select the *#tag* to display the **About #*tag*** page.

Use the About #<tag> page to follow the tag, view a list of conversations and other items, and view a list of related tags that you can add to

To follow a #tag

1. Do one of the following, where *tag* is the #tag you want to follow:

   - Below any microblog or reply that includes the #tag, select **Follow** *#tag*; or if you do not see this option, select the ellipsis and then select **Follow** *#tag*.

Use the links below a conversation to follow tags and people; tags and people you are already following will not be listed

   - Go to the **About** *#tag* page, and select **Follow**.

To stop following a #tag

1. Do one of the following, where *tag* is the #tag you are following:

   - Go to the **#tags I'm following** page, and then below the #tag you want to stop following, select **Stop following**.
   - On any conversation that includes the #tag you are following, select the ellipsis, and then select **Stop following** *#tag*.

Select the ellipsis to display the More Options menu, from which you can stop following a #tag or copy a link to the conversation

   - Go to the **About** *#tag* page, and then select **Stop following this #tag**.

Microblogging

You will find the MicroFeed web part on your Newsfeed page and on team sites. You use this web part to post messages; this is known as *microblogging*. Twitter is an example of a microblogging system.

If you are new to microblogging, you could first review other microblogs, and find and follow people who are microblogging about topics that interest you and notice the tags they use. If they have not locked their microblogs, you could supplement the conversation or ask questions by using the reply link.

When you want to draw specific people's attention to your microblog, you can mention them by prefixing their name with an @ sign. If they have enabled email notifications in their newsfeed settings, they will receive an email letting them know you have mentioned them. They will also see it on their Newsfeed page, when they select the Mentions filter.

You will soon distinguish posts you like most and identify users who provide, significant content, notable ideas, good links, and new information. You can show your appreciation by liking a microblog, which allows you to find them again.

> **TIP** You can monitor the people and tags you follow on your Newsfeed page, as described earlier in this chapter. For more information about searching for people, see Chapter 5, "Search for information and people."

The microblogs are stored in the MicroFeed list that is automatically created on team sites and on your My Site. On team sites, the MicroFeed list inherits its permissions from the site, and therefore any user who is a contributor to the site can start a conversation. When you invite people to your site and want them to be able to add to conversations, select the Contribute permission level.

> **TIP** You can disable the site newsfeed on team sites by deactivating the Site Feed site feature.

On the Newsfeed page, you have the option of sharing your microblog with everyone in your organization or only those people who can access the sites you are following, where the Site Feed site feature is activated. When you share a microblog with a site, the microblog is displayed on the Newsfeed for that site and on the Newsfeed page. On the Newsfeed page, the site name is displayed to the right of your name.

6

You can activate the Site Feed site feature on sites, if it is not already activated. To microblog, you next need to add the MicroFeed web part on a page in the site. The MicroFeed web part is available in the Web Part pane only when the Site Feed site feature is activated in the top-level site of the site collection.

> **SEE ALSO** For information about activating site features, see Chapter 8, "Create and manage sites." For information about how to add web parts to a page, see Chapter 7, "Work with webpages."

To create a microblog

1. In the MicroFeed web part on a SharePoint site or in the **Start a conversation** box on your **Newsfeed** page, enter or insert content.

2. If you want to limit the people who can see your microblog, above the **Start a conversation** box, select the **Share with everyone** arrow, and select a site you are following.

Share with everyone ▾
The Ignite se	everyone
📷	Sites I'm following
Followin	SharePoint 2016
	OOTB Team site
	Partners
	SBS2016
	International Furniture Convention 2016
	Customer Service

Use the Share With Everyone menu to post to a newsfeed on a team site you are following (if the site allows newsfeeds)

> **TIP** When the Site Feed site feature is activated on a site you're already following, it does not immediately appear in the drop-down menu on your Newsfeed page. Stop following the site, and then follow it again to make the site appear in the menu.

3. Select **Post** or press **Enter**.

To reply to a microblog

1. Below the microblog, select **Reply** to open a text box.
2. Enter or insert content.
3. Select **Post** or press **Enter**.

To like a microblog or reply

1. Below the microblog or reply, select **Like**.

To include links in a microblog or reply

> **TIP** You can include a link to a website, webpage, list, library, list item, document or another conversation, or to a video.

1. In a separate browser window or tab, copy the web address of the web component you want to include—for example, by doing one of the following:

   - Right-click the component and select **Copy shortcut** or **Copy link address** or something similar (the exact wording depends on your browser).
   - Copy the web address from the browser address box.
   - On a microblog, select the ellipsis, and then select **Copy a link to a conversation**.

   > **TIP** If you want to include a link to a document, you could copy the document's durable link, as described in Chapter 2, "Navigate SharePoint sites," or its Document ID, as described in Chapter 14, "Manage and monitor content."

2. Return to your microblog, position the cursor where you want to add the link, and paste the copied web address.

3. Optionally, select the web address, and in the window that opens, under **Display as**, enter the text you want displayed, and then select the check mark.

New team site created -> <http://intranet.wideworldimporters.com/sites/teams/>
URL:
http://intranet.wideworldimporters.com/sites/teams/
Display as:
Click here   ×   ✓   ✕

In the microblog, select the web address to open a window that allows you to modify the URL and displayed text

4. In the microblog, select any text to close the window.

To mention a person in a microblog or reply

1. Position the cursor where you want to mention the person, and enter @ followed by at least the first two characters of the person's name to display the autocomplete box.

> Along with @er|
>
> ---
>
> ⓘ FYI, the people you mention will see your post even if they aren't members of OOTB Team site.
>
> ---
>
> Everyone
>
> Erin M. Hagens (HR Manager)

Enter sufficient characters to suggest the name of the person you want to mention

2. Select the name of the person and press **Enter**.

> ✓ **TIP** At first, the names of people you are following are displayed in the autocomplete box. If the name of a person you want does not appear, enter more characters of the person's name; the search then extends to everyone in your organization.

To include a tag in a microblog or reply

1. Position the cursor where you want to include a tag.

2. Enter # and then at least one character of the tag.

3. Do either of the following:

   - If the tag has been previously used, in the autocomplete box that appears, select the tag.

   > I'm organizing the launch of the #m
   >
   > ---
   >
   > #marketing

   Use a #tag when the microblog is not targeted to a specific person, but is about a specific topic

   - If the tag you want to use is new, finish entering the name of the tag.

> ✓ **TIP** When you create a new tag, it is automatically added to the Managed Metadata Service (MMS) metadata term store, under the System, Hashtags hierarchy. For information about MMS, see Chapter 5, "Search for information and people." When you want the hashtag to include more than one word, concatenate the words, as in *#MobileReports*.

To include a picture in a microblog or reply

1. Select the camera icon to open the Choose A Picture dialog.

2. Select **Browse** to open the Open dialog box.

3. Go to the image file you want to add, and then select **Open** to close the Open dialog box.

4. Select **Upload** to close the Choose A Picture dialog and insert the image.

> ✓ **TIP** Pictures are always displayed at the bottom of a microblog or reply.

To delete a microblog

> ⚠ **IMPORTANT** You can only delete microblogs you have created. When you delete a microblog, the whole conversation is deleted; that is, the initial microblog and all replies. The deleted conversation is not moved to the Recycle Bin; therefore, you cannot restore a deleted conversation.

1. Point to the microblog you want to delete, and then select the **x** that appears in the upper-right corner.

2. In the **Get rid of this conversation** dialog, select **Delete it**.

To lock or unlock a conversation

> ⚠ **IMPORTANT** You can only lock or unlock conversations you have created.

1. Go to the microblog you want to lock or unlock, select the ellipsis, and then select **Lock conversation** or **Unlock conversation**.

Work with OneDrive for Business

The OneDrive link on the app launcher takes you to the Documents library on your My Site, also known as your OneDrive for Business library. It is an integral part of both SharePoint Server and Office 365.

You can access your files from your My Site Documents library on your devices by using the OneDrive for Business program, also known as the sync client, for your Windows-based computers, OneDrive for Mac, and OneDrive mobile apps for tablets and smartphones.

> ✓ **TIP** OneDrive for Business is different from OneDrive, also known as *OneDrive personal* or *OneDrive consumer*, which provides a place in the cloud for personal files, separate from the OneDrive for Business Documents library. The cloud storage, OneDrive – personal, is often included if you have a hotmail.com, outlook.com, or live.com email account and is similar to Dropbox, iCloud, Google Drive, and other cloud storage products.

The OneDrive for Business library

The OneDrive for Business library provides a place where you can store your files and documents that is private to you so only you can see them. By default, the library contains a folder named Shared With Everyone that is configured so that everyone in your organization can edit the contents of that folder. You can edit the permissions of this folder, delete it, create a new folder, and choose to share it with your coworkers. Deleting the Shared With Everyone folder reduces the risk of accidentally sharing files with your whole organization.

Most organizations stipulate that you should not use your OneDrive for Business library for group or team files or data that is to be preserved for the long term. Other SharePoint libraries and sites are best suited for that content. This is particularly important in an Office 365 or hybrid OneDrive environment, because when the Office 365 license is removed from you—for example, when you leave your organization—your My Site is deleted, together with all the files and folders in your OneDrive for Business library. In SharePoint 2016, when you leave, your organization can choose to disable your user ID but allow others access to your My Site to move business-critical files that you might have stored in your OneDrive for Business library.

The ribbon is not available in your OneDrive for Business library; however, as in other document libraries, you can do the following:

- Select the commands immediately below the Documents library title to:
  - Create files or folders and upload files.
  - Synchronize the library on your computer.
  - Share a file or folder, which also includes finding out who you have shared a file or folder with.

- You might have to use the More command to open the shortcut menu to complete other activities with selected files and folders, such as opening or downloading a file; renaming, deleting, checking out, or viewing the version history of a file or folder; initiating a workflow; or connecting a folder to Outlook.

> **TIP** A OneDrive for Business library is configured for major versions and is limited to 500 versions of each file.

- Select the ellipsis to the right of the file or folder name to display the callout where you can:
  - Preview the file.
  - Edit and follow the file.
  - Select the ellipsis on the callout to open the shortcut menu.
- Drag the files to the library in the browser window, to where it says Drag Files Here To Upload.
- Select the Recycle Bin link on the Quick Launch to go to the Recycle Bin to restore deleted files and folders.

> **SEE ALSO** For information about working with content in libraries, see Chapter 3, "Work with content in lists and libraries."

In SharePoint 2016, the storage limit for your files in your OneDrive library is set by your IT department. If you are using OneDrive in Office 365, including hybrid OneDrive, the storage limit is set by Microsoft; depending on your organization's Office 365 plan, this could be 1 terabyte (TB) or more. Free OneDrive accounts—that is, personal OneDrive —come with 5 gigabytes (GB), although you can purchase more storage.

> **SEE ALSO** For information about OneDrive for Business storage limits across Office 365 plans, go to *https://technet.microsoft.com/en-gb/library/onedrive-for-business-service-description.aspx*.

The Quick Launch for the OneDrive for Business library is different from the Quick Launch you might see on team sites and contains the following:

- **Search** A box where you can enter keywords to find content.
- **Documents** A link to the default view of your OneDrive for Business library. In Office 365, this link is labeled *Files*.

- **Recent** Displays up to 30 lists and folders that you have accessed recently.

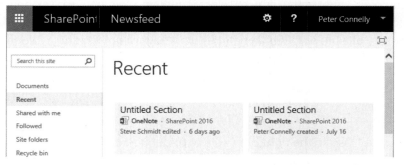

Select Recent on the Quick Launch to view lists and libraries you have recently accessed

- **Shared with me** Displays lists and folders that have been directly shared with you.

- **Followed** Displays the Docs I'm Following page, which lists files you have chosen to follow and suggested documents to follow.

- **Site Folders** Displays a list of sites you have followed and groups you are a member of. When you select a followed site, a list of libraries in that site is displayed; you can then use any of those library links to open the default view of the library. This provides a convenient way to quickly go to a library you are working with. This feature is not currently available in Office 365.

- **Recycle Bin** Opens the Recycle Bin.

> ⚠ **IMPORTANT** At the Ignite conference in September 2016, Microsoft announced new updates to OneDrive for both Office 365 and SharePoint 2016. For more information about the announcement, go to *https://blogs.office.com/2016/09/26/sharepoint-online-sync-preview-headlines-ignite-announcements-for-onedrive/.* The new updates will be rolled out to Office 365 before the end of 2016. The new OneDrive for Business experience for SharePoint 2016 is to be released as part of Feature Pack 1, which will be available in November 2016. If your organization has installed Feature Pack 1, the user experience you see could differ from the one shown in the screenshots in this chapter.

To go to your OneDrive for Business library

1. Do one of the following:

    - In the app launcher, select **OneDrive**.

    - Go to the **Site Contents** page on your My Site, and then select **Documents**.

To sync your OneDrive for Business library to your computer

1. Go to your OneDrive for Business library.

2. Above the list of documents, select **Sync**, and then in the **Sync this library to your device for easy access** dialog box, select **Sync now**.

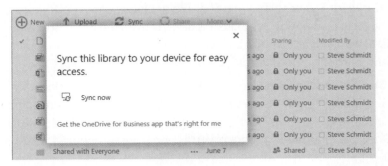

Select Get The OneDrive For Business App That's Right For Me in the Sync dialog box if you do not have the sync client or you need to update your sync client

3. When your browser asks for your permission to open OneDrive or asks whether you mean to switch programs, select **Allow** or **Yes**, whichever option the browser provides.

4. In the **Your files are syncing as we speak** dialog, select **Show my files** if you want to open File Explorer to show the synced library.

> ✓ **TIP** This procedure is very similar to the "To sync a library to your device" procedure in the "Work offline" topic in Chapter 3, "Work with content in lists and libraries." For information about how the sync client and File Explorer work together, see the next section in this topic, "Use the OneDrive for Business sync client."

To access your OneDrive for Business library settings page

1. Go to your OneDrive library, your **About Me** page, or the **Newsfeed** page.

2. On the **Settings** menu, select **Site Content**.

3. Select the ellipsis to the right of **Documents**, and then select **Settings**.

Use the OneDrive for Business sync client

At the time of this writing, there are two OneDrive for Business sync clients:

- **OneDrive for Business Next Generation sync client** This has improved upload limits; however, this new program can currently only be used to synchronize your OneDrive for Business library in SharePoint Online and OneDrive consumer. The Next Generation sync client is already installed if you are using Windows 10 with at least the November 2015 system updates. If you don't have it and want to install it, go to *https://OneDrive.com/download*.

- **The old OneDrive for Business sync client** Use this to synchronize document libraries in SharePoint 2013, SharePoint 2016, and SharePoint Online environments, or your OneDrive for Business library in SharePoint 2013 or SharePoint 2016. To use the old OneDrive for Business program, you'll need to install either Office 2013 or Office 2016.

> **SEE ALSO** For more information about installing the old OneDrive for Business program, go to *https://support.microsoft.com/en-us/kb/2903984*.

Both sync programs can run side by side, which means that you can synchronize one or more SharePoint environments in addition to Office 365 OneDrive for Business and OneDrive consumer.

When you see the synced libraries in File Explorer, having two sync clients can be very confusing:

- The new sync client creates two folders:
  - **OneDrive – Personal**
  - **OneDrive – *<Office 365 tenant name>*** *<Office 365 tenant name>* is usually the name of your company.

  A blue cloud icon is displayed to the right of both folders.

- The old sync client creates two folders:
  - **OneDrive for Business** This is where the files from your synced SharePoint 2016 OneDrive for Business library are stored; it has a blue cloud icon.
  - **SharePoint** This folder is indicated by a SharePoint icon; under it is a subfolder for each synced SharePoint library, regardless of whether the library resides in Office 365 or SharePoint 2016. These subfolders have the naming convention *<site name> - <library name>*. The folder name is limited to 35 characters, with a maximum of 29 characters for the site name.

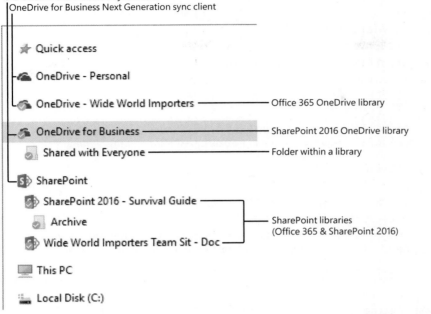

Old OneDrive for Business sync client
OneDrive for Business Next Generation sync client

- Quick access
- OneDrive - Personal
- OneDrive - Wide World Importers ——————— Office 365 OneDrive library
- OneDrive for Business ——————————— SharePoint 2016 OneDrive library
  - Shared with Everyone ——————————— Folder within a library
- SharePoint
  - SharePoint 2016 - Survival Guide
  - Archive ——————— SharePoint libraries
  (Office 365 & SharePoint 2016)
  - Wide World Importers Team Sit - Doc
- This PC
- Local Disk (C:)

You use the two OneDrive for Business sync clients to access Office 365 and SharePoint 2016 libraries

By default, both sets of folders are created in your *%UserProfile%* folder—for example, *C:\Users\steves\OneDrive for Business* and *C:\Users\steves\SharePoint*. You can change this location during installation and after you install the sync client.

You can use the sync client icons in the notification area to manage your synced content:

- The white cloud icon is for OneDrive – Personal content.
- The blue cloud icon is the new sync client.
- The icon showing blue clouds outlined in white is the old sync client.

> **SEE ALSO** To find out which OneDrive sync program you are using, go to *https://support.office.com/en-us/article/Which-OneDrive-sync-client-am-I-using-19246eae-8a51-490a-8d97-a645c151f2ba.*

After the OneDrive for Business sync client is installed on your computer, you can choose to synchronize files from SharePoint libraries and your OneDrive for Business library to your local computer so that you can work offline. It is advisable to check out files before updating them offline. When you modify a file from a synchronized library, the updated file is synchronized back to the SharePoint library when you are next online. You should then check in the file.

You can view the synced files by using File Explorer or by selecting the OneDrive for Business sync client. The OneDrive for Business program is available with Office 2013 and Office 2016 or with an Office 365 subscription that includes Office 2016. You can upload files into your synced libraries by copying and pasting them or by dragging them. You can watch the file icons change to determine when the file is synced to the SharePoint library, as described in the following table.

File icon	Description
	The file is unsynced. You might have just copied the file into the OneDrive for Business folder or SharePoint library folder or you might be offline.
	The file is syncing.
	The file has synced successfully.
	The sync client could not sync the file from your computer to your library. See the "OneDrive for Business limitations" sidebar later in this chapter.

> **TIP** The same icons are used on the OneDrive for Business and SharePoint folders to indicate the sync status of the files in the folder. A red circle with a white x at a folder level indicates that there is a problem with a least one of the files in the folder.

It is not recommended that you sync files when:

- You have sensitive or confidential data in your library and your local computer does not provide mechanisms to restrict access to the files, if you lose your computer or your computer is hacked.
- You are using a shared computer.
- You have more data in your SharePoint libraries and your OneDrive for Business library than storage space on your device.

> **IMPORTANT** When you create, modify, move, or delete a file or folder from your synchronized library on your computer, you are also making those changes in the SharePoint library. You can recover a deleted file from the library's Recycle Bin or from your computer's Recycle Bin.

To open File Explorer to display your OneDrive for Business folder

1. On your computer, do one of the following:

    - Open File Explorer, and then in the navigation pane, select the **OneDrive for Business** folder.

- In the notification area, select the the appropriate blue cloud icon, and then select **Open your OneDrive for Business folder**.

Open your OneDrive for Business folder to see the files that have synced to your computer

- In the notification area, right-click the appropriate blue cloud icon, and then select **Open your OneDrive for Business folder**.

Use the OneDrive For Business menu to manage the syncing of your SharePoint content

File Explorer opens, showing the files synced from your OneDrive for Business library.

> **TIP** To display your OneDrive Personal folder, either open File Explorer and select the OneDrive folder or, in the notification area, select the white cloud icon and then select Open Your OneDrive Personal Folder. For more information about using your personal OneDrive, go to *https://support.office.com/en-US/article/OneDrive-Help-5943c2b9-fafc-4cb4-95c0-9cc73fcabb30*.

> ⚠ **IMPORTANT** The remaining procedures in this chapter detail using the OneDrive for Business sync client and not the new sync client. For more information about setting up your computer to use the new sync client with your OneDrive for Business library in Office 365, go to *https://support.office.com/en-us/article/Set-up-your-computer-to-sync-your-OneDrive-for-Business-files-in-Office-365-23e1f12b-d896-4cb1-a238-f91d19827a16* and *https://support.office.com/en-US/article/OneDrive-for-Business-Help-1eaa32e9-3229-47c2-b363-0a5306cb8c37.*

To open a synced library or folder in your browser

1. In the File Explorer navigation pane, right-click a synced library or folder, select **OneDrive for Business**, and then select **Go to browser**.

Use File Explorer to quickly go to the synced library in your browser

To open the OneDrive for Business Recycle Bin in your browser

1. In the notification area, right-click the icon with blue clouds outlined in white, and select **Manage storage**.

2. Select **Open OneDrive for Business Recycle Bin**.

Use the Manage Storage dialog box to view OneDrive for Business storage and to access the Recycle Bin

To sync to a SharePoint library by using the OneDrive for Business sync client

1. In the notification area, right-click the icon with blue clouds outlined in white, and select **Sync Now**.

To pause syncing

1. In the notification area, right-click the icon with blue clouds outlined in white, and select **Pause syncing**.

> ✓ **TIP** When you look at the OneDrive for Business icon in the notification area, it will now have a red circle with a white x.

To resume syncing

1. In the notification area, right-click the icon with blue clouds outlined in white, and select **Resume syncing**.

To stop syncing a library

1. In the notification area, right-click the icon with blue clouds outlined in white, and select **Stop syncing a folder**.

2. In the **Stop syncing a folder** dialog box, select the library you want to stop syncing, and then select **Stop syncing**.

![Microsoft OneDrive for Business dialog box titled "Stop syncing a folder" with a list of folders: OneDrive for Business (highlighted) and Wide World Importers Team Sit - Doc, with Stop syncing and Cancel buttons.]

Use this dialog box to stop syncing with your OneDrive for Business library or a SharePoint library

3. Select **Yes** to confirm that you permanently want to stop syncing.

4. Select **OK** in the dialog box that states that the library will no longer sync with your PC.

> **TIP** The blue cloud or SharePoint icons will be removed from the folder, and files you've already downloaded will be kept in the folder.

To view the size of your OneDrive for Business (Documents) library

1. On your computer, in the notification area, right-click the icon with blue clouds outlined in white, and select **Manage storage**.

2. Select **View OneDrive for Business storage** to open the Storage Metrics page in your browser.

Or

1. In your browser, display your OneDrive library, and then in the **Settings** menu, select **Site settings**.

2. Under **Site Collection Administration**, select **Storage Metrics**.

Site Settings · Storage Metrics ⓘ

🖥 Site Collection   0.07 GB free of 0.10 GB ▮▭▭▭▭▭

(Page 1 / 1)

Type	Name	Total Size↓	% of Parent	% of Site Quota	Last Modified
📄	Documents	25.2 MB	94.87 % ▮	25.17 % ▮	8/26/2016 9:56 AM
📄	_catalogs	1.2 MB	4.34 % ▮	1.15 % ▮	8/25/2016 5:20 PM
📄	Lists	71 KB	0.26 % ▮	0.07 % ▮	8/25/2016 5:21 PM

Use the Storage Metrics page to see the size of your OneDrive For Business Documents library

> **TIP** To view the storage size of folders on your computer, in File Explorer, right-click the synced folder, and then select Properties.

6

To stop the OneDrive for Business sync client from running on your computer

1. In the notification area, right-click the icon with blue clouds outlined in white, and select **Exit**.

OneDrive for Business limitations

Both OneDrive for Business client sync programs have limitations. Because SharePoint 2016 uses the old OneDrive for Business client sync program, and this book concentrates on SharePoint 2016, this sidebar details limitations that can cause files not to sync between your computer and a SharePoint library or a OneDrive for Business library, when using SharePoint 2016.

SEE ALSO For a list of restrictions for the new sync clients, go to *https://support.microsoft.com/en-us/kb/3125202.*

- **Number of Items that can be synced** 20,000 items (files or folders) across all synchronized libraries. There are also limits to the number of items that can be synchronized for each library type:
  - 20,000 items in a OneDrive for Business library.
  - 5,000 items in a SharePoint library, which includes files and folders.
- **Size limit when syncing files** You can synchronize files up to 2 GB in size.
- **Character limit for files and folders** These limits apply to un-encoded URLs and not to encoded URLs:
  - For SharePoint Server 2013, file names can have up to 128 characters.
  - For SharePoint Online and SharePoint 2016, file names can have up to 256 characters.
  - Folder names can have up to 250 characters.
  - Folder name and file name combinations can have up to 250 characters.
- **Invalid characters**
  - SharePoint 2013:   \ /:*?"<>|#{}%~&
  - SharePoint 2016 and SharePoint Online: \ /:*?"<>|#%

- **Invalid files types or files that will not sync:**
  - File extensions: .tmp, .ds_store, and SharePoint 2016 blocked file types
  - Files: desktop.ini, thumbs.db, ehthumbs.db, any file that is currently open by any program, OneNote notebooks
- **Windows user profile types**

TIP The old OneDrive for Business sync client is not supported if you use a roaming, mandatory, or temporary Windows user profile or when you are using a client session hosted on Windows 2008 Terminal Services or Windows 2012 Remote Desktop Services (RDS).

SEE ALSO For a list of unsupported folder names, go to *https://support.microsoft.com/en-us/kb/2933738*. For information about how to resolve problems with the OneDrive for Business sync client, go to *https://office.microsoft.com/redir/HA104047973.aspx*, , and *https://support.office.com/en-us/article/Fix-OneDrive-for-Business-sync-problems-e12c6a8b-4bbe-4391-9c23-1a52b55a1967*.

6

Skills review

In this chapter, you learned how to:

- Understand your My Site
- Converse and monitor by using the Newsfeed page
- Work with OneDrive for Business

Practice tasks

The practice file for these tasks is located in the SP2016SBS\Ch06 folder.

> ⚠️ **IMPORTANT** You must have sufficient permissions to perform the operations involved in each practice task to complete that practice task. For more information, see Appendix A, "SharePoint 2016 user permissions and permission levels."

Understand your My Site

Go to your Newsfeed page, and then perform the following tasks:

1. Go to the **People I'm Following** page, and follow a person in the **Suggested People** list or someone who is following you who you are not already following.

2. Return to the **Newsfeed** page, and follow one of the trending #tags.

3. Go to the **Sites** page, and pin one of the sites you are following to the top of the list.

Converse and monitor by using the Newsfeed page

Go to your Newsfeed page, and then perform the following tasks:

1. In the **Start a conversation** box, enter, I'm organizing our sponsor booth at the #2016Oslo #furniture #conference. I understand you are attending, and I'm looking for volunteers to help, and then mention at least one person.

2. Post the microblog, and then go to the **About #2016Oslo** page.

3. Add a related tag, choosing an existing hashtag from the suggested list.

4. Go to the **Newsfeed** page to view your recent activity, and delete the microblog you created in step 1.

Work with OneDrive for Business

In your browser, go to your OneDrive, and then perform the following tasks:

1. Start the library sync to your local computer, if you have not already done so.

2. In File Explorer on your local computer, go to the **OneDrive for Business** folder to confirm that the library has synced.

3. Copy the **WideWorldImportersExpenses** document from the practice file folder to your **OneDrive for Business** folder, and sync.

4. Open your **OneDrive for Business** library in your browser and confirm that the library has synced.

Work with webpages

In previous chapters, you learned how to organize your content into site collections, sites, lists, and libraries; however, Microsoft SharePoint sites are similar to other websites in that they can contain multiple webpages. In fact, you could think of storing information in a file, such as a Microsoft Word document or a Microsoft Excel worksheet, as hiding that information. Before a user can see the information in such files, the file has to be downloaded to the user's computer, and then a separate program or app has to be opened to display the contents of the file. With a webpage, your browser displays the information immediately when you select the link to the page. Therefore, it is just as important to place content on pages as it is to use lists and libraries.

This chapter guides you through procedures related to creating pages, adding content to pages, managing pages, and using app parts and web parts.

In this chapter

- Understand SharePoint pages
- Create pages
- Add content to pages
- Manage pages
- Use app parts and web parts

Practice files

For this chapter, use the practice files from the SP2016SBS\Ch07 folder. For practice file download instructions, see the introduction.

Understand SharePoint pages

SharePoint Server includes four types of webpages. The ones you see and can create for a site depend on the site template used to create the site. These are:

- Wiki pages
- Web part pages
- Publishing pages
- Application pages

On team sites and community sites, the two types of pages you will work with are wiki pages and web part pages. Publishing pages are available on sites you create by using one of the publishing site templates, such as the Publishing Portal, Enterprise Wiki, Product Catalog, Publishing Site, Publishing Site with Workflow, or Enterprise Search Center site templates.

You can customize the first three types of pages by using the following tools:

- Your browser
- A SharePoint-compatible webpage-editing tool, such as Microsoft SharePoint Designer 2013
- A professional development tool, such as Microsoft Visual Studio

No one tool can do everything; therefore, it is likely that when you use SharePoint, either in an on-premises installation of SharePoint Server or SharePoint Online, your organization will use all three tools at some point.

Web part pages

Web part pages consist of web part zones that can contain app parts and web parts. Multiple web parts can be added to each zone. After a web part is added to a zone, you can alter the location of the web part within the zone, and you can move the web part from one zone to another. The web part zones are visible only when you are editing a page.

> **TIP** Some zones allow web parts to be stacked in a horizontal direction, whereas others stack them in a vertical direction. The illustration in the Layout section of the New Web Part Page page displays the selected Layout template. If you do not add a web part to a zone, the zone collapses (unless it has a fixed width), and the other zones expand to fill the unused space when you go to the web part page. Therefore, if you currently believe you only need two zones, displayed as two columns, a good choice would be the Header, Footer, 4 Columns, Top Row layout template, because this layout allows for other layout combinations if you need them in the future.

When you create a web part page, you can choose the layout of the zones.

> **IMPORTANT** You cannot change the zone layout after you create the web part page.

Web parts are reusable components that can contain any type of web-based information, including analytical, collaborative, and database information. App parts are used in conjunction with apps you add to your site from your organization's app store or from the online SharePoint Store.

> **TIP** To include free-format static text or images on a web part page, you must use the Content Editor web part (CEWP) or the Image Viewer web part.

App parts can also be used to display content from lists and libraries, so the content dynamically changes as you upload, modify, and delete list items in the lists or files in the libraries. These app parts are used on the web part pages that are created when you create views in your lists and libraries.

> ✅ **TIP** Web part pages can be configured to send data from one web part or app part to another by using a mechanism called a web part connection. This allows you to create interactive pages.

There are a couple of disadvantages of using web part pages: many users find the mechanism of changing such pages not intuitive, and after you create a web part page with a specific layout of web part zones, you cannot change the layout.

Web part pages are the default pages on sites that are created from the Project, Document Center, Record Center, Community Portal, and Compliance Policy Center site templates. On these sites, you need the Add And Customize Pages permission to edit the default web part page. If you do want to create multiple pages on these sites, you can create a wiki page library where you can create wiki and web part pages.

Wiki pages

Wiki pages are easy to use and their layout is easy to change. When you edit the home page of a team site, you'll see that it consists of three content areas, each containing a web part or an app part:

- **Get Started With Your Site** This web part displays five tiles that you can select to quickly complete common SharePoint actions. As you point to each tile, a description of the task is displayed. You can remove this web part by selecting Remove This.

- **Site Feed** This web part displays a newsfeed on your site; its use is also known as *microblogging*. These microblogging conversations are stored in the MicroFeed list.

- **Documents** This app part displays the contents of the Documents library.

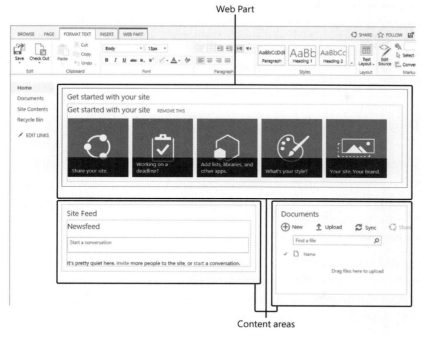

Web Part

Content areas

In the content areas, you can add static text, app parts, and web parts

When you create a team site or community site, SharePoint creates a wiki page library named Site Pages, where webpages are stored and where new pages can be created. The Site Pages wiki library inherits its permissions from the site. Therefore, anyone who is mapped to the Edit permission level at the site level—that is, anyone who is a member of the site's Members SharePoint group—is allowed to change any page or create new pages in the Site Pages library. This is known as open editing. Any member of the site can edit it as he or she wants if, for example, the member thinks the page is incomplete or poorly organized. Therefore, as users share their information, knowledge, experience, ideas, and views, the content evolves. Site members can work together to change or update information without needing to send emails or attend meetings or conference calls. All users are allowed to control and check the content, because open editing relies on the assumption that most members of a collaboration site have good intentions.

Wiki pages can also contain app parts and web parts. Although you cannot use web part connections on wiki pages, the ease with which you can mix free-format static text and images on wiki pages in addition to web parts and app parts make them a popular page choice on team sites.

> ✓ **TIP** Wiki page libraries can be created on any site where the Team Collaboration Lists site feature has been activated. There is a second type of wiki page that you can create when you create a site collection based on the Enterprise Wiki site template. This wiki page is a type of publishing page. For more information about Enterprise Wiki sites, see Chapter 9, "Work with wikis, blogs, and community sites."

Publishing pages

For Internet sites and company portals, when the content on a page is to be viewed by a large number of people, pages might need to go through a formal approval process before users can view them. In such cases, publishing sites and publishing pages are a better choice than team sites and wiki pages. Most visitors to a publishing site want to consume information displayed on the page. They will not be allowed to edit the pages. Only a few users will be able to create, edit, and delete publishing pages.

Publishing pages, also known as Web Content Management (WCM) pages, are stored in the Pages library and are created from publishing templates known as page layouts. After you create a publishing page, you can change the layout of the page by choosing a different layout.

Publishing pages can have both content areas and web part zones. Content areas on a publishing page can be similar to the content areas that you use on a wiki page in that they can contain text, images, app parts, and web parts. However, some content areas can be very restrictive—for example, they might allow you to insert only an image or plain text. The name of the content area usually indicates the type of content you can add. The content area names and the web part zone names are displayed only when you are editing the page. The layout and the type of content you can add to the content areas is dependent on the layout chosen for the publishing page.

Content areas with a grey background are displayed only when you edit the page

Application pages

Application pages, also known as system pages, look very similar no matter which site you go to. Examples of such pages are the List Settings page and the Site Settings page. These pages contain _layouts in their URLs, as in *intranet.wideworldimporters.com /_layouts/15/viewlsts.aspx*, which is the web address for the Site Content page on the Wide World Importers intranet site.

> ✓ **TIP** Application pages cannot be created, modified, or managed by using your browser or SharePoint Designer, so they are not covered in the following topics.

Create pages

The first page displayed on a SharePoint site is known as the home page. This is the page on which all site visitors start. In your organization, the home page might be known as the default page, the welcome page, or the landing page. Home pages tend to aggregate information from elsewhere and direct users to other pages. For instance, in the Quick Launch for a home page, when you select Documents, you are taken to the default view of the Documents library.

There are many reasons why adding content to just the home page is not enough. Although you can add a vast amount of content on one page, this can result in the page taking a long time to render, and it can be difficult for users to find content if they have to scroll down the page many times. Try to compose your content into multiple pages, each with no more than two or three screens of information; and never add content to a page so that users have to scroll to the right to see the content. Link your pages together so that users can navigate easily between them in an organized manner.

There are several methods for creating a new page; however, the recommended method for creating pages that contain content that relates to content on existing pages is to create a forward link, also known as a *wiki link*, by entering the name of the page within two sets of double square brackets. This is quicker and easier than using the Links command on the Insert tab.

> ✓ **TIP** If you want to enter double open or closed square brackets in the content of a page without making a link, enter a backslash before the two brackets, as in \[[or \]].

To create a wiki page

1. Go to the team site where you want to create a new wiki page, and then, on the **Settings** menu, select **Add a page**.

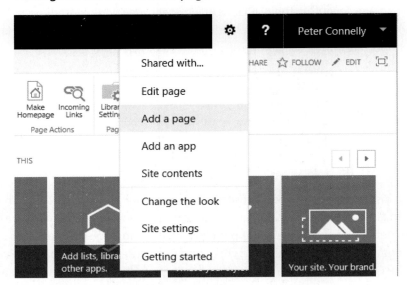

Use the Setting menu to create or edit pages

2. In the **Add a page** dialog, enter the name of your new page.

Enter the name of your page

> **TIP** The name of the page will appear at the top of the page and is also used to create the web address (URL) of the page.

3. Select **Create**.

Or

1. On the home page of your team site or community site, go to the **Page** tab and then, in the **Page Library** group, select **View All Pages** to display the default view of the Site Pages library.

Use the Page tab to manage pages

2. Do one of the following to display the New Item page:

   - Below the title for the Site Pages library, select **New**.

Use the New command below the title of the Site Pages library to create a new page

   - On the **Files** tab, select **New Document**.

3. Enter the name of the page, and then select **Create**.

On the New Item page, enter the name of the new page

To create a web part page

1. On the home page of your team site or community site, go to the **Page** tab and then, in the **Page Library** group, select **View All Pages** to display the default view of the Site Pages library.

2. On the **Files** tab, select the **New Document** arrow (not the button), and then select **Web Part Page**.

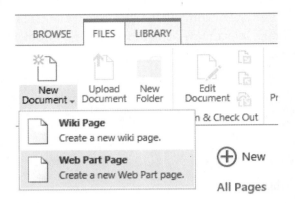

Use the New Document menu to create either a wiki page or a web part page

3. On the **New Web Part Page** page, in the **Name** box, enter the name of your page, and then in the **Layout** section, select the layout template that has the web part zone arrangement you want.

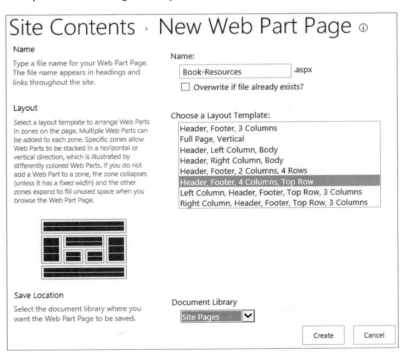

Use the New Web Part Page page to choose a name and zone layout for your webpage

4. In the **Save Location** section, in the **Document Library** list, select **Site Pages**.

> **TIP** Although you can save web part pages in any library, if you want to create wiki links from your wiki pages to a web part page, your web part page must be stored in the Site Pages library.

5. Select **Create**.

To create a publishing page

1. Go to the publishing site where you want to create the publishing page and then, on the **Settings** menu, select **Add a page**.

2. In the **Add a page** dialog, enter the name of your new page, and then select **Create**.

Or

1. Go to the home page of your publishing site.

2. If no tabs are displayed, on the **Settings** menu, select **Show Ribbon**.

3. Go to the **Page** tab, and then, in the **Edit** group, select **New**.

Use the Page tab to create, edit, and manage your page

4. In the **Add a page** dialog, enter the name of your new page, and then select **Create**.

Or

1. Go to the home page of your publishing site.

2. Go to the **Page** tab, and then, in the **Page Library** group, select **View All Pages** to display the default view of the Pages library.

3. On the **Files** tab, select **New Document** to display the Create Page page.

4. In the **Title** box, enter the name of the new page that you want to display to users.

5. In the **Description** box, enter the purpose of the page, including any search keywords that people can use to find the page.

6. Select the **URL Name** box. The name you entered in the Title box appears, with spaces replaced with hyphens.

7. In the **Page Layout** section, select the layout you want to use to control how the content on the page will be displayed.

Create Page

Page Title and Description

Enter a URL name, title, and description for this page.

Title:

> Travel Expenses

Description:

> This page contains companies policy for claiming travel expenses, including mileage rate and parking fees.

URL Name:

Pages/ | Travel-Expenses | .aspx

Page Layout

Select a page layout to control how the page will be displayed.

The article page with body only contains a rich text field.

> (Article Page) Body only
> (Article Page) Image on left
> (Article Page) Image on right
> (Article Page) Summary links
> (Catalog-Item Reuse) Blank Catalog Item
> (Catalog-Item Reuse) Catalog Item Image on Left
> (Enterprise Wiki Page) Basic Page
> (Error Page) Error
> (Project Page) Basic Project Page
> (Redirect Page) Redirect

Check Spelling   Create   Cancel

Use the Create Page page to enter a URL name, title, description, and page layout for the page

8. Select **Check Spelling**.

9. Correct any spelling mistakes, and then select **OK** to close the Spell Checker dialog.

10. Select **Create**.

To create a wiki page or publishing page that is displayed by selecting a forward link

1. On the page where you want to add the forward link, activate edit mode.

2. Positon the cursor where you want to add the link to the page you will create.

3. Enter *[[name of page|words that you want to display on the page for the link]]*. An example is *[[BedroomFurniture|exotic bedroom furniture]]*.

> Wide World Importers import unique furniture, includng [[BedroomFurniture|exotic bedroom furniture]]

Creating a forward link to a page

> **TIP** As you enter the name for the new page, a list of existing pages is displayed. You could select a name from this list to create a forward link to a page you previously created.

4. Save the page. The forward link is indicated by a dotted underline.

Wide World Importers import unique furniture, includng exotic bedroom furniture

A forward link to a page that has not been created is denoted by a dotted underline

5. Select the underlined text to open the Add A Page dialog.

Creating a page from the Add A Page dialog

6. Select **Create**.

Add content to pages

After a page has been created, you can add content, such as text, tables, images, and links to other pages or websites. When you have finished entering your content, save the page. You can re-edit any page at a later time as necessary.

> **TIP** The only way to add content to web part pages is by adding app parts or web parts. This is covered in the "Use app parts and web parts" topic later in this chapter.

Modify pages

To prevent two people from editing a page at the same time, anyone intending to modify content should always check out the page before he or she begins. When you edit a publishing page, the page is automatically checked out to you. You must check out wiki pages and web part pages yourself.

> ✅ **TIP** When another member of your team has checked out a page, the Check Out command on the Page tab is inactive, and a yellow notification area is displayed at the top of the page, stating who the page is checked out to.

The Pages library, where publishing pages are stored, is configured for major and minor (draft) versions. Only users who can edit items can see the draft items; therefore, after you have checked in a page, the page must be published as a major version before visitors to the site can see the amendments you have made to the page.

> 🔍 **SEE ALSO** For more information about checking in, checking out, and versioning, see Chapter 3, "Work with content in lists and libraries."

As you modify a page, you might find that the layout you originally chose does not now suit the content you want to display. On both wiki pages and publishing pages, you can change the page layout.

To activate a wiki or publishing page for editing

1. Go to the page that you want to edit, and then do one of the following:

   - On the **Settings** menu, select **Edit page**.

   - In the upper-right corner of the page, select **Edit**.

   Use the links in the upper-right corner to share a site, follow a site, edit a page, or focus on content

   - On the **Page** tab, select **Edit**.

   Use the Page tab to edit and check out a page

> ✅ **TIP** On publishing pages, if the Page tab is not displayed, on the Settings menu, select Show Ribbon.

To check out a wiki page

1. On the wiki page, on the **Page** tab, select **Check Out**. A yellow notification area is displayed at the top of the page, stating that the page is checked out and editable.

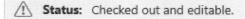

The yellow notification area at the top of a page is used to display the page status

> ✅ **TIP** If you are already editing a wiki page, you can also select Check Out on the Format Text tab.

To check in a wiki page

1. On the wiki page, on either the **Page** tab or the **Format Text** tab, do one of the following:

   - If you have the page checked out, to check in your changes, select **Check In**.

   - If you have the page checked out, to discard any changes you have made to your checked out version and release the checkout, select the **Check In** arrow, and then select **Discard Check Out**.

   - If the page is currently checked out to another user and you have the Override List Behaviors permission, which allows you to check in the page and discard any changes that user might have made to the checked-out version, select **Override Check Out**.

Use the Check In menu to check out, check in, discard a checkout, or override a checkout

To check in and publish a publishing page

1. On the publishing page, do one of the following:

   - In the yellow notification message, select **Check it in**.

   ⚠ **Checked out to you** Only you can see your recent changes. <u>Check it in</u>.

   The yellow notification area displays the status of the page and allows you to check in the page

   - Use one of the options described in the previous procedure, "To check in a wiki page."

2. In the **Check In** dialog, enter a comment, and then select **Continue**.

3. Do one of the following:

   - In the yellow notification message, select **Publish this draft**.

   - On the **Publish** tab, select **Publish**.

To save or discard your modifications to a wiki or publishing page

1. After you have added content to a page, do one of the following:

   - To the right of the tabs, select **Save**.

   When you edit a page, the upper-right Edit link is replaced with Save

   - If you are done adding content to the page, on the **Page** tab or the **Format Text** tab, select **Save**.

   - If you want to save the content you have added so far but intend to continue adding content to the page, on the **Page** tab or the **Format Text** tab, select the **Save** arrow and then select **Save and Keep Editing**.

Use the Save split button to save, keep editing, or discard your modifications

- On the **Page** tab or the **Format Text** tab, select the **Save** arrow, and then select **Stop Editing**. You will then be prompted to save or discard the content you have added to the page. To discard your modification, select **Discard changes**.

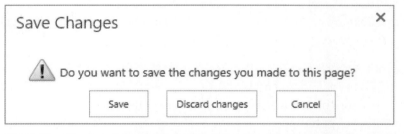

Use the Save Changes dialog to save or discard the changes you have made to a page, or select Cancel to return to editing the page

Format and display content

SharePoint provides you with a What You See Is What You Get (WYSIWYG) environment for adding content to your pages. When a wiki page or publishing page is in edit mode and the cursor is within the body of the page, two tabs are displayed: Format Text and Insert.

 TIP The Format Text and Insert tabs also appear when you enter content by using the Content Editor web part on a web part page.

The commands on these tabs are similar to the commands on the Home and Insert tabs in Word: you use them to format the text, check spelling, and control the layout of the page, and to insert tables, images, videos, audio, hyperlinks, app parts, web parts, and embedded code.

You can also use keyboard shortcuts similar to those in other Office programs. If a tab command has a keyboard shortcut, you can display it by pointing to the command on the tab to display the screen tip.

Screen tips can include the command name, keyboard shortcut, and a description

The Format Text tab

The Format Text tab contains ribbon groups you will not find on the Home tab in Word. These include:

- **Layout** This group appears on the Format Text tab only for wiki pages. Use the Text Layout command to create additional editing areas and to change the structure of your page. You can reformat the page by using any of eight options. For publishing pages, the Layout group is on the Page tab. Developers can create additional publishing page layouts, but no additional wiki page layouts can be added to SharePoint.

You can control the layout of a wiki page

- **Markup** This group provides four commands:
  - **Edit Source** Selecting this command opens a dialog that contains a plain-text box in which you can enter HTML code. The text box displays the HTML tags for the content area where the cursor was located before you selected Edit Source. For example, if your wiki page has a two-column layout and the cursor is in the left column when you select the command, only the HTML for the left column is displayed in the dialog. You will need to know HTML to use this method of entering content on your page, because no IntelliSense help is provided; therefore, you might find it easier to use an HTML editing tool to create the content, and then paste it into the text box. To prevent the entry of malicious code, SharePoint does sanitize user-entered HTML content, so you might find that some of the code you enter is removed when you save the page.

  - **Languages** When you create a SharePoint site, it has a default language. When you enter text in a different language, you can select the text and use this command to tag the language of the text. The SharePoint search functionality can then identify pages that include text in specific languages; some screen reader programs, such as the Job Access With Speech (JAWS) screen reader, use this so they can pronounce words correctly when they read them aloud.

  - **Select** Use this command to select the HTML tag you want to work with. For example, to edit the HTML for a row in a table, place the cursor in a cell in the row, and then select the Select command to display the list of HTML tags that apply to that row, including the row itself and any parent HTML tags, such as for the table or the entire content area. A red dotted line surrounds the area related to the HTML tag when you point to each tag in the Select list. To format or style the row, select the HTML for just the row.

  - **Convert to XHTML** Most SharePoint pages adhere to and generate HTML to the XHTML 1.0 Strict specification; however, when you use the Edit Source command to create HTML, you might introduce errors into the page. By using this command, you might be able to fix those errors.

7

The Insert tab

The Insert tab also contains ribbon groups you will not find on the Insert tab in Word. These include:

- **Media** This group contains two split buttons:

  - **Picture** Use this command to insert a picture from your computer, to reference a web address where a picture is stored, or to reference an image that is stored in a SharePoint library.

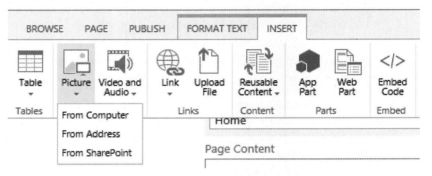

Use the Picture split button to insert a picture on the page

Use the first option, From Computer, when you have stored your image on the hard drive of your computer—for example, drive C. The default location to store images that you use on pages is the Site Assets library; however, you can choose a different library on the site.

> **TIP** The Site Assets library is the place to store files that are needed to brand a site, such as the image files used to display pictures on pages or files that contain team or company information. These are usually not files that team members will collaborate on, so they should be saved in the Site Assets library rather than in, for example, a document library.

Selecting the second option, From Address, opens the Select Picture dialog, in which you must manually enter or paste the URL of the image. To avoid incorrectly entering the URL for the image, which would result in a broken link, open another browser window or tab, navigate to the picture, copy the URL, and then paste the URL into the Address box in the Select Picture dialog.

Selecting the From SharePoint option opens the Select An Asset dialog, which you use to navigate to a SharePoint library where you have previously uploaded an image.

- **Video and Audio** Use this split button to display video and audio on your page. This command provides the same three options as the Picture split button, plus a fourth option, Embed. Using the Embed option is the same as using the Embed Code option in the Embed group on the Insert tab, which is described later in this section.

- **Content** This group appears on the Insert tab only on publishing pages and is detailed in the "Reusable content" section later in this topic.

- **Parts** This group contains two commands, App Part and Web Part. The insertion and configuration of these two components is detailed in "Use app parts and web parts" later in this chapter.

- **Embed** This group contains the Embed Code option, which you can use to embed HTML code to display content not stored in SharePoint, such as content from Bing Maps, Vimeo, and YouTube. Most of these sources provide methods of generating the HTML code you need to embed in your page.

You can also use this option to display the contents of Word, Excel, or PowerPoint files, when Office Online Server (OOS) is installed in your organization. OOS is a separate product from SharePoint; organizations can use it to deliver browser-based versions of Word, PowerPoint, Excel, and OneNote files, among other capabilities.

> **SEE ALSO** For more information about embedding Office documents and PDF files on a website, see "Embed Office documents and PDF files on a website" at *https://aka.ms/Yx8n5e*. For information about embedding an Excel workbook on a webpage, see "Embed your Excel workbook on your web page or blog from SharePoint or OneDrive for Business" at *https://aka.ms/K4c5l6*.

The embedded code is stored in an HTML iFrame tag, which means that your browser can display content stored in SharePoint immediately and it will display the content from the external source when it receives it. If the network connection to the external source is poor or the external source is not responding, you might have unexpected results. For example, if your source is a video source, you could end up with a blank video area on the page, or video buffering or playback problems. When this occurs, it is important to recognize that it is not a

SharePoint issue; you must investigate the network connection and the availability of the external source.

> **IMPORTANT** The insertion of an iFrame on a page could be seen as a potential scripting security risk. A site collection administrator can prevent users from using these commands by selecting HTML Field Security in the Site Collection Administration section on the Site Settings page.

Contextual tabs

When a component has been inserted onto a page and is selected, additional contextual tabs might be displayed. For example, if an image on a page is selected, the Image contextual tab is displayed. You can use the commands on the Image tab to replace the image, enter alternative text, format the borders of the image, position the image on the page, and reduce the area on the page used to display the image.

> **IMPORTANT** The commands in the Size group of the Image tab do not alter the file size of the image; they only place width and height attributes on the <img> HTML tag. Your browser uses these attributes to display the image. For prototyping purposes, this might be adequate; however, the image file could potentially use a large amount of network bandwidth when it is downloaded from SharePoint to your computer, even if the browser then displays the picture at a smaller size than the file's original size. So if you notice that a page takes more time to load than other pages, you might need to look at the size of the image files.

On publishing sites, you need not optimize your images before uploading them into SharePoint, because such sites can use image renditions, as long as your server administrator has configured their use. An image rendition is an optimized, scaled variant generated from the original image. By default, there are four rendition display templates; therefore, after you upload an image, you have the choice of five image sizes on your page: the original size of the image, and a rendition for each display template. You can change the renditions that SharePoint has generated, and if you are a site owner, you can add new rendition display templates.

On a publishing site, on the Image tab, use the Pick Rendition menu to select the image size for an image on your page and to edit the image renditions

To format text on a page

1. On the page whose content you want to format, activate edit mode.

2. On the **Format** tab, use the commands to format the content as you want.

> **TIP** The commands in the Edit, Clipboard, Font, Paragraph, and Styles groups work the same as in any other Office program.

3. Save or save and publish the page.

To change the layout of a wiki page or a publishing page

1. On the page whose layout you want to change, activate edit mode.

2. Do one of the following to display a list of page layouts:

   - If the page is a wiki page, on the **Format Text** tab, in the **Layout** group, select **Text Layout**.

   - If the page is a publishing page, on the **Page** tab, in the **Page Action** group, select **Page Layout**.

3. Select a layout.

4. Save or save and publish the page.

To insert a picture, video, or audio

1. On the page where you want to display the picture, video, or audio, activate edit mode and position the cursor where you want to add the image or file.

2. On the **Insert** tab, select the **Picture** button, and then do one of the following:

   - If the file is on your computer, select **From Computer** to open the **Upload Image** dialog, select **Browse**, navigate to the location on your computer where the file is stored, and select **Open**. In the **Destination** list, select the library where you want to upload the file, and then select **OK**.

   - If the file is on the web, select **From Address** to open the **Select Picture** dialog. Enter the web address for the file you want to use, enter alternative text for the file, and then select **OK**.

   - If the file is already in SharePoint on your site, select **From SharePoint** to open the **Select an Asset** dialog, navigate to the folder or library where the file is stored, select the file, and select **Insert**.

   Or

7

On the **Insert** tab, select the **Video and Audio** button, and then do one of the following:

- If the file is on your computer, select **From Computer** to open the Upload Media dialog, select **Browse**, navigate to the location on your computer where the file is stored, and select **Open**. In the **Destination** list, select the library where you want to upload the file, and then select **OK**.

- If the file is on the web, select **From Address** to open the Link Media dialog. Enter the web address for the file you want to use, and then select **OK**.

- If the file is already in SharePoint on your site, select **From SharePoint** to open the Select An Asset dialog, navigate to the folder or library where the file is stored, select the file, and select **Insert**.

3. Save or save and publish the page.

To format a picture, video, or audio on a page

1. On the page where you want format a picture, video, or audio, activate edit mode.

2. On the **Image or Media** tab, use the commands to format as you want.

3. Save or save and publish the page.

To insert and edit HTML markup

1. On the page where you want to insert and edit web-related code—for example, if you want to insert new HTML tags or modify the properties of the HTML tags—activate edit mode.

2. Do one of the following:

   - To amend code that was generated by using the Format or Insert tab, place the cursor in the content area where the content is displayed, and then on the **Format Text** tab, in the **Markup** group, select **Edit Source**. Amend or enter the code, and then select **OK**.

   - To insert new code that is not directly related to content you inserted by using the Format or Insert tab, such as JavaScript or HTML code snippets, on the **Insert** tab, in the **Embed** group, select **Embed**. Enter the code, and select **Insert**.

3. Save or save and publish the page.

To embed code from another source into a page

1. Navigate to the source of the content (for example, a Bing Map or a YouTube video), and use the source site's tools to generate the code you want to embed.

2. Copy the code to the clipboard.

3. Go to the SharePoint page on which you want to display the content, and activate edit mode.

4. On the **Insert** tab, do one of the following to open the Embed dialog:

   - Select the **Video and Audio** arrow, and select **Embed**.

   - In the **Embed** group, select **Embed Code**.

5. In the text area of the Embed dialog, paste the code from the clipboard, and then select **Insert**.

6. Save or save and publish the page.

Reusable content

On publishing pages, the Insert tab has an extra command, Reusable Content, that you can use to add predefined content to your page—for example, a copyright, a byline, or a quote, such as your company's mission statement. Reusable content is stored in the Reusable Content list at the top-level site of a site collection and can consist of blocks of plain text and HTML elements, such as formatted text, images, tables, and lists. You can use this functionality to create content once, and then allow users who edit pages to reuse these pieces of content.

In the Reusable Content list, you can create categories and folders to help you organize the reusable content items. The items can be designated as automatically updated or not:

- **Automatically updated items** The reusable content is inserted into the page as a read-only reference. When the item is changed in the Reusable Content list, the page content is changed.

- **Not automatically updated items** The reusable content is copied in the page. The page is not updated if the reusable content item is updated in the list.

> ⚠ **IMPORTANT** You must have Contributor permission to add items to the Reusable Content list. To add a reusable content item to your publishing page, you must have read permission to the Reusable Content list. To add or modify a category or folder in the Reusable Content list, you must have the Manage Lists permission.

To create a reusable content category

1. Navigate to the top-level site of your site collection, and then on the **Settings** menu, select **Site contents** to display the Site Contents page.

2. Select **Reusable Content** to display the default view of the Reusable Content list.

3. On the **List** tab, in the **Settings** group, select **List Settings**.

4. Under **Columns**, select **Content Category**.

5. On the **Edit Column** page, under **Type each choice on a separate line**, enter a name for your new category.

6. At the bottom of the page, select **OK**.

To create a reusable content item

1. On the **Site Contents** page, select **Reusable Content**.

2. Do one of the following:

   - Select **new item** to create a new reusable HTML item.

   - On the **Items** tab, select the **New Item** arrow, and then do one of the following:

     - To insert plain text, select **Reusable Text**.

     - To insert another type of content, such as rich text or an image, select **Reusable HTML**.

3. Do the following:

   a. In the **Title** box, enter the title of the reusable content item.

   b. In the **Content Category** list, select a category.

   c. If you want the item to be inserted in a page as a read-only reference, select **Automatic Update**; otherwise, leave this check box cleared.

   d. Enter the reusable content.

   e. If you chose to create a reusable HTML item, format the text and insert HTML elements.

Reusable Content

Title *	Wide World Importers Copyright

Comments

A A͡ | B *I* U | ≡ ≡ ≡ | ⅛ ⅜ ⅜ ⅜ | A ◈ ◄¶ ¶►

Content Category	None ▾
Automatic Update	☑

If this option is selected, the content of this list item will be inserted into web pages as a read-only reference. New versions of this item will automatically appear in the web pages. If the option is not selected, the content of this list item will be inserted into web pages as a copy that page authors can then modify. New versions of this item will not appear in the web pages. Any change to this setting will not affect existing web pages that are using this item.

Show in drop-down menu	☐

Select this option if you want this reusable content item to appear in a drop-down menu available during page editing. This will offer authors a quick way to add this item to a page.

Reusable HTML	Wide World Importers © copyright 2016

Save   Cancel

Use reusable content for content that you find you have to create again and again

4. Select **Save**.

To use a reusable content item on a publishing page

1. On the publishing page where you want to use the reusable content, activate edit mode.

2. On the **Insert** tab, select **Reusable Content**, and then select the reusable content item you want to add to the page.

Manage pages

After you have created several pages, you might need to perform other tasks with them, such as changing the page that is your site's home page, deleting pages, restoring deleted pages, or reviewing the popularity trends of your pages. You can also use alerts to receive email messages whenever a page is changed.

> ✓ **TIP** Like deleted documents and deleted list items, deleted pages are sent to the Recycle Bin. For more information about the Recycle Bin and about using alerts, see Chapter 3, "Work with content in lists and libraries."

Both the Site Pages and Pages libraries have all the features of document libraries, such as history and version management, so the risk of losing your page changes is low. Major versioning is turned on by default for the Site Pages library, and major and minor versioning for the Pages library. You can also use content approval and workflow, and you can restrict the permissions regarding who can edit and publish pages.

> 🔍 **SEE ALSO** For more information about content approval, see Chapter 4, "Make lists and libraries work for you." For more information about workflow, see Chapter 11, "Work with workflows."

To view all pages in either the Pages or Site Pages library

1. Do one of the following:

   - Go to a page, and then, on the **Page** tab, in the **Page Library** group, select **View All Pages**.

   - From the **Site Contents** page, select **Pages** or **Site Pages**.

To make a page the home page for a site

1. Go to the page you want to make the home page.

2. On the **Page** tab, in the **Page Actions** group, select **Make Homepage**.

To display a page's history

1. Go to the page, and then on the **Page** tab, in the **Manage** group, select **Page History**.

The page history displays static content; additions are displayed in a green font and deletions in a red strikethrough font

To compare two versions of a page

1. Display the page history of the page as described in the previous procedure.

2. In the left navigation pane, below one of the versions you want to use in the comparison, in the **Compare with version** list, select a prior version number.

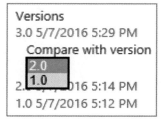

Display what has been added and deleted between one version of the page and another

To revert to a previous version of a page

1. Do one of the following to display the page's version history:

   - Display the page history of the page as described in the "To display a page's history" procedure earlier in this topic, and then select **Version History**.

   - Display all pages as described in the "To view all pages in either the Pages or Site Pages library" procedure earlier in this topic, select the page you want to revert, and then on the **Files** tab, in the **Manage** group, select **Version History**.

2. Select the date and time in the Modified column for the version you want to restore as the current version, and then select **Restore**.

2.0

View

Restore   ide World Importers

Delete   e Are specialist importers

Use the menu to view, restore, or delete a version of a page

3. Select **OK** to confirm that you want to replace the current version of the page with the selected version of the page.

4. Go to the page and, in the yellow notification message, select **Revert to template**.

⚠ The current page has been customized from its template. Revert to template.

The yellow notification message states that the page has been customized from its template

5. Select **OK**. The yellow notification message disappears.

To delete a page

1. Do one of the following:

   - Go to the page you want to delete. On the **Page** tab, in the **Manage** group, select **Delete page,** and then select **OK** to confirm that you want to send the page to the site Recycle Bin.

   - Display all pages as described in the "To view all pages in either the Pages or Site Pages library" procedure earlier in this topic, and then do one of the following:

     - Right-click the page, and then select **Delete**.

     - Select the page, and then on the **Files** tab, in the **Manage** group, select **Delete Document**.

 TIP You cannot delete the home page of a site.

To restore a deleted page

1. Do one of the following to display the Recycle Bin:

   - On the Quick Launch, select **Recycle Bin**.

   - On the **Site Settings** menu, select **Site Content**, and then select **Recycle Bin**.

2. Select the page you want to restore, and then select **Restore Selection**.

3. Select **OK** to confirm that you want to restore the page.

To create an alert on a page

1. Go to the page for which you want to set up an alert.

2. On the **Page** tab, in the **Share & Track** group, select **Alert Me**, and then in the list, select **Set an alert on this page**.

3. In the **New Alert** dialog, select your preferences so that you receive an email based on your specific criteria and frequency, and then select **OK**.

Use app parts and web parts

As you customize your site, you might decide to add information other than static text and images. This information might be stored in lists or libraries or in some other data source. You add such content by using app parts and web parts. You can insert both app parts and web parts on multiple pages, and you can also insert them multiple times on the same webpage.

SharePoint provides built-in app parts and web parts, as detailed in the following table. The category specified in the table is the category name that is displayed when you use the app parts pane. The availability of an app part or web part depends on the type of site you are working with.

Category	Description
Apps	This category contains app parts, which display app information. SharePoint apps are similar to the apps you might find on Facebook or on your smartphone. App parts can also be used to display the contents of list and library apps; each time data in the list or library app changes, the changes are reflected in the app part.
Blog	Use these web parts to help you display and manage blog posts.

Category	Description
Business Data	This category contains web parts related to Business Connectivity Services (BCS) and Microsoft Excel, Visio, and Access.
Community	These web parts are available on community sites. For more information about community sites, see Chapter 9, "Work with wikis, blogs, and community sites."
Content Rollup	These web parts can be used to display content from the current site and from other sites. They include the Content Query, Content Search, and Project Summary web parts.
Document Sets	These web parts can be used to display the contents and properties of document sets. For more information about document sets, see Chapter 14, "Manage and monitor content."
Filters	These web parts can be used to filter the contents displayed by other web parts on the page.
Forms	The web parts in this category can display content from HTML or Microsoft InfoPath forms.
Media and Content	Use these web parts to add content to the page. They include the Content Editor, Script Editor, Image Viewer, and Get Started With Your Site web parts.
Search	These web parts are used with the SharePoint search functionality and on the Search site to display search results and refinements.
Search-Driven Content	These web parts can be used to display the results of a search query.
Social Collaboration	Use these web parts to display socially related content, such as newsfeeds, contact details, and user tasks.
SQL Server Reporting	The web part in this category is used with Microsoft SQL Server Reporting Services.
Miscellaneous	Only one web part is listed in this category: the Case Content web part that is used in the eDiscovery Center.

> **TIP** In addition to built-in web parts, you can create your own web parts by using tools such as Visual Studio. You can also import custom web parts.

All app parts and web parts have a set of common properties that you can use to control the part's appearance and behavior, such as toolbar type, chrome type, the part's height and width, and whether users can minimize it so that only the title is visible.

You can configure the common properties by using either the web part tab or the Appearance, Layout, or Advanced section of the web part tool pane.

Each app part and web part can also have a set of custom properties. These properties might be displayed on a separate contextual tab, or they might be in the web part tool pane, in their own section, or in the Miscellaneous section. For example, if you insert an app part on your page that displays the contents of a list, when you select the check box next to the app part title (in edit mode), three tabs appear on the ribbon: Files, Library, and Web Part.

> ✓ **TIP** If you are having persistent problems with an app part or web part or a web part connection, you can use the Web Part Maintenance page to delete the app part or web part. You can navigate to the Web Part Maintenance page by appending *?Contents=1* to the page's URL; for example, *intranet.wideworldimporters.com/sites/Sales/SitePages /Home.aspx?contents=1.*

To activate a web part page for editing

1. Go to the page you want to edit, and then on the **Page** tab, select **Edit**.

To add an app part to a content area

1. On the page where you want to add an app part, activate edit mode and place the cursor where you want the app part to be displayed.

2. On the **Insert** tab, in the **Parts** group, select **App Part** to open the app parts pane.

3. Select the app you want to add to your page.

Parts	About the part
Documents Form Templates IncomingEmail **Site Assets** Site Pages Test Document library ← →	**Site Assets** Use this library to store files which are included on pages within this site, such as images on Wiki pages. Add part to: Rich Content ▾ Add Cancel

The app parts pane shows an app part for each list or library on the site, in addition to app parts for apps you have installed

4. Select **Add**.

To add a web part to a content area

1. On the page where you want to add the web part, activate edit mode and place the cursor where you want the web part to be displayed.

2. On the **Insert** tab, in the **Parts** group, select **Web Part** to open the web parts pane.

3. Under **Categories**, select a category, and then under **Parts**, select the web part you want to add to your page.

Categories	Parts	About the part
Apps	Apply Filters Button	Current User Filter
Blog	Choice Filter	Filters the contents of Web Parts by using properties of the current user.
Business Data	Current User Filter	
Community	Date Filter	
Content Rollup	Page Field Filter	
Document Sets	Query String (URL) Filter	
Filters	SharePoint List Filter	
Forms		
Upload a Web Part ▼		Add part to: Rich Content ☑
		Add Cancel

When a web part is selected, the About The Part section provides a description of the web part

4. Select **Add**.

To add an app part or web part to a web part zone

1. On the page where you want to add an app part or web part, activate edit mode, and then in the zone where you want to add the app part or web part, select **Add a Web Part** to open the web parts pane.

2. Under **Categories**, select a category, and then under **Parts**, select the web part you want to add to your page.

3. Select **Add**.

To display the Web Part tab and any other contextual tabs for a web part

1. In edit mode, select the check box for the web part by selecting the title bar of the web part.

Site Assets

(+) New   ↑ Upload   ⟳ Share

✓   🗋   Name   Modified   Modified By

Select the web part's title or check box to display contextual tabs

To open the web part tool pane

1. In edit mode, do one of the following:

   • Display the **Web Part** contextual tab, and then select **Web Part Properties**.

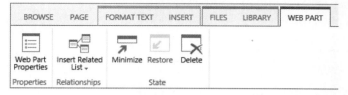

   Use the Web Part tab to open the web part tool pane, create web part connections to related lists, and minimize, restore, or delete the web part

   • Point to the web part, select the arrow on the title bar of the app part or web part, and then select **Edit Web Part**.

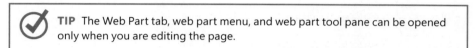

   Use the commands on the menu to minimize, close, or delete the web part or app part or to open the properties pane

> ✓ **TIP** The Web Part tab, web part menu, and web part tool pane can be opened only when you are editing the page.

7

To configure the content that a list or library app part displays

1. Open the web part tool pane as described in the previous procedure.

2. In the web part tool pane, immediately below **List Views**, do one of the following:

   - Select a view that was previously created from the list or library.

   Use the List Views section to select the view you want the
   app part to use and to select the app part toolbar

   - Select **Edit the current view**, and then, if a dialog box opens, select **OK** to save your changes. The Edit View page is displayed. Configure what you want the web part to display, and then select **OK**.

   > **TIP** You configure a view for an app part the same way you configure a view for a list or library. For more information about views, see Chapter 3, "Work with content in lists and libraries."

To move an app part or web part to another location on a page

1. With the page activated for editing, point to the title bar of the app part or web part so that the pointer changes to a four-pointed arrow.

2. Drag the web part to the new area on the page.

To remove an app part or web part from a page

1. Do one of the following:

   - Display the **Web Part** tab, and then in the **State** group, select **Delete**.

   - On the web part's title menu, select **Delete**.

2. Select **OK** to confirm that you want to permanently delete the app part or web part.

To save modifications to a web part page

1. On the web part page, on the **Page** tab, select **Stop Editing**.

7

Skills review

In this chapter, you learned how to:

- Understand SharePoint pages

- Create pages

- Add content to pages

- Manage pages

- Use app parts and web parts

Practice tasks

The practice files for these tasks are located in the SP2016SBS\Ch07 folder.

> ⚠️ **IMPORTANT** You must have sufficient permissions to perform the operations involved in each practice task to complete that practice task. For more information, see Appendix A, "SharePoint 2016 user permissions and permission levels."

Understand SharePoint pages

There are no practice tasks for this topic.

Create pages

Go to a SharePoint team site where you have sufficient rights to create a page, and then perform the following tasks:

1. Create a wiki page named **Wide World Importers**.

2. Position your cursor in the content area, enter **Wide World Importers**, and then on a new line, enter **We are specialist importers of unique furniture [[BedRoomFurniture|bedroom furniture]], [[OfficeFurniture|office furniture]] and [[GardenFurniture|garden furniture]]** to create three wiki links.

3. Save the page.

4. Select the forward links to create the three pages, and on each page, create a link back to the Wide World Importers page before saving each page.

5. Create a web part page named **Kitchen Furniture**, using the **Header, Left Column, Body** layout, and save it in the **Site Pages** library.

6. Stop editing the page, and leave your browser open if you are continuing to the next set of practice tasks.

Add content to pages

Go to the Wide World Importers page and activate it for editing, and then perform the following tasks:

1. Change the page layout to **Two columns with header and footer**.

2. Move the text *Wide World Importers* to the top area and style it as **Heading 1**.

3. In the left column content area, do the following:

   - Insert the **pjcov.jpg** picture from the practice file folder, saving the file in the **Site Assets** library.

   - Create a link to the **Kitchen Furniture** page, and then save the page but continue editing.

4. In the bottom content area, insert the **Wildlife.wmv** video from the practice file folder, saving the file in the **Site Assets** library.

5. Use the commands on the **Media** tab to set the video to **Start Automatically** and use a player style of **Light**.

6. Save and check in the page, leaving your browser open if you are continuing to the next set of practice tasks.

Manage pages

Go to the Wide World Importers page, and then perform the following tasks:

1. View all pages in the **Site Pages** library, and delete the **Kitchen Furniture** page.

2. Display the page history of the **Wide World Importers** page.

3. Compare the current version with version **2.0**, and then restore version **2.0**.

4. Create an alert on the page, retaining the default values.

> **TIP** If SharePoint is not configured to send email messages, an Error page will be displayed. If this page appears, you cannot complete the rest of the steps in this procedure. Check with your SharePoint administrator before you proceed.

5. Activate the page for editing, delete the content in the top content area, and save the page.

6. Check that you have received two emails, one stating that an alert was success-fully created, and another stating that the page was modified.

7. Use **Manage My Alerts** to delete the alert you created on the Wide World Importers page, and then leave your browser open if you are continuing to the next set of practice tasks.

Use app parts and web parts

Go to the Wide World Importers page, and then perform the following tasks:

1. Activate the page for editing, and in the top content area, add an app part for the **Site Assets** library.

2. Open the **Site Assets** web part tool pane.

3. Change the title to Image and Video files and the **Chrome Type** to **Title and Border**, and prevent users from minimizing the app part.

4. Apply your changes.

5. Edit and save the current view so that the **Modified** and **Modified By** columns are not displayed in the app part.

Create and manage sites

8

SharePoint sites are containers for webpages and apps such as lists and libraries, and features and settings that provide the sites' functionality. You can use a site as a single container for your data or you can create as many child sites as you need to make your data easier to find and manage. You will frequently find yourself creating sites to allow a group of people to collaborate. For example, you might create a site to manage a new team or collaborate on a project.

As discussed in Chapter 2, "Navigate SharePoint sites," sites are organized hierarchically within a site collection. There is always one top-level site, and there can be one or more child sites. Typically, a top-level site is created for an entire team and therefore has many visitors (people who only read content), a few members (people who can create and update content), and one or two owners. But as child sites and grandchild sites are created, the total number of visitors typically decreases while the number of people designated as members increases.

This chapter guides you through procedures related to creating sites, managing site users and permissions, sharing sites, changing site themes, creating and using custom site templates, managing site features, managing site content syndication, and deleting sites.

In this chapter

- Create sites
- Manage site users and permissions
- Share sites
- Change site themes
- Create and use custom site templates
- Manage site features
- Manage site content syndication
- Delete sites

Practice files

No practice files are necessary to complete the practice tasks in this chapter.

Create sites

You can provision sites by using site templates. These templates provide site blue-prints by packaging together webpages, apps, navigation, settings, and features that are best suited for different sites' purposes. You can also quickly and easily create personal sites, also known as My Sites, by using Self-Service Site Creation (SSSC).

Create sites

The catalyst for organizing your data into different site containers will often be the same catalyst as for creating multiple subdirectories in a file system. You might have too much information to use a single container and still find what you need easily. If all your files were kept in the root of your hard drive along with the operating system files and other program files, the list of files would be difficult to sort through, work with, and manage. Just as you create subdirectories to organize your file system data, you likely will create child sites to help organize your SharePoint data in logical ways.

The initial site created in a SharePoint site collection is called the top-level site. A top-level site is created from within SharePoint Central Administration because it doesn't have a parent site. Although the functionality of a top-level site is not different from its child sites, it includes administrative links on its Site Settings page to manage the site collection.

To create a child site, you must navigate to the New SharePoint Site page of the site you want to use as the parent site by selecting the New Subsite link in the Subsites section of the Site Contents page.

```
Subsites

⊕ new subsite
```

Select New Subsite to create a new site

> **✓ TIP** Alternatively, you can navigate to the New SharePoint Site page directly from your browser's address bar. See the "The _layouts directory" sidebar later in this section for details about how to gain direct access to your destination directly from a browser's address bar.

The _layouts directory

The administrative pages of a SharePoint 2016 site are kept in a common folder named _layouts/15. By entering the website address in the address bar of your browser, you can navigate quickly to administrative pages that are buried relatively deeply within a site's administrative links.

The following table displays examples of addresses for administrative page links that are typically found on the home page of a SharePoint site.

Website address (URL)	Administrative page
http://[site]/_layouts/15/viewlsts.aspx	Site Contents
http://[site]/_layouts/15/settings.aspx	Site Settings
http://[site]/_layouts/15/newsbweb.aspx	New SharePoint Site

The following table displays the same examples for a child site.

Website address (URL)	Administrative page
http://[site]/[childsite]/_layouts/15/viewlsts.aspx	Site Contents
http://[site]/[childsite]/_layouts/15/settings.aspx	Site Settings
http://[site]/[childsite]/_layouts/15/newsbweb.aspx	New SharePoint Site

Note that the suffix for each website address is the same no matter how deeply you delve into the site hierarchy.

8

On the New SharePoint Site page, you first need to provide a title or name for your new site, a description (optional), and the URL suffix for the new website address.

Provide a title, a description, and a URL name for your new site

When you initially create objects like sites, lists, and libraries in SharePoint, you are establishing two name values: the display name—usually labeled Title or Name—and the URL name. Typically, as is the case with sites, there is an option to provide the URL name separately, after the site has been created. The best practices for specifying a URL name are outlined in the "Naming a URL" sidebar later in this section.

> **TIP** After a site has been created, you can change its title, description, and logo by using the Title, Description, And Logo page, which you can access via a link in the Look And Feel section of the Site Settings page.

After you've provided the title, the optional description, and the URL for your new site, you need to choose how to initially provision your site by using one of the SharePoint 2016 site templates.

Select a site template to base your new site on

Naming a URL

The best practices for naming URLs include the following:

- The URL name should be descriptive, intuitive, and easy to remember.

- The URL name should be concise. There is a limit on the number of total characters available for the entire website address, so you will eventually encounter problems if you consistently use long URL names.

- The URL name should not contain spaces. Spaces in the address bar are replaced with %20 and take up three characters each. Spaces also make the website address difficult to use in an email and difficult for others to read. To reduce frustration and improve readability, an underscore can be used in place of a space.

- The URL name should be used consistently. By default, tasks are found in a list called Tasks, contacts in a list called Contacts, and so on. Similarly, if you frequently create a document library to house proposals, consistently using a name such as Proposals will help others to locate that content. Of course, you cannot have two lists with the same name in a site. Therefore, you may need to differentiate them by putting a prefix on the name, such as Customer_Proposals and Product_Proposals.

It is wise to establish naming conventions as early as possible. This should help prevent unintuitive, verbose, space-laden, and inconsistent objects from being created.

Follow these best practices when initially establishing a URL for objects in SharePoint. For example, providing a URL name of "Todd Rowe" for a new child site would result in a website address like this in the browser's address bar: *http://wideworldimporters/Todd%20Rowe*. Subsequently, providing a URL name of "My Cool Docs" for a new document library within that site would result in the following website address in the browser's address bar: *http://wideworldimporters/Todd%20Rowe/My%20Cool%20Docs*. Notice that replacing the spaces with underscores improves the appearance of the website address: *http://wideworldimporters/Todd_Rowe/My_Cool_Docs*.

8

A site template is used in SharePoint as a blueprint to jump start a new site's usefulness by auto-generating lists, libraries, apps, and webpages that likely will be most useful in a particular situation. SharePoint provides many built-in site templates. Each built-in site template provisions a site structure for a specific purpose, with relevant apps, and webpages prepopulated with web parts that use the navigation best suited for the purpose of the site template.

> **⊘ TIP** The selection of built-in site templates that is available to you for site creation varies depending on the site collection settings in your SharePoint deployment, and on your organization's SharePoint 2016 licensing for on-premises deployments and its SharePoint Online plan for cloud and hybrid deployments.

The built-in site templates are grouped into three categories: Collaboration, Enterprise, and Publishing. Most of the built-in templates are available for both the top-level site and the child sites within the site collection. There are also several templates that can only be used for provisioning the site collection's top-level site.

The following table lists the SharePoint 2016 built-in site templates by category.

Site template name	Site description	Site availability
Collaboration Sites		
Team Site	A collaboration environment for a group of people to work together.	Site collection, site
Blog	A site for a person or team to post ideas, observations, and expertise that site visitors can comment on.	Site collection, site
Developer Site	A site for developers to build, test, and publish Office apps.	Site collection only
Project Site	A site for managing and collaborating on a project. This site template brings all status, communication, and artifacts relevant to the project into one place.	Site collection, site

Site template name	Site description	Site availability
Community Site	A place where community members discuss topics of common interest. Members can browse and discover relevant content by exploring categories, sorting discussions by popularity, or viewing only posts that have a best reply rating. Members gain reputation points by participating in the community—for example, by starting discussions and replying to them, liking posts, and specifying best replies.	Site collection, site
Enterprise Sites		
Document Center	A site to centrally manage documents in an enterprise.	Site collection, site
In-place Hold Policy Center	To satisfy business regulations or compliance requirements, you can place content in sites on hold for a period of time such as a specific number of days, months, or years. You create and manage holds by using an In-place Hold Policy Center.	Site collection only
E-discovery Center	A site to manage the preservation, search, and export of content for legal matters and investigations, and for DLP (data loss prevention) queries.	Site collection only
Records Center	This template creates a site designed for records management. Records managers can configure the routing table to direct incoming files to specific locations. The site also lets you manage whether records can be deleted or modified after they are added to the repository.	Site collection, site
Business Intelligence Center	A central site for presenting business intelligence content in an enterprise,	Site collection, site
Compliance Policy Center	You create and manage the document deletion policies and the DLP policies in the Compliance Policy Center.	Site collection only

8

Site template name	Site description	Site availability
Enterprise Search Center	A site that provides an enterprise-wide search. It includes a welcome page with a search box that connects users to four search results pages: general searches, people searches, conversation searches, and video searches. You can add and customize new results pages to focus on other types of search queries.	Site collection, site
My Site Host	A site used for hosting personal sites (My Sites) and the public People Profile page that displays the newsfeed and profile pages of all users' My Sites. This template is provisioned by a SharePoint administrator only once per User Profile Service Application.	Site collection only
Community Portal	A central site for communities in an enterprise.	Site collection only
Basic Search Center	A site that provides a basic search experience. It includes a welcome page with a search box that connects users to a search results page, and an advanced search page.	Site collection, site
Publishing Sites		
Publishing site	A blank site for expanding your website and quickly publishing webpages. Contributors can work on draft versions of pages and publish them to make them visible to readers. The site includes document and image libraries for storing web publishing assets. Typically, this site has many more readers than contributors.	Site collection, site
Publishing site with workflow	A publishing site that is used to publish webpages with approval workflows. By default, only sites with this template can be created under this site.	Site collection, site

Site template name	Site description	Site availability
Enterprise Wiki	A site for publishing knowledge that you capture and want to share across the enterprise. It provides a content editing experience in a single location for coauthoring content, discussions, and project management.	Site collection, site

All collaboration site templates provision a Quick Launch navigation panel that contains links to the parts of the site. However, the apps and pages are provisioned differently depending on the site's purpose.

The Team Site template provisions a Documents library that is made more visible by placing a web part for it on the site's default home page for easier collaboration. The Blog site template provides a way to publish a type of journal known as a web log or just a blog. The blog owner creates posts on which other users can comment. Each post is a separate content page, and a rollup summary of these pages is typically presented in reverse chronological order (with newest entries listed first) on the home page of the blog site. Blogs are commonly used as news sites, journals, and diaries. A blog focuses on one or more core competencies of the author and is sometimes used as a soapbox for the blog owner to state an opinion. A blog can also be used as a one-way communication tool for keeping project stakeholders and team members informed.

> **SEE ALSO** For more information about blogs, see Chapter 9, "Work with wikis, blogs, and community sites."

> **TIP** Blog site content can be syndicated by using a Really Simple Syndication (RSS) feed. RSS feed–aggregating software allows people to subscribe to the content they are interested in and have new and updated posts delivered to them. By using such a tool, you can aggregate the content from many blogs into one common reader, where posts from selected authors can be sorted, filtered, and grouped. Microsoft Outlook 2010, Outlook 2013, and Outlook 2016 can aggregate RSS feeds; there are also many vendors who give away or sell RSS feed–aggregating software.

The Developer Site template provides a site for developers to create and publish Office apps. The Project Site template provisions a site for collaborating on a project, with all information and artifacts relevant to the project available in one place.

> **SEE ALSO** For more information about working with project sites, see Chapter 10, "Manage work tasks."

The Community Site template provisions an environment for community members to discuss topics of common interest.

> **SEE ALSO** For more information about working with community sites, see Chapter 9, "Work with wikis, blogs, and community sites."

The type of top-level site in the site collection in which your new site will be located defines the list of built-in templates that are available for the new site. For example, the publishing templates are not available in the site collection where the top-level site is a team site. For a site collection where the top-level site is a publishing site, the site templates available for child site creation can be restricted by using the Page Layout And Site Template Settings link on the Site Settings page.

You will likely focus, at least initially, on using the built-in site templates. However, it is also possible to save the websites you create as custom site templates that you and others can then choose from the list of custom site templates on the New SharePoint Site page. A custom site template is a way to package site features and customizations and make them available as a foundation for other sites. When you save a website as a template, a custom site template is created by SharePoint and saved as a file with a .wsp extension. This is done by using the Save Site As Template link in the Site Action section of the Site Settings page of any site. Custom site templates saved in this way are initially available only in the same site collection in which they are saved. The "Create and use custom site templates" topic later in this chapter explains how to copy a saved web template into another site collection. All alterations to an underlying built-in template except security-related settings are retained on those sites that are provisioned by using custom site templates.

After you've selected a site template, you need to choose from the two options for site permissions that are listed on the New SharePoint Site page.

Permissions

You can give permission to access your new site to the same users who have access to this parent site, or you can give permission to a unique set of users.

Note: If you select **Use same permissions as parent site**, one set of user permissions is shared by both sites. Consequently, you cannot change user permissions on your new site unless you are an administrator of this parent site.

User Permissions:

- ◉ Use same permissions as parent site
- ○ Use unique permissions

Set up site permissions

The default option, Use Same Permissions As Parent Site, checks the parent site's permission every time the user visits the child site, to determine what the user is allowed to do on that site. When the permissions on the parent site change over time, the permissions on the child site reflect those changes. The other option is Use Unique Permissions. When you select this option as the site's creator, you break the permission inheritance. You will then be the only user with access to the site, and you will be the site owner with the Full Control permission level.

> ⚠ **IMPORTANT** If you select Use Same Permissions As Parent Site, it is possible that you will have the right to create a new site but not the right to delete it. However, if you select Use Unique Permissions, you become the site owner and, as such, will always have the right to delete the new site.

You also have two other options for assigning permissions to a new site that are less obvious. If you initially select Use Unique Permissions, you will be the only user with access to the site and can make any changes you want. You can then switch to Use Same Permissions As Parent Site, whereby everyone who has access to the parent site (including you) will subsequently have access to the child site by using the permissions assigned on the parent site. If you initially select Use Same Permissions As Parent Site, the parent site's permissions will be used. Yet if you subsequently switch to Use Unique Permissions, all the permissions of the parent site are copied to the child site. This can save you a great deal of time if most of the people who have access to the parent site also need access to the child site.

8

After you assign user permissions to your new site, you need to set up navigation options.

Set up navigation options

Three navigation options can be specified when creating a new site. The first two deal with the visibility of the child site being created within the navigation areas of the parent site. You can choose to show the child site on either the Quick Launch or the top link bar of the parent site, or both. The default of the former is No, and the default of the latter is Yes. In addition, you can specify whether the top link bar of the parent site should display on the top link bar of the new child site. This setting is referred to as navigation inheritance. The default is No.

> **TIP** When you create a grandchild site where the child site above inherits its navigation from the top-level site, the option to show the new site on its parent site top link bar is not available because the top link bar of the parent site is inherited from the grandparent and is therefore locked.

After you have confirmed your choices, SharePoint creates a new site. The new site is listed in the Subsites section of the Site Contents page of the parent site.

> **TIP** SharePoint 2016 provides an additional capability for creating site collections. Fast Site Collection Creation is a mechanism designed to improve provisioning performance of site collections by using a copy operation at the level of the content database. In this scenario, a master copy of a site collection for an enabled template provides the source site collection when a request is made for creating a new site collection. Fast Site Collection Creation can be turned on by using the SharePoint Management Shell.

To create a site

1. On the parent site in which you want to create a child site, on the **Site Contents** page, in the **Subsites** section, select **new subsite**.

2. On the **New SharePoint Site** page, provide the following information for your new site:

   - In the **Title and Description** section, enter the new site's title in the **Title** box and, optionally, enter a description for the site in the **Description** box.

   - In the **Web Site Address** section, complete the new site URL by entering the suffix in the **URL name** box.

   - In the **Template Selection** section, select the site template you want to base your new site on.

   - In the **Permissions** section, select whether your new site will use the same permissions as the parent site or unique permissions. The default is to use the same permissions as the parent site.

   - In the **Navigation** section, select the following:

     - Whether your site will be displayed on the Quick Launch of the parent site. The default is **No**.

     - Whether your site will be displayed on the top link bar of the parent site. The default is **Yes**.

   - In the **Navigation Inheritance** section, select whether the new site should display the top link bar of the parent site. The default is **No**.

3. Select **Create**.

Create personal sites

In SharePoint Server 2016, you can create a personal site to save and share your work, and to work with other people. Your new site will be based on a Team Site template, but it will not inherit either the navigation or the permission settings of any other site. You will be assigned the site owner permissions and will be able to manage site access and share your site with other people.

The site will be created in the location that your administrator has set up for Self-Service Site Creation (SSSC) under a predefined path. In a hybrid environment, the location can be in the cloud. Depending on how SSSC is set up in SharePoint Central

Administration, there might be more than one location available that you can choose from when you create a new site. Your site might be a top-level site in a site collection, or a subsite.

You can create a personal site by using the New link on your Sites page, which is accessible to you via global navigation from any location within your SharePoint on-premises environment.

⊕ new

Select the New link on the Sites page to create a new personal site

> ✓ **TIP** The new site link is visible on the Sites page only when Self-Service Site Creation is turned on in SharePoint Central Administration and you are granted the appropriate permissions to create SSSC sites.

In SharePoint Online, you can create a personal site by using the Create Site on the Sites page, which is accessible via the SharePoint link on the global navigation bar. It is available by default.

+ Create site

Select the Create Site link to create a personal site in SharePoint Online

You only need to provide a name for your new site. The site name will be used as a title for your new site and for the suffix of your site's URL. All other settings are provisioned automatically. Your site will be created in the location your administrator has predefined. Your site will not inherit the permission settings or navigation settings of other sites.

Start a new site   ✕

Give it a name

Find it at http://wideworldimporters/

Create   Cancel

Create a personal site

> ✅ **TIP** Remember to follow the best practices outlined in the "Naming a URL" sidebar when specifying the site name. You can change the site display name after it has been created by using the Title, Description, And Logo link on the Site Settings page.

After the new site has been created, it is added to the list of sites you're following that is displayed on your Sites page, and you can access this site from any location. You can share the site with other users, add content to it, and generally use its capabilities as you would with any other site that you own.

To create a personal site

1. In the upper-right, in the global navigation bar, select one of the following links to go to the Sites page:

   - **Sites** in SharePoint 2016

   - **SharePoint** in SharePoint Online

2. On your **Sites** page, select one of the following links to open the Start A New Site dialog:

   - **new** in SharePoint 2016

   - **Create site** in SharePoint Online

3. In the **Start a new site** dialog, in the **Give it a name** box, enter a name for your new site.

4. Select **Create.**

Manage site users and permissions

After you have created a SharePoint site, you often need to provide or restrict user access to the site or its contents. In SharePoint, a site and its contents can inherit the permission settings of the parent site or have unique permissions. When you assign unique permissions to a site, its permissions are no longer inherited from its parent site. As discussed in Chapter 4, "Make lists and libraries work for you," information in SharePoint is secured at one of four levels: site level, list or library level, folder level, and list item or document level. By default, the site inherits permissions of its parent site; lists and libraries inherit the permissions of the site that contains them; all folders inherit the permissions of the list or library that contains them; and all list items or documents inherit the permissions of the folder that contains them. If you are a site owner, you can change permission settings for the site, which stops permission inheritance for the site.

> **SEE ALSO** For a deeper discussion about list, library, folder, and list item security, see Chapter 4, "Make lists and libraries work for you."

When you create a site, selecting the default option—Use Same Permissions As Parent Site—provides permission inheritance from the parent site to the newly created child site. SharePoint checks the parent site's permission every time the user visits the child site.

If you select the Use Unique Permissions option when creating a new site, SharePoint initially categorizes users of the new site into three SharePoint groups:

- **Visitors** People or groups who only need to be able to read content on a site
- **Members** People or groups who need to be able to create and edit content, but not create subsites or manage site membership
- **Owners** People who are responsible for all aspects of managing and maintaining a site

Selecting the Use Unique Permissions option breaks the permission inheritance and sets you, as the site's creator, with sole access to the new site as its owner. After you select Create on the New SharePoint Site page, the Set Up Groups For This Site page is displayed, from which you can add users to the three groups to provide them with access to the newly created site.

People and Groups ▸ Set Up Groups for this Site

Visitors to this Site

Visitors can **read** content in the Web site. Create a group of visitors or re-use an existing SharePoint group.

( ) Create a new group   ◯ Use an existing group

Members of this Site

Members can **contribute** content to the Web site. Create a group of site members or re-use an existing SharePoint group.

◉ Create a new group   ◯ Use an existing group

Olga Londer

Owners of this Site

Owners have **full control** over the Web site. Create a group of owners or re-use an existing SharePoint group.

◉ Create a new group   ◯ Use an existing group

Olga Londer

Set up group membership for a site that has unique permissions

You can switch between inherited permissions and unique permissions for a site on its Permissions page. On this page, you can select Stop Inheriting Permissions to switch to unique permissions for the site, or Delete Unique Permissions to switch to inherited permissions.

> ✓ **TIP** On a site that inherits permissions, administrators can access the parent site Permissions page by selecting Manage Parent on the site Permissions page, if they have appropriate rights on the parent site.

A site that has unique permissions has no tie to its parent site, so you are allowed to add and remove users from the site regardless of whether they have permissions on any other site. When users are added to a site, they must be added to a SharePoint group or associated with at least one permission level.

> ✓ **TIP** When you create a site with inherited permissions and then break the inheritance, all SharePoint users and groups on the child site remain the same as the users and groups on the parent site. If you don't want to use the same groups as the parent site, you need to create new groups for the child site.

8

SharePoint groups are maintained at the site collection level and represent a collection of users or groups with a defined set of one or more permission levels and a few governing attributes. When a new user or group is added to a SharePoint group, that user or group is granted the permissions of that group in all sites that the group has access to.

> ⚠️ **IMPORTANT** Editing a SharePoint group affects the membership of all sites, lists, folders, and items that are using that SharePoint group.

Think of permission levels as a named collection of permissions that can be assigned to SharePoint groups or individual users. There are several default permission levels in SharePoint 2016: Full Control, Design, Edit, Contribute, Read, Limited Access, Moderate, Approve, Manage Hierarchy, Restricted Read, and View Only.

The following table provides the list of individual permissions and shows the permission levels they are included in by default. The individual permissions are grouped into three categories: site permissions for site access, list permissions for lists and libraries access, and personal permissions for personal web parts and pages.

Permission	Full Control	Design	Edit	Contribute	Read	Limited Access	Moderate	Approve	Manage Hierarchy	Restricted Read	View Only
Site Permissions											
Manage Permissions	x								x		
View Web Analytics Data	x								x		
Create Subsites	x								x		
Manage Web Site	x								x		
Add and Customize Pages	x	x							x		
Apply Themes and Borders	x	x									

Permission	Full Control	Design	Edit	Contribute	Read	Limited Access	Moderate	Approve	Manage Hierarchy	Restricted Read	View Only
Apply Style Sheets	x	x									
Create Groups	x										
Browse Directories	x	x	x	x			x	x	x		
Use Self-Service Site Creation	x	x	x	x	x		x	x	x		x
View Pages	x	x	x	x	x		x	x	x	x	x
Enumerate Permissions	x										
Browse User Information	x	x	x	x	x	x	x	x	x		x
Manage Alerts	x										
Use Remote Interfaces	x	x	x	x	x	x	x	x	x		x
Use Client Integration Features	x	x	x	x	x	x	x	x	x		x
Open	x	x	x	x	x	x	x	x	x	x	x
Edit Personal User Information	x	x	x	x			x	x	x		
List Permissions											
Manage Lists	x	x	x				x		x		
Override List Behaviors	x	x					x	x	x		
Add Items	x	x	x	x			x	x	x		
Edit Items	x	x	x	x			x	x	x		
Delete Items	x	x	x	x			x	x	x		

8

Permission	Full Control	Design	Edit	Contribute	Read	Limited Access	Moderate	Approve	Manage Hierarchy	Restricted Read	View Only
View Items	x	x	x	x	x		x	x	x	x	x
Approve Items	x	x						x			
Open Items	x	x	x	x	x		x	x	x	x	
View Versions	x	x	x	x	x		x	x	x		
Delete Versions	x	x	x	x			x	x	x		
Create Alerts	x	x	x	x	x		x	x	x		x
View Application Pages	x	x	x	x	x	x	x	x	x		x
Personal Permissions											
Manage Personal Views	x	x	x	x			x	x	x		
Add/Remove Private Web Parts	x	x	x	x			x	x	x		
Update Personal Web Parts	x	x	x	x			x	x	x		

> **SEE ALSO** For more information about the individual permissions and permission levels, see Appendix A, "SharePoint 2016 user permissions and permission levels."

When you create a new site based on a site template, SharePoint automatically assigns a predefined set of default SharePoint groups with specific permission levels to the site.

For example, default SharePoint groups in a team site have the following permission levels:

- The Visitors group has the Read permission level.

- The Members group has the Edit permission level.

- The Owners group has the Full Control permission level.

The default SharePoint groups assigned to a site

In addition to Visitors, Members, and Owners groups, a community site includes the Moderators group with a permission level of Moderate, and a publishing site with workflow includes the Approvers group with a permission level of Approve.

The following table shows the default permission levels and associated permissions for Visitors, Members, and Owners groups.

SharePoint Group	Permission level and permissions
Visitors	Read This level includes the following permissions: ■ Open ■ View Items, Versions, Pages, and Application Pages ■ Browse User Information ■ Create Alerts ■ Use Self-Service Site Creation ■ Use Remote Interfaces ■ Use Client Integration Features
Members	Edit This level includes all permissions in Read, plus the following permissions: ■ View, Add, Edit, and Delete Items ■ Manage Lists ■ Delete Versions ■ Browse Directories ■ Edit Personal User Information ■ Manage Personal Views ■ Add, Update, or Remove Personal Web Parts

8

SharePoint Group	Permission level and permissions
Owners	Full Control This level includes all available SharePoint permissions.

Not only can you associate existing SharePoint groups and individual users with permission levels, you can also associate Windows groups (including Active Directory groups and Local Machine groups) with permission levels. This is a very practical approach to providing tight security with minimal maintenance. However, you might not have control over the Windows groups defined in your organization.

> **TIP** You can provide all authenticated users with site access on the site's Permissions page by using the Grant Permissions command and the Everyone group.

Although you can create your own permission levels and even alter all permission levels except for Full Control and Limited, you will likely find the built-in levels to be adequate for most business scenarios. You might also want to provide all users with some level of access to the data on your site—for example, by using permission levels of either Restricted Read or View Only.

The following changes can be made to a permission level:

- Update the name or description
- Add or remove permissions

> **TIP** To change or create permission levels, you must be a site collection administrator or have the Manage Permissions permission on the top-level site in the site collection.

> **IMPORTANT** It is not recommended to make changes to the default permission levels. You can copy a default permission level and change the copy instead. You can't make changes to the Full Control and Limited Access default permission levels, or delete them.

You can assign permission levels directly to individual users, but when you have many users, this approach can make it difficult to track and manage who has access to your site. A better approach is to assign permissions to groups, and then assign individual users to the appropriate groups.

> ✅ **TIP** If anonymous access has been turned on for the Web application in SharePoint Central Administration and has not been denied via the Anonymous User Policy, anonymous users can be granted some access, either to the entire site or to individual lists on a case-by-case basis. This provides the central administrator with the option to decide whether to grant anonymous access for each Web application before its site administrators can begin to turn on this option.

After all users and groups are assigned to various permission levels, it is possible—even likely—that someone will be associated with more than one permission level. Rather than enforcing the most restrictive permission level, all associated rights for a user or a group are aggregated, and the cumulative list of unique rights apply. This can be overridden only by policies created in SharePoint Central Administration.

> ✅ **TIP** It is wise to associate every user in the various child sites in a site collection with at least the Read permission level in the top-level site. Users might be unable to use custom site templates and list templates that have been imported into a site collection unless they are associated with one of the built-in permission levels for the top-level site.

To display the Permissions page for a site

1. On the **Site Settings** page, in the **Users and Permissions** section, select **Site permissions**.

To turn on unique permissions for a site

1. On the **Permissions** page of the site, on the **Permissions** tab of the ribbon, select **Stop Inheriting Permissions**.

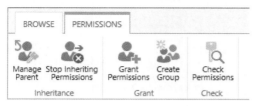

Select Stop Inheriting Permissions to create unique permissions for your site

2. In the warning message that appears, asking you to confirm your action, select **OK**.

3. On the **Set Up Groups** page, in each section, do one of the following:

   • If you want to keep using the default group, select **Use existing group**.

- If you want to create a new group, select **Create a new group**. Then, in the two boxes, do the following:

   a. In the first box, enter the new name for the group or keep the default name.

   b. In the second text box, enter the names of the members of the new group, separated by semicolons. You can also use the Browse button in the lower-right corner of the box to browse to the users and groups in your organization and add them to the new group.

   c. Validate the names by selecting the Validate Names button (the icon of a person with the check mark in the lower-right corner of the box).

Create a new Members group and add users

4. When you're done, select **OK**.

To restore permissions inheritance for a site

1. On the **Permissions** page of the site, on the **Permissions** tab, select **Delete Unique Permissions**.

Select Delete Unique Permissions to restore inheritance from the parent site

2. In the message that appears, asking you to confirm that you want to remove unique permissions, select **OK**.

To manage permissions for a parent site

1. Go to a site that has inherited permissions, and whose parent site's permissions you want to manage.

2. Display the **Permissions** page.

3. On the **Permissions** tab, select **Manage Parent**.

To check user permissions for a site

1. On the **Permissions** page for the site, on the **Permissions** tab, select **Check Permissions**.

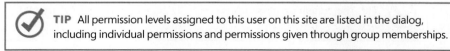

Check access to your site

2. In the **Check Permissions** dialog, enter the user name you want to check permissions for, and select **Check Now**.

> ✅ **TIP** All permission levels assigned to this user on this site are listed in the dialog, including individual permissions and permissions given through group memberships.

3. Check the permission levels for the user listed at the bottom of the **Check Permissions** dialog, and then select **Close** when you're done, to return to the Permissions page.

To grant user permissions for a site

1. On the **Permissions** page for the site, on the **Permissions** tab, select **Grant Permissions**.

8

Grant user permissions for your site

2. In the **Share** dialog, make sure that **Invite people** is selected, and then in the **Enter names or email addresses** box, enter the names or email addresses of the people or groups to whom you want to grant access.

3. Select **Show options**, and in the **Select a permission level** list, select the permission level you want to grant to the people and groups defined in step 2.

> **TIP** The default permission level in the Select A Permission level list is Edit.

4. Do one of the following:

   • In the **Include a personal message** box, add text for an optional email message that will be sent to everyone in the Invite People box.

   • If you don't want to send the email, clear the **Send an email invitation** check box.

5. Select **Share** to apply your changes and return to the Permissions page.

To change the user permissions for a site

1. On the **Permissions** page for the site, in the **Name** list, select the check box next to the name of the user or group for which you want to change the permission level.

> **TIP** You can only change permissions for a site that has unique permissions.

2. On the **Permissions** tab, select **Edit User Permissions**.

Team Site   ✎ EDIT LINKS

Permissions ▸ Edit Permissions

Users or Groups
The permissions of these users or groups will be modified.

Users:
   Team Site Members

Choose Permissions
Choose the permissions you want these users or groups to have.

Permissions:
- ☐ Full Control - Has full control.
- ☐ Design - Can view, add, update, delete, approve, and customize.
- ☑ Edit - Can add, edit and delete lists; can view, add, update and delete list items and documents.
- ☐ Contribute - Can view, add, update, and delete list items and documents.
- ☐ Read - Can view pages and list items and download documents.
- ☐ View Only - Can view pages, list items, and documents. Document types with server-side file handlers can be viewed in the browser but not downloaded.

Modify permissions for existing site users and groups

3. On the **Edit Permissions** page for this user or group, under **Permissions,** choose the permission level you want this user or group to have.

4. Select **OK** to apply your changes and return to the Permissions page.

To remove user permissions for a site

1. On the **Permissions** page for the site, in the **Name** list, select the check box next to the name of the user or group that you want to remove the permissions from. You can select multiple users and groups.

> **TIP** You can remove user permissions only for a site that has unique permissions.

2. On the **Permissions** tab, select **Remove User Permissions**.

3. In the message box that appears, asking you to confirm that you want to remove permissions from these users or groups, select **OK**.

To remove a user from a group on a site

1. On the **Site Settings** page, in the **Users and Permissions** section, select **People and groups**.

2. On the **People and Groups** page, in the **Groups** section at the top of the Quick Launch, select the group you want to remove the user from.

3. On the group page, select the user you want to remove. Then, on the **Actions** menu located above the list of users, select **Remove users from group**, and then select **OK** in the confirmation message that appears.

To create a permission level

1. Go to the top-level site in the site collection in which you want to create a new permission level.

> ✓ **TIP** To create or make changes to permission levels, you must belong to a SharePoint group that includes the Manage Permissions permission. By default, you have this permission if you belong to the top-level Site Owners group or if you are a site collection administrator.

2. Display the **Permissions** page for the site.

3. On the **Permissions** tab, select **Permission Levels**.

Manage permission levels for a site collection

4. On the **Permission Levels** page, select **Add a Permission Level**.

Create a permission level

5. On the **Add a Permission Level** page, in the **Name and Description** section, provide the name and the optional description for your new permission level.

6. In the **Permissions** section, select the check boxes next to the list, site, and personal permissions that you want your new permission level to include.

7. When you're done, select **Create**.

To make changes to a permission level

1. Display the **Permissions** page for the top-level site in the site collection in which you want to make changes to a permission level.

2. On the **Permissions** tab, select **Permission Levels**.

3. On the **Permission Levels** page, click or tap the name of the permission level you want to edit.

> **TIP** Be sure to click or tap the link; do not select the check box next to the name.

4. On the **Edit Permission Level** page, do any of the following:

   - In the **Name and Description** section, change the name or the optional description for this permission level.

   - In the **Permissions** section, add or remove permissions for the permission level by selecting or clearing the check boxes next to the list, site, and personal permissions.

> **TIP** You can't make changes to the Full Control and Limited Access default permission levels.

5. When you're done, select **Submit**.

To delete a permission level

1. Display the **Permissions** page for the top-level site in the site collection in which you want to delete a permission level.

2. On the **Permissions** tab, select **Permission levels**.

3. On the **Permission Levels** page, select the check box next to the permission level that you want to delete.

8

TIP You can't delete the Full Control and Limited Access default permission levels.

4. Select **Delete Selected Permission Levels**, and if a confirmation box appears, select **OK**.

To make a copy of a permission level

1. Display the **Permissions** page for the top-level site in the site collection that contains the permission level you want to make a copy of.

2. On the **Permissions** tab, select **Permission Levels**.

3. On the **Permission Levels** page, click or tap the name of the permission level you want to copy.

 TIP Be sure to click or tap the link; do not select the check box next to the name.

4. On the **Edit Permission Level** page, scroll down to the bottom of the page and select **Copy Permission Level**.

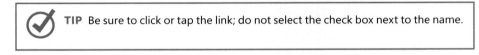

Copy Permission Level

5. On the **Copy Permission Level** page, do any of the following:

   - In the **Name and Description** section, change the name or the optional description for your new permission level.

   - In the **Permissions** section, add or remove permissions for the permission level by selecting or clearing the check boxes next to the list, site, and personal permissions.

6. When you're done, select **Create**.

Share sites

After you've created a site, you can give other people access to this site by using the Share command from any page on the site. If email has been turned on for your SharePoint deployment, you also have the option of sending a message to let people know that they have access to your site.

Sharing a site means granting access permissions to the users and groups you want to use your site. You can assign different levels of access to different people. For example, when you share your site with users who have the Edit permission level, they can create and modify the site content, including lists and libraries.

> ⊘ **SEE ALSO** For more information about sharing individual documents and folders, see Chapter 4, "Make lists and libraries work for you."

> ⚠ **IMPORTANT** If you want to share your site with external users outside of your organization—for example, in a hybrid environment—before you can share the site, your global administrator must turn on external sharing and set the appropriate permissions in SharePoint Online. You need to be a site owner or have Full Control permissions to share a site with external users.

When you share your site by using the Share command, the Share dialog is displayed. In the Share dialog, you can add a user to the SharePoint group that has the permission level that you are assigning to the user. For example, you can assign the Edit level to the user, which will add the user to the Members group.

If your site inherits permissions from its parent site, when you add users to your new site, they will also have access to the parent site and the sites that share permissions with it. Because of this, you will need to be an owner of the parent site to be able to share the new child site with other people. If you are not the site owner, you can still use the Share command to invite people to the site, but your request will be sent to the site owner for approval.

If you are the site owner, you can allow the users in the Members group to share the site, and the individual files and folders. You can also can set up the mail address where the access requests are sent for approval. You can manage these settings by using Access Requests Settings in the Permissions page of the site.

8

Manage access request settings

The Share command can also be used to see the list of people a site has been shared with.

If a site has been shared with a user and you want to revoke access to the site for this user, you can do so by removing the permissions for the site from this user by using Remove User Permissions in the Permissions page of the site.

To share a site

1. Go to a page in the site, and in the upper-right of the page, select **Share**.

2. In the **Share** dialog, make sure that **Invite people** is selected, and then in the **Enter names or email addresses** box, enter the names or email addresses of the people or groups to whom you want to grant access.

3. Select **Show options**, and in the **Select a permission level** list, select the permission level you want to grant to the people and groups defined in step 2.

> ✓ **TIP** The default permission level in the Select A Permission Level list is Edit.

4. Do one of the following:

   - In the **Include a personal message** box, add text for an optional email message that will be sent to everyone in the Invite People box.

   - If you don't want to send the email, clear the **Send an email invitation** check box.

5. Select **Share** to apply your changes and return to the site.

To see who has access to a site

1. Go to any page in the site, and in the upper-right of the page, select **Share**.

2. In the **Share** dialog, select **Shared with**.

View a list of users and groups the site is shared with

3. In the **Share** dialog, view the list of people who have access to the site, then do either of the following:

- Select **Advanced** to go to the site Permissions page to manage site access.
- Select **Close** to return to the site.

Change site themes

The look and feel of the default blue SharePoint sites are all right initially, but eventually you might find that your sites start to look too similar to each other. You might want to differentiate your sites by the way they are presented to the user. In SharePoint, you can apply themes to your sites. Themes can radically affect display items such as colors, text, background images, banners, and borders. There are many built-in themes available from which to choose. You can set up a theme for a site by using the Change The Look link on the Site Settings page.

Select a theme design

Each SharePoint site can have its own theme, or you can set several sites so that they all have a common theme and are related visually. For the built-in themes, you can change the background graphics, the color scheme, the site layout, and the fonts.

To set up a theme for a site

1. On the **Site Settings** page for the site, select **Change the look**.

2. On the **Change the look** page, select the theme you want to use.

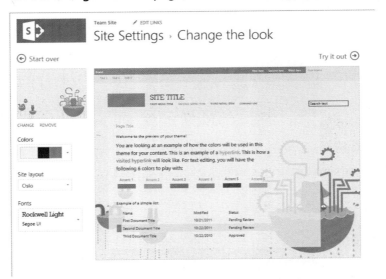

Customize the theme design

3. In the left panel of the theme design page, you can customize the theme design by doing any of the following:

   - To change the background, select **Change** and browse to the new image you want to use. To remove the background image, select **Remove**.

   - To change the colors used in the design, in the **Colors** list, scroll through the color schemes, and select the one you want to use.

   - To change the layout of the site, in the **Site layout** list, select a new layout.

   > ✓ **TIP** The site layouts for themes are based on the available master pages for your site. For example, the Seattle site layout displays the Quick Launch, whereas the Oslo site layout does not. In the Oslo layout, the links from the Quick Launch replace the links in the top link bar.

   - To change the font, in the **Fonts** list, select a new font.

4. When you're done, select **Try it out** to display a preview of your site with its new theme.

5. In the preview screen, do either of the following:

   - If you like the look, select **Yes, keep it** to apply the changes and return to the Site Settings page.

   - If you don't like the design, select **No, not quite there** to return the theme design page, and then repeat steps 3 through 5.

Create and use custom site templates

After working with a site, you might want to save it just the way it is so that it can be re-created over and over again. SharePoint facilitates this by allowing anyone with a Design permission level or higher to save a site as a custom site template. Custom site templates provide a way of packaging up a set of changes to an underlying built-in site template and making that package available as a template for new sites. Custom site templates behave in much the same way as built-in templates, in that they provision lists, document libraries, and webpages prepopulated with web parts that are best suited for the purpose of the template. In fact, nearly everything you can set up in a site except security-related information is saved in a custom site template, including its theme and navigation. The contents of all lists and libraries can also be included.

There are a few site capabilities that are not supported and that can't be saved in site templates. The following list distinguishes the supported and non-supported capabilities:

- **Supported** Lists, libraries, external lists, data source connections, list views and data views, custom forms, workflows, content types, custom actions, navigation, site pages, master pages, modules, and web templates

- **Unsupported** Customized permissions, running workflow instances, list item version history, workflow tasks associated with running workflows, people or group field values, taxonomy field values, publishing sites and pages, and stapled features

A custom site template allows you to create a solution and then share that solution with your peers, the broader organization, or outside organizations. Custom site templates are used to deploy solutions in other sites or to provide site consistency

8

within an organization. A custom site template is saved as a Web Solution Package file with a .wsp extension in the Solutions Gallery of the site collection. Only the current site is saved as the template; the subsites below the site are not saved.

> ⚠️ **IMPORTANT** A site template file is limited to 50 megabytes (MB).

A user with sufficient permissions to create a child site can select the custom site template from the Custom tab in the Template Selection section on the New SharePoint Site page.

You can save a site as a template by using the Save As Template page that is accessible via the Save Site As Template link on the Site Settings page.

Team Site   ✏ EDIT LINKS

Site Settings › Save as Template ⓘ

File Name
Enter the name for this template file.

File name:

Name and Description
The name and description of this template will be displayed on the Web site template picker page when users create new Web sites.

Template name:

Template description:

Include Content
Include content in your template if you want new Web sites created from this template to include the contents of all lists and document libraries in this Web site. Some customizations, such as custom workflows, are present in the template only if you choose to include content. Including content can increase the size of your template.

Caution: Item security is not maintained in a template. If you have private content in this Web site, enabling this option is not recommended.

☐ Include Content

Save a site as a template

> ⚠️ **IMPORTANT** Saving sites as templates is not supported on publishing sites. If your site has the publishing infrastructure turned on, you can't use the site template feature. The Site Settings page does not display the Save Site As Template link for publishing sites.

After it has been saved, a custom site template is made immediately available throughout the entire site collection in which it is saved. The site template file can be downloaded from the Solutions Gallery of the current site collection and redeployed to other site collections.

TIP To make a custom site template available for site creation in a site collection, you must ensure that the file containing the template is available and activated in the Solutions Gallery of the site collection.

The steps to save and redeploy your site template in another site collection are as follows:

1. Save the site as a template in the solution gallery of its site collection.

2. Download the template .wsp file from the solution gallery of its site collection.

3. Upload the template .wsp file to a solution gallery of a site collection you want to redeploy it to.

    TIP You can upload a .wsp file to the same site collection or to different site collections in the same or different SharePoint environments.

4. Activate the site template in the new site collection. After the template has been activated, it becomes available for site creation within the new site collection and is displayed on the Custom tab in the Template Selection section of the New SharePoint Site page.

You can also download a .wsp file from the Solutions Gallery and then open it in another environment or program such as Microsoft Visual Studio, and further customize it there.

 TIP The .wsp files used to create the sites for the practice tasks for this book are custom site templates saved to files.

To save a site as a template

1. On the site's **Site Settings** page, in the **Site Actions** section, select **Save site as template**.

2. On the **Save as Template** page, do the following:

   - In the **File Name** section, in the **File name** box, enter a name for the template file.

   - In the **Name and Description** section, in the **Template name** and **Template description** boxes, enter a name and optional description for the template.

   - In the **Include Content** section, select the **Include Content** check box to include the content of the site in the site template.

3. Select **OK** to save the template. If all of the components on the site are valid, the template is created, and a confirmation page is displayed.

A site template has been created

4. On the confirmation page, do one of the following:

   - Select **OK** to return to your site.

   - Select **solution gallery** to go to the saved site template in the Solution Gallery.

    TIP When a custom site template is created and saved in the Solutions Gallery, it is activated within the site collection.

To download a site template file

1. On the top-level site of the site collection that contains the site template, display the **Site Settings** page, and in the **Web Designer Galleries** section, select **Solutions** to open the Solution Gallery.

   Click or tap the template you want to download

2. On the **Solution Gallery** page, click or tap the site template name, and then in the **Do you want to save *template file*?** bar that appears, display the **Save** menu and select **Save As**.

3. In the **Save As** dialog, browse to the location where you want to save the template .wsp file, select **Save**, and then close the message box that confirms the file download.

To upload a site template to a site collection

1. On the top-level site of the site collection, display the **Site Settings** page, and in the **Web Designer Galleries** section, select **Solutions**.

2. On the **Solution Gallery** page, on the **Solutions** tab of the ribbon, select **Upload Solution**, and then, in the **Add a document** dialog, select **Browse**.

Add a document   ×

Choose a file   [   ] Browse...

☑ Overwrite existing files

OK   Cancel

Browse to the site template file you want to upload

3. In the **Choose File to Upload** dialog box, select the site template file you want to upload, select **Open**, and then, in the **Add a document** dialog, select **OK** to perform the upload.

To activate a site template

1. On the top-level site of your site collection, display the **Site Settings** page, and in the **Web Designer Galleries** section, select **Solutions**.

2. On the **Solution Gallery** page, select the template you want to activate by clicking or tapping in its leftmost column.

3. On the **Solutions** tab of the ribbon, in the **Commands** group, select **Activate**.

4. In the **Activate Solution** dialog, on the **View** tab, in the **Commands** group, select **Activate**.

8

Activate a site template

To deactivate a site template

1. On the top-level site of your site collection, display the **Site Settings** page, and in the **Web Designer Galleries** section, select **Solutions**.

2. On the **Solution Gallery** page, select the template you want to deactivate by clicking or tapping in its leftmost column.

3. On the **Solutions** tab of the ribbon, in the **Commands** group, select **Deactivate**.

4. In the **Deactivate Solution** dialog, on the **View** tab, in the **Commands** group, select **Deactivate**.

To remove a site template from a site collection

1. On the top-level site of the site collection, display the **Site Settings** page, and in the **Web Designer Galleries** section, select **Solutions**.

2. On the **Solution Gallery** page, deactivate the template you want to delete.

3. On the **Solutions** tab of the ribbon, in the **Commands** group, select **Delete**. Select **OK** in the dialog that appears, to confirm that you want to remove the template.

> **TIP** When a site template is deleted from the Solution Gallery, it is moved into the Recycle Bin. It can be restored from the Recycle Bin within the time period that is set for keeping items in the Recycle Bin. The default time period is 30 days for SharePoint 2016 and 93 days for SharePoint Online.

Manage site features

SharePoint features provide site capabilities by grouping together chunks of functionality that developers and administrators can activate to make the combined functionality available. This can be done at one of four scope levels, as follows:

- **Farm level** These features are activated for all sites in the entire SharePoint Foundation farm and are managed by the farm's central administrators.

- **Web application level** These features are activated for all sites where the web address is the same. For instance, all sites that start with *http://wideworldimporters* would be managed under the same web application. These features are also managed by the farm's central administrators.

- **Site collection level** These features are activated only for sites within a specified site collection. Management of these features is accomplished from the top-level site of the site collection and is typically distributed to the site collection administrators.

- **Site level** These features are activated only for the site in which the activation is performed. Management of these features can be done by anyone with the Full Control permission level on the site.

A feature needs to be installed and activated in order to provide its functionality. For example, there are several built-in features that are installed and activated by default in a site collection in which the top-level site is a team site. These features include a Team Collaboration Lists feature that provides collaboration capabilities for a team site by making document libraries and several lists available, a Site Feed feature that provides the site with newsfeed capability, and others. Each SharePoint feature is identified by a numeric, globally unique identifier (GUID).

> **SEE ALSO** For a complete list of built-in SharePoint 2016 site features with corresponding GUIDs, see *https://gallery.technet.microsoft.com/office/SharePoint-2016-Features-8b181fec.*

The site features are managed from the Site Features page, which you can navigate to via the Manage Site Features link on the Site Settings page.

8

Following Content	Enable users to follow documents or sites.	Deactivate	Active
Getting Started	Provides a tile view experience for common SharePoint site actions.	Deactivate	Active
Getting Started with Project Web App	This feature creates an instance of the Promoted Links list with items about how to get started with your Project Web App site.	Activate	
Hold	This feature is used to track external actions like litigations, investigations, or audits that require you to suspend the disposition of documents.	Activate	
Metadata Navigation and Filtering	Provides each list in the site with a settings pages for configuring that list to use metadata tree view hierarchies and filter controls to improve navigation and filtering of the contained items.	Activate	

Activate or deactivate site features

A feature must be installed and activated in scope on your SharePoint server farm before you can begin working with it. For example, when a custom site template is deployed in a site collection, the Web Template feature that provides its functionality is created and activated in the site collection. It is this feature that allows the new template to appear on the Custom tab in the Template Selection section of the New SharePoint Site page.

> **TIP** A custom site template includes a list of activated features from the originating site. If these features are not activated at the intended parent site when the creation of a new site is attempted, SharePoint 2016 will not create a site and will generate an error message that includes the GUID of the missing feature.

To activate or deactivate a feature for a site

1. Display the site's **Site Settings** page.

2. In the **Site Actions** section, select **Manage site features**.

3. On the **Site Features** page, scroll to the feature, and do one of the following:

   - To activate the site feature, select **Activate** to the right of the feature.

   - To deactivate the site feature, select **Deactivate** to the right of the feature, and then on the confirmation page, select **Deactivate this feature** to confirm your action.

Manage site content syndication

Really Simple Syndication (RSS) is a standard way to make new or modified content available to readers of a SharePoint list or document library. After you subscribe to an RSS feed (the XML emitted from a web request), you can use an RSS aggregator, also known as a reader, to check for new or modified content as often as you want.

> **TIP** There are different types of RSS readers, including standalone readers, browsers such as Internet Explorer, and email programs. Outlook 2010, Outlook 2013, and Outlook 2016 can be used as RSS aggregators.

RSS feeds come at periodic intervals and appear in an RSS reader. You can use RSS to receive updates in a standardized format from several sites at the same time. The reader gathers all updates into a common pool of data that can be searched, sorted, filtered, and grouped by the aggregator as directed. This can be a useful way to roll up data entered into a SharePoint list. By default, every web application in SharePoint is configured to allow RSS feeds for all site collections that they contain.

Site collection administrators can specify whether RSS feeds are allowed on lists and libraries in the sites within the site collection by using the RSS page available via the RSS link in the Site Settings page. By default, RSS feeds are allowed. Each site can then subsequently specify whether RSS feeds are allowed on lists and libraries in the site; they are also allowed by default. If RSS feeds are turned off for a site, no lists in this site are allowed to provide their data in the form of an RSS feed.

Set up RSS feeds for a site

If sites do allow feeds, several attributes can be defined that will be included in every feed, as follows: copyright, managing editor, webmaster, and time to live. The time to live defines a period in minutes that instructs the RSS reader to wait at least this long before checking for updates. A shorter period increases the frequency of requests from RSS readers to a site. A longer duration can help reduce the number of RSS reader requests.

To configure RSS feed for a site

1. On the site's **Site Settings** page, in the **Site Administration** section, select **RSS**.

2. On the **RSS** page, in the Enable RSS section, do either of the following:

   - To enable RSS, select the **Allow RSS Feeds In This Site** check box, and then in the **Advanced Settings** section, enter the attributes for the feed in the following boxes:

     - Copyright
     - Managing Editor
     - Webmaster
     - Time To Live (minutes)

   - To disable RSS, clear the **Allow RSS Feeds In This Site** check box.

3. When you are done, select **OK** to apply the changes and return to the Site Settings page.

Delete sites

There will be times when you want to remove a site that you either created in error or no longer need. SharePoint automatically generates all the necessary user interface elements to create, review, update, manage, and delete your sites.

> ⚠ **IMPORTANT** You need to have Full Control permissions to delete a site or subsite.

When you delete a site, you're also deleting all content and user information that is part of the site, including documents, document libraries, lists, and list data. When you delete a top-level site, you delete all subsites within the site collection and all of the content within those subsites.

When a site is deleted, it is sent to the site collection's Recycle Bin. The site can be restored from the site collection's Recycle Bin to its original location only by an administrator of the site collection.

To delete a site

1. On the site's **Site Settings** page, in the **Site Actions** section, select **Delete this site**.

2. On the **Delete This Site** page, select **Delete** to confirm the deletion request, and then in the confirmation box that appears, select **OK**.

Delete a site when you no longer need it

3. On the confirmation page, select **Go Back To Site** to return to the parent site.

Skills review

In this chapter, you learned how to:

- Create sites
- Manage site users and permissions
- Share sites
- Change site themes
- Create and use custom site templates
- Manage site features
- Manage site content syndication
- Delete sites

Chapter 8

Practice tasks

No practice files are necessary to complete the practice tasks in this chapter.

> ⚠ **IMPORTANT** You must have sufficient permissions to perform the operations involved in each practice task to complete that practice task. For more information, see Appendix A, "SharePoint 2016 user permissions and permission levels."

Create sites

Go to your SharePoint site and perform the following tasks:

1. Create a subsite that uses the following settings:

Title	Buyers
Description	Site for general buyer collaboration
URL name (suffix)	buyers
Template	**Team Site**
Permissions	**Use same permissions as parent site**
Display this site on the Quick Launch of the parent site?	**No**
Display this site on the top link bar of the parent site?	**Yes**
Use the top link bar of the parent site?	**No**

2. Confirm that you can navigate to your new site by selecting a link on the top link bar of the parent site.

3. Create a personal site with the name **Vendors**.

4. Go to the **Sites** page and validate that your new site has been added to the list of sites you are following.

Manage site users and permissions

Continuing on your SharePoint deployment, perform the following tasks:

1. Go to the **Buyers** site.

2. Turn on unique permissions for the **Buyers** site and set up the following groups:

Visitors to this site	**Use existing group**
Members of this site	**Create a new group**, with the following settings

Name	**Buyers Members**
Members	Add users and groups from your environment
Owners of this site	**Create a new group**, with the following settings
Name	**Buyers Owners**
Members	Add a user to be a co-owner of the site with you

3. Remove site permissions from all users and groups inherited from the parent site, so that only your new groups, Buyers Members and Buyers Owners, have permissions to the site.

4. Grant **Design** permissions to a user.

5. Check permissions for the user you granted permissions to in step 4.

Share sites

Continuing on your SharePoint deployment, perform the following tasks:

1. Go to the **Vendors** site.

2. Share the site with a user or a group you want to invite to your site with **Read** permissions, such as:

    *   The **Everyone** group for on-premises deployment.

    *   The **Everyone except external users** group for SharePoint Online.

> **TIP** Turn off email notifications when sharing your new site.

Change site themes

Continuing on your SharePoint deployment, perform the following tasks:

1. Go to the **Buyers** site.

2. Change the site theme to **Sea Monster**. Select the design choices that you like most for the background graphics, color scheme, site layout, and fonts.

Create and use custom site templates

Continuing on your SharePoint deployment, perform the following tasks:

1. On the **Buyers** site, save the site as a template with the following settings:

File name	Buyers
Template name	Buyers Site
Template description	Sea Monster themed site created by buyers

2. Go to the parent site for the **Buyers** site.

3. Create a new subsite with the following settings:

Title	Finance
Description	Site for Finance Department
URL name (suffix)	finance
Template	Buyers Site
Permissions	Use same permissions as parent site
Display this site on the Quick Launch of the parent site?	No
Display this site on the top link bar of the parent site?	Yes
Use the top link bar of the parent site?	No

4. Confirm that the new **Finance** site is identical to the **Buyers** site, with the **Sea Monster** theme applied.

Manage site features

Continuing on your SharePoint deployment, perform the following tasks:

1. Go to the **Finance** site.

2. Verify the feed functionality by positioning your cursor in the newsfeed box, entering **Hello World!**, and then selecting **Post**.

Verify the site newsfeed functionality

3. Deactivate the **Site Feed** site feature for the **Finance** site.

4. Go to the home page of the **Finance** site. Confirm that the newsfeed box and the **Post** button are no longer available, and that your post has also been removed.

5. Activate the **Site Feed** site feature.

6. Go to the home page of the site and confirm that the newsfeed box is displayed and that site feed functionality is available.

Manage site content syndication

Continuing on your SharePoint deployment, perform the following tasks:

1. Go to the **Vendor** site.

2. Set up RSS feed with the following settings:

Copyright	2016
Managing Editor	Enter your name
Webmaster	Enter your best friend's name
Time To Live (minutes)	90

Delete sites

Continuing on your SharePoint deployment, perform the following tasks:

1. Delete the **Finance** site.

2. Confirm that the link to the **Finance** site is no longer available in the top link bar of the parent site.

Work with wikis, blogs, and community sites

Wikis, blogs, and community sites allow users to quickly publish content for consumption by designated groups of consumers. For example, you can designate whether the consumers are your entire organization or only part of it.

Blogs contain frequent posts and are traditionally used for personal journals or observations but are increasingly being used by teams to share information. Wikis allow groups of users to collect knowledge about a particular content area or event. Blog posts, after they have been written, are rarely updated, whereas wikis are continually updated with more content and supporting links.

Community sites offer a forum experience that uses discussions and answers. Knowledge sharing is encouraged through a reward system for quality and quantity of contribution.

This chapter guides you through procedures related to creating wiki libraries; creating and using Enterprise Wiki sites; creating and managing blog sites; creating, managing, and deleting blog posts; creating and managing community sites, and using community sites.

In this chapter

- Create wiki libraries
- Create and use Enterprise Wiki sites
- Create and manage blog sites
- Create, manage, and delete blog posts
- Create and manage community sites
- Work with community sites

Practice files

For this chapter, use the practice file from the SP2016SBS\Ch09 folder. For practice file download instructions, see the introduction.

Create wiki libraries

The very first ever wiki (pronounced *wee-kee*) site, WikiWikiWeb, was created for the Portland Pattern Repository in 1995 by Ward Cunningham, who devised a system that uses a browser to create webpages quickly and allows users to freely create and edit page content. *Wiki* is the Hawaiian word for *quick*, and because Hawaiian words are doubled for emphasis, *wikiwiki* means *very quick*. One wiki implementation is Wikipedia, from Wikimedia Foundation, Inc. (*wikipedia.org*), which is an encyclopedia-like website that has inherited many of the non-encyclopedic properties of a wiki site.

> **TIP** *WikiWikiWeb* is the proper name of the concept, for which the terms *wiki* and *wikis* are abbreviations.

In SharePoint, the wiki system of creating webpages quickly is incorporated into both collaboration and publishing sites. On team and community sites, wiki pages are stored in a wiki page library named Site Pages. On publishing sites, you can use the wiki method of creating and linking pages within the content areas on publishing pages.

Sites such as those created from the Project or Document Center site templates do not automatically contain wiki libraries; however, you can either create a new wiki page library on such a site or activate the Wiki Page Home Page site feature to create the Site Pages wiki page library and set your site's home page to a wiki page.

> **SEE ALSO** For information about using the wiki system to create new pages, and about adding content to pages, see Chapter 7, "Work with webpages."

Wikis are a great knowledge repository, allowing users to collaborate on content and agree on ways of working, in addition to documenting work-specific terms. When content is specific to a team or project, you could create the wiki page library on the team's or project's site. When the information is important to all users in your organization, and when you want to require content approval before allowing the content to be viewed, consider using an Enterprise Wiki site, which is detailed in the next topic.

When a wiki page library contains many pages, instead of linking one page to the next page, you could group pages into categories. If you display these categories on your site's home page, visitors can quickly find pages for a specific topic.

> **TIP** Wiki page libraries contain a Wiki Content column that you can use in your app parts or views to display the contents of wiki pages.

An Enterprise Wiki site automatically provides a mechanism that allows you to categorize your wiki pages; however, a wiki page library does not. A solution would be to add one or more columns to your wiki page library to categorize your pages, and then use an app part on your site's home page, configured to display the pages grouped by category.

Welcome to your wiki library!
You can get started and add content to this page by clicking **Edit** at the top of this page, or you can learn more about wiki libraries by clicking How To Use This Library.

What is a wiki library?

Wikiwiki means quick in Hawaiian. A wiki library is a document library in which users can easily edit any page. The library grows organically by linking existing pages together or by creating links to new pages. If a user finds a link to an uncreated page, he or she can follow the link and create the page.

In business environments, a wiki library provides a low-maintenance way to record knowledge. Information that is usually traded in e-mail messages, gleaned from hallway conversations, or written on paper can instead be recorded in a wiki library, in context with similar knowledge.

Other example uses of wiki libraries include brainstorming ideas, collaborating on designs, creating an instruction guide, gathering data from the field, tracking call center knowledge, and building an encyclopedia of knowledge.

When a wiki page library is first created, its home page provides information on how to add content to the wiki page library and what a wiki page library is

> **TIP** If your team wants to brainstorm on a project, collect reference material, take notes, or share meeting minutes, you should consider using a Microsoft OneNote notebook for the team. For more information about using SharePoint to share OneNote notebooks, see Chapter 12, "Collaborate with Office programs by using SharePoint."

To create a wiki page library

1. Do one of the following to display the Your Apps page:
   - From the **Settings** menu, select **Add an app**.
   - On the Quick Launch, select **Site Contents**, and then select **add an app**.

2. On the **Your Apps** page, under **Apps you can add**, select **Wiki Page Library** to open the Adding Wiki Page Library dialog box.

> **TIP** If the Wiki Page Library is not listed, check that the site has the Team Collaboration Lists site feature activated (see Chapter 8, "Create and manage sites").

3. In the **Name** text box, enter a name for your wiki page library, and then select **Create**.

To activate a Wiki Page Home Page site feature

1. Sign on as a site owner, and on the **Settings** menu, select **Site settings** to display the Site Settings page.

2. Under **Site Actions**, select **Manage site features**.

3. On the **Site Features** page, to the right of the **Wiki Page Home Page** site feature, select **Activate**. You might need to scroll down the page.

To add categories to a wiki page library

1. Do one of the following to display the Create Column page:

   - Display one of the pages in the wiki page library, such as the home page. Then, on the **Page** tab, select **View All Pages** to display the default view of the wiki page library. On the **Library** tab, select **Create Column**.

   - Display the default view of the wiki page library. On the **Library** tab, select **Library Settings** to display the Settings page, and then in the **Columns** section, select **Create column**.

   - On the **Site Contents** page, point to the wiki page library, select the ellipsis that appears, and then select **Settings** to display the Settings page. In the **Columns** section, select **Create column**.

2. On the **Create Column** page, in the **Column name** box, enter a name for the column, such as *Category*, and under **The type of information in this column is**, select **Choice**.

> ⚠ **IMPORTANT** You can use a variety of column types for a category column. This procedure is an example that uses the Choice column type. For more information about creating columns and column types, see Chapter 3, "Work with content in lists and libraries."

3. In the **Type each choice on a separate line** box, delete the three predefined generic choices, and then enter the categories you want to use in your wiki page library, on separate lines.

4. Select **OK**.

> ✓ **TIP** When you create a category column to a wiki page library, it is not obvious, to wiki contributors that they need to categorize their page; therefore, you need to tell them to use the following procedure to categorize their pages.

To categorize a wiki page

1. Go to the wiki page you want to categorize, and then on the **Page** tab, in the **Manage** group, select **Edit Properties**.

2. In the **Category** list, select one of the categories.

Use the edit properties page to change the name of the wiki page and to categorize the page

3. Select **Save**.

To add an app part to a page to display wiki pages grouped by category

1. On the page where you want to add the app part that displays wiki pages by category, activate edit mode and then place the cursor where you want the app part to be displayed.

2. On the **Insert** tab, in the **Parts** group, select **App Part** to display the app parts pane.

3. Select the wiki page library that contains the category column you want to group pages by, and then select **Add**.

4. On the **Page** tab, select the **Save** arrow (not the button), and select **Save and Keep Editing**.

5. Do one of the following to display the web part tool pane:

   - On the **Web Part** contextual tab, select **Web Part Properties**.

   - Point to the app part, select the arrow on the title bar of the app part, and then select **Edit Web Part**.

6. In the properties pane, immediately below **List Views**, do one of the following:

   - If you previously created a view that displays wiki pages grouped by category, select that view and then, in the properties pane, select **OK**. Save the page.

   - Select **Edit the current view** and then, if a dialog box opens, select **OK** to save your changes. Then, on the **Edit View** page, scroll down to the **Group By** section and expand it. In the **First group by the column** box, select **Category**, and then under **By default, show groupings**, select **Expanded**.

9

At the bottom of the page, select **OK**.

Use the Group By section to display the wiki pages by category

Create and use Enterprise Wiki sites

Microsoft envisaged that organizations would use an Enterprise Wiki when they required a large, centralized knowledge repository that used strict content control and had the ability to use a workflow to establish an approval process. You create an Enterprise Wiki by using the publishing Enterprise Wiki site template at the top-level site of a site collection or subsite. Enterprise Wikis use publishing pages.

Enterprise Wikis can contain content similar to what wiki libraries contain; however, they provide additional capabilities, such as the following:

- The top of the page contains the date the page was last modified and the name of the person who modified it.

- When you upload an image or a file, the default location is the Images library. An Enterprise Wiki site does not have a Site Assets library. An Enterprise Wiki site contains other libraries in which you can store files: Documents, Site Collection Documents, and Site Collection Images libraries.

- You are limited to two page layouts: Basic Page and Basic Project Page. Additional page layouts can be created by using the Design Manager, which can be accessed from the Settings menu.

- You can categorize and rate the page, without the need to do any configuration. The categorization of Enterprise Wiki pages uses the Managed Metadata Service (MMS) and Term Store, which allows you to define categories once centrally and then reuse them throughout the organization in multiple site collections.

> **TIP** You cannot automatically convert or migrate wiki pages to Enterprise Wiki pages or vice versa without the help of a developer. You can copy and paste the content between the two page types; however, content such as app parts or web parts might need to be recreated. If the new wiki page is created in a library on a different site, you cannot copy an app part from the original site to that library, in which case you might need to consider using a web part, such as the Content Query web part or Content Search web part. Also, if you are migrating content from pages on one site to pages on another site and you have included images on a page, the location where the images are stored remains the same—for example, the Images library. Users on the new site might not have Read access to the Images library; therefore, you might have to upload the images, for example, to the Site Assets library and then insert the images on the new page.

To create an Enterprise Wiki site

> **IMPORTANT** Creating a top-level site of a site collection as an Enterprise Wiki site, by using either the SharePoint 2016 Central Administration website or Windows PowerShell, is outside the scope of this book. However, if Self-Service Site Creation (SSSC) is turned on, you might be able to create an Enterprise Wiki site as a top-level site of a site collection. For information about SSSC, see Chapter 8, "Create and manage sites." This procedure allows you to create an Enterprise Wiki subsite. This requires the SharePoint Server Publishing Infrastructure site collection feature, which is usually activated when the top-level site of a site collection is created by using a publishing site template. Activating this site collection feature on a team site is not supported by Microsoft; therefore, usually you cannot create an Enterprise Wiki site as a subsite of a team site.

1. Go to the site where you want to create an Enterprise Wiki site as a subsite.

2. To display the Site Contents page, do one of the following:

   - From the **Settings** menu, select **Site Contents**.

   - On the Quick Launch, select **Site Contents**.

3. At the bottom of the **Site Contents** page, and under **Subsites**, select **new subsite**.

On the Site Contents page, you can add an app and create subsites

4. On the **New SharePoint Site** page, in the **Title** box, enter the name of the site, and in the **URL name** box, enter the website address.

5. In the **Template Selection** section, select the **Publishing** tab, if it is not already active, select **Enterprise Wiki**, and then select **Create**.

> **TIP** If the Publishing tab is not displayed, check to make sure that you are creating the subsite in a site collection where the SharePoint Server Publishing Infrastructure site collection feature is activated.

The SharePoint search functionality uses the words entered in the title, description, and website address boxes to calculate the relevancy of this site against the keywords a user enters into the search box

To add categories to an Enterprise Wiki site

> ⚠️ **IMPORTANT** The categorization of Enterprise Wiki pages uses MMS and the Term Store, which must be created by your SharePoint server administrator. If the server administrator did not create the MMS service application or no applicable terms are created in the Term Store, you will not be able to categorize your pages. For information about MMS, see Chapter 5, "Search for information and people."

1. Display one of the pages on your Enterprise Wiki site, and on the **Page** tab, select **Library Settings**.

2. In the **Columns** section, select **Wiki Categories** to display the Edit Column page.

3. In the **Term Set Settings** section, select the arrow to the left of **Managed Metadata Service** to display the term set groups. (Your organization might have a different name for the MMS.)

4. Select the arrow to the left of the term set group that contains the term set you want to use for the category names, and then select the term set you want to use.

9

Use the Term Set Settings page to select one or more terms or a term set

5. In the **Default Value** section, to the right of the **Default value** box, select the **Browse for a valid choice** icon to open the Select : Default dialog box.

6. Select the term you want to select as the default, and then select **Select**.

Select : Default   ×

New items are added under the currently selected item. Add New Item

- ▲ Department
  - HR
  - IT
  - Marketing
  - Not known at the moment
  - Not known at the moment
  - Not known at the moment
  - Training

Select >>   IT:

When you create an Enterprise Wiki page, the value term you select in the Select : Default dialog box is the category for the page

7. Select **OK** to close the Select : Default dialog box.

Default Value

Enter the default value for the column

Default value:

IT:

When the Select : Default dialog box closes, the selected value populates the Default Value box

8. Select **OK** to close the Edit Column page.

To categorize an Enterprise Wiki page

⚠ **IMPORTANT** Before you can categorize pages, the previous procedure must have been completed.

1. Go to the page you want to categorize, and then on the **Page** tab, in the **Manage** group, select **Edit Properties**.

2. To the right of the **Wiki Category** box, select the **Browse for a valid choice** icon to open the Select Wiki Categories dialog box.

3. Select the term or terms you want to use, and then select **Select**.

4. Select **OK** to close the dialog box.

5. Select **Save**.

To rate an Enterprise Wiki page

1. Go to the page your want to rate, and then to the right of the page, select one to five stars.

Last modified at 5/29/2016 7:45 PM by ☐ Peter Connelly [Edit this page]

Use the Enterprise Wiki to create a single, go-to place for knowledge sharing and project management across the enterprise. Enterprise Wikis are simple to use, flexible, and lightweight in features. They are quick and easy to create, and you can

Page Rating
★ ★ ★ ☆ ☆ | 1
Categories
HR

Ratings help content owners and wiki authors easily see which topics are considered popular by the readers

Create and manage blog sites

A web log, known as a blog, is a personal journal or commentary shared on a website. Blogging refers to publishing thoughts, in formal essays or more informal formats, on a blog website; a person who does this is called a blogger. The thoughts shared on the blog website are called posts or articles, which are stored in a list named Posts.

Although the logical location for your blog site is on your personal site, also known as your My Site, often a team leader creates a blog site below the team site, and asks team members to record their weekly activities on the team blog. Blogs can also be used by organizations and departments to replace the sending of emails or newsletters; an example is the Microsoft Office Blogs site, *blogs.office.com*, which aggregates blog posts.

> ⚠ **IMPORTANT** If you are using Office 365, you might experience a different blog experience than is described in this topic.

Blog posts can be categorized to help users find past conversations. The first task you should complete after a blog site is created is to add categories that reflect the blog posts you will create. For example, the Microsoft Office Blogs sites use three types of categories for their posts:

- **Products you use** These include Office 365, OneDrive, SharePoint, and Sway.
- **Where you use Office** Possible options include Business, Dev, Home, School, and on-premises.
- **What you want to see** Possible options include customer stories, events, video shows, updates, and podcasts.

Blogs are also indexed so that visitors can search through old blogs and learn from past conversations. Bloggers write blogs frequently, often on a daily basis. Some blogs allow visitors to comment on the blog, provide feedback, and ask questions.

A blog site's home page is a web part page consisting of three web part zones, which can more clearly be seen when the page is in edit mode:

- **Quick Launch** This area contains:

  - **Categories** This section contains links to words or phrases that you use to categorize your posts. The words or phrases are saved in a list named Categories. When your site is first created, the list contains three sample categories: Events, Ideas, and Opinions.

  - **Archives** This section provides links to older items, organized by the month in which they were created.

- **Left** This is the main part of the page. It contains one web part, which displays the 10 most recent posts, in reverse chronological order. Each post states the time it was published, and, depending on the blog post layout, at the bottom of the post is the name of the person who published the post, along with its category. Selecting the category link on this line displays a page on which all similarly categorized posts are listed. This behavior is the same as selecting a link under Categories on the Quick Launch.

- **Right** This area contains three web parts:

  - **Blog Tools** This web part allows blog owners and the site owner to create and manage posts, manage comments and categories, and launch blogging apps. It also includes an option for changing the layout of the main part of the page to one of three options: Basic, Boxed, and Inline.

Blog tools
Create a post
Manage posts
Manage comments
Manage categories
Launch blogging app
Change post layout:
Basic ⌄

Use the Blog Tools web part to manage posts, comments, and categories, and to change the layout of the page.

- **About This Blog** When you first create a blog site, this is a Content Editor web part (CEWP) containing an image and some static text, which can be changed. The web part is configured to hide its title, About This Blog, which you will only see when the page is in edit mode.

- **Blog Notifications** This web part allows visitors to your blog site to register for blog post notifications by using RSS feed or alerts.

To create a personal blog site

1. Select your picture in the upper-right corner, and then select **About me** to display your profile page.

2. On the Quick Launch, select **Blog**.

> **TIP** If this is the first time you have selected About Me, the Blog link on the Quick Launch is not displayed. Refresh the webpage until the link appears. For more information about your personal site, see Chapter 6, "Work with My Sites and OneDrive for Business."

> **IMPORTANT** If you are using Office 365, a link to your personal blog might not be displayed on the Quick Launch, but a link to all your posts might be displayed in the body of your profile page.

To create a team blog site

1. Go to the site where you want to create the new blog site as a subsite.

2. Do one of the following to display the Site Contents page:
   - From the **Settings** menu, select **Site Contents**.
   - On the Quick Launch, select **Site Contents**.

3. Scroll to the bottom of the **Site Contents** page, and then under **Subsites**, select **new subsite**.

4. On the **New SharePoint Site** page, in the **Title** box, enter the name of the site, and in the **URL name** box, enter the website address.

9

5. Select the **Collaboration** tab, if it is not already active, and then select **Blog**.

> **TIP** If the Collaboration tab is not displayed, or the Blog site template is not displayed on the Collaboration tab, check to make sure that you are creating the subsite in a site collection where the usage of the Blog site template is allowed. For information about creating sites, see Chapter 8, "Create and manage sites."

6. Select **Create**.

To change a blog image and description for a blog site

1. On the home page of the blog site, activate edit mode.

> ⊙ **SEE ALSO** For information about using web part pages and adding content to pages, see Chapter 7, "Work with webpages."

2. In the **About this blog** web part, select the image to activate the Format Text, Insert Image, Table Layout, Design, Insert, and Web Part contextual tabs.

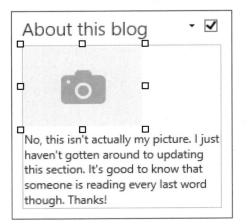

Use the Content Editor web part to describe the purpose of the blog site

3. Do one of the following to replace or modify the properties of the image.

   - On the **Image** tab, make the selections you want.

   - On the **Insert** tab to the right of the **Format Text** tab, select **Picture**, and then insert an image by following the "To insert a picture, video, or audio" procedure in Chapter 7, "Work with webpages."

4. To modify the description, delete or modify the existing text, or format the text, use the commands on the **Format Text** tab.

5. Save the page.

To create a category for a blog site

1. Do one of the following to display the new item page:

   - On the Quick Launch, under **Categories**, select **Add category**.

Categories
   Events
   Ideas
   Opinions
   ADD CATEGORY

Use the Categories section on the Quick Launch to add new categories

   - On the home page of the blog site, in the **Blog tools** web part, select **Manage categories**, and then select **new item**.

   - Go to the **Site Contents** page, select the tile to the left of **Categories**, and then select **new item**.

2. In the **Title** box, enter the name of the category, and then select **Save**.

To modify a category for a blog site

1. Do one of the following to display the default view of the Categories list:

   - On the home page of the blog site, in the **Blog tools** web part, select **Manage categories**.

   - Go to the **Site Contents** page, and select the tile to the left of **Categories**.

2. Do one of the following:

   - Click or tap to the left of the category, and then on the **Items** tab, in the **Manage** group, select **Edit Item**.

   - Right-click the category, and then on the menu, select **Edit Item**.

3. Modify the category, and then select **Save**.

9

To delete a category for a blog site

1. Display the default view of the **Categories** list, as described in the previous procedure.

2. Do one of the following:

   - Click or tap to the left of the category, and then on the **Items** tab, in the **Manage** group, select **Delete Item**.

   - Right-click the category, and then on the menu, select **Delete Item**.

Create, manage, and delete blog posts

A blog post is the method by which you share your opinions and knowledge. You must remember that, as a blogger, you are responsible for the commentary you post, and you can be held personally liable if your posting is considered defamatory, obscene, or libelous, or if it is non-attributed copyrighted content. As with posting information on a wiki, you should practice good manners and understatement.

Many blogging apps are available for creating blog posts, including Microsoft Word, OneNote (you will need to have Word installed to publish by using OneNote), Windows Live Writer, and browsers.

> **TIP** Microsoft has released Windows Live Writer as an open source project on GitHub, under the MIT license at *openlivewriter.org*.

To link a blog site with a blogging app

> **IMPORTANT** This procedure uses Word, but other blogging apps could be used. To use other blogging apps, open those apps first and then connect to your SharePoint blog site. Some of the steps might vary depending on the blogging app you use.

1. On the home page of the blog site, in the **Blog Tools** web part, select **Launch blogging app** to open the New SharePoint Blog Account dialog box. The web address of the blog site is listed in the Blog URL box.

Use the New SharePoint Blog Account dialog box to enter your blog site sign on details and to specify where to upload pictures

2. Select **Picture Options** if you want to change where images are stored, and then select **OK** to close the Picture Options dialog box.

> ✓ **TIP** You can choose to save pictures on your SharePoint blog site or your own server, or you can choose not to upload pictures when you publish a blog post. When you configure Word to use the SharePoint blog site, it will store pictures in the Photos library.

3. Select **OK**. A Microsoft Word dialog box opens, warning that when Word sends information to the blog service provider, it might be possible for other people to see that information, including your user name and password.

4. Select **Yes** to close the Microsoft Word dialog box. Another Microsoft Word dialog box opens, stating that the account registration was successful.

The Microsoft Word dialog box confirms that your account details were used successfully to sign you on to the blog site

5. Select **OK**. Now, when a blog post is opened in Word, the Blog Post tab is active.

The Blog group on the Blog Post tab provides easy access to the home page of your blog site, where you can assign a category to the blog post, open an existing blog, manage accounts, and publish the blog

To create a blog post by using a browser

> ⚠ **IMPORTANT** You can create, modify, or delete a blog post only if you are a member of the blog site.

1. Do one of the following to display the Posts - New Item page:

   - On the home page of the blog site, in the **Blog tools** web part, select **Create a post**.

   - On the home page of the blog site, in the **Blog tools** web part, select **Manage posts**, and then select **new item**.

   - Go to the **Site Contents** page, select the tile to the left of **Posts**, and then select **new item**.

2. In the **Title** box, enter the title of your post.

3. In the **Body** box, enter the content of the post, using the tools on the **Format Text** tab and the **Image** tab to format the content and to insert tables, pictures, links, and embedded code.

4. In the **Category** list, select one or more categories, and then select **Add**.

In the Category list, you can select consecutive categories by selecting the first category, holding down the Shift key, and selecting the last category, or you can select nonconsecutive categories by holding down the Ctrl key and then selecting each category

5. In the **Published** section, select a date and time in the future, if you do not want the post to be immediately seen by users who only have Read access to the blog site.

6. Do one of the following;

   - On the **Edit** tab, select **Save As Draft** to publish the post at a later time.

   - On the **Edit** tab, select **Publish**.

   - At the bottom of the page, select **Publish**.

   > **TIP** If you decide that you no longer want to create a new post, select Cancel on the Edit tab or at the bottom of the page.

To modify a blog post

> ⚠ **IMPORTANT** You can create, modify, or delete a blog post only if you are a member of the blog site.

1. Go to the blog post you want to modify. Then at the bottom of the post, select the ellipsis, and then select **Edit**.

Categories
    Mobile

    News

    OneDrive

    Outlook

    SharePoint Updates

    Visio

    ADD CATEGORY

Archives
    May

    April

Welcome to the WWI's technology blog

Sunday, May 29, 2016

Welcome to the new technology blog! Wide World Importers are continually using technology to gain a competitive advantage over our competitors. We in the IT team, wish to share, on an on-going basis, how the technology will improve the efficiency of the business and keep costs down. Please provide feedback to our posts using the comments section.

by Peter Connelly at 10:14 PM in News

0 comments | Like   Email a link   •••

Edit

Use the ellipsis menu to select the Edit command

2. Modify the post, and then select **Save As Draft** or **Publish**, as described in the previous procedure.

Or

1. Do one of the following to display the default view of the Posts list:

    • On the home page of the blog site, in the **Blog tools** web part, select **Manage posts**.

    • Go to the **Site Contents** page, and select the tile to the left of **Posts**.

2. Do one of the following to activate edit mode:

    • Click or tap to the left of the category, and then on the **Items** tab, in the **Manage** group, select **Edit Item**.

    • Right-click the category, and then on the menu, select **Edit Item**.

3. Modify the post, and then select **Save As Draft** or **Publish**, as described in the previous procedure.

To delete a blog post

> ⚠ **IMPORTANT** You can create, modify, or delete a blog post only if you are a member of the blog site.

1. Do one of the following:

   - Display the default view of the Posts library, as described in the previous procedure, and then do one of the following:

     - Click or tap to the left of the category, and then, on the **Items** tab, in the **Manage** group, select **Delete Item**.

     - Right-click the category, and then, on the menu, select **Delete Item**.

   - Go to the post you want to delete, activate edit mode, and then, on the **Edit** tab, select **Delete Item**.

2. Select **OK** to send the blog post to the Recycle Bin.

> ✅ **TIP** You can delete a blog post when you are modifying it; on the Edit tab, in the Actions group, select Delete Item.

To edit, check the spelling of, or delete your blog post comment

1. Go to the blog post where you created the comment. If the comments are not displayed, select **comment** below the post.

2. Below your comment, select **Edit**.

3. On the **Comments** page, do one of the following:

   - Modify your comment, and then on the **Edit** tab, or at the bottom of the post, select **Save**.

   - On the **Edit** tab, select **Spelling**.

> ✅ **TIP** Select the Spelling arrow (not the button) to check spelling by using a language other than the default language for the site.

   - On the **Edit** tab, select **Delete Item**.

To manage blog post comments

> ⚠ **IMPORTANT** When you are a member of the blog site, use this procedure to manage comments added to any blog post; otherwise, use the "To edit, check the spelling of, or delete your blog post comment" procedure earlier in this topic.

1. On the home page of the blog site, in the **Blog tools** web part, select **Manage comments**, and then do one of the following:

   - Click or tap to the left of the comment and then, on the **Items** tab, in the **Manage** group, select **Edit Item** or **Delete Item**.

   - To the right of the comment, select the **Edit** icon.

2. Modify your comment, and then do one of the following:

   - On the **Edit** tab, or at the bottom of the post, select **Save**.

   - On the **Edit** tab, in the **Actions** group, select **Delete Item**.

   - On the **Edit** tab, select **Spelling**.

To add a comment to a blog post

1. Do one of the following to go to the blog post you want to comment on:

   - If the post is displayed on the home page, go to that page.

   >  **TIP** The 10 most recent blog posts are displayed on the home page.

   - Find the blog post by using the search box.

   - On the Quick Launch, select **Archives**, or one of the links below **Archives**, and locate the blog post in the list.

2. Select the title of the blog post, and below the post, place your cursor in the **Add a comment** box.

   > **TIP** If the Add A Comment box is not displayed, select Comments below the post.

3. Enter your comment, and then select **Post**.

by **Peter Connelly** at 10:14 PM in News
Like   Comment   •••

---

0 comments

There are no comments for this post.

Great to see the team blog, and I look forward to your posts.

Post

Add comments that illustrate what the blogger is saying, or a point the blogger has missed, but always be courteous

To like a blog post

1. Do one of the following to go to the blog post you want to like:

   • If the post is displayed on the home page, go to that page.

   • Find the blog post by using the search box.

   > ⊙ **SEE ALSO** For information about using the search box, see Chapter 5, "Search for information and people."

   • On the Quick Launch, select **Archives**, or one of the links below **Archives**, and locate the blog post in the list.

2. Below the post, select **Like**.

Create and manage community sites

Community sites offer a forum experience to categorize discussions around subject areas and connect users who have expertise or who are seeking information about particular subject areas. This is different from My Sites and Team sites, which are centered on people and their primary work tasks.

Such communities could span your entire organization and could be based on job roles, such as doctors, trainers, firefighters, or project managers; or they could be based on subject areas, such as preschool, publications, or project management. Other communities might be focused on a narrow group of users, especially when the content is strategic or sensitive, or both.

Users can find communities by searching or by using the community portal. A community site is created from the Community Site site template, and can be created as the top-level site of a site collection or as a subsite; the Community Portal is created by using the Community Portal site template, which is only available if you are using the enterprise edition of SharePoint Server; it is a top-level site of a site collection, and there can only be one Community Portal per organization.

> **TIP** Some organizations, particularly if they are using Office 365, might consider using other community apps such as Yammer instead of community sites.

Community Portal

On the home page of a Community Portal, a Content By Search web part displays new communities and tracks community statistics such as creation date, number of members, discussions, and replies. Only sites created from the Community Site template are listed, ordered by the number of posts, replies, and members. Posts have a higher weight than replies and members; therefore, a community with a smaller number of very active users is considered more popular than a larger, less active community. From the Community Portal's home page, you can quickly find more information about a community or follow a community site by displaying a callout, which you can do by selecting the ellipsis to the right of the community site.

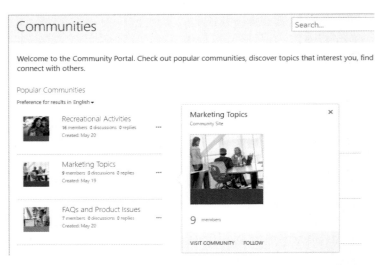

Use the Community Portal to find all the community sites in your organization

Community site pages and web parts

A community site contains four lists—Discussions, Categories, Badges, and Community Members—and four wiki pages, which contain several web parts that might or might not be visible, depending on the permissions of the user. The wiki pages are the following:

- **Home** This page contains the app parts that display the contents of the Discussions and Community Members lists and Community Tools, Join, and What's Happening web parts. Use the Discussions app part on the home page to create new discussions, and use the views to see the recent discussions, your discussions, featured discussions, unanswered and answered questions, and "What's hot," which shows the most active discussions.

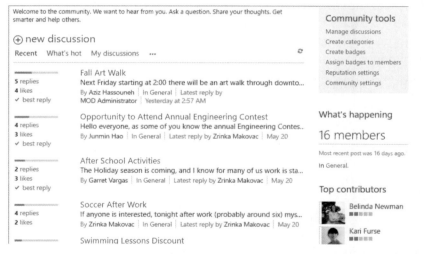

Use the home page to find discussions, see what's happening, and view the top contributors—and if you are a moderator or site owner, manage the community

- **Categories** This page contains the app parts that display the contents of the Categories and Community Members lists and the Community Tools and What's Happening web parts. Use this page to find discussions by selecting a category.

- **Members** This page contains the Community Members app part and the Community Tools, Join, and My Membership web parts. Use this page to find members. You can sort the members list by Top Contributor, New Members, A-Z, or Z-A.

9

- **About** This page displays information about the community and includes the Community Member app part and the Community Tools, Join, What's Happening, and Community Members web parts, and a web part that displays a link to the RSS feed for the site.

> ✓ **TIP** You can customize any of these wiki pages by adding text, images, app parts, or web parts. For information about editing and adding content to wiki pages, see Chapter 7, "Work with webpages." You can also change the look and feel of your community site. For more information about customizing sites, see Chapter 8, "Create and manage sites."

The main community web parts are:

- **About This Community** This web part displays the community description and properties such as the date the community was established.

- **Community Tools** This web part is visible only to community owners and moderators. Use links displayed in this web part to set policies for group membership, set up and manage discussion categories, define the points system for community participation, assign badges, and define how offensive content will be handled. You can also manage community settings by using the links in the Site Setting page, in the Community Administration section.

- **Join** This web part allows non-members to join the community. This web part is not displayed if you are already a user of the members group.

- **My Membership** This web part displays your reputation and membership information.

- **What's Happening** This web part displays the number of members of the community site.

> ✓ **TIP** Community features can be added to any site by activating the Community Site feature; however, sites that are not created from the Community Site site template will not be listed on the Community Portal site. For information about activating site features, see Chapter 8, "Create and manage sites."

Permissions and Auto Approval

Access to and discoverability of community sites are determined by how you con-figure permissions and auto approval. A community site collection comes with four SharePoint groups, and each group is mapped to a different permission level:

- **Community Members** This group is mapped to the Contribute permission level and allows users to start discussions, reply to discussions, earn reputation points, and nominate replies as "best reply." When you want anyone in your organization to be able to contribute to the community, grant membership permissions to everyone. Members have Read access only to the Categories and Members lists.

> **TIP** Only one reply can be marked as a best reply for a discussion.

- **Community Moderators** This group is mapped to the Moderate permission level, which allows users to create and manage discussion categories, monitor and act upon member complaints, assign badges to members, and determine reputation ratings.

- **Community Owners** This group is mapped to the Full Control permission level and allows users to have full control over a community, to create and delete communities, assign permissions, participate in discussions, assign badges to members, and perform moderation tasks.

- **Community Visitors** This group is mapped to the Read permission level and allows users to follow discussions but doesn't allow them to participate in discussions.

If you want everyone in your organization to be able to view the community site, add Everyone to the Community Visitors group; users who want to actively contrib-ute to the community can identify themselves by requesting to join the community. Alternatively, you can prevent view access, but turn on access request at the site level; users can then request access to the community site and you can decide whether to allow them access and which group to add them to.

> **SEE ALSO** For information about access request, see Chapter 8, "Create and manage sites."

9

You can turn on auto approval to provide automatic access to a user who has requested to join, and then later you can explicitly assign the new member to the appropriate community group.

> ✓ **TIP** Community moderators, site owners, and site collection administrators are the only users who can manage community membership.

To create a community site

1. Go to the site where you want to create a new community site as a subsite, and then do one of the following to display the Site Contents page:

   - On the **Settings** menu, select **Site contents**.
   - On the Quick Launch, select **Site contents**.

2. Select **new subsite**.

3. On the **New SharePoint Site** page, in the **Title** box, enter the name of your community.

4. In the **Description** box, enter a brief descriptions of the purpose of the community.

5. In the **URL name** box, enter the site name.

>  **SEE ALSO** For information about naming a URL, see Chapter 8, "Create and manage sites."

6. In the **Template Selection** section, select the **Collaboration** tab if it is not already selected, and then select **Community Site**.

7. Complete the other options as required.

> ⚠ **IMPORTANT** If you want to use the four community SharePoint groups detailed in this topic (Community Members, Community Moderators, Community Owners, and Community Visitors), and your parent site does not contain those groups, select Use Unique Permissions. Otherwise select the option that best suits your needs.

8. Select **Create**.

> 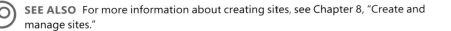 **SEE ALSO** For more information about creating sites, see Chapter 8, "Create and manage sites."

To create a community site discussion category

1. Do one of the following to display the Categories list:

   - On the home page of the community site, in the **Community tools** web part, select **Create categories** to display the Admin View, and then select **new item** or, on the **Items** tab, select **New Item**.

   - From the **Settings** menu, select **Site Settings**, and then under **Community Administration**, select **Community Settings** to display the Admin View, and then select **new item** or, on the **Items** tab, select **New Item**.

   - Go to the **Site Contents** page, select the tile to the left of **Categories** to display the Category Tiles view, and then on the **Items** tab, select **New Item**.

2. In the **Category Name** box, enter the name of the category.

3. Enter a description for the category, and enter the URL and description of a category picture. (This step is optional.)

4. Select **Save**.

To modify or delete a community site discussion category

1. Display the **Categories** list as described in the previous procedure.

2. Do one of the following:

   - Select **edit** to display the list in Quick Edit view, and then modify or delete the categories you want.

   - Click or tap to the left of the category, and then on the **Items** tab, select **Edit Item** and then modify the item, or select **Delete Item**.

   - Right-click the category, and then from the menu, select **Edit Item** and then modify the item, or select **Delete Item**.

> **SEE ALSO** For more information about editing and deleting list items, see Chapter 3, "Work with content in lists and libraries."

To configure community settings

1. Go to your community site, and do one of the following to display the Community Settings page:

   - On the home page, from the **Community tools** web part, select **Community settings**.

9

- From the **Settings** menu, select **Site Settings**, and then under **Community Administration**, select **Community Settings**.

2. In the **Established Date** section, if your community existed before the community site was created, select the date when the community was started.

3. If your community site is the top-level site of a site collection, select the **Auto-approval for permission requests** check box to allow new members to join without administrator or moderator approval.

4. In the **Reporting of offensive content** section, select the **Enable reporting of offensive content** check box if you want community members to report abusive content to administrators and moderators.

Use the Community Settings page to select the date the community was created, allow users to join the community without approval from site owners and moderators, and turn on reporting of offensive content

5. Select **OK**.

To manage reported content

> ⚠️ **IMPORTANT** This procedure is only valid when the Reporting Of Offensive Content option is turned on. Members cannot see reported content; only members of the Moderators or Owners group will be able to see reported content by using this procedure.

1. Go to your community site, and do one of the following:

- On the home page, from the **Community tools** web part, select **Review Reported Posts**.

- From the **Settings** menu, select **Site Settings**, and then under **Community Administration**, select **Manage Reported Posts**.

2. Click or tap to the left of the discussion, and then, on the **Moderation** tab, do one of the following:

   - Select **Review Reports** to review reported content along with comments left by the members who found it offensive.

   - Select **Edit Post** to edit the contents of the item.

   > **TIP** The number of times this item has been reported cannot be modified.

   - Select **Delete Post**, and then select **OK** to confirm deletion, if you consider the item inappropriate. This will also delete any reports and comments.

   > **TIP** The deleted post is moved to the Recycle Bin.

   - Select **Dismiss Report**, and then select **OK** to approve the discussion item. All associated reports will be deleted.

Select a post, and then use the commands on the Moderation tab to manage the post

To add users to groups

> 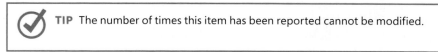 **IMPORTANT** The four community SharePoint groups (Community Members, Community Moderators, Community Owners, and Community Visitors) are only created and assign the different permission levels detailed in this topic if your community site uses unique permissions, is created as a top-level site of a site collection, or is a subsite inheriting from a site in which the community groups were created.

1. From the **Settings** menu, select **Site settings**, and then under **Users and Permissions**, select **People and groups**.

2. On the Quick Launch, select **More**, and then select the group to which you want to add users.

3. Select **New**, and then add the people you want to add. Select **Share**.

> (search icon) **SEE ALSO** For information about managing permissions on sites, see Chapter 8, "Create and manage sites."

To configure or modify the reputation settings

1. Go to your community site, and do one of the following:

   - On the home page, from the **Community tools** web part, select **Reputation Settings**.

   - From the **Settings** menu, select **Site Settings**, and then under **Community Administration**, select **Reputation Settings**.

2. In the **Rating settings** section, do one of the following:

   - Select **Yes** to allow members to apply ratings to discussions and replies, and then select either **Likes** (to turn on like/unlike rating) or **Star Ratings** (to allow users to vote by assigning one to five stars).

   - Select **No** to prevent members from rating content.

Rating settings	Allow items in this list to be rated?	
Specify whether or not items in this list can be rated.	⦿ Yes	○ No
When you enable ratings, two fields are added to the content types available for this list and a rating control is added to the default view of the list or library. You can choose either "Likes" or "Star Ratings" as the way content is rated.	Which voting/rating experience you would like to enable for this list?	
	⦿ Likes	○ Star Ratings

Use the Rating Setting section to specify whether posts can be rated or not

3. In the **Member achievements point system** section, select **Enable member achievements point system** to award points for community participation, and then enter the number of points to reward members.

Member achievements point system		
Within the community you can allow members to collect points based on their participations.	☑ Enable member achievements point system	
	Specify the point values for the following activities	
	Creating a new post	10
	Replying to a post	10
	Member's post or reply gets liked or receives a rating of 4 or 5 stars	10
	Member's reply gets marked as 'Best Reply'	100

Use the Member Achievements Point System section to turn on member achievements and to specify the point values for tasks

4. In the **Achievement level points** section, enter the number of points members must acquire to be promoted to each level.

Achievement level points			
As members accumulate points, they can reach specific levels as milestones of achievement. Specify the number of points required for members to reach each achievement level.	Specify achievement levels		
	Level 1	More than	0
	Level 2	More than	100
	Level 3	More than	500
	Level 4	More than	2500
	Level 5	More than	10000

Use this section to specify the number of accumulated points a member has to reach for each achievement level

5. In the **Achievement level representation** section, do one of the following:

- Select **Display achievement level as an image**.
- Select **Display achievement level as text**, and enter text for levels 1 to 5.

Achievement level representation		
Specify whether achievement levels are represented as a series of boxes or as a textual title. You can customize the title for each level.	● Display achievement level as image ■■■■■ ○ Display achievement level as text Specify a title for each level	
	Level 1	Level 1
	Level 2	Level 2
	Level 3	Level 3
	Level 4	Level 4
	Level 5	Level 5

Use this section to specify whether the achievement levels are to be displayed as a series of boxes or as a textual title

6. Select **OK**.

To create a badge

1. Go to your community site, and then, from the **Community tools** web part, select **Create badges**.

2. Select **new item** or, on the **Items** tab, select **New Item**.

3. Enter a name for the badge, and then select **Save**.

To edit or delete a badge

1. Go to your community site, and then from the **Community tools** web part, select **Create badges**.

   - Select **edit** to display the list in Quick Edit view, and then modify or delete badges.

   - Click or tap to the left of the badge, and then on the **Items** tab, select **Edit Item** and then modify the badge, or select **Delete Item**.

   - Right-click the badge, and then from the menu, select **Edit Item** and then modify the badge, or select **Delete Item**.

> **SEE ALSO** For more information about editing and deleting list items, see Chapter 3, "Work with content in lists and libraries."

To assign a badge

1. Go to your community site, and do one of the following:

   - On the home page, from the **Community tools** web part, select **Assign badges to members**.

   - Go to your community site, and on the **Settings** menu, select **Site Settings**. Under **Community Administration**, select **Manage Members** to display the Admin View.

2. Click or tap to the left of the member to whom you want to award the badge.

3. On the **Moderation** tab, select **Give Badge**, and then select a badge from the list.

4. Select **Save**. The badge will be displayed beneath the member's name on all discussions and replies and in any web parts, such as Top Contributors, in which the member is listed.

To monitor community members

1. Go to your community site, and on the **Settings** menu, select **Site Settings**.

2. Under **Community Administration**, select **Manage Members** to display the Admin View.

3. Use the other views—**Members View**, **New Members**, **Top Contributors**, and **Single Member View**—to display information on members and their ongoing activity.

To mark or unmark a discussion as featured

1. Go to your community site and do one of the following:

    - On the home page, from the **Community tools** web part, select **Manage discussions**.

    - Go to your community site, and on the **Settings** menu, select **Site Settings**. Under **Community Administration**, select **Manage Discussions**.

2. Click or tap to the left of the discussion, and then on the **Moderation** tab, select **Mark as Featured**, or **Unmark as featured**.

Work with community sites

You can use a community site to meet with like-minded people to share and discuss topics of common interest; you can discover content by using categories, sorting by popularity, or viewing those posts that have a best reply. If you are a member of a community, you can start discussions and reply to them, like posts, and specify best replies for those discussions you created. The more you contribute, the higher your reputation in the community, because your contributions earn reputation points. At times, you might be recognized as a valued contributor, and you might be "gifted" a badge by the community site owners or moderators.

Open communities provide automatic membership to all users in an organization; other community sites might be configured to require you to join. Depending on the configuration of the community site, your request to join might be approved automatically or might have to go through an approval process.

To join a community site

1. Go to the community site you want to join, and on the right side of the page, select **Join this community**.

To view membership information

1. On the Quick Launch, select **Members**. On the right side of the page, the **My membership** web part displays information about your community participation, such as when you joined, your reputation, and the number of discussions you have posted.

To leave a community

1. Go to the community site you want to leave, and on the Quick Launch, select **Members**.

2. On the right side of the page, at the bottom of the **My membership** web part, select **Leave this community**.

To add a discussion

1. On the community site's home page, select **new discussion**.

2. In the **Subject** box, enter the discussion title.

3. In the **Body** box, enter the contents of your discussion, using the commands on the **Format Text** tab and the **Insert** tab to format the content and to insert tables, pictures, videos, audio, links, and embedded code.

4. Select the **Question** check box if you want other members of the community to answer to your post.

5. Select a category from the **Category** list, and then select **Save**.

To review discussions by category

1. On the Quick Launch of the community site, select **Categories** to display the category tile view.

2. Select the views, **A-Z**, **Z-A**, **What's hot**, and **Recent**, to review the categories.

3. Select the tile of the category you are interested in, to list the posts in that category.

> **TIP** The discussions can be sorted by using the Recent, What's Hot, and My Discussions views, and if you select the ellipsis, by Unanswered Questions, Answered Questions, and Featured views.

4. Select the discussion title to display the discussion content and replies.

To edit, check the spelling of, or delete your discussion

1. Do one of the following to go to the discussion:

   - Go to the community site's home page or the categories page, and select **My discussions** to find your discussion.

- In the search box, enter a keyword or keywords to find your discussion.

2. Select the title of the discussion.

3. At the bottom of the discussion, select the ellipsis to display the discussion menu, and do one of the following:

   - Select **Edit**, make your changes, and then, on the **Edit** tab or at the bottom of the post, select **Save**.

   > **TIP** If, while modifying the discussion, you then decide you want to delete the discussion, on the Edit tab, in the Actions group, select Delete Item.

   - Select **Delete**.

Use the discussion menu to edit or delete discussions, create alerts, mark a discussion as featured, report a discussion to the moderator, or display information about a discussion that has been reported for offensive content

Or

On the **Edit** tab, select **Spelling** to check the spelling of your discussion.

> **TIP** You can select the Spelling arrow (not the button) to check spelling by using a language other than the default language for the site.

To reply to a discussion

1. Go to the discussion you want to reply to by using the home page, the category page, or the search box, and then selecting the title of the discussion.

2. At the bottom of the discussion, select **Reply**.

9

3. Enter your reply, and then select **Reply**.

 TIP You can reply to the discussion or to any replies that other community members have added.

To assign or unassign a reply as a best reply

 IMPORTANT Only the author of the discussion or a moderator can mark a reply as a best reply.

1. Go to the discussion and find the reply you want to work with.

2. Select the ellipsis, and then select either **Best reply** or **Remove best reply**.

Peter Connelly
great question

May 29   Like   Reply   •••

Jack Creasey
some text

May 29   Like   Reply

Edit

Best reply

Delete

Report to moderator

Add a reply

Use the reply menu to edit or delete a reply, select the reply as a best reply, report the reply to the moderator, or display information about a reply that has been reported to the moderator

To delete a reply

 IMPORTANT Only the author of the reply or a moderator can delete a reply.

1. Go to the discussion and find the reply you want to delete.

2. Select the ellipsis, and then select **Delete**.

To rate a discussion

 IMPORTANT This procedure will work only if the community owner has turned on discussion rating.

1. At the bottom of the discussion that you want to rate, do one of the following (the available option depends on how the community owner has configured the community site):

   - Select **Like**.

   - Select one to five stars.

To monitor featured discussions

1. On the community site's home page, in the **Discussions List** web part, select the ellipsis, and then select **Featured**.

2. Select the discussion title to review the item.

To monitor answered or unanswered discussions

1. On the community site's home page, in the **Discussions List** web part, select the ellipsis, and then select **Answered questions** or **Unanswered questions**.

2. Select the discussion title to review the item.

To track discussions

1. At the bottom of the discussion you want to track, select the ellipsis. and then select **Alert me**.

2. Complete the options as required, and then select **OK**.

Skills review

In this chapter, you learned how to:

- Create wiki libraries

- Create and use Enterprise Wiki sites

- Create and manage blog sites

- Create, manage, and delete blog posts

- Create and manage community sites

- Work with community sites

9

Practice tasks

The practice file for these tasks is located in the SP2016SBS\Ch09 folder.

> ⚠️ **IMPORTANT** You must have sufficient permissions to perform the operations involved in each practice task to complete that practice task. For more information, see Appendix A, "SharePoint 2016 user permissions and permission levels."

Create wiki libraries

Go to your SharePoint team site and perform the following tasks:

1. Create a wiki page library named **WWI Company History**, and then go to the home page of the wiki page library.

2. Create a **Category** column with five choices: **1876-1911**, **1912-1946**, **1947-1979**, **1980-2001**, **2002-Present**.

3. Edit the properties of the wiki page library's home page, and categorize it as **2002-Present**.

4. Edit the home page, deleting all the content, and then enter **The history of Wide World Importers** and format it by using the **Heading 1** style.

5. On a separate line, add the **WWI Company History** app part to the home page.

6. Save and keep editing the page.

7. Configure the **WWI Company History** app part to display wiki pages, grouped by category. In the app part, do not display the **Modified By**, **Modified**, **Created By**, and **Created** columns; and display the wiki pages, sorted by their name.

> ### The history of Wide World Importers
> WWI Company History
> ⊕ New   ⬆ Upload   ⟳ Share
>
> ✓   ⬜   Name
>
> ▲ **Category : (1)**
>   📄 How To Use This Library ✿   •••
>
> ▲ **Category : 2002-Present** (1)
>   📄 Home ✿   •••

Configure the Category app part to display wiki pages to suit your needs

8. Leave your browser open if you are continuing to the next set of practice tasks.

Create and use Enterprise Wiki sites

Go to a SharePoint publishing site where you have sufficient rights to create an Enterprise Wiki site as a subsite, and then perform the following tasks:

1. Create an Enterprise Wiki site named **SharePoint Guidelines**, with the following description: **This site explains how Wide World Importers are using SharePoint 2016 and provides guidelines on how to use SharePoint. It also contains a knowledge base where you can find answers to frequently asked questions, who to contact, and their roles and responsibilities.** Use a URL of **WWI-Guidelines**.

2. Select a term set for the **Wiki Categories**, selecting one of the terms as the default category.

3. Categorize the home page of the Enterprise Wiki site as one of the terms.

4. Stop editing the page, and leave your browser open if you are continuing to the next set of practice tasks.

Create and manage blog sites

Go to a SharePoint site where you have sufficient rights to create a blog site as a subsite, and then perform the following tasks:

1. Create a blog site with the title **IT team blog** and a URL of **IT-Blog**.

2. Leave your browser open if you are continuing to the next set of practice tasks.

Create, manage, and delete blog posts

Go to the blog site you created in the previous set of practice tasks, and then perform the following tasks:

1. Remove the categories that were created when the site was created, and add the following new categories: **Mobile, News, OneDrive, Outlook, SharePoint, Updates,** and **Visio.**

2. Delete the **Welcome to my blog** post.

3. Create and publish a new blog post titled, **Welcome to the WWI's technology blog** with a body of **Welcome to the new technology blog! Wide World Importers are continually using technology to gain a competitive advantage**

over our competitors. We in the IT team wish to share, on an on-going basis, how the technology will improve the efficiency of the business and keep costs down. Please provide feedback to our posts using the comments section. Categorize the post as **News**.

4. Add the following comment to your blog post: **Great to see the team blog, and I look forward to your posts.**

5. Delete the comment.

6. Leave your browser open if you are continuing to the next set of practice tasks.

Create and manage community sites

Go to a site where you have sufficient rights to create a community site as a subsite, and then perform the following tasks:

1. Create a community site with the title **WWI Furniture Product Ideas & Questions** and a URL name of **Furniture-Products**.

2. Modify the reputation settings so that members achieve **5** points for creating a new post, and the achievement level 1 is represented as **Beginner**.

3. By using the **Site Contents** page, go to the **Sites Assets** library and upload the **Sale.jpg** file from the practice file folder.

4. Get the image's web address by selecting the ellipsis to the right of the image file to display the callout, and then right-clicking the URL and selecting **Copy**.

5. Create a new category named **Sales**, with a description of **Sales ideas and questions**, and use the image's web address as the category picture.

6. Leave your browser open if you are continuing to the next set of practice tasks.

Work with community sites

Go to a site where you are a community member, and then perform the following tasks:

1. Create a new discussion with **Eco recommended retail prices** as the subject, and body text of **When will WWI's recommended retail price list be available for the Eco furniture line?**, identified as a question and categorized as **Sales**.

2. Reply to the discussion, and then mark the reply as a best reply.

Manage work tasks

SharePoint Server 2016 provides a lightweight project management system, where tasks and subtasks are stored in task lists and can be managed with Microsoft Project or Outlook, and you can keep them in sync. Microsoft Project Server extends the capabilities of Project and gives organizations a central location to store project information.

This chapter guides you through procedures related to creating and managing project sites; working with tasks, subtasks, and the timeline; and managing projects by using SharePoint and Project Professional.

In this chapter

- Create and manage project sites

- Work with tasks, subtasks, and the timeline

- Manage projects by using SharePoint and Project Professional

Practice files

No practice files are necessary to complete the practice tasks in this chapter.

Create and manage project sites

There are two types of project sites: ones that you can create by using the Project Site site template, and ones that you can create if your organization is using Project Server 2016, known as the Project Web App (PWA) site. Both can be used in conjunction with Project Professional 2016 to build and manage projects.

SharePoint 2016 project sites

When you create a project site, in addition to a document library and a site assets library, two other lists are created—Tasks (with a timeline) and Calendar—and the Project Summary web part is added to the home page.

Use the Project Summary web part on the project site home page to identify late and upcoming tasks

You can use the Project Summary web part to quickly monitor your projects' health. It contains two sections:

- On the left side, project tasks are displayed by the number of days left until the task's due date. When the task list contains no task items, the text "Get organized. Edit the task list" is displayed; when you select Edit, the task list is displayed in Quick Edit view.

- On the right side, you can display either the timeline or the upcoming tasks pane, where tasks are displayed in the order of their due date. You use the arrows in the upper-right corner to switch between the two.

You can also use the Project Summary web part to add tasks to the list and edit the list. When you add a Project Summary web part to a site that does not contain a task list, the web part displays a link that you can select to create a task list.

Many teams and projects do not initially create project sites, but use team sites and then later find that they need the extra project-related components on their site. Of course, you could manually create a task app, and then a calendar app, and then add the Project Summary web part to your home page; however, the easier way to add these components to any site is by activating a site feature.

> **TIP** A site created from the Project Site site template automatically activates the Project Functionality site feature.

A disadvantage of using a project site is that, unlike a team site, a project site does not use wiki pages, and the project site's home page is a web part page saved in the root of the website; therefore, you need to be a site owner to modify the page. A project site home page contains three web part zones: Top, Left, and Right.

> **SEE ALSO** For information about creating task and calendar lists, see Chapter 3, "Work with content in lists and libraries."

You might see other components on your project site, depending on the installation of other Microsoft server products in your organization:

- When SharePoint is bound to Microsoft Office Online Server 2016, a Microsoft OneNote notebook is created, allowing your team members to quickly capture and organize information about the project.

- If SharePoint is connected to Microsoft Exchange Server 2016, a project site can include a site mailbox for unified communication about the project as it progresses.

- If a project site in a site collection is associated with Project Server 2016, the Tasks list can be added to the Project Web App site.

> **SEE ALSO** For information about using OneNote and Outlook with SharePoint, see Chapter 12, "Collaborate with Office programs by using SharePoint."

10

To create a project site

1. Go to the site where you want to create the new project site as a subsite.

2. To display the Site Contents page, do one of the following:

   - From the **Settings** menu, select **Site Contents**.

   - On the Quick Launch, select **Site Contents**.

3. Scroll to the bottom of the **Site Contents** page, and then under **Subsites**, select **new subsite**.

4. On the **New SharePoint Site** page, in the **Title** box, enter the name of the site, and in the **URL name** box, enter the website address.

   > (Q) **SEE ALSO** For information about naming a URL, see Chapter 8 "Create and manage sites."

5. Select the **Collaboration** tab, if it is not already active, and then select **Project Site**.

6. Select **Create**.

   > ✓ **TIP** If the Collaboration tab is not displayed, or the Project Site site template is not displayed on the Collaboration tab, check to make sure that you are creating the subsite in a site collection where the usage of the Project Site site template is allowed. For information about creating sites, see Chapter 8, "Create and manage sites."

To add project features to a team site

1. Sign on to the team site as a site owner, and then do one of the following:

   - If the site displays the **Get Started With Your Site** web part, select **Working on a deadline?**

Use the tile on the Get Started With Your Site web part to activate the project functionality features

In the **Working on a deadline?** dialog, select **Add Them**.

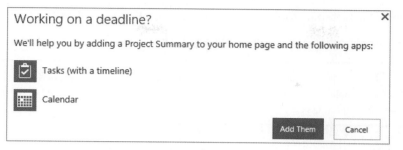

Use this dialog to quickly add a task list and calendar list to your site, and add the Project Summary web part to your site's home page

 TIP If the project functionality has previously been installed, a dialog that allows you to add another task or calendar list opens

- On the **Settings** menu, select **Site settings** to display the Site Settings page, and then under **Site Actions**, select **Manage site features**. Then, on the **Site Features** page, to the right of the **Project Functionality** site feature, select **Activate**. You might need to scroll down the page.

To add a Project Summary web part to a page

1. On the page where you want to add the web part, activate edit mode and then do one of the following to open the Web Parts pane:

   - On a wiki page or publishing page, place the cursor where you want the web part to be displayed, and then on the **Insert** tab, in the **Parts** group, select **Web Part**.

   - On a web part page, in the zone where you want to add the web part, select **Add a Web Part**.

2. Under **Categories**, select **Content Rollup**, and then under **Parts**, select **Project Summary**.

3. Select **Add**.

 TIP If the current site does not have any task lists, the web part will display the text, "Click to create a new task list."

To modify the properties of a Project Summary web part

1. Open the web part tool pane as described in Chapter 7, "Work with webpages."

2. In the properties pane, under **Primary Task List**, select one of the site's task lists.

> **TIP** The primary task list is used for the due date countdown and items on the timeline. Tasks that are included on the timeline are not included in the list of late and upcoming tasks.

Configure the Project Summary web part properties so that you can quickly monitor your projects

3. Under **Headlines**, if you want to display a timeline, select the **Timeline** check box.

> **SEE ALSO** For information about how to format the timeline and add items to it, see the "Format the timeline" section later in this chapter.

4. If you want to display tasks items that are not completed that have a due date prior to the current date, select the **late** check box, and then optionally complete the following:

    a. To the right of **late**, select **edit** to display the Lists To Include In Late Panel dialog.

    b. Select one or more task lists, and then select **OK**.

Lists to Include in Late Panel ✕

Select which lists you would like to include in the Late panel. Unfinished items from the selected lists that are due prior to the current date will appear in this panel.

☐ IFC16 Tasks
☑ Tasks - *Primary Task List*

| OK | Cancel |

Use this dialog to select task lists whose late items you want to include in the Late panel

5. If you want to display those items that are due today or later in the Upcoming panel, select the **upcoming** check box, and then optionally do the following:

   a. To the right of **upcoming**, select **edit** to display the Lists To Include In Upcoming Panel dialog.

   b. Select one or more calendar and task lists.

   c. Enter the number of upcoming days (the default is 14), and then select **OK**.

Lists to Include in Upcoming Panel ✕

Select which lists you would like to include in the Upcoming panel. Items from the selected lists that are due today or later will appear in this panel.

☑ Calendar
☐ IFC16 Tasks
☑ Tasks - *Primary Task List*
Show items for the following number of upcoming days: 14

| OK | Cancel |

In the Upcoming panel, you can display calendar items and task items that are due in the upcoming days

6. Modify other web part properties as needed, and then, at the bottom of the properties pane, select **OK**. Save the page.

> ⊘ **SEE ALSO** For information about webpages and adding web parts to them, see Chapter 7, "Work with webpages."

Project Server 2016 Project Sites

Project Server 2016 is the Microsoft on-premises solution for project portfolio management (PPM) and includes demand management features that organizations can use to manage work from inception until work is completed.

10

> **TIP** Project Server 2016, unlike previous versions of Project Server, does not need to be installed separately from SharePoint Server 2016; it is installed with SharePoint Server 2016 Enterprise, although it is licensed separately. After you have installed SharePoint Server 2016 Enterprise, you can configure Project Server 2016. For more information about planning, installing, configuring, operating, and managing Project Server 2016, see *https://aka.ms/Ypuma1*.

The main browser-based interface to Project Server is the Project Web App site, which you can use to manage one or more projects. A Project Web App site can be created as the top level of a new site collection, or you can add a Project Web App site as a subsite to an existing site collection.

> **TIP** Only one Project Web App site can be created per site collection.

However, unlike with past versions, there are no webpages that you can use to create a Project Web App site, either as the top-level site of a site collection or as a subsite, or to activate the Project Web App site collection features. Your SharePoint Server administrator will need to use Windows PowerShell to make Project Server capabilities available.

Project Web App sites have all the features of the SharePoint Project Site discussed previously. A task list in a Project Web App is very similar to the task list in SharePoint—you can add tasks, subtasks, and the timeline by using the same methods. However, Project Web App sites offer much greater scheduling capabilities.

Before you create and manage any projects, you will need to configure the Project Web App site, by using the PWA Settings page and the visual tiles on the Project Web App's home page. You will need to create project-related components, such as Cost Codes, Departments, and Resources.

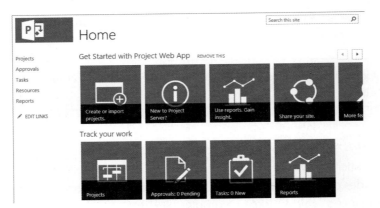

Use the tiles on a newly created Project Web App site to get started and to track your work

On the Quick Launch of a newly created Project Web App site, there are links to five pages:

- **Projects** Known as the Project Center, this page is used to view the overall project schedule and lists all project sites. Depending on your permissions, you can use this page to create new projects, open projects, check in and check out projects, manage project timelines, and view a project's Gantt view.

- **Approvals** Known as the Approval Center, this page is the central location for timesheets and task status.

- **Tasks** Known as the Task Center, this page is used to view and manage all assigned tasks across all projects that are published in a Project Web App site.

- **Resources** Known as the Resource Center, this page is used to manage people, materials, or costs that are required to complete a project.

- **Reports** Known as the Reports Center, this page provides several predefined reports, such as Deliverables, IssuesAndRisks, and MilestonesDueThisMonth.

> 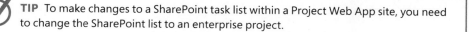 **TIP** There are no links on the Quick Launch of a Project Web App site for the Site Contents page or the Recycle Bin. To display the Site Contents page, from the Settings menu, select Site Contents. The Site Contents page includes a link to the Recycle Bin.

Your Project Web App site might have many more links on its Quick Launch, such as Timesheet, Strategy, Issues And Risks, and Server Settings. You can make more links available by displaying the Quick Launch page from the PWA Settings page.

Projects that can be managed with a Project Web App site can come from a variety of sources, including:

- Microsoft Project Professional project plans (.mmp files).
- SharePoint task lists.
- Projects created directly in Project Web App.

SharePoint task lists can be included as read-only in the Project Center, so that you can track these tasks in reports generated through the Project Web App site, and users can update their tasks on SharePoint sites. When you use this approach, you can also take SharePoint tasks into consideration when you review a resource's workload.

> **TIP** To make changes to a SharePoint task list within a Project Web App site, you need to change the SharePoint list to an enterprise project.

10

> ⚠ **IMPORTANT** Full coverage of Project Server 2016 is beyond the scope of this book. For more information, see *https://products.office.com/project*, *https://blogs.technet.microsoft.com/projectsupport*, *https://social.technet.microsoft.com /Forums/projectserver/*, and *https://blogs.office.com/product/project*.

To administer a Project Web App site

1. On the **Settings** menu for the Project Web App site you want to manage, select **PWA Settings**.

Work with tasks, subtasks, and the timeline

You can use the task management capabilities within a SharePoint task list to create tasks, which can have child tasks known as subtasks. Tasks and subtasks can be added to a timeline view, thereby providing a visualization of important tasks. You can also add the Timeline web part to a page, to display a timeline view of task items from a task list from any site within any site collection.

> ⚠ **IMPORTANT** In SharePoint Server 2013, the tasks view on your personal site provided a central location where you could manage your tasks, whether they were assigned to you in SharePoint, Outlook, or Project Server. This is not available in SharePoint Server 2016 or in Office 365, because the ability to create the Work Management service application and the ability to synchronize with Exchange and Project Server have been removed. However, if you are using one of the Office 365 Enterprise E1–E5, Business Essentials, Premium, or Education subscription plans, you might consider using Microsoft Planner. You can use Planner to create new plans; organize, assign, and collaborate on tasks; set due dates; update statuses; and share files; while visual dashboards and email notifications keep everyone informed on progress. For more information about Microsoft Planner, see *https://products.office.com/business/office-365-planner*.

Manage tasks and subtasks

The easiest and quickest way to create a project plan is to use Quick Edit. You can also paste a list of tasks from a Microsoft Excel spreadsheet. As you work with your list of tasks and subtasks, those with due dates listed in red are late. After you mark a late task as complete by selecting the check box to the left of the task, the due date no longer appears as red text.

	✓	Task Name		Due Date	Assigned To

⊕ new task or edit this list

All Tasks   Calendar   Completed   ⋯   Find an item 🔍   SAVE THIS VIEW

	✓	☑	Task Name		Due Date	Assigned To
		☐	Define project scope ⚹	⋯	Monday	☐ Peter Connelly
		☐	Create draft project plan ⚹	⋯	5 days from now	☐ Peter Connelly
		☐	⊿ **Kickoff activity** ⚹	⋯	June 17	☐ Peter Connelly
		☐	Book meeting room ⚹	⋯	Tomorrow	☐ Peter Connelly
		☑	~~Identify attendees~~ ⚹	⋯	Saturday	☐ Peter Connelly
		☐	Create agenda ⚹	⋯	Today	☐ Peter Connelly

Use the task list as a lightweight project management tool

After you add tasks to your list, you might want to change the way they are structured. You can indent or outdent a task to indicate a subtask, or a subtask of a subtask; move a task or subtask up or down in the list, or permanently delete a task or subtask from the list.

When you create a task list, several views are created that allow you to manage tasks. These views are All Tasks, Calendar, Completed, Gantt Chart, Late Tasks, My Tasks, and Upcoming. You can amend these views and create new views.

> 🔍 **SEE ALSO** For information about creating and editing items in a task list and views, see Chapter 3, "Work with content in lists and libraries."

To create a subtask

1. Select the ellipses to the right of the task item that you want to use as the parent task, and then, in the callout that opens, select **Create Subtask**.

Use the callout to display information about a task item, such as the task item's due date, a link to the task item, and task-related commands

To indent or outdent tasks

1. Click or tap to the left of one or more task items, ensuring that you are not selecting the check boxes that are displayed to the left of the items, and then do one of the following:

   - On the **Tasks** tab, in the **Hierarchy** group, select **Indent** or **Outdent**. The new position of the task item is displayed, and the list is displayed in Quick Edit mode.

Use the commands in the Hierarchy group of the Tasks tab to modify the structure of your project

   - If the task list is in Quick Edit, press **Alt+Shift+Right Arrow** to indent the tasks, or **Alt+Shift+Left Arrow** to outdent the tasks.

To move a task up or down in the task list

1. Click or tap to the left of an item or items, ensuring that you are not selecting the check box that is displayed to the left of the items, and then do one of the following:

   - On the **Tasks** tab, in the **Hierarchy** group, select **Move Up** or **Move Down** to move the item within the list.

   - If the task list is in Quick Edit, press **Alt+Shift+Up Arrow** to move the task up in the list, or press **Alt+Shift+Down Arrow** to move the task down in the list.

Format the timeline

On the timeline, tasks or subtasks without a start date, or those that have a start date but no due date, appear as diamonds. In Gantt charts, a diamond is traditionally used to indicate a project milestone, which is a major event in the project, and can be used to monitor the project's progress. Therefore, for most tasks, you could add a start date and a due date, and then add tasks with a due date but no start date, to identify milestones in your project.

> ✓ **TIP** On the timeline, when you select a task with no start date (that is, one that is currently displayed as a diamond) and then select Display As Bar on the Timeline tab, the Define Project Scope dialog is opened. You can then enter a Start Date to display the task as a bar.

A task with a start date and a due date can appear as a bar in the timeline that spans those dates, or you can choose to display it as a callout above the timeline. Using callouts is particularly useful when you have created subtasks in your task list as a way to communicate project phases, or for tasks that have several subtasks. Each task could be displayed as a callout, and subtasks as bars.

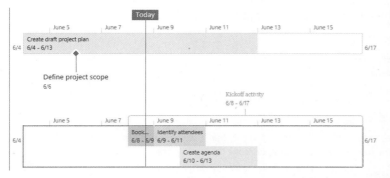

Format the timeline so you and your team can quickly track important project tasks

You can have more than one timeline, allowing you to group similar tasks. Each timeline includes dates across the top to mark the timescale, task dates, and a marker indicating today's date. You can include the overall project start and finish dates, or choose to hide any of the default date indicators. You can also select the format for the task start dates and due dates.

After you have added tasks to the timeline and dragged them to arrange them in an order that represents your project, you can lock the timeline width so others can see the timeline the way you want them to. When the timeline width is not locked, the width will vary based on the size of the user's browser window.

To add a task or subtask to a timeline

1. On the task list that contains the task or subtask, do one of the following:

   - Click to the left of the task or subtask that you want to add to the timeline, and then, on the **Tasks** tab, in the **Actions** group, select **Add to Timeline**.

   - To the right of the task or subtask, select the ellipsis to open the callout, and then select **Add to Timeline**.

To remove a task or subtask from a timeline

1. In the timeline, select the task or subtask bar, diamond, or callout, and then do one of the following:

   - On the callout, select **Remove from Timeline**.

   - On the **Timeline** tab, in the **Current Selection** group, select **Remove from Timeline**.

To display a task as a callout on a timeline

1. In the timeline, select the task or subtask bar.

2. On the **Timeline** tab, in the **Current Selection** group, select **Display as Callout**.

Use the commands in the Current Selection group of the Timeline tab to remove a task from the timeline, display the task as a bar or callout, or move the task to different timeline bars

To configure the display of dates on a timeline

1. Select the title of the timeline, and then, on the **Timeline** tab, in the **Show/Hide** group, select the check boxes of any of the following:

   - **Task Dates** Select this check box to display the start date and due date for each task within the task's bar or next to the task's diamond.

   - **Today** Select this check box to display an indicator on the timeline for the current date.

   - **Start & Finish** Select this check box to display a start date at the beginning of the timeline, and a finish date at the end of the timeline. These dates relate to the earliest task start date and the latest task due date.

   - **Timescale** Select this check box to display markers at dated intervals across the top of the timeline.

To configure the date format for bars and diamonds

1. Select the title of the timeline, and then, on the **Timeline** tab, in the **Show\Hide** group, select **Date Format**.

2. From the menu, select a date format.

Use the Date Format menu to select a date format for the bars and diamonds on a timeline

To configure a timeline to only show a specific date range

1. Select the title of the timeline, and then, on the **Timeline** tab, in the **Show\Hide** group, select **Set Date Range**.

2. In the **Set Timeline Dates** dialog, select **Set custom dates**, and then select a start and finish date.

Use the Set Timeline dialog to restrict the tasks displayed on the timeline to a specific date range

3. Select **OK**.

To change the color used to fill the background of a timeline

1. In the timeline, select a space that does not represent a task or subtask.

2. On the **Timeline** tab, select **Highlight Color**, and then select a color from the picker.

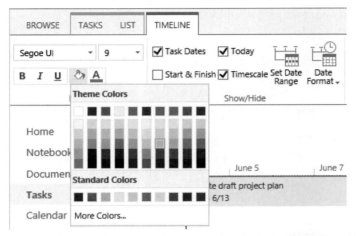

Use the Highlight Color picker to fill the background of a time bar and a task bar

To change the font of a timeline

1. Select the timeline, and then, on the **Timeline** tab, in the **Font** group, use the tools to change the font face, size, format, and color.

> **TIP** Changing the font for the timeline affects all timeline bars and is only visible when you have selected the Start & Finish check box.

To add a timeline bar to a timeline

1. Select the timeline, and then, on the **Timeline** tab, in the **Timeline Bar** group, select **Add**.

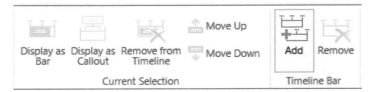

Use the Add and Remove commands in the Timeline Bar group to add or remove additional timeline bars

> **TIP** You can have up to 10 timeline bars on a timeline.

To move a task between timeline bars within a timeline

1. In the timeline that contains the task you want to move, select the task's bar, callout, or diamond.

2. On the **Timeline** tab, in the **Current Selection** group, select either the **Move Up** or **Move Down** command.

> **TIP** When you select a task in the topmost timeline bar and then select Move Up, the task moves to the last displayed timeline bar. Similarly, when you select a task in the bottom timeline bar and then select Move Down, the task moves to the topmost timeline bar.

To remove a timeline bar from a timeline

1. Select the timeline bar you want to remove, and then, on the **Timeline** tab, in the **Timeline Bar** group, select **Remove**.

> **TIP** There must be at least one timeline bar on a timeline; therefore, you cannot remove the last timeline bar on a timeline.

To change the font of a task bar or callout

1. In the timeline, select the task bar or callout.

2. On the **Timeline** tab, in the **Font** group, change the font, size, format, and color.

To change the color used to fill in a task bar or line surrounding a callout

1. In the timeline, select the task bar or callout.

2. On the **Timeline** tab, in the **Font** group, select **Highlight Color**, and then select a color.

> **TIP** The color used to fill a diamond is also used for the line drawn between the diamond and the task name.

To lock the timeline width

1. Select the timeline, and then on the **Timeline** tab, in the **Actions** group, select **Lock Timeline Width**.

10

To turn the timeline view on or off for a task list

1. Go to the task list for which you want to turn the timeline view on or off, and activate edit mode.

2. Open the **Task** web part tool pane, as described in Chapter 7, "Work with webpages."

3. Under **List Views**, select or clear the **Show timeline** check box.

Use the web part tool pane to configure the display of the timeline on the task list view

> ✅ **TIP** When the web part tool pane is displayed, the timeline within the web part is not displayed, regardless of whether the check box is selected. Only when the page is saved will your changes take effect.

4. At the bottom of the web part tool pane, select **OK**, and then save the page.

To add and configure a Timeline web part

1. On the page where you want to add the web part, activate edit mode, and place the cursor where you want the web part to be displayed.

2. On the **Insert** tab, in the **Parts** group, select **Web Part** to open the web part pane.

3. Under **Categories**, select **Content Rollup**, and then under **Parts**, select **Timeline**.

4. Select **Add**, and then open the web part tool pane for the web part.

5. Under **Data Source**, in the **Web URL** box, enter the name of the website that contains the task list you want to display on the timeline, and then select **Verify URL** to ensure that you have entered a valid web address. The page will refresh, and the text *Valid URL* is displayed above Verify URL. If you get any other message, repeat the previous step, checking the URL you provided.

6. In the **Source** list, select the task list whose items you want to display on the timeline.

Use the Timeline web part tool pane to configure the web part to display the task items from a specific task list, either from the same site or from another site

7. Change other web part properties as needed, and then at the bottom of the web part tool pane, select **OK**.

Manage projects by using SharePoint and Project Professional

Like many other Office applications, Project Professional 2016 includes a set of templates that you can use to jump start the creation of a project plan. It provides a grid similar to an Excel worksheet, which allows for quick management of tasks, measurement of progress, and resource allocation. It also includes reports that adhere to industry guidelines; however, many people find Project Professional complicated to use. By synchronizing tasks between SharePoint and Project, project managers who understand Project can use it to manage their projects, and project members can use content in SharePoint task lists, making this approach a lightweight project management tool for tracking and managing tasks.

There are two methods of synchronizing your tasks between SharePoint and Project, both of which are available with SharePoint Server 2013, SharePoint Server 2016, and SharePoint Online through Project Professional 2013, Project Professional 2016, and Project for Office 365:

- You can create a task list in SharePoint and then import those task items to a new Project plan.
- You can create the project plan in Project and then create a new SharePoint site that contains a project summary and timeline, a task list, and a calendar. Synchronizing also saves the .mpp file to the site assets for future editing.

> **IMPORTANT** The person synchronizing the tasks must be part of the SharePoint Owners group, or at the least have designer permissions, on the existing site or parent site where the new subsite is to be created.

With a synchronized task list, site members can view, add, edit, and report the status of their tasks. You can even view your tasks list in other views, including calendar and Gantt Chart view.

SharePoint does not provide active scheduling; however, when a SharePoint task list is synchronized with Project, you can then edit the task list within Project by using the Project feature set and scheduling capabilities. You would then resynchronize the task list to SharePoint, so the rest of your team can see the results.

> **SEE ALSO** Full coverage of Project Professional 2016 is beyond the scope of this book. For more information about Project Professional 2016, see *Microsoft Project 2016 Step By Step* by Carl Chatfield and Timothy Johnson (Microsoft Press, 2016).

To sync a project plan to a new SharePoint site by using Project Professional

1. Open your project by using Project Professional, select the **File** tab on the ribbon, and then select **Save As**.

2. In the **Save and Sync** list, select **Sync with SharePoint** to display the Sync With SharePoint Tasks List pane.

Use the Sync With SharePoint Tasks List pane to sync with a new SharePoint site or an existing one

3. In the **Sync with** list, select **New SharePoint Site** if it is not already selected, and then, in the **Project name** box, enter a name for the project.

4. In the **Site Address** list, enter or select the address of the SharePoint site where you want to create the new SharePoint site as a subsite.

5. Select **Save**.

   A Sync With Tasks Lists dialog box opens, displaying the site creation and the progress of the task synchronization process. Your project plan is saved in the new site's site assets library.

   > ✓ **TIP** You might have to provide a user name and password before your new SharePoint site can be created. Also, when your project plan contains resources (people) that do not exist in SharePoint, a Microsoft Project dialog box opens, reminding you that these users will remain assigned to the tasks in your project plan.

To sync a SharePoint task list with a Project Professional project plan

1. In Project Professional, open a project plan, select the **File** tab on the ribbon, and then select **Save As**.

2. In the **Save and Sync** list, select **Sync with SharePoint** to display the Sync With SharePoint Tasks List pane.

3. In the **Sync with** list, select **Existing SharePoint Site**.

4. In the **Site Address** list, enter the address of the SharePoint site that contains the task list whose items you want to import.

5. Select **Verify Site** to populate the Tasks List list.

> **TIP** You might have to provide a user name and password before the Task List can be populated.

6. In the **Tasks List** list, select the name of the task list you want to link to your project plan.

7. Select **Save**.

8. If you synced the SharePoint task list to a different project plan file, a Microsoft Project dialog box opens. Select **OK**.

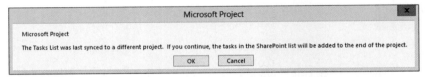

Select OK to add the tasks in the SharePoint list to the end of the project

A Sync With Tasks Lists dialog box opens, displaying the site creation and the progress of the task synchronization process.

> **IMPORTANT** Your project plan is saved in the site's site assets library, with the name <site name> - <task list name>.mpp. If the site assets library already contains a file by that name, the file will be overwritten, with no warning message. However, the site assets library is configured for major versions; therefore, you will be able to restore the previous version of the project plan, if necessary.

To sync a task list from a SharePoint site to Project Professional project plan

1. In your browser, go to the task list you want to sync.

2. On the **List** tab, in the **Connect & Export** group, select **Open with Project**.

Use the commands in the Connect & Export group on the List tab to sync a task list with Project, connect a task list to Outlook, analyze items in a list by using Excel, and work with a list in Access

> **TIP** You might have to provide a user name and password before your Task list will open in Project Professional.

A notification appears, stating that new tasks were created in Manually Scheduled mode (this is also known as "User-Controlled Scheduling").

3. Make your changes in Project, and then select **File** to display the Info page.

4. Select **Save** to save and sync your project.

> **TIP** The project plan will be saved to the site's site assets library by using the <site name> - <task list name>.mpp naming convention.

To find information about a synchronized project plan

1. With the project plan opened in Project Professional, select **File** to display the Info page, and review the information displayed below **Save and Sync Your Project**.

Info

Customer Service-Tasks

http://intranet.wideworldimporters.com » project » Customer Service » SiteAssets

Save

Save and Sync Your Project
Last saved: 08/06/16 19:29
SharePoint site: http://intranet.wideworldimporters.com/
project/Customer Service

Synced with tasks list: Tasks

Map Fields

Manage Accounts

Project Web App Accounts
You're not connected to Project Web App

Project Information

Start Date	Today
Finish Date	12/09/2016
Schedule from	Start
Current Date	Today
Status Date	Today
Project Calendar	Standard
Priority	500

10

Use the links in the Save And Sync Your Project section to find out when the project plan was last saved and the SharePoint site it was saved to, and to modify the Project fields that will be synced with the corresponding SharePoint task list columns

> **TIP** You can use the link in the Save And Sync Your Project section to open the SharePoint site in the browser.

Skills review

In this chapter, you learned how to:

- Create and manage project sites
- Work with tasks, subtasks, and the timeline
- Manage projects with SharePoint and Project Professional

Chapter 10

Practice tasks

No practice files are necessary to complete the practice tasks in this chapter.

> ⚠️ **IMPORTANT** You must have sufficient permissions to perform the operations involved in each practice task to complete that practice task. For more information, see Appendix A, "SharePoint 2016 user permissions and permission levels."

Create and manage project sites

Go to your SharePoint team site and perform the following tasks:

1. Create a project site named **International Furniture Convention 2016**, with the description **Use this site to coordinate activities to ensure WWI takes advantage of being a lead sponsor at IFC 2016** and a URL of **IFC16**.

2. Change the properties of the **Project Summary** web part so that it displays upcoming tasks for the next seven days.

3. Leave your browser open if you are continuing to the next set of practice tasks.

Work with tasks, subtasks, and the timeline

Go to the project site you created in the previous set of practice tasks, and then perform the following tasks:

1. Add three task items, assigned to you, with the following values:

Task name	Start date	Due date
Define project scope	No date	Today – 2 days
Create draft project plan	Today's date	Today + 5 days
Kickoff activity	Today's date	Today + 10 days

2. The first task should be automatically added to the timeline. Add the other two task items to the timeline, and configure the kickoff activity as a callout.

3. Create the following three items as subtasks to the kickoff activity task item.

Task name	Start date	Due date
Book meeting room	Today's date	Tomorrow's date
Identify attendees	Tomorrow's date	Today + 3 days
Create agenda	Today + 2 days	Today + 5 days

4. Add the three subtasks to the timeline, and fill the three bars with different colors.

5. Leave your browser open if you are continuing to the next set of practice tasks.

Manage projects with SharePoint and Project Professional

Start Project Professional, and then perform the following tasks:

1. Create a project plan based on the Customer Service online template.

> **TIP** Use the Search For Online Templates box on the New page, and enter the *Customer* keyword to find the template.

Project Professional comes with several project templates that you can use as a starting point for your project plan; however, there are a vast number of project templates that you can use online

2. Sync with the task list on the site you created in the first practice task, and then save. Wait while SharePoint and Project are updated.

3. From the **New** page of Project, open your SharePoint site in your browser and verify the following:

   - Tasks from the project plan are displayed in the task list and on the timeline.

   - The project plan was uploaded to the site assets library.

4. Go to the task list, open it with Project, and review the task items—for example, in the Gantt Chart view.

Work with workflows

You can use SharePoint to help you complete business tasks. SharePoint comes with several built-in human-centric workflow templates that you can associate with lists and libraries and that work well with approval decisions. Site owners can easily create workflows from these templates with little or no training. This means that success in automating business processes depends not on the technology but on the site owner's knowledge of the tasks and the people needed to complete the business process.

This chapter guides you through procedures related to using built-in workflows, interacting with workflows, and managing workflows. You will learn the fundamental elements of a workflow and what workflow templates are provided by default in SharePoint Server 2016. You will use your browser to learn how to create, delete, and modify workflows, and how to track the status of workflows that are currently running. You will also learn how to associate workflow templates with content types.

In this chapter

- Automate business processes by using SharePoint
- Use built-in workflows
- Interact with workflows
- Manage workflows

Practice files

No practice files are necessary to complete the practice tasks in this chapter.

Automate business processes by using SharePoint

Automating frequently run or time-consuming business processes allows you to make efficient use of your time and the time of your team. When you adopt SharePoint in your organization, the initial productivity boom can become a management burden as more content is added to the SharePoint installation and the amount of work required to maintain the content increases. By creating SharePoint workflows, you can remove some of this burden by automating parts or all of your old and new business processes.

Previous chapters introduced you to how SharePoint can help you complete your work with the use of the following:

- **RSS Feeds** You use these to find information from a variety of sources on an ad-hoc basis.

- **Alerts** You use these for regular notifications of new, modified, or deleted content.

- **Content approval** Along with versioning, this allows you to manage content and who can see content that is classified as draft.

However, none of these three methods allows you to automate business processes beyond a one-step process. You could combine these methods—for example, by using content approval with alerts to provide a lightweight workflow that sends you emails when your team members change a document, thereby approving documents to a specific timescale. However, such a solution can help with only a few of your business processes.

Imagine that you want to ask multiple people their opinion of a document or a webpage before publishing it. SharePoint provides two other methods to help automate such a process:

- **Workflows** Used to automate and track processes that require human intervention, such as notifying users when their action is required to move the process forward. Such processes could take days, weeks, or months to complete and might need to wait for an event or another process to complete. SharePoint provides several methods of creating workflows, some with just the use of your browser, and others that require an additional tool, such as Microsoft SharePoint Designer or Visual Studio.

- **Event Receivers** Used to automate processes that require no human intervention, such as moving job applications from one document library to a series of other document libraries for some purpose. These are also known as machine-centric workflows. Event receivers can only be created by a developer using Visual Studio.

Workflows and event receivers cannot automate a task unless someone takes the time to define exactly how the task should be automated, nor can they track the status of information stored on paper documents. They also cannot force users to perform a particular task. You must have a clear understanding of how the business process operates. If you do not understand how to complete a business process manually, you will not be able to describe the business process in sufficient detail to automate that process.

Therefore, you need to complete some planning and startup tasks to automate a process. To ensure that you can achieve the productivity improvement you want, you must understand what SharePoint has to offer. You don't necessarily want to automate every little process in your organization; you want to automate processes that are predictable, those where the startup cost of creating a workflow is offset by the benefit of reengineering the process. You must also ensure that your team is happy with the new process that the automated process will provide.

> **TIP** Professional developers and information workers can use SharePoint Designer and Microsoft InfoPath to build lightweight business applications. InfoPath 2013 and SharePoint Designer 2013 are the last versions of these products. Microsoft will continue to support custom workflows built with SharePoint Designer and hosted on SharePoint Server 2016 and SharePoint Online. InfoPath 2013 and SharePoint Designer 2013 match the support life cycle for SharePoint Server 2016, which extends until 2026. SharePoint Designer is a free product available at *https://www.microsoft.com/en-us/download/details.aspx?id=35491*.

11

Use built-in workflows

You can use SharePoint Server 2016 and SharePoint Online to run two types of workflows:

- **SharePoint 2010 workflows** These are the same as you might have used in SharePoint 2010 and use a workflow engine internal to SharePoint.

- **SharePoint 2013 workflows** These use a highly scalable workflow framework that is implemented by a piece of software called the Workflow Manager. The Workflow Manager is installed separately to SharePoint 2016 by your server administrators.

You can build either type of workflow by using SharePoint Designer 2013, Visual Studio, or a third-party tool. Also, in the same way that you base a new site, list, or library on a template, you can use your browser to create a new workflow based on a workflow template.

Activate workflow templates

SharePoint Server 2016, like SharePoint Server 2013 and SharePoint Online, includes several built-in SharePoint 2010 workflow templates designed for file or list management tasks; these are known as list workflow templates. There are no built-in site workflow templates or SharePoint 2013 workflow templates.

No special software is needed to create workflows by using these workflow templates. You only need a browser. A workflow template is a very good starting point in getting SharePoint to help with business processes that you might currently complete manually. If these templates do not meet your needs or you want to create SharePoint 2013 workflows, you must use either SharePoint Designer 2013, Visual Studio, or a third-party tool.

A SharePoint 2010 list workflow template can be created for a specific content type or for any content type. The templates can be associated not only with lists and libraries but also with content types.

SharePoint Server 2016 contains the following SharePoint 2010 workflow templates:

- **Three-state** Used to track items or files.

- **Approval – SharePoint 2010** Routes a document for approval. Approvers can approve or reject the document, reassign the approval task, or request changes to the document.

- **Collect Feedback – SharePoint 2010** Routes a document for review. Reviewers can provide feedback, which is compiled and sent to the person who initiated the workflow when the workflow has completed.

- **Collect Signatures – SharePoint 2010** Gathers signatures needed to complete a Microsoft Office document.

- **Publishing Approval** A variant of the Approval workflow template associated with the Pages library on publishing sites; used to approve the publishing of pages.

- **Disposition Approval** Used to manage document expiration and retention by allowing participants to decide whether to retain or delete expired documents.

- **Group Approval** A variant of the Approval workflow template; available only in East Asian versions of SharePoint Server.

- **Translation Management** Used to translate documents. This earlier workflow template was first introduced in Microsoft Office SharePoint Server 2007 and is still available in SharePoint Server 2016 when your SharePoint server administrators activate it by using Windows PowerShell. More information on the Translation Management workflow can be found at *office.microsoft.com /en-us/sharepoint-server-help/use-a-translation-management-workflow-HA010154430.aspx*.

> **SEE ALSO** For more information about SharePoint Server 2010 workflows, see the Microsoft TechNet article at *https://technet.microsoft.com/en-us/library /cc263134.aspx*; for information about content type and workflow planning, see the article at *https://technet.microsoft.com/en-us/library/cc262735.aspx*.

Most of the built-in workflow templates are for approval workflows. You can use these workflow templates, for example, to approve vacation requests, change requests, or expenses. Before creating a workflow, you need a list or library where your team members can detail their vacations, change requests, or expenses. For a vacation approval process, the team leader could create a list based on the calendar list template and then associate the *Approval – SharePoint 2010* workflow template with the list. As members of your team create items in this list to represent vacation requests, the items progress through the vacation request approval process.

For example, assume that there are four people who need to submit their vacation requests. The first person, Peter, has submitted his vacation request, it has completed the approval process, and it has a status of *Workflow completed*. A second person, Bill,

11

and a third person, Todd, have submitted their vacation requests, each of which has a status of *Pending*. Each vacation request has its own instance of the workflow that progresses the item through the approval process. Bill's vacation request is waiting for the department manager, whereas Todd's vacation request is waiting for the team leader. A fourth person, Jeff, is still completing his vacation request, and therefore there is no workflow instance associated with it.

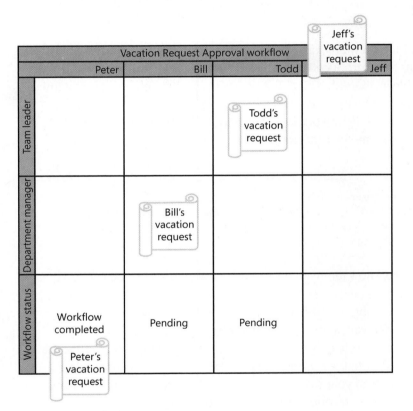

An approval workflow

Workflow site collection features

When your site collection administrator activates features at the site collection level, workflow templates are made available to all sites in that site collection. For example, the *Workflows* site collection feature must be activated if you want to use any of the workflow templates that have *SharePoint 2010* appended to their name. These three workflow templates are also known as reusable workflows because they can be modified by using SharePoint Designer 2013. They also contain a Microsoft Visio visualization of the workflow.

Not all of the workflow-related site collection features are activated on each site collection; therefore, if you want to use one of the built-in workflow templates, your site collection administrator might need to activate a feature. The following table lists the five workflow-related site collection features and their status on publishing and collaboration sites.

Site collection feature	Publishing sites	Collaboration sites
Disposition Approval workflow	Active	Active
Publishing Approval workflow	Active	Deactivated
SharePoint 2007 workflows	Deactivated	Deactivated
Three-state workflow	Deactivated	Active
Workflows	Active	Deactivated

11

SEE ALSO For more information about features, see Chapter 8, "Create and manage sites."

TIP The SharePoint Server 2007 workflow templates are available only on sites that were upgraded from SharePoint Server 2007 to SharePoint Server 2010, then upgraded to SharePoint Server 2013, and then upgraded to SharePoint Server 2016.

To activate a workflow site collection feature

1. Sign on as a site collection administrator and navigate to the top-level site of the site collection.

2. On the **Settings** menu, click **Site settings** to display the Site Settings page.

3. Under **Site Collection Administration**, click **Site collection features**.

```
Site Collection Administration
Recycle bin
Search Result Sources
Search Result Types
Search Query Rules
Search Schema
Search Settings
Search Configuration Import
Search Configuration Export
Site collection features
Site hierarchy
Site collection navigation
Search engine optimization settings
```

Use the Site Collection Administration section to manage components, such as workflow-related site collection features

4. On the **Site Collection Features** page, to the right of the site collection feature you want to use, click **Activate**. You might need to scroll down the page.

Three-state workflow		Activate
Use this workflow to track items in a list.		
Video and Rich Media		Activate
Provides libraries, content types, and web parts for storing, managing, and viewing rich media assets, like images, sound clips, and videos.		
Workflows		Activate
Aggregated set of out-of-box workflow features provided by SharePoint.		

Features, including workflows, are listed alphabetically on the Site Collection Features page

Add a workflow

To create a SharePoint workflow, you first need to identify the people who will fulfil the following roles:

- **Workflow creator** A business analyst or someone with SharePoint experience who knows the business process and creates the workflow or workflow template by using a workflow application, such as SharePoint Designer 2013.

- **Workflow editor** A business analyst or someone with SharePoint experience who knows the business process and creates a workflow by adding a workflow template to a list, library, or content type. To add a workflow template to a list or library, the workflow editor must be mapped to the *Manage Lists* permission. To add a workflow template to a content type, the workflow editor must be a member of the *Site Owners* SharePoint group.

- **Workflow initiator** A user who starts an instance of the workflow on a document or list item. The user must be mapped to the *Edit Item* permission on the list or library.

- **Workflow participant** A user who is assigned tasks in the workflow. Workflow participants must have at least *View Item* permission to the list item or document that they are asked to review, and *Edit Item* permission to the Workflow Task list.

The availability of a workflow within a site varies, depending on where it is added:

- When a workflow template is added directly to a list or library, only those list items or files in that list or library are processed by the workflow.

- When a workflow template is added to a list content type, only items or files of that content type are processed by the workflow.

- When a workflow template is added to a site content type, that workflow is available for any items or files of that content type in every list and library where an instance of that site content type was added. To make a workflow available across many lists or libraries in a site collection for items of a specific content type, add that workflow template directly to a site content type at the top site of the site collection.

- To make a workflow process list items and files across multiple lists and libraries in a site, use a site workflow.

11

When you create a workflow, you need to provide a name, the workflow task and history lists, and how the workflow is to start. You can specify these options on the Add A Workflow page, also known as the *association form* or *page*.

Some workflow templates, such as the Approval - SharePoint 2010 workflow template, require additional information, such as the names of the approvers, whether the approvers are to be contacted sequentially or in parallel, and the content of the email to be sent to the approvers. These additional options are displayed on the second association page when you click Next on the Add A Workflow page.

Workflow name

When you create a workflow, you must give it a name. This will be the name of the column that contains the workflow status. When a list or library workflow is created from a workflow template, the workflow name must not match any of the list's column names. When you create a workflow in SharePoint Designer, the workflow name must be unique across the whole site.

Select the workflow template and type a workflow name

Workflow task and history lists

With human-centric workflows, there must be a mechanism for interacting with users. This is achieved by using emails, task items, and information stored in the workflow history list. You should create a new task list for each workflow you create. This will be essential when you have many documents or list items progressing through the workflow. Each workflow should also have its own workflow history list.

You do not have to create a new task list or a new history list prior to creating the workflow. When you create the workflow, on the Add A Workflow page, you can choose to create a new task list or history list, or both.

Task List		
Select the name of the task list to use with this workflow, or create a new one.	Select a task list: Tasks (new) ▾	Description: A new task list will be created for this workflow.
History List		
Select the name of the history list to use with this workflow, or create a new one.	Select a history list: Workflow History (new) ▾	Description: This workflow will use a new history list.

Select an existing task list and history list, or choose to create new task and history lists

When a task list and a history list do not already exist for the site, the task list will be named *Tasks*, and the history list will be named *History*. Otherwise, the name of the new task list will take the format of *workflow name* Tasks, as in *Vacation Request Approval Tasks*.

The workflow history list is a hidden list and is not shown on the Site Contents webpage. You can display this list in your browser by appending /lists /*<workflow history list name>*/ to your site's Uniform Resource Locator (URL); for example, *wideworldimporters/lists/workflow history*.

> **TIP** By default, SharePoint removes all task items and history list items associated with completed workflows that are more than 60 days old. This is done for performance reasons. Therefore, you cannot rely on items in either of these lists for auditing purposes. You could export the contents of these lists periodically to Microsoft Excel and create reports to analyze the workflow process. For a more complex archiving solution, see the "Archiving Your SharePoint Workflow History Lists" blog post at *whitepages.unlimitedviz.com/2011/09 /archiving-your-sharepoint-workflow-history-lists*.

11

Start options

Workflows can be started manually or automatically. Manually starting a workflow allows you to run the workflow when needed; additionally, each time you manually start the workflow, you can change some of the workflow settings. The advantage of automatically starting an instance of the workflow is that no one has to remember to manually start the workflow. An instance of the workflow is created every time a start option event is triggered.

When you create a workflow by using the Approval – SharePoint 2010 workflow template, the following start options are available:

- **Manually** Users must have the Edit Items permission to manually start an instance of the workflow on the list item or file. You can restrict the ability to manually start workflows to those users who have the Manage Lists permission.

- **Automatically** You can have the workflow automatically start at any of these events:

  - When a list item or file is created.

  - When a list item or file is changed.

  - When a major version of an item or file is published. When you choose this option, an instance of the workflow is not automatically started when a minor version of a file is saved; therefore, to use this option, you must configure the library with major and minor versioning enabled. See Chapter 4, "Make lists and libraries work for you," for more information on how to configure a library to use major and minor versions.

Not all SharePoint workflows have these same start options. For example, the Three-state workflow template can create workflows that use the first two types of start options. You select the start option when you create the workflow—that is, when you add a workflow template to a list, library, or content type.

Complete the configuration

To complete the configuration of a new workflow, you might have to enter additional information on a second association page. This allows you to customize the work-flow to meet your business needs. For example, for the approval workflow templates, you can configure multiple approvers and whether the approvers are involved in the process one at a time (serial) or at the same time (parallel). You can have one or multiple stages of approval tasks, where the approvers for each stage can be assigned in series or in parallel. When you have multiple stages, the stages are performed sequentially.

> **SEE ALSO** For more information about SharePoint 2010 approval workflows, see *support.office.com/en-US/article/ All-about-Approval-workflows-078C5A89-821F-44A9-9530-40BB34F9F742.*

To add a workflow to a list or library

1. On the **List** or **Library** tab, in the **Settings** group, click the **Workflow Settings** arrow (not the button), and then click **Add a Workflow** to display the Add A Workflow page.

   > **TIP** The name of the tab depends on the type of list or library you are working with. For example, in a Calendar list, the tab is named Calendar.

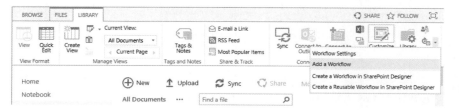

On the Workflow Settings menu, click Add a Workflow

2. On the **Add a Workflow** page, select a workflow template, and then in the **Name** box, enter a new name for this workflow.

   > **TIP** If the workflow template you want to use doesn't appear in the list, check that the relevant feature is activated at the site collection level. Alternatively, the workflow template might be associated with a specific content type. If this is the case, see the "To add a workflow that is associated with a content type" procedure later in this topic.

11

3. In the **Select a task list** list, do one of the following:

   - Select **Tasks (new)** if the site does not contain a task list.

   - Select **New task list** to create a new task list.

   - Select a task list if one has already been created.

4. In the **Select a history list** list, do one of the following:

   - Select **Workflow History (new)** if no workflow history list exists for the site.

   - Select **New history list** to create a new history list.

   - Select a previously created history list.

5. In the **Start Options** section, select one or more check boxes to specify how the workflow can be started.

On the Add A Workflow page, select one or more Start Options

6. If the workflow has a second association page, click **Next** to display the second association page, which you can complete as needed; otherwise, click **Save**.

To add a workflow that is associated with a content type

1. On the **List** or **Library** tab, in the **Settings** group, do one of the following to display the Workflow Settings page:

   - Click **Workflow Settings**.

   - Click **List Settings** (on the **List** tab) or **Library Settings** (on the **Library** tab) to display the List Settings or Library Settings page, and then, in the **Permissions and Management** section, click **Workflow Settings**.

2. On the **Workflow Settings** page, in the **Show workflow associations of this type** list, do one of the following:

   - Select **This List** to add a workflow template associated with any content type.

   - Select a specific content type to add a workflow for that content type.

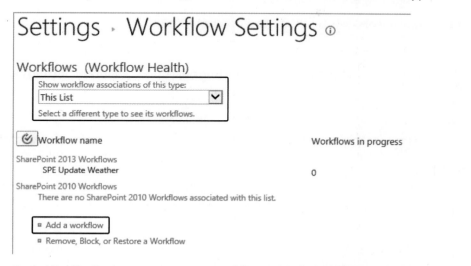

Settings ▸ Workflow Settings ⓘ

Workflows (Workflow Health)

Show workflow associations of this type:

| This List ▾ |

Select a different type to see its workflows.

☑ Workflow name	Workflows in progress
SharePoint 2013 Workflows	
SPE Update Weather	0
SharePoint 2010 Workflows	
There are no SharePoint 2010 Workflows associated with this list.	

▫ Add a workflow
▫ Remove, Block, or Restore a Workflow

On the Workflow Settings page, you can see workflow associations and add a workflow

3. Click **Add a workflow** to display the Add A Workflow page.

4. On the **Add a Workflow** page, complete your selections as described in the previous procedure.

To associate a workflow template to a site content type

1. On the **Settings** menu, click **Site settings** to display the Site Settings page.

2. In the **Web Designer Galleries** section, click **Site Content Types**.

3. Click the content type with which you want to associate the workflow, to display the Site Content Type page.

> ✓ **TIP** When a content type is inherited from a parent site, the name of the content type is not a link to the Site Content Type page. Click the hyperlink in the Source column to display the Site Content Type page of the parent site, and then click the link for the content type.

11

4. In the **Settings** section, click **Workflow settings**.

5. Click **Add a workflow** to display the Add A Workflow page.

6. On the **Add a Workflow** page, complete your selections as described in the previous procedure.

To associate a workflow template to a list content type

1. Open the list or library where the content type was previously added.

2. On the **List** or **Library** tab, in the **Settings** group, click **Library Settings** to display the Settings page.

3. In the **Content Types** area, click the name of the content type.

 TIP If the Content Types section is not displayed, click Advanced Settings, and then select Allow Management Of Content Types.

4. Click **Workflow settings**, and then click **Add a workflow** to display the Add A Workflow page.

5. On the **Add a Workflow** page, complete your selections as described in the previous procedure.

To complete the second association page

⚠ **IMPORTANT** The second association page differs depending on the workflow template you have chosen. This procedure is an example that uses the Approval - SharePoint 2010 workflow template. The options you see might be different depending on the workflow template you are using.

1. In the **Approvers** section, do the following:

 TIP This is the only section you need to complete.

   a. In the **Assign To** text box, enter the name of one or more approvers or groups, separated by semicolons, and then to the right of the text box, click the **Check Names** icon.

   b. In the **Order** list, select either **One at a time (serial)** or **All at once (parallel)**.

c. Click **Add a new stage** if you require more than one assignment stage.

Settings · Change a Workflow · Expenses Approval ⓘ

Approvers	Assign To		Order
	Peter Connelly; Todd Rowe	👤 📇	One at a time (serial) ▾

☐ Add a new stage
Enter the names of the people to whom the workflow will assign tasks, and choose the order in which those tasks are assigned. Separate them with semicolons. You can also add stages to assign tasks to more people in different orders.

Enter the approvers to the workflow

2. Optionally, do any of the following:

- In the **Expand Group** section, if a group is specified in the Approvers section, do one of the following:

  - If you want each member of the group to be assigned a task, leave the check box selected.

  - If you want to assign one task to the entire group, clear the check box. An email is sent to each member of the group, and any member can claim and complete the single task.

- In the **Request** text box, enter the text you want approvers to see in the email and task items.

Expand Groups	☑ For each group entered, assign a task to every individual member and to each group that it contains.
Request	Please review the expenses file.
	This message will be sent to the people assigned tasks.

Select Expand Group and enter text in the Request section

- In the **Due Date for All Tasks** section, select a single date by which all tasks are due.

> **TIP** When you have chosen to start workflow instances automatically, you should not specify a date in this section, because this is a static date and is not relative to the start date and time of the workflow instance. A due date will override the task duration.

11

- In the **Duration Per Task** section, enter the duration allowed to complete each task.

- In the **Duration Units** section, select **Day(s)**, **Week(s)**, or **Month(s)**.

Due Date for All Tasks	
	The date by which all tasks are due.
Duration Per Task	2
	The amount of time until a task is due. Choose the units by using the Duration Units.
Duration Units	Day(s)
	Define the units of time used by the Duration Per Task.

Select the duration for the tasks

- In the **CC** text box, enter the name of the person who should receive an email each time an instance of this workflow is started or completed.

- In the **End On** sections, select either or both of the check boxes for ending the workflow:

  - On first rejection

  - If the document changes

- In the Enable Content Approval section, select the **Update the approval status after the workflow is completed** check box when you have configured the list to use content approval.

CC	Erin M. Hagens
	Notify these people when the workflow starts and ends without assigning tasks to them.
End on First Rejection	☑ Automatically reject the document if it is rejected by any participant.
End on Document Change	☑ Automatically reject the document if it is changed before the workflow is completed.
Enable Content Approval	☐ Update the approval status after the workflow is completed (use this workflow to control content approval).
Save	Cancel

Select carbon copy, workflow termination, and content approval options

3. Click **Save**.

Interact with workflows

After a workflow has been created, an instance of the workflow can be started that sends a list item or file through the process. While the instance of the workflow is running, it will send emails and assign tasks that need to be completed. You can monitor progress, make adjustments, and terminate the instance of the workflow when needed by using the workflow status page.

Start, monitor, and terminate workflow instances

Depending on the configuration of your workflow, you can start a workflow instance either by starting the workflow manually or by uploading, modifying, or creating a new item or document.

When you start a workflow manually, a page known as the initiation page might be displayed. On this page, you can modify how your file or list item is processed by the workflow. Any changes you make to the initiation page apply only to how the workflow processes that list item or file. It does not affect how other list items or files are processed.

> ⚠ **IMPORTANT** A workflow cannot be started on an item or file that is checked out, nor can a workflow be started on an item or file when the workflow is already in a pending state for that item or file. For example, assume that two workflows—Expenses Approval and Vacation Requests—are created on a list that has four items. Each item can have an instance of the Expense Approval workflow and the Vacation Request workflow running, making a total of eight workflow instances. However, you cannot start two instances of the Expense Approval workflow on the same item.

11

The workflow status of the item or file is displayed in a list column, which is automatically added to the default view of the list or library when the workflow is created. You can use this lookup column to display the workflow status page.

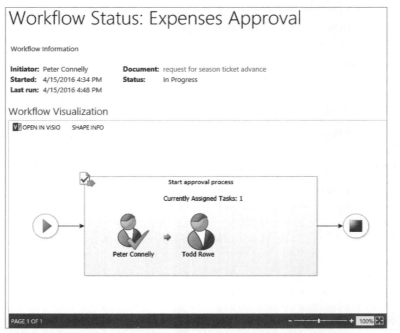

Workflow Status: Expenses Approval

Workflow Information

Initiator: Peter Connelly   **Document:** request for season ticket advance
Started: 4/15/2016 4:34 PM   **Status:**   In Progress
Last run: 4/15/2016 4:48 PM

Workflow Visualization

OPEN IN VISIO   SHAPE INFO

Start approval process

Currently Assigned Tasks: 1

Peter Connelly   Todd Rowe

PAGE 1 OF 1   100%

Find the status of the workflow on the Workflow Status page

You can use the workflow status page to:

- Find information about this instance of the workflow, such as who initiated the workflow and when it was started.

- Open the file or list item being processed by the workflow.

- Monitor the progress of the item or file through the workflow by using the Task section and Workflow History section; for example, to find who is holding up the completion of the workflow.

- Make adjustments to the instance of the workflow. For example, for an Approval – SharePoint 2010 workflow, you can:

  - Add or update approvers.

  - Cancel all approval tasks.

  - Update active tasks.

- End the workflow instance.

On the workflow status page, you might see a Visio visualization of the workflow. When you are using the Approval – SharePoint 2010 workflow, the Visio diagram displays an image of a person for each person involved in the approval process. A right-pointing arrow between the person images indicates a serial approval process, whereas a dot indicates a parallel approval process.

> ⚠ **IMPORTANT** A person image with a green check mark indicates that the person has completed his or her task. It does not indicate how the person completed that task. The outcome of the task can be found in the Tasks section of the workflow status page or in the task list associated with the workflow.

A Visio representation of the workflow is available only when all of the following are true:

- You are using a reusable workflow—that is, a workflow created by using one of the workflow templates with *SharePoint 2010* appended to its name or a workflow that was created by using SharePoint Designer 2013.

- You are using the Enterprise edition of SharePoint Server or, in SharePoint Online, you are using the Enterprise (E3 and E5) plans or SharePoint Online Plan 2.

- The SharePoint Server administrator has configured Visio Services.

- The SharePoint Server Enterprise feature is activated at the site collection and site levels.

> 🔍 **SEE ALSO** For more information about SharePoint features in Office 365, see *https://technet.microsoft.com/en-GB/library/jj819267.aspx#bkmk_tableo365*.

You can also use the workflow status page to terminate the workflow instance when an item or file no longer needs to be processed by the workflow, thereby avoiding having people waste time completing unnecessary tasks.

> ✓ **TIP** When you are using a publishing approval workflow on a publishing site, you can use the Publish tool tab to manually start, monitor, and cancel workflow instances.

11

To manually start a workflow instance on a list or library

1. Display the list or library that contains the list item or file for which you want to start the workflow instance.

2. Do one of the following:

   - To select the list item or file, click the area to the left of the list item or file for which you want to start a workflow, and then on the **Items** or **Files** tab, in the **Workflows** group, click **Workflows**.

To manually start a workflow, on the Files tab, click Workflows

   - Right-click the item's name, click **Advanced**, and then click **Workflows**.

✓	📄	Name			Modified	Modified By
✓	📄	request for season ticket advance ⚹	•••		About a minute ago	☐ Peter Connelly

Open in Excel
Download
View in Browser
Share
Rename
Delete
Copy
Version History
Properties
Advanced ▶

Shared With
Compliance Details
Check Out
Follow
Workflows

On the List Item menu, click Workflows

3. On the **Start a New Workflow** page, in the **Start a New Workflow** area, click the workflow that you want to run.

Choose a workflow to start

4. On the **Change a Workflow** page, on the initiation form, make any changes that you want to apply to this specific instance of the workflow.

5. Click **Start**.

Or

1. On a publishing site with workflow, display the page you want to manually submit for approval.

2. If the ribbon is hidden, on the **Settings** menu, click **Show Ribbon**.

3. To open the initiation form, on the **Publish** tab, click **Submit**.

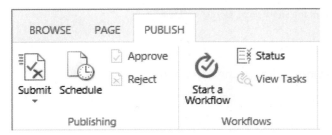

On the Publish tab, click Submit to approve a publishing page

4. At the bottom of the initiation page, click **Start**.

11

To manually start a workflow by using a Microsoft Word, Excel or PowerPoint document

1. Navigate to a library where a workflow has been added, and open a document.

2. Click the **File** tab to display the Backstage view, and then click **Share** to display the Share page.

3. In the **Workflows** area, click the workflow name, and then click **Start Workflow**.

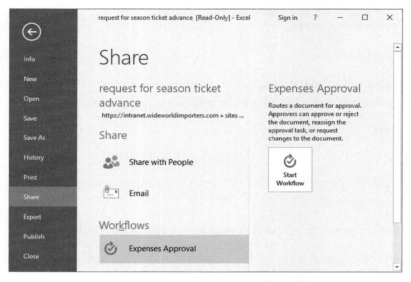

In the backstage view, from the Share page, start a workflow

To manually start a site workflow

1. Do one of the following to display the Site Contents page:

   - On the **Quick Launch**, click **Site Content**.

   - On the **Settings** menu, click **Site Content**.

2. Click **Site Workflows**.

From the Site Contents page, you can display the Site workflows page

3. On the **Start a New Workflow** page, in the **Start a New Workflow** area, click the workflow that you want to run.

To monitor a workflow instance on a list item, file, or page

1. Display the list or library that contains the list item or file for which you want to monitor the workflow instance.

2. Do one of the following to display the Workflow Status page:

- In the column that was added when the workflow was created, click **In Progress**.

On the Workflow Status page, you can find the progress of workflows

- Click to the left of the list item or file to select it, and then, on the **Items** or **Files** tab, in the **Workflows** group, click **Workflows**.

- Right-click the item's name, click **Advanced**, and then click **Workflows**. In the **Running Workflows** area, click the name of the workflow.

Or

1. On a publishing site with workflow, display the page whose workflow you want to monitor.

2. if the ribbon is hidden, click the **Settings** icon, and then click **Show Ribbon**.

3. On the **Publish** tab, click **Status**.

To monitor a site workflow

1. On the **Site Contents** page, click **Site Workflows**.

2. On the **Workflows** page, in the **Workflows (Workflow Health)** area, click the name of the site workflow to display the Workflow Status page.

11

To terminate a workflow instance

1. Display the list or library that contains the list item or file for which you want to terminate the workflow instance.

2. Do one of the following to display the Workflow Status page:

    *   In the column that was added when the workflow was created, click **In Progress**.

    *   Click to the left of the list item or file to select it, and then, on the **Items** or **Files** tab, in the **Workflows** group, click **Workflows**.

    *   Right click the item's name, click **Advanced,** and then click **Workflows**. In the **Running Workflows** area, click the name of the workflow.

3. In the **If an error occurs or if this workflow stops responding, you can end it** area, click **End this workflow**.

> If an error occurs or if this workflow stops responding, you can end it.
> ▫ End this workflow.

On the Workflow Status page, you can end workflows

Or

1. On a publishing site with workflow, display the page whose workflow you want to terminate.

2. If the ribbon is hidden, click the **Settings** icon, and then click **Show Ribbon**.

3. On the **Publish** tab, click **Cancel Approval**.

Complete workflow tasks

After a workflow instance is started, you need to respond to task actions assigned to you by reviewing the workflow status page, by navigating to the tasks list, or by clicking Open This Task, if the workflow sent you an email.

Reply   Reply All   Forward

Open this Task...

| | test workflow <sp2016@wideworldimporters.com> | Peter Connelly | 16:34 |

Tasks - Please approve request for season ticket advance

Action Items

Task assigned by Peter Connelly on 4/15/2016.

Due by None

Approval started by Peter Connelly on 4/15/2016 4:34 PM
Comment: Please review the expenses file.

To complete this task:
1. Review request for season ticket advance.
2. Perform the specific activities required for this task.
3. Use the **Open this task** button to mark the task as completed. (If you cannot update this task, you might not have access to it.)

An example of an email sent by a workflow

Different workflows require you to complete different task actions. You might be notified of these task actions by email in addition to a task item in the workflow task list. You should review the list item or file and then complete the task.

> **TIP** If the workflow is associated with a document library, when you open an Office document, you will see a message bar that informs you that you have been assigned a workflow task.

The tasks used by the workflow might look different than the task items from a tasks list created by using the Tasks list template. Often when a workflow is added to a list or library, a new content type is associated with the workflow's task list. For example, when you create a workflow from the Approval - SharePoint 2010 workflow template,

11

the Approval Workflow Task content type is associated with the task list. This allows users to complete the task by using the following options:

- Approve

- Reject

- Cancel

- Request Change

- Reassign Task

> ✓ **TIP** Request Change allows you to ask another user a question regarding the approval process and the list item or file you need to review. After the other person has sent his or her response, control of the approval process returns to you. The Reassign Task option allows you to delegate the approval process to another person. For example, if you should not be part of the approval process because you have moved to a different position or another person is now the Team Leader, you would use this option.

To view all workflow task items

1. Display the list or library where the workflow was created, and then display the workflow status page.

2. In the **Tasks** section, in **This workflow created the following tasks. You can also view them in** *<task list>*., click the name of the task list.

	Assigned To	Title	Due Date	Status	Related Content	Outcome
	Peter Connelly	Please approve request for season ticket advance ⊡ NEW	4/17/2016	Completed	request for season ticket advance	Approved
	Todd Rowe	Please approve request for season ticket advance ⊡ NEW	4/17/2016	Not Started	request for season ticket advance	

Tasks
This workflow created the following tasks. You can also view them in Tasks.

The Tasks section of the workflow status page

To complete a workflow task

1. Display the list or library where the workflow was created, and then display the workflow status page.

2. In the **Tasks** section, in the **Title** column, click the name of the task assigned to you.

3. On the **Tasks** page, review the information and, if necessary, click the link to the right of **This workflow task applies to**, to view the related list item or file.

Tasks: Please approve request for season ti‹

✕ Delete Item

⊘ This workflow task applies to request for season ticket advance.

Status	Not Started
Requested By	Peter Connelly
Consolidated Comments	Approval started by Peter Connelly on 4/15/2016 4:34 PM Comment: Please review the expenses file. These are the comments of the requestor and all previous participants.
Due Date	4/17/2016
Comments	
	This message will be included in your response.

[Approve] [Reject] [Cancel] [Request Change] [Reassign Task]

An example of the approval workflow tasks form

4. Click a button to reflect your decision.

Manage workflows

As you use a workflow, you might find that it does not match your business needs—perhaps your team leader has changed, or a third level of approval is required, or the business process is no longer needed for your team. Therefore, you will need to modify the workflow as time progresses.

> **TIP** You cannot change the workflow template that a workflow was created from.

If you need to make significant changes to a workflow, you can avoid confusing your users by creating a new workflow rather than modifying the existing workflow. You can disable the old workflow, thereby preventing users from starting new instances of the workflow but allowing currently running instances of the workflow to complete. When all workflow instances have completed, you can delete the workflow.

For SharePoint 2013 workflows, you can use the Workflow Health page to display all workflows for a site and the status of their associated workflow instances. Click the Information icon (the *i* in a circle), to find more information. From the Workflow Health page you can quickly navigate to the Change A Workflow page by clicking the workflow name.

Site Settings ▸ Workflow Health ⓘ

Site workflow status: **Connected**

Workflow name	Started	Suspended	Canceled	Terminated	Completed	Total
HA_Copy Person To Title						
HA_Copy Person To Title	0	0	0	0	2 ⓘ	2 ⓘ
Ideas						
Ideas	0	0	0	0	0	0
SharePoint 20123 Workflow test						
There are no workflows.						
SPE Update Weather						
SPE Update Weather	0	0	0	0	1 ⓘ	1 ⓘ

Workflow Health page for SharePoint 2013 workflows

To monitor all SharePoint 2013 workflows for a site

1. Do one of the following to display the Workflow Settings page:

   - On the **List** or **Library** tab, in the **Settings** group, click **Workflow Settings**.

   - On the **List** or **Library** tab, in the **Settings** group, click **Library Settings**, and then under **Permissions and Management**, click **Workflow Settings**.

   - On the **Settings** menu, click **Site Settings**, and then on the **Site Settings** page, in the **Site Administration** area, click **Workflow Settings**.

2. To the right of **Workflows**, click **Workflow Health** to display the Workflow Health page, from which you can monitor your workflows.

Settings ▸ Workflow Settings ⓘ

Workflows (Workflow Health)

Show workflow associations of this type:

This List ▾

Select a different type to see its workflows.

To display the Workflow Health page, click Workflow Health

To modify a list workflow

1. Display the **Workflow Settings** page for the list or library where the workflow was created.

2. Do one of the following:

   • In the **Show workflow associations of this type** list, select **This List** to display workflows created from workflow templates associated with any content type.

   • Select a specific content type to display workflows created from a workflow template associated with a specific content type.

3. Under either **SharePoint 2013 Workflows** or **SharePoint 2010 Workflows**, click the name of the workflow you want to modify.

ⓖ Workflow name	Workflows in progress
SharePoint 2013 Workflows	
There are no SharePoint 2013 Workflows associated with this list.	
SharePoint 2010 Workflows	
Expenses Approval	1
▫ Add a workflow	
▫ Remove, Block, or Restore a Workflow	

The Workflow Name section of the Workflow Settings page

4. The same association page that was used when the workflow was created is displayed. Make and save your changes.

11

To modify a list content type workflow

1. Open the list or library where the workflow was added to the content type.

2. On the **List** or **Library** tab, in the **Settings** group, click **Library Settings** to display the Settings page.

3. In the **Content Types** area, click the name of the content type.

 TIP If the Content Types section is not displayed, click Advanced Settings, and then select Allow Management Of Content Types.

4. In the **Settings** area, click **Workflow settings,** and then click the name of the workflow you want to modify.

5. The same association page that was used when the workflow was created is displayed. Make and save your changes.

To modify a site content type workflow

1. Navigate to the site where the content type is defined.

2. On the **Settings** menu, click **Site settings** to display the Site Settings page.

3. In the **Web Designer Galleries** area, click **Site Content Types**.

4. Click the content type where the workflow was created.

5. In the **Settings** area, click **Workflow settings**.

6. Click the name of the workflow you want to modify.

7. The same association page that was used when the workflow was created is displayed. Make and save your changes.

8. Optionally, on the **Workflow Settings** page, click **Update all related content types with these workflow association settings**, and then in the dialog box warning that workflow customizations on related content types will be lost, click **OK**.

To disable a workflow

1. On the **Workflow Settings** page, click **Remove, Block, or Restore a Workflow**.

2. To the right of the workflow name, click **No New Instances**.

> **TIP** This action is reversible. To re-enable the workflow, navigate to this page and select Allow.

To delete a workflow

1. On the **Workflow Settings** page, click **Remove, Block, or Restore a Workflow**.

2. To the right of the workflow name, click **Remove**.

> ⚠ **IMPORTANT** When you delete a workflow, all running instances are immediately terminated. The column for that workflow is deleted and no longer appears in the default view for the list or library. There is no method of displaying the workflow status page for a list item or file, and all items in the related Tasks list are deleted.

Skills review

In this chapter, you learned how to:

- Automate business processes by using SharePoint

- Use built-in workflows

- Interact with workflows

- Manage workflows

11

Practice tasks

No practice files are necessary to complete the practice tasks in this chapter.

> **IMPORTANT** You must have sufficient permissions to perform the operations involved in each practice task to complete that practice task. For more information, see Appendix A, "SharePoint 2016 user permissions and permission levels."

Automate business processes by using SharePoint

There are no practice tasks for this topic.

Use built-in workflows

Open a SharePoint Team site where you would like to add a workflow template to a document library, and then perform the following tasks:

1. Add the **Approval - SharePoint 2010** workflow template to the library, giving it the name Expenses Approval.

2. On the second association page, do the following:
   - Assign two valid users to the workflow and check their names.
   - Add Please review the expenses file and set the duration per task to 2 days.

3. Save the template, and leave the browser open if you are continuing to the next set of practice tasks.

Interact with workflows

Upload a document to the document library if the library does not already contain one, and then test the workflow by performing the following tasks. This procedure asks you to approve and reject tasks; if you are not a site owner, on the initiation page, change the two approvers to your user ID.

1. Manually start the **Expenses Approval** workflow on a document.

2. Display the **Workflow Status** page to monitor the instance of the workflow that was started.

3. Approve the task.

4. From the **Workflow Status** page, view all task items.

5. In the default view of the **Tasks** list, click the task item that has the title **Please approve** *<document name>* and that has no value in the **Outcome** column, where *<document name>* is the name of your document.

6. Reject the task item.

7. Display the default view of the library, and click **Rejected** in the **Expenses Approval** column.

    On the Workflow Status: Approval Workflow page, in the Workflow Information section, the workflow instance has a status of Rejected.

Workflow

In the Tasks section, the two tasks have a status of Completed, and in the Workflow History section, there are six events: a Workflow Initiated event, two Task Created events, two Task Completed events, and a Workflow Completed event.

Date Occurred	Event Type	User ID	Description	Outcome
4/12/2016 3:49 PM	Workflow Initiated	Peter Connelly	Approval was started. Participants: Erin M. Hagens;Jeff Teper	
4/12/2016 3:49 PM	Task Created	Peter Connelly	Task created for Erin M. Hagens. Due by: None	
5/2/2016 11:16 AM	Task Completed	Erin M. Hagens	Task assigned to Erin M. Hagens was approved by Peter Connelly. Comments:	Approved by Peter Connelly
5/2/2016 11:16 AM	Task Created	Peter Connelly	Task created for Jeff Teper. Due by: None	
5/2/2016 11:16 AM	Task Completed	Jeff Teper	Task assigned to Jeff Teper was rejected by Peter Connelly. Comments:	Rejected by Peter Connelly
5/2/2016 11:16 AM	Workflow Completed	Peter Connelly	Approval was completed.	Approval on Connecting to the Virtual Lab Environment v6 has successfully completed. All participants have completed their tasks.

The Workflow History section shows the workflow's events

Leave the browser open if you are continuing to the next set of practice tasks.

Manage workflows

Open the default view of the document library where you associated the workflow template, and then perform the following tasks:

1. Modify the **Expenses Approval** workflow so that a workflow instance will start when a new document is created.

2. Upload a new document to the library.

   The default view of the document library refreshes, displaying the new document that you uploaded with an Expenses Approval status of In Progress.

    TIP If the Expenses Approval column is empty, refresh the browser.

3. By using the **Workflow Status** page, terminate this workflow instance.

   The Workflow Status page refreshes, and in the Workflow Information section, the workflow has a status of Canceled. There are no task items listed in the Tasks section, and in the Workflow History section, the last event in the list has an event type of Workflow Canceled.

4. Display the default view of the library and notice that the document has an Expenses Approval status of Canceled.

5. Delete the workflow from the library.

Collaborate with Office programs by using SharePoint

Microsoft SharePoint Server 2016 provides the collaborative backbone to the Microsoft Office 2016 programs, Office Online apps, and mobile Office apps. Both Office Online apps and mobile Office apps provide a subset of the capabilities and functionality of Office programs. However, if you need to quickly view content or give a presentation by using your smartphone or tablet, you should consider using the platform-specific Office mobile apps.

> ✓ **TIP** To use the full functionality of the mobile apps, you will need an Office 365 or personal Microsoft OneDrive account.

This chapter guides you through procedures related to editing documents by using Office, sharing OneNote notebooks, importing and exporting data in Microsoft Excel spreadsheets to and from SharePoint lists, connecting Microsoft Outlook with SharePoint lists and libraries (thereby storing SharePoint content as a local copy that is available offline), using SharePoint with Outlook and Skype for Business, and using Microsoft Access with SharePoint.

In this chapter

- Edit documents in Office
- Share OneNote notebooks with SharePoint
- Import data from and export data to Excel spreadsheets
- Work with SharePoint content in Outlook
- Integrate Access with SharePoint

Practice files

For this chapter, use the practice files from the SP2016SBS\Ch12 folder. For practice file download instructions, see the introduction.

> **TIP** You can complete many of the tasks documented in this chapter by using earlier versions of Office programs; however, the steps and screenshots in this chapter were created by using Office 2016. If you use Office 2010 or Office 2013, your steps and screenshots will be slightly different. For steps on using Office 2010, see *Microsoft SharePoint Foundation 2010 Step by Step*, by Olga Londer and Penelope Coventry (Microsoft Press, 2011). For steps on using Office 2013, see *Microsoft SharePoint 2013 Step by Step*, by Olga Londer and Penelope Coventry (Microsoft Press, 2013).

Edit documents in Office

When you share a file, saving it directly from its Office program to SharePoint allows you to keep one definitive copy of that file. If you save a document to a SharePoint library, your team does not have to find all the different copies of the same document and worry about whether they are editing the most up-to-date copy of that file.

The combination of SharePoint and Office reduces your dependency on using your browser to complete tasks. Together, SharePoint and Office provide a variety of methods for collaborating, whether you are co-authoring a spreadsheet, commenting on the contents of a document, processing a business plan by using a workflow, or categorizing your documents by using metadata stored in document library columns. When you store your files within SharePoint, Office provides your team with a similar experience in Microsoft Word, Excel, PowerPoint, Visio, and OneNote, and provides a Save To SharePoint option in each of these programs.

> **SEE ALSO** For more information about using Office programs and Office Online, in particular Word and Word Online, see Chapter 3, "Work with content in lists and libraries." For information about co-authoring, see "Co-author by using Office and Office Online" later in this topic. For information about using a workflow from within Word, see Chapter 11, "Work with workflows."

View and change file properties

In previous versions of Office, you could use the Document Information Panel (DIP) with Word, PowerPoint, and Excel to view and change the properties for an individual file. These properties, also known as metadata, are details about a file. They are stored in the document, and they have the advantage of allowing you and your team to filter, sort, identify, and search for documents in SharePoint. It is often a struggle to encourage users to tag documents with metadata, and the DIP encouraged users to quickly and easily track and edit metadata for a document even as they continued to work in the Office program.

The DIP has been removed from Office 2016 programs. To view and edit the metadata within Word 2016, Excel 2016, and PowerPoint 2016, you can use the Info page that is available when you select the File tab. In Word, you can also embed metadata in the body of the document by using quick parts, also known as *property controls*. You can use quick parts to track and edit metadata as you work in a document; the metadata is then saved into the document library columns when the document is saved.

To add a quick part to a Word document

1. Place the cursor in the document where you want to add a quick part.

2. On the **Insert** tab, in the **Text** group, select **Quick Parts**.

3. Select **Document Property**, and then select the name of the property you want to add.

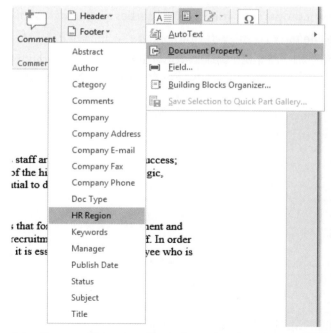

Select Document Property to choose from a list of properties you can insert in your document

> ✓ **TIP** Another useful Word quick part is AutoText, which allows you to store content in the Quick Part Gallery that you can use again and again.

12

To update a Word document property by using a quick part

1. In the document, select the quick part control that references the property you want to change.

2. Change the information.

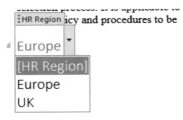

The quick part displays the SharePoint column name, and allows you to enter or select content, depending on the column type

> **TIP** You can use the Developer tab in Word to open the Control Properties dialog box, in which you can lock a quick part control so that it cannot be deleted.

To update a Word document property by using the Properties section of the Info page

1. In Word, select the **File** tab to display the Info page.

2. If all of the properties are not listed under **Properties** on the right side of the page, at the bottom of the right side, under **Related Documents**, select **Show All Properties**.

3. Point to the right of the property you want to update, and make your change.

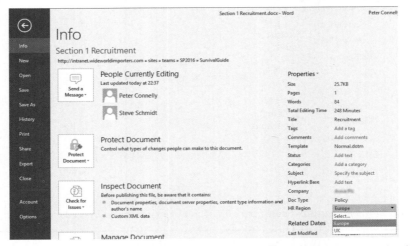

Some document library column types can't be edited directly in the Properties section; in such cases, you use the Show Details link to open the Web Files Properties dialog box

Co-author by using Office and Office Online

When you edit documents by using Office, you have the option of either locking the editing to a single user at a time by using the Check Out/Check In mechanisms or opening the file to multiple users for real-time co-authoring, without interfering with each other's changes. You can use the Office co-authoring feature when storing documents in SharePoint 2016, SharePoint Online in Office 365, your personal OneDrive, or OneDrive for Business. It can be used in libraries only when checkout is not used.

> **TIP** In Microsoft OneNote notebooks, version information is stored within the notebooks themselves, which is different than how Word and PowerPoint store their version information; therefore, you should not enable minor versioning when storing OneNote notebooks in a SharePoint library, because this will interfere with the synchronization and versioning capabilities of OneNote.

The co-authoring functionality in each Office product is similar; however, there are some differences, as detailed in the following table. Only when you use those Office products listed with a "Yes" in the respective SharePoint column can you co-author documents.

Office product	SharePoint 2013	SharePoint 2016	SharePoint Online in Office 365
Word 2010-2016	Yes	Yes	Yes
Word Online	Yes*	Yes**	Yes
PowerPoint 2010-2016	Yes	Yes	Yes
PowerPoint Online	Yes*	Yes**	Yes
Excel Online	Yes*	Yes**	Yes
OneNote 2010-2016	Yes	Yes	Yes
OneNote Online	Yes*	Yes**	Yes
Visio 2013-2016	Yes	Yes	Yes

* Co-authoring is available only with the Office Online products when Office Web Apps server is installed.

** Co-authoring is available only with the Office Online products when Office Online Server is installed.

> **IMPORTANT** Co-authoring, or working on a spreadsheet at the same time with other people, is available in Excel Online but not in Excel 2016 (or earlier) for Windows.

Office programs and SharePoint are designed to minimize any performance or scalability issues that might be associated with co-authoring documents; therefore, only when more than one author is editing the document does the Office program send or download co-author information from the server. Office programs are designed to reduce the frequency of synchronization actions related to co-authoring when the server is under a heavy load or when a user is not actively editing a document.

> **SEE ALSO** For more information about co-authoring, see Chapter 4, "Make lists and libraries work for you."

Real-time co-authoring

When you edit a Word or PowerPoint document at the same time that other people are working in it, you will see where they are editing. This is known as *real-time co-authoring* and is supported when all co-authors are using either Word 2016 or Word Online in Office Online Server, or PowerPoint 2016 or PowerPoint Online in Office Online Server. Word, PowerPoint, and OneNote also support real-time typing, which allows you to see where others are working and what they are typing.

With real-time typing, you can see where others are working and what they are typing as they type

In the status bar of the Office 2016 programs—that is, not the Office Online products—you might see a message that says Updates Available which means that if you save the document now, it will be updated with the changes that others have saved.

You can configure whether others can see your changes by using the Share pane, which is displayed when you select Share in the upper-right corner (in Word, you can also configure this in the Word Options dialog box, on the General Tab).

The Automatically Share Changes options are:

- **Always**   Others who have agreed to share their changes will always be able to see yours.

- **Ask Me**   If this is the first time you have used real-time co-authoring, you will be asked whether you want to automatically share your changes as they happen. Select Yes to always allow automatic sharing. (Clear the Don't Ask Me Again check box if you don't want to be asked about this the next time you open a document.)

- **Never**   Only you will be able to see your changes until you save your document, and you will not be able to see other users' changes; how-ever, you will be able to see who has the document open.

In Word 2016, use the Real-Time Collaboration Options section of the Word Options dialog box to configure how you want Word to share your changes

12

Visio co-authoring

Visio uses the same Office Document cache as Word and PowerPoint for co-authoring .vsdx files. When more than one user is editing a Visio file, the Visio program displays an icon on the status bar indicating the number of users editing the file. Select the icon to display a list of authors.

When a user edits a shape, a person icon is added to the upper-right corner of the shape, to inform you that someone else is editing the shape. Select the person icon to display the name of the person. Shapes that have been deleted by someone else display an exclamation mark in a square box along with a small red cross in the lower-right corner of the box.

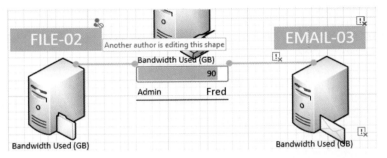

Person icons and exclamation icons indicate shapes that other users are amending or have deleted

> ✓ **TIP** Developers can create Visio templates that do not allow co-authoring.

Visio does not stop multiple users from editing the same shape; therefore, a more correct name for this feature would be collaborative authoring.

Share OneNote notebooks with SharePoint

You can use OneNote to store information in notebooks, which are organized in pages and sections. OneNote is included as a desktop program as part of Office 2016 and is available as a Universal Windows Platform app that is part of Windows 10. OneNote apps are also available for Apple and Android devices.

> **TIP** If you have a OneNote notebook stored on your local computer and you want to open it by using your smartphone or tablet, you'll need to first share the notebook to OneDrive or SharePoint.

OneNote 2016, OneNote 2013, and OneNote 2010 use the same file format (.one); therefore, if you have notebooks that were created in previous versions of OneNote, you can open and edit them in any of these versions. However, the newer notebook format is not backward-compatible; for example, you cannot use a notebook you created in OneNote 2016, OneNote 2013, or OneNote 2010 in OneNote 2007 or OneNote 2003.

OneNote integrates with other Office programs, such as Outlook—you can flag a note in OneNote and use the Outlook Tasks command on the Home tab to turn it into an Outlook task, you can send a OneNote page as an email message, or you can send an entire notebook as a OneNote file or as a PDF file as an email attachment.

> **TIP** If you are new to OneNote, you might want to look at *OneNote 2016 Tips & Tricks*, which is a free eBook that can be found at *https://support.office.com/en-us/article /eBook-OneNote-2016-Tips-Tricks-4e08cf8b-dc37-4229-bdef-1f580220b6f5*.

You can store OneNote notebooks to your computer's local drive and to your personal OneDrive, to your OneDrive for Business and in SharePoint libraries, thereby sharing the information in the notebook with your team in a central place and allowing easy access to the notebook from any device.

> **SEE ALSO** For information about OneDrive for Business, see Chapter 6, "Work with My Site and OneDrive for Business."

12

OneNote Online

If you have a personal OneDrive account or Office Online Server installed alongside SharePoint Server, or if you are using Office 365, OneNote is also available as a web-based app known as OneNote Online. If this is the case, when you create a team site, a OneNote shared notebook is automatically created as part of the site. With OneNote Online, you can see updates as they happen, see who did what on the page by selecting the Show Authors command on the View tab, and share a notebook by sending a link instead of an email attachment.

Share notebooks by using SharePoint

By sharing a notebook in a SharePoint library, you can use the document management features detailed in this book to manage and share your notebooks. You can manage who has permission to view the notebook or contribute notes. You can store additional information about the notebook or its pages, such as the department name or project number. You can also track versions of the notebook, so that people can view or restore an earlier version if needed, and you can use alerts or RSS Feeds to be informed when the content changes.

> **TIP** OneNote backs up your notebook files automatically each week and keeps two backup copies. If you take a lot of important notes, you can back up your notebooks more often by using the Save & Backup settings in the OneNote Options dialog box. If you share your notebook by using OneDrive for Business or SharePoint, your IT department will also maintain copies of the shared notebook.

When you or another user changes the content in a notebook, OneNote automatically saves and syncs the notebook on SharePoint. You can also sync notebooks manually. OneNote also maintains a separate offline copy of the notebook on each user's computer, thereby allowing you to edit the notebook locally, even when you are disconnected from the network. The next time you connect to the shared notebook, OneNote merges your changes with everyone else's.

> **IMPORTANT** If the document library where your OneNote notebook is stored requires files to be checked out before editing, OneNote cannot save changes to the notebook; therefore, always ensure that the Require Check Out setting is not selected for the document library where notebooks are stored. For information about the Require Check Out setting, see Chapter 4, "Make lists and libraries work for you." Other causes of synchronization errors are when the library is enabled for minor versions, or one or more columns are configured as required and do not have a default value, or the SharePoint site collection that contains the library has exceeded its storage quota.

> **TIP** OneNote Class notebooks are widely used by organizations, particularly those in the education sector, and were designed for Office 365. For information about the OneNote Class notebook, go to *onenoteforteachers.com*. To download the OneNote Class Notebook add-in, go to *https://microsoft.com/en-us/download/details.aspx?id=51934*. For information about integrating OneNote Class notebooks with your Learning Management System (LMS), go to *onenote.com/lti*.

To create a SharePoint library in which to save OneNote notebooks

> ⚠️ **IMPORTANT** You can save OneNote notebooks in any type of library. This procedure sets the New command on the File tab to create a OneNote notebook. This is useful if you do not have Office Online Server installed and the common file type for a document library is a OneNote notebook.

1. In SharePoint, do one of the following to display the Your Apps page:
   - On the **Settings** menu, select **Add an app**.
   - On the Quick Launch, select **Site Contents**, and then select **add an app**.

2. On the **Your Apps** page, under **Apps you can add**, select **Document Library** to open the Adding Document Library dialog.

3. Select **Advanced Options** to display the New page.

4. In the **Name** box, enter a name for the library.

5. In the **Document Template** list, select **Microsoft OneNote 2010 Notebook**, and then select **Create**.

> ✅ **TIP** Although the name of the document template is OneNote 2010, the format of the notebook has not changed between OneNote 2010 and OneNote 2016, so you can use this document template whether you use OneNote 2010, OneNote 2013, or OneNote 2016.

To create a OneNote notebook in a SharePoint library by using your browser

1. If you have Office Online Server installed and connected to your SharePoint server, or if you are using Office 365, go to the SharePoint library where you want to create the OneNote notebook.

2. Select **new**, and then select **OneNote notebook**.

12

If you have Office Online Server installed, you can quickly create Word, Excel, PowerPoint, and OneNote files

3. In the **Name** text box, enter the name of your notebook, and then select **OK**.

Or

1. Go to the SharePoint library where you want to create the OneNote notebook, and do one of the following:

    *   If the document library is associated with a OneNote notebook document template, on the **Files** tab, select **New**.

    *   If a content type that is associated with a OneNote notebook document template has been added to the library, on the **Files** tab, select the **New** arrow, and then select that content type.

2. In the dialog box that opens, select the option that allows OneNote to open. (The form of this dialog box and option depends on your browser. For example, if you are using Internet Explorer, select **Allow**; if you are using Google Chrome, select **Launch Application**; or if you are using Microsoft Edge, select **OneNote** or **OneNote 2016**. The OneNote program starts and opens the Unpack Notebook dialog box.

3. In the **Name** box, enter the name of your notebook, and in the path list, enter the web address of the SharePoint library.

4. Select **Create**.

To create a OneNote notebook in a SharePoint library by using OneNote

1. Open OneNote 2016, select the **File** tab, and then on the **New** page, select **Other Web Location** or **Browse**. Then do one of the following to open the Create New Notebook dialog box:

   - Under **Recent Folders**, select a SharePoint library where you have previously created or opened other OneNote notebooks.

   - Select **Browse**.

2. If the Create New Notebook dialog box does not display the contents of the SharePoint library where you want to store your team notebook, in the **Notebook Name** box, enter the web address of the SharePoint site, and press **Enter** to go to the document library on the SharePoint site.

3. In the **Notebook Name** box, enter a meaningful, descriptive name for the new notebook, and then select **Create**.

4. In the **Microsoft OneNote** dialog box, do one of the following:

   - Select **Invite people** if you want to share the notebook.

   - Select **Not now** to keep the notebook unshared for now.

To manually sync a notebook

1. In OneNote, select the notebook list, and then do one of the following to the notebook you want to sync:

   - Right-click the notebook, and then select **Sync This Notebook Now**.

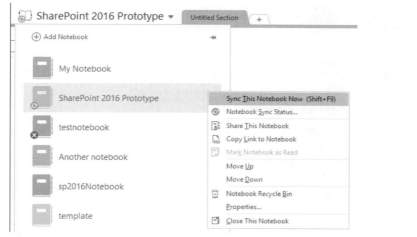

If a syncing error occurs, select the error icon for more information

12

- Select the notebook and press **Shift+F9**.

- Right-click the notebook, select **Notebook Sync Status**, and in the **Shared Notebook Synchronization** dialog box, to the right of the notebook, select **Sync Now**.

- Select the **File** tab. On the **Info** page, select **Settings** to the left of the notebook, and then select **Sync**.

To configure notebook synchronization

> ⚠️ **IMPORTANT** Using these settings affects all notebooks.

1. In OneNote, do one of the following to open the Shared Notebook Synchronization dialog box:

   - Select the **File** tab, and then on the **Info** page, select **View Sync Status**.

   - Right-click the notebook, and select **Notebook Sync Status.**

2. Under **How should we sync your notebooks**, select either **Sync automatically whenever there are changes** or **Sync manually**.

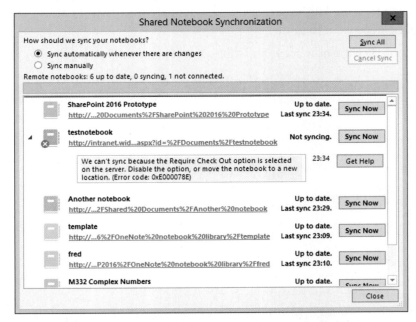

Use the dialog box to configure how you want to sync your notebooks, to manually sync a notebook, and to investigate syncing errors

Import data from and export data to Excel spreadsheets

You can use Excel 2016, much like previous versions of Excel, to export and import data to and from SharePoint lists. You can create a SharePoint list via your browser by importing an Excel spreadsheet, or from within Excel by exporting an Excel table. You can copy (export) the contents of a SharePoint list or library, or the results of a survey, to an Excel spreadsheet.

The web query that exports the contents from the list or library creates an Excel table named *Table_owssvr* and maintains a connection between the content in the list or library and the content in the table, making the table an external table or linked object. Changes you make to data in your Excel worksheet do not synchronize with the list or library on your SharePoint site; that is, only a one-way synchronization occurs from the SharePoint site to Excel. Any changes you make to data in the Excel spreadsheet are lost when you next refresh the external table content.

> ✅ **TIP** When you export a SharePoint library, Excel represents the documents in the list with hyperlinks that point to the documents on the SharePoint site. Similarly, attachments on list items are replaced with hyperlinks. In the Excel spreadsheet, select this link to open the file.

Similarly, when you create a SharePoint list from within Excel, you have an option to create the data within Excel as an external table; after the SharePoint list is created, you cannot link the spreadsheet to the SharePoint list. Therefore, if you want to synchronize updates between the list and the spreadsheet, be sure to select the Create A Read-Only Connection To The New SharePoint List check box. When you use your browser to create a SharePoint list from Excel data, the option to create an external table in Excel is not available.

To create a SharePoint list from an Excel spreadsheet by using your browser

1. In SharePoint, on the **Your Apps** page, under **Apps you can add**, select **Import Spreadsheet** to display the New page.

2. In the **Name** box, enter a name for the list, and optionally enter a description of the list in the **Description** box.

3. Select **Browse** to open the Choose File To Upload dialog box, and go to the folder that contains your spreadsheet.

12

4. Select your spreadsheet, and then select **Open**.

5. On the **New** page, select **Import**.

You can save time when you create a list by importing an Excel spreadsheet

Excel opens your spreadsheet and opens the Import To Windows SharePoint Services List dialog box.

6. In the **Range Type** list, select **Table Range**, **Range of Cells**, or **Named Range**, as appropriate, and then in the **Select Range** list, select the data you want to copy to your SharePoint list.

You can also convert an Excel workbook to an InfoPath form template that you can then use for a Forms library

> **TIP** If you import a range of cells from an Excel spreadsheet and want the Excel column names to become the SharePoint list column names, you should first edit the spreadsheet and convert the range of cells to an Excel table.

7. Select **Import** to create the list.

> ✓ **TIP** The new SharePoint list is not configured to appear on the Quick Launch.

To create a SharePoint list from within Excel

1. If the data in your Excel spreadsheet is not already formatted as an Excel table, complete the following:

   a. In Excel, select any cell within the data you want to create the list from.

   b. On the **Home** tab, in the **Styles** group, select **Format as Table**, and then select a table style.

Use this method when you already have the data in Excel and you want to create a SharePoint list during the synchronization process

   c. In the **Format As Table** dialog box, change the range of cells if necessary, and optionally select the **My table has headers** check box.

> ✓ **TIP** If your data does not contain headers, Excel creates them for you and labels them as Column1, Column2, and so on.

   d. Select **OK**.

12

2. Select any cell within your Excel table if one is not already selected, so that the Table Tools Design tab is displayed.

3. In the **External Table Data** group, select the **Export** arrow, and then select **Export Table to SharePoint List**.

4. In the **Export Table to SharePoint List – Step 1 of 2** dialog box, in the **Address** box, enter the name of the SharePoint site to which you want to export the data.

5. Select **Create a read-only connection to the new SharePoint list** if you want to create a one-way synchronization connection between the Excel table data and the data in the SharePoint list.

6. In the **Name** box, enter the name of the SharePoint list, and optionally, in the **Description** box, enter a description for the SharePoint list.

In the Address box, enter the web address for the new SharePoint list

7. Select **Next** to open the Export Table To SharePoint List – Step 2 Of 2 dialog box.

Excel removes formulas during the export process; therefore, you might consider deleting columns and creating calculated columns after you complete the export and the data is in SharePoint

> **TIP** Excel checks the data in each column to ensure that the data belongs to a data type supported by SharePoint. If it doesn't, Excel usually applies the Text data type to each column. Excel also checks whether each column contains only one type of data. If a column contains a mixture of data types, such as numbers and text, Excel chooses Text as the data type. At this point, you can select Cancel, correct erroneous data, and then restart the export process.

8. Select **Finish**, and then select **OK** to close the Microsoft SharePoint Foundation dialog box that confirms that the table was successfully published.

> **TIP** The new SharePoint list is not configured to appear on the Quick Launch.

To export the contents of a SharePoint list or library to an Excel spreadsheet

> **TIP** The export process exports only the columns and rows contained in the list's current view; if none of the views contain the data that you want to export, you must create a new view to meet your needs. Alternatively, you can choose one of the existing views, export the list to a spreadsheet, and then delete the unwanted data.

1. Go to the list or library, and on the **List** or **Library** tab, in the **Connect & Export** group, select **Export to Excel**.

> ✓ **TIP** If a message dialog box opens stating that to export a list you must have a Microsoft SharePoint Foundation–compatible program, and you have Excel 2016 installed, select OK.

You will see either a File Download dialog box or a notification message at the bottom of your browser that ask whether you want to open or save owssvr.iqy.

2. Select **Open**. Excel opens a new workbook that contains one worksheet named *owssvr*.

3. In the **Microsoft Excel Security Notice** dialog box, select **Enable**.

Enable the web query that exports the contents of the SharePoint list

To refresh external table data

1. In Excel, select one cell within your external table, and then on the **Table Tools Design** tab, in the **External Table Data** group, select **Refresh**.

To modify the external table data refresh behavior

1. Select one cell within your external table, and then do one of the following to open the Connection Properties dialog box:

   - On the **Table Tools Design** tab, in the **External Table Data** group, select the **Refresh** arrow, and then select **Connection Properties**.

   - On the **Data** tab, in the **Connections** group, select **Connections**. In the **Workbook Connections** dialog box, select **owssvr**, if it is not already selected, and then select **Properties**.

2. Make your changes, and then select **OK**.

Work with SharePoint content in Outlook

You can use Outlook to access and update content in SharePoint, and to share information within SharePoint across multiple sites. You can maintain shared items from calendars, contacts, and task lists, in addition to previewing and editing documents. You can also receive notifications about changes to content stored in SharePoint.

When you are using an Office program with a document stored in SharePoint, SharePoint Online in Office 365, or OneDrive for Business, if you point to the name of the author of the document or the name of a co-author, that person's contact information is displayed. If you have Skype for Business installed, the contact information includes options to start an instant message, a call, or a video call, or send an email.

Connect SharePoint lists and libraries to Outlook

You can connect SharePoint calendar, task, contact, and external lists; discussion forums; and most libraries with Outlook, as long as the Offline Client Availability option is set to Yes on the list settings Advanced Settings page. SharePoint permissions are used to decide which items and files you can access in Outlook. The items and files from SharePoint do not increase the size of your Inbox on your mail server because a copy of this content is saved in an Outlook Data File on your computer.

> ⚠️ **IMPORTANT** At the time of writing, there are known issues when connecting external lists with Outlook with SharePoint 2016 and Office 365. Currently only when you use Outlook 2013 with SharePoint 2016 can you connect external lists. In Office 365, whether you use Outlook 2016 or Outlook 2013, you cannot connect external lists with Outlook.

12

After you connect a list or library to Outlook, if you have permissions to edit list items in the SharePoint list, you can modify items from that list from within Outlook. Similarly, if you have permissions to view a document in a SharePoint library, you can view a preview of the contents of the file from the connected library in the Outlook reading pane. However, you do not edit the contents of a file within Outlook; to edit the file, you double-click the file in Outlook to open it in the appropriate program. When you do so, you will be modifying an offline copy of that document, known as a *cached copy*. When you have completed your modifications, you can choose to save the document to the SharePoint library.

> ⚠️ **IMPORTANT** During offline editing, another user could modify the same document, so it is recommended that you always check out your document before you edit it.

You disconnect a list or library from Outlook by using a delete command. This does not delete the SharePoint list or library, but it does remove the related list or library from Outlook on all computers you use.

You can also share a connection with others by right-clicking the list or library name in Outlook and then selecting Share This Folder.

To connect a list or library to Outlook

> ⚠ **IMPORTANT** This procedure can be used with SharePoint libraries and lists that were created by using the following list templates: Calendar, Contacts, Discussion Board, External List, and Tasks.

1. Go to a list or library you want to connect to Outlook.

2. On the **List**, **Library**, or **Calendar** tab, in the **Connect & Export** group, select **Connect to Outlook**.

3. If an **Internet Explorer - Security Warning** dialog box appears asking whether you want to allow this website to open a program on your computer, select **Allow**.

4. If another **Internet Explorer - Security Warning** dialog box appears, telling you that a website wants to open web content using this program on your computer, select **Allow**.

5. A Microsoft Outlook dialog box appears, telling you that you should only connect lists from sources you know and trust. Optionally select **Advanced** to open a SharePoint List Options dialog box, and in the **Folder Name** box, enter a new name for the list as it will be shown in Outlook, and then select **OK**.

Enter a meaningful name for your SharePoint list, so that the purpose of the list and its originating site are obvious in Outlook

6. In the **Microsoft Outlook** dialog box, select **Yes**.

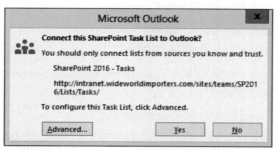

Use the Advanced button to enter a new name, display the list on other computers, and update the subscription

> ✓ **TIP** When you connect a list or library to Outlook, it appears in the related area of the Outlook Navigation pane: calendars appear in the My Calendar pane under Other Calendars; tasks appear in the My Tasks pane under Other Tasks; contacts appear in the My Contacts pane under Other Contacts; and libraries and discussion forums appear in the Mail pane under SharePoint lists. When you connect external lists to Outlook, they are created in the SharePoint External Lists folder.

To disconnect a SharePoint list or library from Outlook

1. In Outlook, do one of the following:

    *   In the mail navigation pane, under **SharePoint lists**, right-click the SharePoint library or discussion board, and select **Delete Folder**.

Use the Delete Folder option to disconnect the SharePoint list or library

- In the calendar navigation pane, under **Other Calendars**, right-click the SharePoint calendar list, and select **Delete Calendar**.

- In the contacts navigation pane, under **Other Contacts**, right-click the SharePoint contact list, and select **Delete Folder**.

- In the task navigation pane, under **Other Tasks**, right-click the SharePoint task list, and select **Delete Folder**.

2. In the **Microsoft Outlook** dialog box that appears, select **Yes**.

Before you remove a connected list or library from Outlook, to prevent the loss of changes you made since the last Send/Receive, resync Outlook with SharePoint

Work with SharePoint calendars in Outlook

You can work with multiple calendars when using Outlook, thereby enabling you to create calendars for specific purposes, such as having one for work and one for your personal life. By using Outlook, you can view several calendars at the same time. When you view and scroll multiple calendars, they all display the same date or time period. This feature is particularly useful if you have connected a SharePoint calendar list to Outlook. When you do so, you create an Outlook Calendar folder in which a copy of the data from the SharePoint list is stored locally. In this way, you can keep track of any calendar items in a SharePoint list from the Outlook Calendar folder, even if you are not connected to the network.

To display a connected SharePoint calendar list in Outlook

1. In Outlook, in the calendar navigation pane, select the check box to the left of the connected SharePoint calendar list.

To overlay calendars

1. In Outlook, in the calendar content area, select the left arrow on the calendar tab.

Overlay calendars to see a unified view of your events and appointments

To copy a calendar item to or from a SharePoint calendar list

1. In the calendar navigation pane, display the source calendar and the SharePoint calendar.

2. Select the calendar item you want to copy, and drag the item onto the other calendar.

To move a calendar item to or from a SharePoint calendar list

1. Complete the copy procedure as described previously, and then delete the calendar item from the original calendar.

Use contacts and tasks with Outlook and SharePoint

When you connect a SharePoint contacts list to Outlook, you create an Outlook contacts folder. Similarly, when you connect a SharePoint task list, you create a task folder. You can then copy the contact and task information from your other Outlook contact and tasks folders into the connected SharePoint contact and task lists. The new contacts and tasks are added to the SharePoint lists the next time Outlook synchronizes with SharePoint. You can use this technique to create a definitive contacts list and a tasks list, which you can access in Outlook, even when you are not connected. You can also use the contacts in the connected contact lists in your emails.

To copy contacts or tasks from Outlook to a SharePoint contacts or task list

1. In Outlook, do one of the following:

    • In the contacts navigation pane, under **My Contacts**, select **Contacts**, and then select one or more contacts.

    • In the task navigation pane, under **My Tasks**, select **To-Do List** or **Tasks**, and then select one or more tasks.

> ✓ **TIP** You can select multiple items by holding down the Shift key or the Ctrl key while clicking the mouse button. Press Ctrl+A to select all contacts.

2. On the **Home** tab, in the **Actions** group, select **Move**, and then select **Copy to Folder**.

12

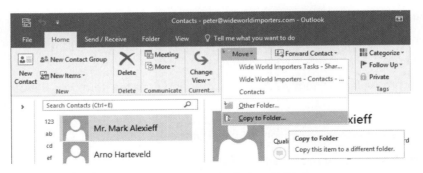

You can use the Move menu to move or copy contacts or tasks

3. In the **Copy Items** dialog box, expand **SharePoint Lists**, select a SharePoint list you previously connected to Outlook, and then select **OK**.

You can also drag to copy contacts and tasks

✅ **TIP** For contact items, you can also right-click one of the selected contacts and then, from the menu, select Move and then select Copy To Folder to open the Copy Items dialog box. You can also drag contacts and tasks from one folder to another.

To move contacts or tasks from Outlook to a SharePoint contacts or task list

1. In Outlook, do one of the following:

   - In the contacts navigation pane, under **My Contacts**, select **Contacts**, and then select one or more contacts.

- In the task navigation pane, under **My Tasks**, select **Tasks**, and then select one or more tasks.

2. On the **Home** tab, in the **Actions** group, select **Move** and then select the respective connected SharePoint list.

Or

Do one of the following to open the Move Items dialog box:

- On the **Home** tab, in the **Actions** group, select **Move**, and then select **Other Folder**.

- Press **Ctrl+Shift+V**.

Expand **SharePoint Lists**, select a SharePoint list you previously connected to Outlook, and then select **OK**.

> ✓ **TIP** For contact items, you can also right-click one of the selected contacts and then, from the menu, select Move, and then select the connected SharePoint list, or select Other Folder to open the Move Items dialog box.

To move or copy an item from a SharePoint list to an Outlook folder

> ⚠ **IMPORTANT** This procedure can be used to move contact information from a SharePoint contact list to your Outlook Address Book, and to move a task item from a SharePoint task list to an Outlook tasks folder.

1. Do one of the following:

- In the contacts navigation pane, under **Other Contacts**, select the connected SharePoint contacts list, and then select one or more contacts.

- In the task navigation pane, under **Other Tasks**, select the connected SharePoint task list, and then select one or more tasks.

2. Follow the procedures described earlier in this section to move or copy items between lists and folders.

Manage notifications

Outlook supports Really Simple Syndication (RSS) feeds so that you can subscribe to and stay updated on the latest news sites and blogs. You can manage your RSS feeds in Outlook just like other mail by flagging them for follow-up, assigning them a specific color, or automating any process by using Rules. You can also manage all of your SharePoint alerts from one Outlook dialog box.

12

To add a SharePoint list RSS feed to Outlook

1. Go to the list or library whose RSS feed you want to subscribe to, and on the **List** or **Library** tab, in the **Share & Track** group, select **RSS Feed**.

2. Right-click **Subscribe to this feed**, and then select **Copy Shortcut** (or if you are not using Internet Explorer, the equivalent option in your browser).

3. Open Outlook, if it is not already open.

4. In the mail navigation pane, right-click **RSS Feeds**, and then select **Add a New RSS Feed**.

5. In the **New RSS Feed** dialog box, in the **Enter the location of the RSS Feed** box, press **Ctrl+V** to paste the shortcut that you copied in step 2.

6. Select **Add**.

7. In the **Microsoft Outlook** dialog box, optionally select **Advanced** to enter a meaningful name for the RSS feed as it will be shown in Outlook, and then select **OK**.

8. Select **Yes** to close the Microsoft Outlook dialog box.

To create a new SharePoint alert by using Outlook

1. Select the **File** tab, and then on the **Info** page, select **Manage Rules & Alerts** to open the Rules And Alerts dialog box.

2. Select the **Manage Alerts** tab, and then select **New Alert**.

Use the options in the Rules And Alerts dialog box to create Outlook rules and manage alerts

3. In the **New Alert** dialog box, select a SharePoint site from the list under either **Sources currently sending me alerts** or **Sources I have visited**, or, in the **Web site Address** box, enter the name of the SharePoint site for which you want to create the alert, and then select **Open**.

Select a SharePoint site that currently sends you alerts or one that you have visited, or enter the web address of a SharePoint site

4. On the **New Alert** page that opens in your browser, select one of the lists or libraries, and then select **Next**.

5. Complete the page so that you receive alerts as needed, and then select **OK**.

> **SEE ALSO** For more information about managing alerts, see Chapter 3, "Work with content in lists and libraries," and Chapter 4, "Make lists and libraries work for you."

Integrate Access with SharePoint

The combination of SharePoint and Microsoft Access 2016 makes it easy for you to build desktop databases by using SharePoint. By doing so, users who do not possess the skills or privileges to be a Microsoft SQL Server database administrator can still obtain the manageability and stability benefits of storing data on the server while retaining the ease of use of Access 2016.

The level of server functionality integrated into Access 2016 increases when it is used in combination with an Access app hosted in SharePoint Server 2016 Enterprise Edition running Access Services, which was first introduced with SharePoint Server 2013 and Access 2013.

In Access 2016, as in Excel and previous versions of Access, you can export and import data both to and from SharePoint lists; however, if you do not want to maintain two copies of that data, one in Access and one in SharePoint, you can link to data that is physically located external to Access.

In an Access app, a table linked to a SharePoint list only provides a read-only connection, whereas a table linked to a SharePoint list in an Access desktop database provides two-way synchronization, so you can work with the SharePoint data offline and then synchronize the changes when you reconnect.

> **SEE ALSO** For information about the new Access app features introduced with SharePoint 2016, go to *https://technet.microsoft.com/en-us/library /mt346121%28v=office.16%29.aspx#access*.

Work with an Access app in your browser

You can use Access 2016 to create and design an Access app; you use your browser to add, edit, view, and delete data stored in the Access app. Similar to SharePoint lists and libraries, Access apps can be displayed on the SharePoint Quick Launch and on the Site Contents page.

When you select an Access app, the Access app page is displayed. It includes a Back To Site link in the upper left of the page; when selected, this link displays the home page of the SharePoint site where the Access app was created. You can select the cog icon in the upper right of the page to customize the app in Access.

The Access app page is divided into several elements:

- **Tables** Similar to the Quick Launch in your SharePoint team site, this area displays Access app tables.

- **Views** This area displays a list of views associated with the table that is currently selected in the table selector element. Most tables include a List and a Datasheet view.

- **Filter text box** This can be used to search and filter data displayed in the view. Access Services does not search for sequences of characters within a word.

- **Action bar** This bar displays buttons that you can use to add, delete, edit, save, and cancel changes. The action bar is the same for each view; however, Access Services enables and disables the buttons depending on what actions are actually available for the view. For example, when the detailed pane is in view mode, the Add, Delete, and Edit buttons are enabled. When the item detailed pane is in edit mode, the Add, Delete, and Edit buttons are disabled, and the Save and Cancel buttons are enabled.

- **Item pane** This pane displays two fields and an optional thumbnail image from an Image data type field. The values for the field are for the items stored in the table that is currently selected in the table selector element. The item pane displays a scroll bar if there are more items to display.

- **Item detailed pane** This displays fields for the item that is currently selected in the item pane. The item detailed pane only displays those fields that are configured to be visible in the view you select in the view selector. Depending on the action bar button you select, you can view, create, modify, and delete properties of an item by using the item detailed pane.

- **Related items** This area displays items from other tables that are related to the item displayed in the item detailed pane. A tab is displayed for each related table. When there are no related tables, this element is not displayed.

An Access page lets you view and enter data

> **TIP** In your browser, you can use keyboard shortcut keys to navigate between tables, views, and items. For example, when your cursor is focused on the table selector, use the Down Arrow and Up Arrow keys to highlight table names. Press Enter to select the highlighted table. Use Tab or Shift+Tab to move your focus to the table selector and to each of the view names in the view selector. Press Ctrl+N to create a new item and Ctrl+E to edit an item.

> **SEE ALSO** Full coverage of Access apps is beyond the scope of this book. For information about Access apps, see *Microsoft Access 2013 Inside Out* by Jeff Conrad, (Microsoft Press, 2013).

Skills review

In this chapter, you learned how to:

- Edit documents in Office

- Share OneNote notebooks with SharePoint

- Import data from and export data to Excel spreadsheets

- Work with SharePoint in Outlook

- Integrate Access with SharePoint

Practice tasks

The practice files for these tasks are located in the SP2016SBS\Ch12 folder.

> ⚠️ **IMPORTANT** You must have sufficient permissions to perform the operations involved in each practice task to complete that practice task. For more information, see Appendix A, "SharePoint 2016 user permissions and permission levels."

Edit documents in Office

Go to your SharePoint team site, and then perform the following tasks:

1. Create a document library named **Survival Guide**.
2. Create a choice column named **HR Region** containing the choices **Europe** and **UK**, configured as a drop-down menu. Ensure that the **HR Region** column is added to the default view of the library.
3. Create a Word document in the library.
4. Open the document in Word and add a quick part to display the **HR Region** property.
5. In the quick part, select **Europe**, and then save your document.
6. Close Word. In your browser, you should see the value *Europe* in the HR Region column for the document.
7. Leave your browser open if you are continuing with the next set of practice tasks.

Share OneNote notebooks with SharePoint

If you have Office Online Server installed, go to the Survival Guide library you created in the previous set of practice tasks; otherwise, create a new document library with OneNote as the default document template. Then perform the following tasks:

1. Create a OneNote notebook named **Recruitment Tips & Tricks**.
2. If you have the notebook opened in OneNote Online, open in the OneNote program and then create a page named **Interview Questions**. In the body of the page, enter **What is your greatest strength?**
3. Manually sync your notebook, and then close OneNote.
4. Leave your browser open if you are continuing with the next set of practice tasks.

Import data from and export data to Excel spreadsheets

Go to your SharePoint team site, and then perform the following tasks:

1. Create a SharePoint list named **FurniturePrice** by using the Excel **Furniture_ Price.xslx** spreadsheet from the practice file folder, with a description of **This list contains the furniture items in stock together with their unit prices.**

Select the **Stock!FurniturePriceTable** table range.

2. Change the list name to Furniture Price, and ensure that the list is displayed on the Quick Launch.

3. Export the **Furniture Price** list to Excel and add a new row that has the following values: Garden lounger, Bianca, wood, 5, 10.

4. Refresh the external table data. The spreadsheet is updated with a copy of the data from the Furniture Price list on the SharePoint site. Your changes to data in the Excel spreadsheet are lost. Discard the workbook.

5. Open the **Sales_Figures.xlsx** workbook from the practice file folder, and format the data in the workbook as a table.

6. Export the table to your SharePoint site as a read-only connection, with a list name of SalesFigures and a description of This list contains furniture sales for this year.

7. Open the new list in your browser, and review the data in the list.

8. Leave your browser open if you are continuing with the next set of practice tasks.

Work with SharePoint content in Outlook

Go to your SharePoint team site. If you do not have a contacts list, create a contacts list by following the steps in the "To create a list" procedure in Chapter 3, "Work with content in lists and libraries," which explains how to create a list. Add at least two contacts to the list, and then perform the following tasks:

1. Connect your contact list to Outlook, and name the folder WideWorldImporters – Contacts.

2. Copy two contacts from your Outlook **My Contacts** address book to the **WideWorldImporters – Contacts** folder.

3. Move one of the contacts from the **WideWorldImporters – Contacts** folder to your **My Contacts** address book.

4. Get the web address of your contact list and add it in Outlook as a RSS Feed.

> **TIP** When you have completed this practice task, you might want to disconnect the contacts list from Outlook and remove the contacts list as an RSS Feed.

Integrate Access with SharePoint

There are no practice tasks for this topic.

Work with business intelligence

Business intelligence (BI) is a set of tools and capabilities that work together to turn large amounts of data into meaningful information for better decision making. SharePoint 2016 provides a BI platform that puts power in the hands of the users, providing self-service capabilities for collaborative data exploration, visualization, and presentation experiences for gaining better and deeper insights.

The BI capabilities provided in SharePoint 2016 and Microsoft Office Online Server integrate with Excel 2016 to explore and visualize data. You can build data models and create a wide range of scorecards and dashboards in Excel, including PowerPivot tables and charts, that you can then publish to SharePoint.

SharePoint 2016 BI functionality includes Power View, an ad hoc reporting tool you can use to build interactive and intuitive reports and animations to visually explore data. You can create a variety of interactive charts and tables, and add timeline controls, filters, and slicers so that users can drill further into the data.

This chapter guides you through procedures related to getting started with SharePoint BI, shaping your data, creating and publishing PowerPivot dashboards, displaying PowerPivot dashboards in web parts, building visualizations by using Power View, and displaying Power View reports in web parts.

In this chapter

- Get started with SharePoint BI
- Shape your data
- Create and publish PowerPivot dashboards
- Display PowerPivot dashboards in web parts
- Build visualizations by using Power View
- Display Power View reports in web parts

Practice files

For this chapter, use the practice file from the SP2016SBS\Ch13 folder. For practice file download instructions, see the introduction.

Get started with SharePoint BI

The BI tools and components in SharePoint 2016 work together so that you can explore, visualize, and share information in interactive reports, scorecards, and dashboards. In addition to the server-side services, they include SharePoint sites, libraries, and content types that are specifically designed for providing self-service BI functionality.

> ⚠ **IMPORTANT** Full SharePoint BI capabilities are included in SharePoint 2016 Enterprise when it is installed with Microsoft SQL Server 2016 Enterprise in on-premises deployments. For the full range of BI capabilities in SharePoint Server 2016, including Excel integration, you also need to have Office Online Server (OOS) installed and activated in your deployment.

In SharePoint 2016, self-service BI goes beyond individual insight. All self-service BI capabilities are extended into a collaborative BI platform that you can use to share insights and work together to develop insights even further. For example, you can view and interact with data in Power View visualizations and in Excel workbooks that have been published to SharePoint 2016 sites in your browser by using Excel Online.

On the server side, SharePoint 2016 relies on Office Online Server, which connects to SQL Server 2016 Analysis Services (SSAS) and SQL Server 2016 Reporting Services (SSRS) servers to provide PowerPivot and Power View capabilities.

> 🔍 **SEE ALSO** For more information about deploying SQL Server 2016 PowerPivot and Power View features in SharePoint 2016, go to *https://go.microsoft.com/fwlink/?LinkId=717341*.

SharePoint 2016 BI server-side components also include PerformancePoint Services and Microsoft Visio Services. By using PerformancePoint Services, you can create centrally managed interactive dashboards that display key performance indicators (KPIs) and data visualizations in the form of scorecards, reports, and filters.

By using Visio Services, you can view visual diagrams and share them to SharePoint sites. You can create and publish diagrams that are connected to data sources and that can be configured to refresh data to display up-to-date information. The diagrams can be viewed on multiple devices, which means that you can view Visio documents without having the Visio client application installed on your device. Visio diagrams can also be rendered within the Microsoft Visio Web Access web part.

For SharePoint Online, the BI features are supported in several SharePoint Online and Office 365 plans, such as P2, E3, E4, E5, and O365 Education. The BI features in SharePoint Online are more limited compared to those available in SharePoint 2016 on-premises deployments. For example, SQL Server Reporting Services (SSRS) Integrated Mode is not available. You can publish PowerPivot and Power View reports created in Excel, but you cannot build a Power View report in SharePoint Online.

> 🔍 **SEE ALSO** For more information about the BI features that are included in the SharePoint Online and Office 365 subscription plans, go to *https://technet.microsoft.com/en-GB/library/jj819267.aspx.*

> ✅ **TIP** Office 365 also provides the Microsoft Power BI suite of business analytics tools to analyze data and share insights. The Power BI suite includes the Power BI online service and the Power BI Desktop application, which provide a powerful BI platform and functionalities. The Power BI functionalities are not fully compatible with those provided by SharePoint and Excel. The Power BI Desktop files have a .pbix extension and can be published to the Power BI online service. At the time of writing, the .pbix files are not integrated with SharePoint. For more information about Power BI, go to *https://powerbi.microsoft.com.*

In addition to the server-side components, SharePoint 2016 BI provides site and library templates that include the BI self-service capabilities, such as the Business Intelligence Center site, the PowerPivot site, and the PowerPivot Gallery library.

> ✅ **TIP** The Enterprise Search Center site includes a built-in vertical search results page named Reports, which searches the index of BI-related reports and provides previews of the search results for quick reference.

> ⚠️ **IMPORTANT** The PowerPivot site and PowerPivot Gallery are not available in SharePoint Online.

13

The Business Intelligence Center is an enterprise SharePoint site that is designed to support enterprise-wide BI applications. It provides multiple libraries, web parts, and content types that are optimized for BI self-service applications. By using the Business Intelligence Center, organizations can centrally store and manage data connections, reports, scorecards, dashboards, and web part pages.

Business Intelligence Center

Business Intelligence Center

Empower the people in your organization to gain insights with ease using familiar tools. Learn More

Explore and Analyze Data
Create powerful data mash-ups of millions of rows of data from various sources using PowerPivot.

Design Interactive Reports
Create presentation-ready reports that tell a compelling story using Excel and Power View.

Share Dashboards
Publish dashboards that users can interact with using Excel Services.

Use the Business Intelligence Center to centrally store and manage reports and dashboards

The PowerPivot site is a collaboration SharePoint site that includes BI capabilities with PowerPivot and Power View features. It is similar to the Team site, but in addition to the default Documents library, it also provides a PowerPivot Gallery, which is a document library that has additional functionalities that are designed to support BI applications.

> **TIP** The PowerPivot capabilities include server-side data refresh processing, collaboration, and management support for PowerPivot workbooks. For these capabilities to be available in your SharePoint 2016 deployment, you need to install Microsoft SQL Server 2016 PowerPivot for SharePoint 2016, which is available as a free download from *https://www.microsoft.com/en-us /download/details.aspx?id=52675*.

When the PowerPivot site feature is active in the site collection, the PowerPivot site template becomes available in the New SharePoint Site page when you create a new site in the site collection.

Select a template:

| Collaboration | Enterprise | Custom |

Team Site
Blog
PowerPivot Site
Project Site
Community Site

Create a new PowerPivot site

The PowerPivot Gallery is a special-purpose library in SharePoint that you can use to view and update Excel workbooks that contain PowerPivot data. It also includes options for configuring a data refresh schedule and creating a Power View report based on a published PowerPivot workbook. The PowerPivot Gallery is deployed as a part of a PowerPivot site and is displayed on its Quick Launch.

You can also add the PowerPivot Gallery to an existing team site. When PowerPivot for SharePoint 2016 is deployed in a site collection, the PowerPivot Gallery app is added to the list of available apps for all sites in the site collection and is listed on the Your Apps page on the team site.

Add a PowerPivot Gallery

When you publish an Excel workbook to the PowerPivot Gallery, you can use different library views to display the worksheets. When the workbook is uploaded to the PowerPivot Gallery, it is displayed in the Gallery view, which allows you to focus on individual worksheets in the workbook by displaying a sheet in the viewing area.

Use a Gallery view to browse through the worksheets in an Excel workbook

In the Theatre view, the viewing area is centered, with individual worksheets revolving to the front as you focus on them. In the Carousel view, you can browse through the worksheets by clicking or tapping left and right arrows. The All Documents view displays the list of files in the PowerPivot Gallery. This view is useful for managing files.

> **TIP** The PowerPivot Gallery views—such as the Gallery, Theatre, and Carousel views—require Microsoft Silverlight to display the workbooks. Client devices must have Silverlight installed to use the PowerPivot Gallery.

Although the PowerPivot Gallery is specially designed for BI reports, when the PowerPivot site feature is active, the PowerPivot for SharePoint capabilities can also be used in a generic document library, such as the default Documents library, to view and update the Excel workbooks that contain PowerPivot data.

You can choose to display one or more worksheets or the individual named items in the workbooks by using the browser view options in Excel. The default is to display an entire workbook with all worksheets.

When you choose to display a worksheet, an entire worksheet is displayed in Excel Online, similar to how it looks in Excel. This view works well for dashboards that are created in Excel, because you can see all the charts and tables on the screen in a single view. When you use a filter, all displayed items that are connected to that filter are refreshed. If you've identified more than one worksheet in the workbook to be displayed, the additional worksheets are shown as tabs across the bottom of the screen that you can select to view another worksheet.

View an entire worksheet in Excel Online

When you choose to display a named item, such as a chart, a table, or a range of cells, the item is displayed in the center of the screen in Excel Online, and additional parameters, such as filters, can be displayed as thumbnail images along the right side of the screen. When you use a filter, the displayed chart or table is refreshed. This view works well for individual charts and tables.

Product Sales	Date			2015 Total			2016 Total	Grand Total
	⊟ 2015				⊟ 2016			
Product	⊕ H1	⊕ H2			⊕ H1	⊕ H2		
⊕ Arm chairs	53779.48	90240.37	144019.85		75159.52	110349.14	185508.66	329528.51
⊕ Cabinets	91959.33	90081.58	182040.91		33531.64	90889.91	124421.55	306462.46
⊕ Chairs	169543.38	144668.09	314211.47		199341.16	193811.16	393152.32	707363.79
⊕ Chests of drawers	112156.86	144431.56	256588.42		77533.93	147512.66	225046.59	481635.01
⊕ Desks	144798.75	181780.81	326579.56		122831.9	92105.42	214937.32	541516.88
⊕ Sofas	72320.01	105817.1	178137.11		59868.37	79711.25	139579.62	317716.73
⊕ Tables	161458.26	215261.55	376719.81		167664.2	155898.93	323563.13	700282.94
⊕ Wall units	124044.39	79545.72	203590.11		56479.55	132853.09	189332.64	392922.75
Grand Total	930060.46	1051826.78	1981887.24		792410.27	1003131.56	1795541.83	3777429.07

Display an individual named item in Excel Online

To publish worksheets or named items in an Excel workbook to a document library

1. In Excel, open the workbook that you want to publish to a SharePoint document library. Select the **File** tab, and on the **Info** page, select **Browser View Options** to open the Browser View Options dialog box.

2. In the **Browser View Options** dialog box, do one of the following:

   - To publish worksheets, on the **Show** tab, in the drop-down list, select **Sheets**. Then select the check boxes next to the worksheets that you want to display, and select **OK**.

Select worksheets to publish to SharePoint

- To publish named items, on the **Show** tab, in the drop-down list, select **Items in the Workbook**. Then, select the check boxes next to the named items that you want to publish. If there are additional filters and slicers to be displayed, on the **Parameters** tab select **Add**, and then select the filters. Select **OK** to confirm and return to the **Parameters** tab. When you are done, select **OK** in the **Browser View Options** dialog box.

3. Save and close the workbook.

4. Upload the workbook to a document library.

To create a PowerPivot Gallery in a team site

1. In a team site where you want to create a PowerPivot Gallery, on the **Your Apps** page, select the **PowerPivot Gallery** app.

2. In the **Adding PowerPivot Gallery** dialog, in the **Name** box, enter the name of the new gallery, and then select **Create**.

Adding PowerPivot Gallery	✕
Pick a name You can add this app multiple times to your site. Give it a unique name.	Name: _____
Advanced Options	Create Cancel

Create a PowerPivot Gallery

3. On the Quick Launch, select your new gallery. If Silverlight is not installed on your device, a message appears prompting you to install Silverlight. Click or tap the message to download Silverlight and start the setup wizard. Follow the wizard to install Silverlight, and then select **Close** on the **Installation Successful** page.

> **TIP** When a new PowerPivot Gallery is created, its link is added to the Recent section of the Quick Launch. If you want the link to be permanent, you can edit the Quick Launch to move the link from the Recent section into another area on the Quick Launch.

To switch views in a PowerPivot Gallery

1. In the PowerPivot Gallery, on the **Library** tab, in the **Manage Views** group, under **Current View**, select the arrow to display a list of views.

Switch between views in the PowerPivot Gallery

2. Select the view you want to switch to.

To create a PowerPivot site

1. In the parent site where you want to create a PowerPivot site, on the **Site Contents** page, select **new subsite**.

2. On the **New Site** page, enter the name and URL for the new site.

3. In the **Template** section, on the **Collaboration** tab, select **PowerPivot site**.

4. Select the permissions and navigation options you want, and then select **Create** to confirm the new site creation.

Shape your data

When you work with business intelligence, there are three main steps to consider:

1. Identify the data sources for your reports and establish connections to them.

2. Organize the data from these multiple sources to build a coherent data model.

3. Build and share reports based on that data model.

The first two steps are dedicated to identifying and shaping your data into an aggregate data model so that you can then build insightful and compelling reports for better decision making. Your BI report is as insightful as the data model it is based on.

13

With data models that are supported in SharePoint 2016 and Excel 2016, you can bring data from a variety of sources into one cohesive data set, and then use it to create charts, tables, reports, and dashboards. A data model is essentially a collection of data from multiple sources with relationships between different fields, which you can create and organize by using PowerPivot for Excel. Typically, a data model includes one or more tables of data. To build a data model, you can sort, organize, and calculate the data and create relationships between different tables.

When you create a data model in Excel, in addition to data that is native to Excel, you can also combine data from one or more external data sources. SharePoint and OOS support a subset of the external data connections that you can create from Excel. The external data connections that are supported in SharePoint Server 2016 and OOS include connections to the following data sources:

- SQL Server tables

- SQL Server Analysis Services cubes

- OLE DB and ODBC data sources

- OData data sources

> **TIP** To use data from external data sources that are not supported in SharePoint 2016 and OOS, you might be able to import a snapshot of the data into Excel, and then use it in your data model as data native to Excel.

To build a data model, you can use the PowerPivot add-in for Excel that is included in Excel 2016. With PowerPivot for Excel, you can import data from external sources, if needed, and build relationships between disparate data so that you can work with the data as a whole.

> **TIP** If you do not see the PowerPivot tab in Excel, you might need to enable the PowerPivot for Excel add-in.

PowerPivot provides the data-modeling engine in Excel that is used to create data relationships and hierarchies to design your data model according to your business requirements.

Create data relationships in a PowerPivot data model

After you have created a data model in Excel, you can use it as a source to create multiple charts, tables, and reports. For example, you can use Excel 2016 to create interactive PivotChart reports and PivotTable reports, or you can use Power View to create interactive visualizations such as pie charts, bar charts, bubble charts, line charts, and many others.

> **SEE ALSO** For more information about building data models in Excel 2016, go to *https://support.office.com/en-us/article/Create-a-Data-Model-in-Excel-87E7A54C-87DC-488E-9410-5C75DBCB0F7B*.

13

You can use SharePoint Server 2016 BI capabilities to view and use published workbooks that contain data models. You collect data in a data model, and then use it for reports and scorecards that you can publish and share. You can use SharePoint permissions to control who can view and use the reports, scorecards, and workbooks that you have published. SharePoint and Office Online Server retain connectivity to external data sources and refresh the data so that the reports, scorecards, and workbooks remain up to date.

To enable the PowerPivot for Excel add-in

1. In Excel 2016, select the **File** tab, and then select **Options** to open the Excel Options dialog box.

2. In the **Excel Options** dialog box, select **Add-ins**.

3. Select **COM Add-ins**, and then select **Go**.

4. In the **COM Add-ins** dialog box, select **Microsoft Power Pivot for Excel** from the list of available add-ins, and then select **OK**.

Enable the PowerPivot for Excel add-in

5. Verify that the **PowerPivot** tab is available.

To explore a data model in an Excel workbook

1. In Excel, on the **PowerPivot** tab, in the **Data Model** group, select **Manage** to open the data model in Data View.

2. In Data View, explore the data in each table and do the following:

   - View the formulas in the calculated fields by pointing to each calculated field column. The calculated fields are displayed in a different color than the rest of the fields in the table.

   - Move between tables in the data model by using the tabs at the bottom of the view.

3. On the **PowerPivot** tab, in the **View** group, select **Diagram View** to switch to the Diagram View.

4. Explore the data model diagram by doing the following:

   - Explore the relationships between tables and connections between the related fields.

   - Identify whether data hierarchies are set up in the tables by scrolling down within the table boxes to view the hierarchies.

5. When you're done, switch to the Excel workbook by clicking or tapping the Excel icon in the upper-left corner of the PowerPivot window.

Create and publish PowerPivot dashboards

By using PowerPivot for Excel, you can combine data from multiple sources and build PivotTable reports and PivotChart reports for information analysis, which you can then publish to SharePoint as interactive dashboards.

After you create a data model, you can use it to build PivotTables and PivotCharts in an Excel workbook. The workbook can then be published to a SharePoint site, where the PowerPivot server components provide server-side query processing of PowerPivot data in Excel workbooks that you access from SharePoint sites.

> **SEE ALSO** For more information about building PivotTables in Excel 2016, go to *https://support.office.com/en-US/article/Create-a-PivotTable-in-Excel-2016-to-analyze-worksheet-data-c875f798-78cf-49a2-9f79-c842dcdd2869*. For more information about building PivotCharts in Excel 2016, go to *https://support.office.com/en-US/article/Create-a-PivotChart-in-Excel-2016-for-Windows-b7668cdd-1981-4271-9ce1-9de5a71c230a*.

When you publish a workbook with PowerPivot data to a PowerPivot Gallery or to a general document library, SharePoint creates pages to display its PowerPivot items in Excel Online. The published workbooks can contain embedded PowerPivot data or have a connection to PowerPivot data that is published in a different workbook in the same library. SharePoint 2016 and OOS include the data model functionality that you use to interact with PowerPivot dashboards in a browser. You can view, sort, filter, and interact with PivotTables and PivotCharts in the Excel Online app in your browser as you would if you were using the Excel client application. You can show or hide the PivotTable or PivotChart Fields panel, depending on whether you want to modify the reports in Excel Online.

Publish a PivotChart to SharePoint

13

When you want to publish an individual PivotTable or PivotChart, you must set up the browser viewing options in Excel to point to the named table or chart with the associated filters that users would interact with. You then publish the workbook to a PowerPivot Gallery or a document library on the SharePoint site to create an interactive PowerPivot dashboard.

> ⚠ **IMPORTANT** For on-premises deployments, you must publish to a SharePoint 2016 server that has Microsoft SQL Server 2016 PowerPivot for SharePoint 2016 installed and to a site that has the PowerPivot site collection feature activated. If you publish to a server or a site that does not have PowerPivot server-side capabilities, the data will not load when you open the workbook from a library.

To publish a PivotChart or PivotTable to SharePoint

1. In Excel, open the workbook where the PivotChart or PivotTable is located.

2. Open the **Browser View Options** dialog box.

3. On the **Show** tab, select **Items in the Workbook**, and then select the name of the PivotChart or PivotTable you want to publish.

Publish a chart to SharePoint

4. If there are additional filters that you want to add, on the **Parameters** tab, select **Add**, then select the filters for the table or chart. After you've selected all filters, select **OK** to confirm and return to the **Parameters** tab.

5. Select **OK** in the **Browser View Options** dialog box, and then save and close the workbook.

6. Upload the workbook to a document library or a PowerPivot Gallery.

7. Open the workbook in Excel Online to display the PivotChart or PivotTable with the appropriate filters for user interaction.

To analyze the data in a PowerPivot dashboard

1. Display the Pivot Table or the PivotChart you want to work with.

2. If necessary, minimize the **Fields** pane to provide more space for the table or chart.

3. Do any of the following:

   • To drill down into data in the PivotTable, use the plus and minus buttons to expand and condense the sections in the table.

   • To analyze the data by using the PivotChart, use various combinations for the available filters. For example, you can select different combinations of parameters for the horizontal and vertical axes by using their drop-down lists in the chart control. Within each parameter, you can select different values to filter the data further.

Display PowerPivot dashboards in web parts

After you have published a PivotTable and a PivotChart to a SharePoint site, you can display them in a webpage by using an Excel Web Access web part. An Excel Web Access web part is a container that displays Excel content in a SharePoint site. You don't have to open the workbook for viewing; in the web part, the content is displayed as part of the page. The web part connects to the published workbook to obtain the data and present the PowerPivot charts and tables to the users.

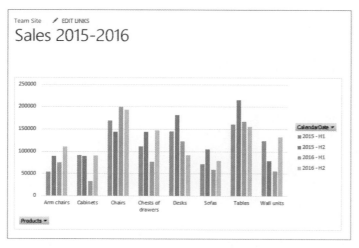

Publish PowerPivot reports in an Excel Web Access web part

13

> **TIP** Web parts are server-side controls that run in the context of SharePoint site pages and provide additional features and functionalities. For an in-depth discussion of web parts, see Chapter 7, "Work with webpages."

You can create a dashboard-style webpage by adding several Excel Web Access web parts to the same page to display different PowerPivot charts and tables side by side. Each web part is independent, and filters applied in one report do not affect another. The PowerPivot charts and tables displayed in web parts on the same page can be from different Excel workbooks, but all workbooks must be published to SharePoint.

To publish a PivotTable or PivotChart in an Excel Web Access web part

1. Open the SharePoint page where you want to publish a PivotTable or a PivotChart in a web part for editing.

2. Do the following to add the Excel Web Access web part to the page:

   a. Position your cursor in a zone in the page content area where you want to add the web part, and then on the **Insert** tab, select **Web Part**.

   b. In the **Categories** pane that appears near the top of the page, select **Business Data**.

Add an Excel Web Access web part to a webpage

   c. In the **Parts** pane, select **Excel Web Access**, and then select **Add** to add the web part to the page.

3. Connect to a workbook that contains the PowerPivot dashboard by doing the following:

   a. In the **Excel Web Access** web part, select **Click here to open the tool pane**.

Connect to the workbook that contains the PowerPivot report

IMPORTANT The PivotChart or PivotTable must be available for browser viewing in the published workbook.

   b. In the tool pane, in the **Workbook Display** section in the **Workbook** box, do one of the following:

- Enter the URL for the workbook.

- Select the ellipsis (...) button, then in the **Select an Asset** dialog, browse to the workbook that you want to use, and then select **Insert**.

   c. In the **Named Item** box, enter the name of the PivotChart or PivotTable you want to display.

4. If you want options for modifying the PivotChart and PivotTable to be displayed within the web part, including the Fields pane, in the **Navigation and Interactivity** section, select **PivotTable & PivotChart Modification**. If you want users to be able to explore the report but not modify it, leave this option unchecked which is the default.

5. In the **Appearance** section, in the **Chrome Type** list, select **None**.

6. Specify settings for the web part in other sections, if required. When you're done, at the bottom of the tool pane, select **OK** to apply your changes and close the pane.

7. On the **Page** tab, select **Save** to save the webpage and return to browse mode. Check the page in and then publish it to make the page available to the site users.

Build visualizations by using Power View

13

Power View in SharePoint 2016 is a browser-based Silverlight application. By using Power View, you can present and share insights with others in your organization through interactive presentations. Power View in SharePoint 2016 provides a highly interactive, browser-based data exploration, visualization, and presentation experience. By using Power View, you can create interactive reports with intuitive charts, grids, and filters that provide the ability to visually explore data and easily create interactive visualizations to help define insights.

Power View is available as a standalone version in SharePoint 2016 on-premises deployments and as a native feature in Excel 2016. Power View in Excel 2016 supports HTML5, whereas Power View for SharePoint requires Silverlight to be installed on the user's device.

> ⚠️ **IMPORTANT** You can publish Excel Power View reports to SharePoint Online for viewing as a part of an Excel workbook, but you cannot create Power View reports in SharePoint Online and Office 365. The BI capabilities in Office 365 are available in the Power BI platform, but they are not compatible with SharePoint at the time of writing. For more information about the Power BI platform, see *https://powerbi.microsoft.com*.

> ✅ **TIP** In SharePoint 2016, Power View is a feature of the SQL Server 2016 Reporting Services Add-in for Microsoft SharePoint Products.

Power View reports in SharePoint 2016 provide views of data from data models based on PowerPivot workbooks published in a PowerPivot Gallery, or models deployed to SSAS instances. Each page within a Power View report is referred to as a *view*. In Power View, you can quickly create a variety of interactive and intuitive visualizations, including tables and matrices, and pie, bar, and bubble charts.

With Power View, you can plot your data on a map and create sets of multiple interconnected charts.

Create interactive visualizations by using Power View

Power View uses the metadata in the underlying data model to compute the relationships between the different tables and fields. Based on these relationships, Power View provides the ability to filter one visualization, and at the same time highlight another visualization in a current view. In addition to filters, you can use slicers to compare and evaluate your data from different perspectives. When you have multiple slicers in a view, the selection for one slicer filters the other slicers in the view.

> ⚠️ **IMPORTANT** Power View reports on SharePoint are separate files that have the .rdlx file format. In Excel, Power View sheets are part of an Excel .xlsx workbook. The .rdlx file format is not compatible with the .xlsx format. In other words, you cannot open a Power View .rdlx file in Excel. Equally, SharePoint cannot open Power View sheets in an Excel .xlsx file. The .rdlx file format is also not compatible with the .rdl files that you create in SQL Server Report Builder or SQL Server Reporting Services (SSRS). You cannot open .rdl reports in Power View, and vice versa. Additionally, the .rdlx file format is not compatible with the .pbix file format of the Power BI Desktop application.

The Power View design environment in SharePoint 2016 is similar to the Power View tab in Excel 2016. You can open a published worksheet in the Power View design mode from the PowerPivot Gallery.

> ✓ **TIP** Power View uses SharePoint 2016 permissions to control access to Power View reports.

A Power View report in SharePoint 2016 can contain multiple views that are all based on the same data model. However, each view has its own visualizations and filters. In design mode, you can copy and paste between the views, and you can also duplicate views.

Power View in SharePoint 2016 has two presentation modes: a reading mode and a full-screen mode. In the presentation modes, the ribbon and other design areas are hidden to provide more space for the reports, which are still fully interactive.

To open a workbook data model in Power View

1. In the PowerPivot Gallery, in the upper right of the workbook gallery view, select the **Power View** icon to open the workbook data model in the Power View design environment.

Open the workbook in Power View Design mode

13

To switch between design and presentation modes in Power View

1. In the Power View design environment, do one of the following:

   - To switch from the reading mode to the design mode, in the upper right of the page, select **Edit Report**.

   - To switch from the design mode to the reading mode, on the **Home** tab, in the **Display** group, select **Reading Mode**.

   Reading Mode   Full Screen

   Select the presentation mode for the Power View report

   - To switch to from the design mode to the full-screen mode, on the **Home** tab, in the **Display** group, select **Full Screen**.

   - To switch from the reading mode to the full-screen mode, in the upper right of the Power View report, select **Full Screen**.

To save a Power View report

1. In the Power View design environment, in design mode, select the **File** tab and then select **Save As**.

2. In the **Save As** dialog box, select the URL of the Power Pivot Gallery or another location that you want to save the report to, and then enter the name of the file that will contain the report. Select **Save** to save the report.

> **TIP** A Power View report is saved as a file with the .rdlx extension. The file is separate from the .xlsx workbook that contains the data model the report is based on.

To open a Power View report from a PowerPivot Gallery

1. Open the PowerPivot Gallery that contains the report.

2. Select the report snapshot to open it in the Power View environment.

To add a view to a Power View report

1. Open a report in the Power View environment and switch to the design mode.

2. On the **Home** tab, in the **Insert** group, select **New View** to add a view page.

**New
View** ▾

Create a new view in Power View report

To create a chart in Power View

1. In the Power View design mode, open the view you want to add a chart to.

2. Build a table that would provide a base for your chart by doing the following:

   a. In the **Fields List** pane, locate the first field you want to include in the table and drag it to the view. Power View builds a table in which a column displays the values of the field.

   b. Locate the second field in the **Fields List** pane and drag it to the table you created for the first field. When the table is highlighted, drop the field. Power View calculates the data and displays a table with two columns.

3. On the **Design** tab, in the **Visualizations** group, in the **Charts** section, select the chart type that you want to create, such as a pie chart, column chart, or bar chart.

> **TIP** The choice of virtualizations in the Charts section is contextual: the list displays only the virtualizations that can be used with the selected data. For example, all charts are unavailable if there are no aggregated numeric values in the data.

4. To add a slicer to a pie chart, in the **Fields List**, locate the field that you want to slice by, and then drag it to the **Slices** area at the bottom of the **Field List** pane.

13

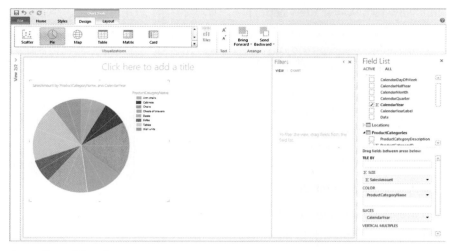

Create Power View charts

To create a Power Map with pie charts

1. In the Power View design mode, open the view you want to add a map to.

2. Build the table that will provide data for the pie charts you want to display on the map by doing the following:

    *   In the **Fields List** pane, locate the field that will define the size of a "whole pie" circle in each location, and drag it to the design surface view. Power View draws a table with the actual data displayed in a column.

    > **TIP** Power View in SharePoint 2016 supports two-dimensional (2D) charts plotted on maps. Power View in Excel 2016 supports both 2D and 3D charts for Power Maps.

    *   In the **Fields List** pane, locate a field that would define the geographic location of the charts on the map and drag it to the table to add this field. Power View calculates the data and displays a new table with two columns.

    > **TIP** Power Map requires at least one geographic value per row of data. This could be a Latitude/Longitude pair, City, Country/Region, Zip code/Postal code, State/Province, or Address. The accuracy of Power Map depends on the geographic data you provide. For more information about how to prepare your data model, go to *https://support.office.com/en-us/article/Get-and-prep-your-data-for-Power-Map-67e19f9a-22b8-4b89-a604-3ebb49a368e5*.

3. On the **Design** tab, in the **Visualizations** group, select **Map**. Power Map uses Bing to geocode your data based on its geographic properties. If a privacy warning appears in the yellow bar under the ribbon, stating that some of the data needs to be geocoded by sending it to Bing, select **Enable Content** to confirm that you would like to proceed.

4. A map visualization appears in the view, with the "whole pie" circles plotted in the locations identified. To show the pie charts instead of the circles, in the **Fields List** pane, identify the field that would define the sectors of the pie circles and drag it to the **Color** area at the bottom of the pane.

Σ SIZE
Σ SalesAmount ▼
LOCATIONS
⊕ CityName ▼
LONGITUDE   LATITUDE
COLOR
ProductCategoryName ▼

Set up fields that contain data for plotting pie charts on the map, such as their size, location, and colors

5. The map is redisplayed with pie charts for each location and a legend in the upper right of the view page. The legend lists the values of the field you configured in the previous step for the pie sectors, with each value mapped to its sector color in the pie charts.

To move among views in a Power View report

1. Do one of the following:

   - In the design mode, select one of the preview images in the **View** pane on the left of the screen to move to that view.

   - In the reading and full-screen presentation modes, select the navigation arrows in the lower-right corner of the page view to move among views.

Display Power View reports in web parts

Power View reports can be integrated into SharePoint site pages by using web parts. Two generic web parts provided by SharePoint 2016 can be used to display the Power View reports on a webpage: the Page Viewer web part and the Silverlight web part.

13

The Page Viewer web part is a general-purpose web part that retrieves and displays a webpage by using a hyperlink. You can easily add this web part to new and existing pages to display Power View reports. When you need to display a report for users to analyze and explore data, the Page Viewer web part can come in useful.

Display Power View reports in the Page Viewer web part

> ⚠ **IMPORTANT** The Page Viewer web part uses the HTML <IFRAME> element and therefore cannot be used in browsers that don't support IFrames.

The Silverlight web part is a container for Silverlight applications. It can be used to display the Power View environment.

To display a Power View report in a Page Viewer web part

1. Open for editing the SharePoint page where you want to display a Power View report in a web part.

2. Do the following to add the Page Viewer web part to the page:

    a. Position your cursor in a zone in the page content area where you want to add the web part, and then on the **Insert** tab, select **Web Part**.

    b. In the **Categories** pane that appears near the top of the page, select **Media and Content**.

Add a Page Viewer web part to a page

   c. In the **Parts** pane, select **Page Viewer**, and then select **Add** to add the web part to the page.

3. Link to the Power View report by doing the following:

   a. In the **Page Viewer** web part, select **open the tool pane**.

Link to the Power View report webpage

   b. In the web part tool pane, in the **Link** section, provide a link to the Power View report by doing the following:

     i. Open a new tab or window in your browser and navigate to the Power View report you want to display. In the Power View environment, set up a view page the way you want it to appear in the web part. For example, switch to the reading mode and display the view page that you want to appear in the web part when it first appears on the web-page. When you're done, copy the URL from the browser address bar.

     ii. Return to the **Page Viewer** tool pane, and select the ellipsis to the right of the link box to open the text editor. Delete any text from the text box, and then paste the Power View report URL in the text box (by right-clicking in the text box and selecting **Paste**).

```
http://wideworldimporters/_layouts/15/Repor
tServer/AdHocReportDesigner.aspx?RelativeRe
portUrl=%2fwideworldimporters%2fPowerPivot%
2520Gallery%2fSalesPerformance.rdlx&ViewMod
e=Presentation&ReportSection=ReportSection
```

Copy the Power View report URL and paste it into the text editor

iii. To provide a better user experience when the report is displayed in a web part, you can hide the top tool bar in the Power View page (the bar that includes the Edit Report and the Full Screen options) by adding a *PreviewBar* parameter to the URL. In the text editor, at the end of the URL, add **&PreviewBar=False**.

iv. In the text editor, select **OK** to insert the URL into the Link box in the web part tool pane.

> **TIP** You can verify the URL by selecting Test Link above the Link box. The URL is tested in a new browser tab.

4. In the **Appearance** section of the web part tool pane, in the **Chrome Type** list, select **None**.

5. Specify other settings in the web part tool pane if required. When you're done, at the bottom of the pane, select **OK** to apply your changes and close the pane.

6. On the **Page** tab, select **Save** to save the webpage and return to the browse mode. Check the page in, and then publish it to make the page available to the site users.

Skills review

In this chapter, you learned how to:

- Get started with SharePoint BI

- Shape your data

- Create and publish PowerPivot dashboards

- Display PowerPivot dashboards in web parts

- Build visualizations by using Power View

- Display Power View reports in web parts

Practice tasks

The practice file for these tasks is located in the SP2016SBS\Ch13 folder.

> ⚠ **IMPORTANT** You must have sufficient permissions to perform the operations involved in each practice task to complete that practice task. For more information, see Appendix A, "SharePoint 2016 user permissions and permission levels."

Get started with SharePoint BI

Open Excel 2016, then go to your SharePoint site and perform the following tasks:

1. In your SharePoint site, create a new PowerPivot Gallery named **PowerPivot Gallery**. Upload the **SalesData.xlsx** Excel workbook to the PowerPivot Gallery.

2. In the PowerPivot Gallery, do the following:

   a. Open the workbook in the default Gallery view.

   b. Switch the PowerPivot Gallery view to the Carousel view, and open the **SalesData.xlsx** workbook in this view.

   c. Switch back to Gallery view.

3. In Excel, open the **SalesData.xlsx** workbook. Publish the following worksheets to the **Documents** library on your SharePoint site:

   - Sales

   - Products

   - SalesPivot

4. In the **Documents** library, open the **SalesData.xlsx** workbook in Excel Online, and then do the following:

   - In the SalesPivot worksheet, expand the **Chairs** category in the table and view how this change is reflected in the chart.

   - Condense **H1** and **H2** for year **2015** into a single column and view how the chart changes to reflect your actions in the table.

   - Explore the data further by expanding or condensing rows and columns in the table and viewing how these changes are reflected in the chart.

- Change some data in the Sales worksheet, and then view the changes reflected in the table and chart. You might need to refresh the table to see the changes; you can do so by right-clicking the table and selecting **Refresh**.

 TIP If a security prompt appears, confirm that you want to refresh the workbook.

5. Close Excel Online when you're done.

Shape your data

Continuing in Excel 2016, perform the following tasks:

1. In the **SalesData.xlsx** workbook, go to the Power Pivot tab and explore the data model.

2. In the diagram view, do the following:

   a. Review the table relationships and field connections:

      - Between the **Sales** and **Shops** tables.

      - Between the **Sales** and **Dates** tables.

      - Between the **Sales** and **Products** tables.

      - Between the **Shops** and **Locations** tables.

      - Between the **Products** and **Product Categories** tables.

   b. In the **Dates** table box, scroll down to display the **Calendar** hierarchy that establishes the relationships between the columns in the **Dates** table. For example, a date is a part of a month, which in turn is a part of a quarter, which in turn is a part of a half year, which in turn is a part of a year.

   c. In the **Products** table box, scroll down to explore the **Products** hierarchy that establishes relationships between the **ProductName** and **ProductCategory** fields.

3. In the data view, in the **Products** table, analyze the formula in the **ProductCategory** calculated column.

Create and publish PowerPivot dashboards

Continuing in Excel 2016 and your SharePoint site, perform the following tasks:

1. In Excel, save the **SalesData.xlsx** workbook as SalesDataPivotChart.xlsx in the same folder. Publish the PivotChart named **Sales 2015-2016** in the **SalesDataPivotChart.xlsx** workbook to the **Documents** library on your SharePoint site.

2. Analyze the data in the PivotChart in Excel Online by doing the following:

   - Filter the **Products** on the horizontal axis so that only the **Tables** sales data is plotted on the chart.

   - Filter the **Calendar** to see only the **2016** sales data in the chart.

   - Experiment with adding more filters to the horizontal and vertical axes to drill further into the data.

3. Close Excel Online when you're done.

Display PowerPivot dashboards in web parts

Continuing in Excel 2016 and your SharePoint site, perform the following tasks:

1. Add a page to your site and name it **MyDashboard**. In the new page that opens for editing, in the **Title** area at the top of the page, add a space between the words, so that the title reads **My Dashboard**.

   Title

   My Dashboard

   Give your dashboard a title

2. On the **My Dashboard** page, publish a PivotTable in the Excel Web Access web part, with the following settings:

   - **Workbook Display** section

     - **Workbook**   **SalesData.xlsx** in the **Documents** library

     - **Named Item**   Product Sales

   - **Toolbar and Title Bar** section

     - **Type of Toolbar**   None

   - **Appearance** section

     - **Height**   Select **Yes**; enter **300** for the height in pixels

     - **Chrome Type**   None

3. Publish a PivotChart in the second Excel Web Access web part in the **My Dashboard** page, with the following settings:

   - **Workbook Display** section

     - **Workbook**   **SalesData.xlsx** in the **Documents** library

     - **Named Item**   Sales 2015-2016

- **Toolbar and Title Bar** section
    - **Type of Toolbar**   None
- **Appearance** section
    - **Height**   Select **Yes**; enter **350** for the height in pixels
    - **Chrome Type**   None

4. Check in and publish the **My Dashboard** page on your site. Validate that the table and chart are interactive and that users can analyze the data.

Publish PowerPivot dashboards in web parts

Build visualizations by using Power View

Continuing in your SharePoint site, perform the following tasks:

1. In the PowerPivot Gallery, open the **SalesData.xlsx** workbook data model in Power View.

2. Switch from the reading mode to the design mode.

3. Create a Power Map with sales data pie charts plotted at store locations, using the following data fields for plotting the pie charts on the map:

    *   Size of a pie circle

        SalesAmount field in the **Sales** table

    *   Location

        CityName field in the **Locations** table

    *   Categories for the sectors (mapped to different colors in the chart)

        ProductCategoryName field in the **ProductCategories** table

4. At the top of the view page, in the title area, enter Sales Performance.

5. Switch to the reading view and explore the map visualization you've built by doing the following:

    *   Call out a particular product category by selecting the category in the legend; for example, **Chairs**. The colors for other categories in the pie charts are dimmed, so that the sales performance for the Chairs category is easily identifiable in all locations.

    *   Point to a pie chart in a city location to display the sales data for the location.

    *   Experiment with selecting different filters in the upper right of the view page to further drill into the data.

6. Add a view to your Power View report. In the new view, create two connected visualizations, a pie chart and bar chart, by doing the following:

    a. Create a pie chart that displays the sales amount by product category for all stores sliced by year, to complement the pie charts for individual stores on the map on the first view page. Set up the pie chart so that it is based on the following data fields:

        *   Size of the whole pie

            SalesAmount field in the **Sales** table

        *   Categories for the sectors (mapped to different colors in the chart)

            ProductCategoryName field in the **ProductCategories** table

        *   Slicer

            CalendarYear field in the **Dates** table

    b. Create a bar chart that displays the sales amount by the product material, such as Oak, Pine, Cherry, Leather, and Metal. When the material filter is selected in the bar chart, the selection will filter the pie chart.

The bar chart is based on the following data fields:

- Values for the horizontal axis

  SalesAmount field in the **Sales** table

- Categories for the vertical axis

  ProductMaterial field in the **Products** table

7. At the top of the view, in the title area, enter Sales Comparison.

8. To filter the pie chart based on the selection in the bar chart, in the bar chart, click or tap a bar for a material; for example, **Oak**. Other bars in the bar chart become dimmed. The pie chart displays only the parts that apply to oak furniture, with the other parts dimmed.

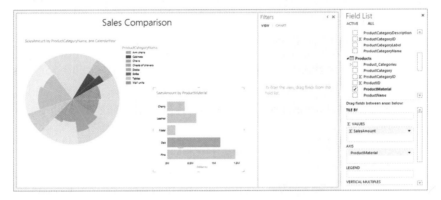

Create interconnected charts in Power View

9. Switch to the **Sales Performance** view page. Verify that the visualization in the first view is unchanged and displays the pie chart diagrams for all product materials; in other words, the first view has not been affected by the **ProductMaterial** filter in the second view.

10. Save the Power View report to the Power Pivot Gallery with the name SalesPerformance.rdlx.

Display Power View reports in web parts

Continuing in your SharePoint team site, perform the following tasks:

1. Add a new page to your site and name it HelloWorld. On the new page that opens for editing, in the **Title** area at the top of the page, add a space between the words, so that the title reads Hello World.

2. On the **Hello World** page, display a Power View report in the Page Viewer web part, with the following settings:

    - **Page Viewer** section, **Link** box

      Provide a URL of the first view page in the **SalesPerformance.rdlx** report that you created in the previous section. Append the **&PreviewBar=False** parameter to the URL to hide the top toolbar in the Power View page.

    - **Appearance** section

        - **Height**   Select **Yes**; enter **600** for the height in pixels
        - **Width**   Select **Yes**; enter **600** for the width in pixels
        - **Chrome Type**   **None**

    > **TIP** When you are done, select OK in the web part tool pane to save your settings and return to the webpage.

3. Check in and publish the **Hello World** page on your site. Verify that you can move between the views and that the views are interactive.

Navigate view pages in a Power View report in a Page Viewer web part

Manage and monitor content

Much of this book has concentrated on organizing content in lists, libraries, sites, and site collections, where access to content is secured by using permissions. This chapter looks at other ways to manage and monitor content, including retaining and expiring content; using sites such as the Document Center, Records Center, In-Place Hold Policy Center, eDiscovery Center, and Compliance Center; and using features such as document IDs, document sets, the Content Organizer, information management policies, and auditing.

This chapter guides you through procedures related to managing documents, storing and managing records, and protecting data.

In this chapter

- Manage documents
- Store and manage records
- Protect data in SharePoint

Practice files

For this chapter, use the practice files from the SP2016SBS\Ch14 folder. For practice file download instructions, see the introduction.

Manage documents

SharePoint Server is an Enterprise Content Management (ECM) system that can store millions of documents that can be retrieved at a high rate. In earlier chapters of this book, many of the basic ECM components were described, such as multiple file uploads; opening with Explorer; major and minor versioning; checking in and checking out; durable URLs; content approval; the synchronization of offline files; the ability to define data (metadata) at the site, site collection, and enterprise levels by using site columns; content types and enterprise content types; keywords and term sets; and the authoring, branding, and controlled publishing of web content known as Web Content Management (WCM).

Create enterprise content management sites

SharePoint Server provides many site templates that can be used to create sites targeted to managing enterprise-wide content, such as:

- **Document Center** A site to centrally manage documents.

- **Records Center** A site designed for records management. Records managers can configure the routing table to direct incoming files to specific locations.

- **In-Place Hold Policy Center** A site to manage policies to preserve content for a fixed period of time.

- **eDiscovery Center** A site to manage the preservation, search, and export of content for legal matters and investigations.

> **TIP** You can search and locate files by using the Records Center's eDiscovery features or by creating sites from the eDiscovery Center site template.

- **Compliance Policy Center** A site that allows you to manage policies that can delete documents after a specified period of time.

> **TIP** These five site templates can be used to create top-level sites of a site collection. Only the Document Center and Records Center can be used to create subsites.

Many of the features available in these sites, such as document IDs, document sets, and the Content Organizer, can be made available in any library.

To create a Document Center or a Records Center as a subsite

1. Go to the **Site Contents** page of the site where you want to create the subsite.

2. At the bottom of the **Site Contents** page, under **Subsites**, select **new subsite**.

3. On the **New SharePoint Site** page, in the **Title** box, enter the name of the site, and in the **URL name** box, enter the website address.

4. In the **Template Selection** section, select the **Enterprise** tab, if it is not already active, and then select **Document Center** or **Records Center**.

5. Select **Create**.

To activate or deactivate a site collection feature

1. Go to the top-level site of your site collection.

2. On the **Settings** menu, select **Site Settings**, and then under **Site Collection Administration**, select **Site collection features**.

> **TIP** If you do not see the Site Collection Administration section, you are not a Site Collection Administrator. If you see Go To Top Level Site Settings, you are not at the top-level site of the site collection.

3. On the **Site Collection Features** page, scroll to the feature and do either of the following:

   - To activate a feature, select **Activate** to the right of the feature.

   - To deactivate a feature, select **Deactivate** to the left of the feature, and then select **Deactivate this feature** to confirm your action.

Work with document IDs

The web address of a file stored in a library consists of the library's URL and the file name. When you move a file to different library, the file's web address is now the new library's URL and the file name; therefore, if you created links to the file when it was stored in the first location, they no longer work when the file is moved. Also, if you submit content to, for example, a records center, the file is given a new web address and you will not be able to find the file by using the original URL. In these scenarios,

14

you might consider using the site collection Document ID feature or consider the file's durable URLs, as described in the "Navigate lists and libraries" topic of Chapter 2, "Navigate SharePoint sites."

> ⚠ **IMPORTANT** When you activate the Document ID Service feature, existing documents in your site collection might not be assigned document IDs immediately, because by default the SharePoint document ID–related jobs are configured to run nightly.

After the Document ID Service feature is activated, new hidden site columns are added to the Document and Document Set content types, and then the changes to those content types are sent to the sites within the site collection, so that the columns are added to all libraries that use those content types. Each document in those libraries receives a unique ID known as the *document ID*.

> ✓ **TIP** When the Document ID Service feature is activated, the Find By Document ID web part is made available in the Search category in the Web Part pane. Use this web part on a page when you want to display the properties of the document by referencing its document ID.

A document ID consists of two parts:

- A prefix, which can be randomly generated or can be specified on the Document ID settings page. You should ensure that every site collection that uses the document ID feature has a unique prefix; otherwise, duplicate document IDs could exist.
- Two numbers—the ID of the library where the document was created, and the item ID of the file in the library.

An example of a document ID is *SP2016SBS-3-9*. The library Document ID column contains a URL to the file that uses the document ID and has a format similar to *http://wideworldimporters/_layouts/DocIdRedir.aspx?ID=SP2016SBS-3-9*. When you select this URL, the SharePoint search functionality is used to find the file; therefore, the URL might not work until the file has been added to the search index. The default search scope used to find files is *All Sites*, which you can change if additional search scopes have been created.

If you deactivate the Document ID Service feature, you will no longer see the Document ID Settings link on the Site Settings page. Document IDs will not be created for new files. In libraries, the Document ID column is not deleted, so that the document IDs for existing files are preserved even after deactivation; however, if you try to look up a file by its document ID, you will get the error message, "This Site Collection is not configured to use document IDs."

To turn document IDs on or off for a site collection

 IMPORTANT An automated process, which by default is scheduled to run daily, completes the document ID configuration.

1. On the **Site Settings** page for the site collection, under **Site Collection Administration**, select **Document ID settings**.

    ✓ **TIP** If the Document ID Settings link is not displayed, verify that the Document ID Service site collection feature is activated. See the "To activate or deactivate a site collection feature" procedure earlier in this topic.

2. Do either of the following, and then select **OK**:

   - Select the **Assign Document IDs** check box to turn on the use of document IDs.

   - Clear the **Assign Document IDs** check box to turn off the use of document IDs.

Document ID Settings

Assign Document IDs

Specify whether IDs will be automatically assigned to all documents in the Site Collection. Additionally, you can specify a set of 4-12 characters that will be used at the beginning of all IDs assigned for documents in this Site Collection, to help ensure that items in different Site Collections will never get the same ID. Note: A timer job will be scheduled to assign IDs to documents already in the Site Collection.

Configuration of the Document ID feature is scheduled to be completed by an automated process.

☑ Assign Document IDs

Begin IDs with the following characters:

`SP2016SBS`

☐ Reset all Document IDs in this Site Collection to begin with these characters.

Document ID Lookup Search Scope

Specify which search scope will be used to look up documents using their IDs.

Use this search scope for ID lookup:

`All Sites ▾`

On the Document ID Settings page, you can turn on or off the use of Document IDs in every document library in the site collection

To configure the document ID settings

 IMPORTANT You do not have to complete any of the tasks unless you want to change the defaults.

1. Open the **Document ID Settings** page for the site collection.

    ✓ **TIP** If the Document ID Settings link is not available on the Site Settings page, verify that the Document ID Service site collection feature is activated. See the "To activate or deactivate a site collection feature" procedure earlier in this topic.

14

2. Turn on the use of document IDs as described earlier in this topic, if necessary.

3. Make any of the following changes, and then select **OK**:

   - In the **Begin IDs** box, enter a minimum of 4 and a maximum of 12 characters for the document ID prefix.

   - In the **Use this search scope for ID lookup** box, select the search scope to be used to look up documents.

   - If you have changed the document ID prefix and want all document IDs in the site collection to begin with the prefix characters, select the **Reset all Document IDs in this Site Collection to begin with these characters** check box.

> ⚠ **IMPORTANT** This will impact the integrity of any previously documented document ID URLs such as those for files, emails, and webpages.

To find the document ID of a file

1. In the library where the file is stored, click or tap to the left of the file.

2. On the **Files** tab, select **View Properties**. SharePoint displays the document's properties, including the document ID.

Name	induction pack.doc
Title	
Document ID	SP2016SBS-845020134-1
Version: 1.0	
Created at 8/27/2016 10:33 PM by ☐ Peter Connelly	
Last modified at 8/27/2016 10:33 PM by ☐ Peter Connelly	Close

View the properties of a file to find its document ID and the link to the file

> ✓ **TIP** To easily see the document ID assigned to any file in a library, display the Document ID column for any view.

Create and modify document sets

As you perform a business process, you might find that you always work with three or four related files, such as a product sheet, a product proposal PowerPoint presentation, and an Excel workbook with supporting financial information. To group those files together, you could categorize the files by using metadata in a column or store them in a folder; alternatively, you could group the files together as one item or set by using the Document Set feature.

Documents · 2016 Oslo Bedroom Furniture

2016 Oslo Bedroom Furniture

View All Properties
Edit Properties

⊕ New   ⬆ Upload   ⟳ Sync   ⟳ Share   More ⌄

Find a file   🔍

✓	☐	Name		Modified	Modified By
		2016 Oslo Bedroom Furniture - WWI_Presentation ⌗	···	A few seconds ago	☐ Peter Connelly
		2016 Oslo Bedroom Furniture - WWI_ProductSheet ⌗	···	A few seconds ago	☐ Peter Connelly

Drag files here to upload

Use a document set to group related files, which can be created at the same time and managed as a single entity

After you group files as a document set, you can specify the column values—that is, metadata—on each item within the set or, alternatively, just once, in which case the metadata is then shared across the items, making it easier to tag and manage content.

You can run workflows on each item of a set or on the document set as a whole; for example, you could use an approval workflow to specify that a document set that represents a legal case must be signed off before it can be used in court.

> 🔍 **SEE ALSO** For information about how to integrate document sets with your SharePoint Server document management solutions, go to "Plan document sets in SharePoint Server 2013" at *https://technet.microsoft.com/en-us/library/ff603637.aspx*. For information about adding or modifying site columns on a document set content type, see the "To add an existing site column to a content type," "To add a new site column to a content type," and "To associate a document template with a content type" procedures in the "Work with content types" section in Chapter 4, "Make lists and libraries work for you." For information about adding a document set content type to a library, see the "To add a content type to a list or library" procedure in the same section.

14

To create a document set content type

1. On the **Site Settings** page for the site where you want to create the document set content type, under **Web Designer Galleries**, select **site content types** to display the Site Content Types page, and then select **Create**.

2. On the **New Site Content Types** page, in the **Name** box, enter a name for your document set. You can also enter a description, which will be used as the description on the New button.

3. In the **Select parent content type from** list, select **Document Set Content Types**, and in the **Parent Content Type** list, select **Document Set**, if it is not already selected.

4. Do either of the following:

   - Select **Existing group**, if it is not already selected, and then select a group from the list.

   - Select **New group**, and then enter the name of the new group.

Use the New Site Content Type page to create a document set content type

5. Select **OK**. The Site Content Types page for your document set content type is displayed.

To display the document set settings page for a document set content type

1. Go to the **Site Settings** page for the site where the document set content type was created, and then under **Web Designer Galleries**, select **Site content types**.

2. On the **Site Content Types** page, select the document set you want to modify, and then under **Settings**, select **Document Set settings**.

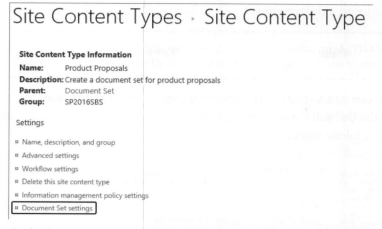

Site Content Types › Site Content Type

Site Content Type Information
Name: Product Proposals
Description: Create a document set for product proposals
Parent: Document Set
Group: SP2016SBS

Settings

□ Name, description, and group
□ Advanced settings
□ Workflow settings
□ Delete this site content type
□ Information management policy settings
□ Document Set settings

On the Site Content Types page, select Document Set Settings to go to the Document Set Settings page, where you can modify or add new site columns to the document set

To configure the content types that are allowed for a document set

1. On the **Document Set Settings** page for the document set you want to configure, in the **Allowed Content Types** section, under **Available Site Content Types**, select the content types you want to allow, and then select **Add**.

Site Content Type › Document Set Settings

Allowed Content Types

Select from the list of available site content types to add them to the Document Set.

Select site content types from:
All Groups

Available Site Content Types:

Audio
Basic Page
Discussion
Dublin Core Columns
Form
Image
JavaScript Display Template
Link to a Document
List View Style

Add >

< Remove

Content types allowed in the Document Set:

Document

Description:
Upload an audio file.

Group: Digital Asset Content Types

Add site content types from the list of available site content types

2. At the bottom of the page, select **OK**.

14

To add default files to a document set

> ⚠️ **IMPORTANT** . Any modifications you make to the Default Content section only affect new document sets. Existing document sets are not affected.

1. On the **Document Set Settings** page for the document set you want to configure, in the **Default Content** section, select a content type, and in the **Folder** box, enter a folder name.

In the Default Content section, you can configure settings to have new Document Sets you create automatically contain specific files

2. Select **Browse** to open the Choose File To Upload dialog box, navigate to the file you want to use, and then select **Open**.

3. To add another default file, select **Add new default content**, and repeat the two previous steps.

> ✅ **TIP** To remove a file, select Delete to the right of the Browse button.

4. Select or clear the **Add the name of the Document Set to each file name** check box.

5. At the bottom of the page, select **OK**.

To select a document set's columns whose values are to be used by all files in the document set

1. On the **Document Set Settings** page for the document set you want to configure, in the **Shared Columns** section, select the check box to the left of each column whose values you want to automatically synchronize to all files contained in the document set.

2. At the bottom of the page, select **OK**.

To select which column to show on the Welcome Page

1. On the **Document Set Settings** page for the document set you want to configure, in the **Welcome Page Columns** section, under **Available columns**, select one or more columns you want to show, selected in the order you want them to appear on the welcome page, and then select **Add**.

2. At the bottom of the page, select **OK.**

To customize the Welcome Page for a document set

1. On the **Document Set Settings** page for the document set you want to configure, in the **Welcome Page** section, select **Customize the Welcome Page** to open the Welcome Page web part page in a new browser tab.

2. On the **Page** tab, select **Edit Page**.

3. To modify and save the document set Welcome Page, use the procedures in Chapter 7, "Work with webpages."

4. When you have completed all your changes to the Welcome Page, return to the **Document Sets Settings** page, and select the **Update the Welcome Page of Document Sets inheriting from this content type** check box.

You will not see the changes you have made to your Welcome Page until you select the check box

5. At the bottom of the page, select **OK.**

To force updates to all content types that inherit from your document set content type

1. On the **Document Set Settings** page for the document set you want to configure, in the **Update List and Site Content Types** section, select **Yes**.

2. At the bottom of the page, select **OK.**

To create a new document set

1. Go to a library where a document set content type has been added.

2. On the **Files** tab, select the **New Document** arrow, and then select the document set content type you want to use.

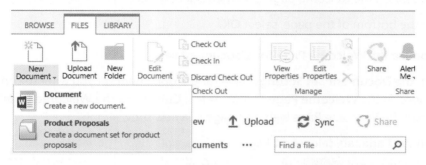

Select the New Documents command on the Files tab to add new files and document sets

Set up the Content Organizer

The Content Organizer is very useful when you have users who are confused about where to store files. It also helps you manage library and folder sizes and resolve duplicate file names.

You can use the Content Organizer to automatically move documents by using rules based on content type site columns. The content types must be based on the Document content type; that is, this functionality affects files and not list items. The target location can be a library or a folder in a library, which can be in the site where the rule is defined, in another site, or in a different site collection.

> **TIP** Document sets can be routed after the content type is added to the target location. To facilitate the move, the organizer zips (compresses) the document sets. Documents cannot be routed to a document set, nor can pages be redirected.

As with document IDs and documents sets, you need to activate a feature to use this functionality; however, the Content Organizer is a site feature and is activated at the site level. It is automatically activated on a Records Center; therefore, you can use this feature to route records.

You can configure the Content Organizer so that when a user uploads files to a target library, the files are redirected and stored in the Drop Off Library, which is created when the Content Organizer site feature is activated. The files then enter the submission process. The user who uploads the file does not have to have contributor access to the target location; however, the user's ID is used for the Modified By property on the file in the target location. Any files that do not match a rule or that are missing metadata will remain in the Drop Off Library.

> **TIP** You can upload files directly into the Drop Off library; alternatively, you can email files to the library or use the Custom Send To Destination option, as described in the "Work with advanced settings" topic in Chapter 4, "Make lists and libraries work for you."

To configure the Content Organizer

1. On the **Settings** menu, select **Site Settings**, and then under **Site Administration**, select **Content Organizer Settings**.

> **TIP** If the Content Organizer Settings link is not displayed, verify that the Content Organizer site feature is activated. For information about how to activate or deactivate the Content Organizer site feature, see the "To active or deactivate a feature for a site" procedure in the "Manage site features" topic in Chapter 8, "Create and manage sites."

2. On the **Content Organizer Settings** page, do any of the following:

   - In the **Redirect Users to the Drop Off Library** section, select the check box if you want files that are uploaded to target locations to be moved to the Drop Off Library, where they will be tested against the criteria specified in one or more Content Organizer rules.

   > **TIP** Users must use the Upload command in the target library. Files that are created in the library or that are uploaded by being dragged to the library will not be submitted to the organizer. Also, when there are no rules pointing to a library, files uploaded to that library will be directly stored in that library and not sent to the drop-off library.

   - In the **Sending to Another Site** section, select the check box to allow rules to route files to another site or site collection.
   - In the **Folder Partitioning** section, do the following:
     - Select the check box to automatically create subfolders when the target location has too many items.
     - In the **Number of items in a single folder** box, enter the number of items you want to allow.
     - In the **Format of folder name** box, enter the name of the folder, which should include *%1*, where *%1* will be replaced by the date and time the folder is created.

14

- In the **Duplicate Submissions** section, to specify what should occur when a file with the same name already exists in a target location, select either **Use SharePoint versioning** or **Append unique characters to the end of duplicate file**.

> ✓ **TIP** If versioning is not enabled in the target library, duplicate files will have unique characters appended to the end of their names, regardless of the setting selected in this section.

- In the **Preserving Context** section, select the check box to save the original audit log and properties, if they are included with the submissions.
- In the **Rule Managers** section, specify rule managers and select or clear the check boxes to email rule managers when submissions do not match a rule or when content has been left in the Drop Off Library.

Rule Managers

Specify the users who manage the rules and can respond when incoming content doesn't match any rule.

☑ E-mail rule managers when submissions do not match a rule
☑ E-mail rule managers when content has been left in the Drop Off Library
Enter users or groups separated by semicolons:

Peter Connelly

Rule Managers must have the Manage Web Site permission to access the content organizer rules list from the site settings page.

Number of days to wait before sending an e-mail: 3

Submission Points

Use this information to set up other sites or e-mail messaging software to send content to this site.

Web service URL: http://intranet.wideworldimporters.com/sites/teams/SP2016/_vti_bin/OfficialFile.asmx
E-mail address:

In the Rules Managers section, specify users who manage the rules and who can respond

3. At the bottom of the page, select **OK**.

To create Content Organizer rules

1. On the **Settings** menu, select **Site Settings**, and then under **Site Administration**, select **Content Organizer Rules** to display the Content Organizer Rules list.

> ✓ **TIP** The Content Organizer Rules list has three views: Group By Content Type, All Items, and Group By Target Library. It is a hidden list, and therefore it is not displayed on the Site Contents page. You can go to the list only from the link on the Site Settings page. If the link is not displayed, verify that the Content Organizer site feature is activated.

2. Select **new item**, and then in the **Rule Name** section, in the **Name** box, enter the name of the rule.
3. In the **Rule Status And Priority** section, do one of the following:
   - Select **Active** and then select the rule's priority.

- Select **Inactive** if you think you might need the rule again in the future.

 TIP If a submission matches multiple rules, the rule with the higher priority is used. Priorities range from 1 (Highest) to 9 (Lowest).

4. In the **Submission's Content Type** section do the following:

   - Select the content type group and content type to determine the properties that can be used in the conditions of the rule you are creating.

   - Optionally, select the **This content type has alternate names in other sites** check box, enter the alternate name in the **Add alternate name** box, and select **Add**.

Submission's Content Type *	
By selecting a content type, you are determining the properties that can be used in the conditions of this rule. In addition, submissions that match this rule will receive the content type selected here when they are placed in a target location.	Content type: Group: Document Content Types ▾ Type: Document ▾ Alternate names: ☐ This content type has alternate names in other sites: Add alternate name: [ ] Add Note: Adding the type "*" will allow documents of unknown content types to be organized by this rule. List of alternate names: Document [ ] Remove

In this section, you select a content type to determine the properties that you use in conditions

 TIP When you use an asterisk (*) as the alternate name, any document whose content type is unknown will be organized by this rule.

5. In the **Conditions** section, do the following:

   a. In the **Property** list, select a property.

   b. In the **Operator** list, select an operation.

   c. In the **Value** list, enter a value.

   d. Optionally, select **Add another condition** and repeat steps a through c.

Conditions	
In order to match this rule, a submission's properties must match all the specified property conditions (e.g. "If Date Created is before 1/1/2000").	Property-based conditions: Property: Name ▾ X Operator: begins with ▾ Value: [Holiday] (Add another condition)

A submission must match all the specified property conditions to match a rule

14

509

6. In the **Target Location** section, either enter the URL for a library or select **Browse** and navigate to the library you want to route files to.

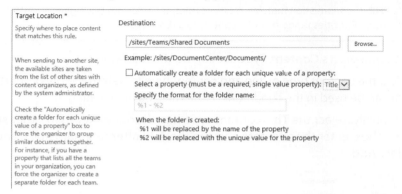

In the Target Location section, you specify where to place content that matches the rule and force the organizer to group similar documents together

> ✓ **TIP** If a message box opens stating that the content type you chose (in step 4 in this procedure) is not added to the library, select OK, add the content type to the recipient library, and then repeat step 4.

7. Optionally, select the **Automatically create a folder for each unique value of a property** check box, select a property, and then specify the format of the folder name.

8. Select **OK**.

Store and manage records

SharePoint provides a variety of records management mechanisms that you can use to enforce legislation and regulations dictated by external organizations such as auditors, and to satisfy data protection and legal processes. You can place records on hold, associate retention and expiration information management policies with content, and search and locate files, all by using the eDiscovery features, in a Records Center or in a site created from the eDiscovery Center site template.

> 🔍 **SEE ALSO** For more information about the eDiscovery Center, see the "Protect data in SharePoint" topic later in this chapter.

One way an organization can manage records is to create a Records Center, which is the organization's central repository for document retention and record declarations. Site owners can also configure in-place records management for libraries within their sites. When a library is configured to allow the manual declaration of records, records can be stored alongside active files, which is not the case in the Records Center. This way you can store and manage records across multiple sites in many site collections without moving them to a Records Center, thereby avoiding the need for you and other users to learn a new location for the files.

Any file in a library can be declared as a record. This can be done manually, via a workflow, or as part of an information management retention policy. The file is then protected from changes or deletion, and the library where the file is stored cannot be deleted.

To configure in-place records management, you first need to activate the feature at the site collection level. You can then configure record declaration at the site collection level or at a list or library level to make the Declare/Undeclared Record command visible on the ribbon.

> **TIP** The implementation of records management in an organization is not a trivial activity; it needs careful planning and the creation of a file plan.

> **TIP** To activate the In Place Records Management feature for a library, use the "To activate or deactivate a site collection feature" procedure earlier in this chapter.

To configure in-place records management at the site collection level

1. On the **Site Settings** page, under **Site Collection Administration**, select **Record declaration settings**.

2. On the **Record Declaration Settings** page, do the following:

   a. In the **Record Restrictions** section, select the restriction to place on the item or file after it has been declared as a record.

   Record Restrictions

   Specify restrictions to place on a document or item once it has been declared as a record. Changing this setting will not affect items which have already been declared records. Note: The information management policy settings can also specify different policies for records and non-records.

   ○ No Additional Restrictions
      Records are no more restricted than non-records.
   ○ Block Delete
      Records can be edited but not deleted.
   ◉ Block Edit and Delete
      Records cannot be edited or deleted. Any changes will require the record declaration to be revoked.

   Selecting Block Edit And Delete restriction locks the item; a padlock icon is associated with the item to visually show that it is locked

14

b. In the **Record Declaration Availability** section, select whether all lists and libraries in this site collection should allow manual declaration of records.

Record Declaration Availability	
Specify whether all lists and libraries in this site should make the manual declaration of records available by default. When manual record declaration is unavailable, records can only be declared through a policy or workflow.	Manual record declaration in lists and libraries should be: ○ Available in all locations by default ⦿ Not available in all locations by default

When manual record declaration is not available, only a policy or a workflow can declare items and files as records

c. In the **Declaration Roles** section, select which user roles can manually declare and undeclare an item or a file as a record.

Declaration Roles	
Specify which user roles can declare and undeclare record status manually.	The declaration of records can be performed by: ⦿ All list contributors and administrators ○ Only list administrators ○ Only policy actions Undeclaring a record can be performed by: ○ All list contributors and administrators ⦿ Only list administrators ○ Only policy actions

Specify which user roles can manually declare or undeclare records

3. Select **OK**.

To configure in-place records management for a list or library

1. Go to the **List Settings** or **Library Settings** page for the list or library.

2. In the **Permissions and Management** section, select **Record declaration settings**.

3. In the **Manual Record Declaration Availability** section, select one of the options to set the list or library to allow or prevent the manual declaration of records.

Manual Record Declaration Availability	
Specify whether this list should allow the manual declaration of records. When manual record declaration is unavailable, records can only be declared through a policy or workflow.	⦿ Use the site collection default setting: Do not allow the manual declaration of records ○ Always allow the manual declaration of records ○ Never allow the manual declaration of records
Automatic Declaration Specify whether all items should become records when added to this list.	☐ Automatically declare items as records when they are added to this list.

At a list or library level, you can allow or prevent the creation of records

4. In the **Automatic Declaration** section, select or clear the check box to configure whether items or files should be declared as records when they are added to the list or library.

5. Select **OK**.

To declare an in-place record

1. Click or tap to the left of the item or file, and then on the **Files** tab, in the **Manage** group, select **Declare Record**.

2. Select **OK** to confirm that you want to declare the selected item or file as a record.

To display compliance details

1. Right-click the item or file, select **Advanced**, and then select **Compliance Details** to open the Compliance Details dialog box.

![Compliance Details dialog box]

Compliance Details - WWI_Financials -- Webpage Dialog ☒

Use this dialog to determine what retention stage an item is in. You can also take action to keep this item in compliance with organizational policy.

Retention Stages

Event	Action	Recurrence	Scheduled occurrence date

This item is not subject to a retention policy

Name	WWI_Financials.xlsx
Content Type	Document
Folder Path	Proposals
Exemption Status	Not Exempt Exempt from policy
Hold Status	Not on hold You cannot add/remove item from hold.
Record Status	Declared record on 8/31/2016 Undeclare record
Audit Log	Generate audit log report

Close

The Compliance Details dialog box displays the retention stage of an item or file, information about its hold or record status, and more

 TIP In the Compliance Details dialog box, you can exempt an item or file from having a policy applied.

14

Protect data in SharePoint

SharePoint 2016 contains features similar to those in Microsoft Office 365. Your organization can create an eDiscovery Center to identify content, a Compliance Center in which deletion polices and Data Loss Protection (DLP) polices can be managed, and an In-Place Hold Policy Center in which you can create and manage time-based in-place hold policies.

The core component for protecting data in SharePoint is policies, some of which you can create at a site collection, site, list, or library level; others are created on the top-level site of a site collection and are used on some or all of the SharePoint content in your organization.

The policies you can use in SharePoint are detailed in the following table.

Policy	Created/ Configured in	Assigned to	Assigned by
eDiscovery in-place hold	eDiscovery Center	All content	eDiscovery Center site collection owners
Time-based in-place hold	In-Place Hold Policy Center	Site collections	In-Place Hold Policy Center site collection owners
			Site collection owners
In-place record	Records Center	Lists	Site collection owners
	Site collection	Libraries	List owners
	Site		
Data Loss Protection	Compliance Policy Center	Site collections	Compliance Policy Center members
Document deletion	Compliance Policy Center	Site collection templates	Compliance Policy Center members
		Site collections	Site collection owners
		Sites	
Site closure	Site collection	Sites	Site collection owners
			Site owners

Policy	Created/ Configured in	Assigned to	Assigned by
Information management	Content types Lists Libraries Folders	Content types in a content type hub Site content types Lists Libraries Folders	Site collection owners Site owners List owners

eDiscovery Center

Usually organizations have only one eDiscovery Center. The eDiscovery Center is where legal teams create eDiscovery cases and Data Loss Protection (DLP) queries. A *case* is a set of sources, queries, and perhaps in-place holds. When your organization identifies content it is interested in, you can create a case to discover that content, and then configure an eDiscovery in-place hold, which lasts until it is removed.

> ✓ **TIP** The results of the query can be exported in the industry-standard Electronic Data Reference Model (EDRM) XML data format, which can then be imported into EDRM review tools.

> 🔍 **SEE ALSO** For more information about eDiscovery cases, go to *https://support.office.com/article/Plan-and-manage-eDiscovery-cases-d955aeb8-0d48-4291-a8e2-f3b84f17943f.*

Data loss protection queries

DLP was rolled out first in Microsoft Exchange 2013 and Exchange Online, later to SharePoint Online, and now to SharePoint 2016. A DLP query works the same as an eDiscovery case query, except that the DLP query can be configured to find content with a minimum amount of sensitive information. For example, a DLP query can return content that is stored anywhere in SharePoint content that contains at least one US bank account number. You can export the results of your query as a .csv file, which you could analyze by using Excel.

14

New DLP Query ✕

Choose the template corresponding to the type of content you want to find:
Learn more about these templates.

U.S. Personally Identifiable Information (PII) Data
U.S. Gramm-Leach-Bliley Act (GLBA)
PCI Data Security Standard (PCI DSS)
U.K. Financial Data
U.S. Financial Data
U.K. Personally Identifiable Information (PII) Data
U.K. Data Protection Act
U.K. Privacy and Electronic Communications Regulations
U.S. State Social Security Number Confidentiality Laws
U.S. State Breach Notification Laws

Microsoft Exchange uses 80 built-in sensitive information types, also known as templates; SharePoint Online uses 51, and SharePoint 2016 uses 10 templates

DLP queries use the search index to find sensitive data; therefore, the effectiveness of DLP is dependent on the content's inclusion in the search index and on the accuracy of the content crawling process.

> **SEE ALSO** For more information about data loss prevention in SharePoint 2016, go to *https://support.office.com/en-gb/article/Overview-of-data-loss-prevention-in-SharePoint-Server-2016-80f907bb-b944-448d-b83d-8fec4abcc24c*.

Document deletion policies

Document deletion policies are created in the Compliance Policy Center and can contain one or more delete rules. A delete rule can specify the time period until deletion (which can be calculated by using the Created or Modified properties) and whether the document should be permanently deleted or moved to the Recycle Bin.

Use the Compliance Policy Center to create policies to help you prevent the deletion of SharePoint content and delete content that you do not want

After a deletion policy is created, it can be assigned to:

- A site collection template, which means that it will be applied to sites already created from that site template and sites that will be created in the future.
- A specific site collection, thereby overriding any polices assigned to the site template.

Similar to permissions, navigation, and other site features, deletion policies are inherited. When a site owner selects a document deletion policy, all the sites below that site inherit the policy; however, if a subsite owner selects a different policy, the inheritance will be broken from that point down in the site hierarchy, and the new policy will apply to the subsite and all its subsites.

Use document deletion policies when your organization needs to automatically delete unstructured content, such as OneDrive for Business and team sites; in this way, deletion policies work together with records management or information management policies, which are best suited to structured data and content types.

> ⊘ **SEE ALSO** For more information about document deletion policies in SharePoint 2016, go to *https://support.office.com/en-gb/article/Overview-of-document-deletion-policies-in-SharePoint-Server-2016-cbbb1a8b-9f30-41cb-8110-36f33f90a1e6.*

Data loss protection policies

DLP allows your organization to define rules and policies to protect sensitive data, such as national insurance (NI) or credit card numbers. Documents that breach a policy rule are blocked so that users cannot view them, and an email is sent to the author informing him or her of the issue.

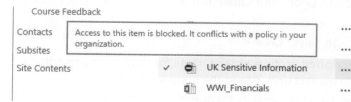

A no-entry icon is associated with a file or item that is blocked

14

Time-based in-place hold polices

Time-based in-place hold policies are created in the In-Place Hold Policy Center site; you can use them to preserve SharePoint content for a fixed period of time, based on the date it was created or modified. Content that is placed on hold is preserved; however, you can continue to edit it.

> **SEE ALSO** For more information on in-place hold in SharePoint 2016, go to *https://support.office.com/en-gb/article/Overview-of-in-place-hold-in-SharePoint-Server-2016-5e400d68-cd51-444a-8fe6-e4df1d20aa95*.

Define and apply a site policy

Site closure and deletion are the concepts upon which site policies are based. A closed site does not appear on pages that include aggregated content; however, you can still modify the content if you have taken note of its URL. The primary purpose of closing a site is to eventually delete the site after a planned amount of time, thereby defining the lifecycle of the site and helping reduce site proliferation. Closed sites are particularly useful when self-service site creation is in use.

Site policies are created at the site collection level, by the site collection owner, and can be applied by site owners at the site level.

> **TIP** When you define site policies in a content type hub, you can publish policies across site collections.

To create a site policy

1. Activate the **Site Policy** site collection feature, if it is not already active.
2. On the **Site Settings** page, under **Site Collection Administration**, select **Site Policies**.
3. On the **Site Policies** page, select **Create**.
4. In the **Name and Description** section, enter a name for the policy, and enter a description to help site owners understand the purpose of the policy.
5. In the **Site Closure and Deletion** section, do one of the following:
   - Select **Do not close or delete site automatically**. If you select this option, when the policy is applied to a site, the site owner must delete the site manually.

- Select **Delete sites automatically** and then, in the **Deletion Event** section, do the following:

  - Select either **Site created date** or **Site closed date**.

  - Enter the amount of time in days, months, or years after the deletion event to specify when the site will be deleted.

  - Optionally, select the check box to send a notification to the site owner, enter the amount of time to send the notification before the site is due to be deleted. You can also set options for follow-up notifications.

  - Optionally, select the check box to allow site owners to postpone the deletion for a specified amount of time.

- Select **Close and delete sites automatically**, enter the **Close Event** and the amount of time to wait after the site was created before closing the site, and then complete the **Deletion Event** section.

Site Closure and Deletion

You can configure how sites under this policy are closed and eventually deleted automatically.

When a site is closed, it is trimmed from places that aggregate open sites to site members such as Outlook, OWA, and Project Server. Members can still access and modify site content until it is automatically or manually deleted.

○ Do not close or delete site automatically.

○ Delete sites automatically.

● Close and delete sites automatically.

Close Event:

Site created date + [5] [years ▾]

Deletion Event:

Site closed date + [6] [months ▾]

☑ Send an email notification to site owners this far in advance of deletion:

[3] [months ▾]

☑ Send follow-up notifications every:

[14] [days ▾]

☑ Owners can postpone imminent deletion for:

[1] [months ▾]

A site policy specifies the conditions for automatically closing and deleting sites

6. If you want the top-level site and all subsites to be set as read-only when the top-level site of the site collection is closed, in the **Site Collection Closure** section, select **The site collection will be read-only when it is closed**.

7. Select **OK**.

To apply a site policy to a site

1. On the **Site Settings** page for the site where you want to use the site policy, under **Site Administration**, select **Site Closure and Deletion**.

2. On the **Site Closure and Deletion** page, select a site policy, and then select **OK**.

14

To manually close a site

1. On the **Site Closure and Deletion** page for the site, select **Close this site now**, and then select **OK**.

Site Closure	This site will be closed on: 7/12/2021 2:26 PM
When a site is closed, it is trimmed from places that aggregate open sites to site members such as Outlook, OWA, and Project Server.	Close this site now
Site Deletion	This site will be deleted on: 1/12/2022 2:26 PM
Deleting a site deletes the site, its shared mailbox and all documents, emails and tasks associated with the site.	Postpone deletion of this site for 1 month.
Site Policy	WWI site policy
Select the appropriate policy for this site. Site policies are configured by your administrator and define the rules for closing and deleting the site.	

The site closure and deletion dates on the page are approximations, because a SharePoint time job, that, by default runs weekly, closes or deletes them

To postpone the deletion of a site

1. On the **Site Closure and Deletion** page for the site, select **Postpone deletion of this site**, and then select **OK**.

To open a closed site

1. On the **Site Closure and Deletion** page for the site, select **Open this site**, and then select **OK**.

Work with information management policies

Organizations use information management policies to control and track things like how long content is retained or what actions users can take with that content.

> **TIP** You cannot specify an information management policy for a core content type. Core content types are installed when a site collection is created. You must create a content type that is derived from a core content type and apply an information management policy to the derived content type.

An information management policy is a set of rules that can be set on the following SharePoint components:

- **A site collection** An information policy set on a site collection applies to all documents of a specific type on all sites within the site collection. You first create a content type policy template, also known as a site collection policy, and then apply the template to content types. The templates can be exported and then imported to other site collections.

> **TIP** You can centrally create a policy on a content type that is saved in a site known as the *content type hub*. The policy can then be published across site collections by using the Managed Metadata Service.

- **A site content type** When the content type is created at the site collection level, an information management policy set on that content type affects all items and files created from that content type, in all lists and libraries, on all sites in the site collection. When the content type is created in a subsite, the information management policy affects all items or files created from that content type, in all lists and libraries on the subsite and any subsites below that site.

- **A content type added to a specific list or library** Lists and libraries inherit the content type information management policies from the site where the content types were created. You can edit these content type information management policies in a list or library, and then only your modified information management policies affect those items or files created from that content type in that list or library.

- **A list or library** This type of policy is known as a *location-based retention policy* or a *list-based* or *library-based retention schedule*. When you create an information policy for a list or library, all items or files in the list, library, or folder, regardless of which content type they were created from, are affected by the policy.

> **TIP** By default, when you create a content type, an empty information management policy is created. You do not have to create one; you only need to edit the one that was created when the content type was created. To create a list-based or library-based retention schedule, you need to switch from using site content types to a location-based retention policy, also known as *Library And Folder*.

14

To display the Information Management Policy Settings page for a list or library

1. On the **List Settings** or **Library Settings** page for the list or library, under **Permissions and Management**, select **Information management policy settings** to open the Information Management Policy Settings page.

Settings · Information Management Policy Settings ⓘ

Library Based Retention Schedule

By default, a library will enforce the retention schedule set on its content types. Alternatively you can stop enforcing content type schedules and instead define schedules on the library and its folders.

Source of retention for this library: **Content Types** (Change source)

Content Type Policies

This table shows all the content types for this library, along with the policies and expiration schedules for each type. To modify the policy for a content type, click its name.

Content Type	Policy	Description	Retention Policy Defined
Document	None		No
Folder	None		No

On the Information Management Policy Settings page, you can edit content type policies, stop enforcing content type schedules, and define your own schedules

To turn on or off a location-based retention policy

1. Activate the **Library and Folder Based** site collection feature, if it is not already activated.

2. On the **Information Management Policy Settings** page for the list or library, to the right of **Source of retention**, select **Change source**.

> **✓ TIP** When a location-based retention policy is turned on, Or Configure List (or Library) Schedule will be appended to the link.

3. In the **Source of Retention** section, on the **Edit Policy** page, do the following:

   a. To turn on location-based retention, select **Library and Folders**.

Source of Retention

Configure how items in this library receive a retention schedule. Select **Content Types** if this site uses retention schedules on site level content types. This will ensure that this library complies with the site's information policy.

Alternatively, select **Library and Folders** if you want to define schedules on the library and its folders. Those schedules will be enforced regardless of any schedules defined on the content types.

○ Content Types
◉ Library and Folders

Use the Source Of Retention section to configure how items receive a retention schedule

b.   Select **OK** in the message box that opens, confirming that you want to ignore all content type retention schedules, and by doing so you might be overwriting policies defined by your site administrator.

c.   Complete the "To create or modify a retention policy" procedure later in this topic.

Or

a.   To turn off location-based retention, select **Content Types**.

b.   Select **OK** in the message box that opens, stating that when content type–based retention schedules are used, any existing library-based or folder-based schedules are ignored.

4.   Select **Apply**, and then select **OK** to return to the Information Management Policy Settings page.

To display the Edit Policy page

1.   Do the following:

a.   For a content type template, activate the Site Policy site collection feature, if it is not already active.

b.   On the **Site Settings** page, under **Site Collection administration**, select **Content Type Policy Templates**.

c.   Select **Create** or select **Define A Policy**.

Or

a.   For a site content type policy, go to the **Site Settings** page, and under **Web Designer Galleries**, select **Site content types**. Then select the content type for which you want to display the edit policy page.

b.   On the **Site Content Types** page, select **Information management policy settings**.

Or

a.   For a content type policy for a list or library, go to the **Information Management Policy Settings** page.

b.   In the **Content Type Policies** section, select the content type.

14

2. In the **Administrative Description** box and the **Policy Statement** box, enter the description and statement you want.

> ✓ **TIP** The administrative description is displayed to list managers when they are configuring policies on a list or content type. The policy statement is displayed to users when they open items subject to the policy. The policy statement should explain which policies apply, and any special information that users need to be aware of.

3. Turn on one or more retention, auditing, barcodes, or labels policies as described in the following procedures.

4. Select **OK**.

To turn on retention for a content type

> ⚠ **IMPORTANT** If the Library And Folder Based Retention feature is active, list administrators can override content type policies with their own retention schedules. To prevent this, deactivate the Library And Folder Based Retention site collection feature.

1. Display the **Edit Policy** page for the content type or content type template.

2. In the **Retention** section, select **Enable Retention**.

   Retention

   Schedule how content is managed and disposed by specifying a sequence of retention stages. If you specify multiple stages, each stage will occur one after the other in the order they appear on this page.

   Note: If the Library and Folder Based Retention feature is active, list administrators can override content type policies with their own retention schedules. To prevent this, deactivate the feature on the site collection.

   ☑ Enable Retention

   Specify how to manage retention:
   Items will not expire until a stage is added.
   Add a retention stage...

   Use a retention policy to define how long to retain content

3. Complete the following procedure.

To create or modify a retention policy

1. In the **Retention or Retention Schedule** section of the **Edit Policy** page for the content type for which you want to create or modify a policy, do one of the following to open the Stage properties dialog box:

   - To add a new stage, select **Add a retention stage**.
   - To add a stage above another stage, point to the stage, select the arrow that appears, and then select **Add Stage Above**.

From the stage menu you can edit, delete, and create a stage

- To edit a stage, point to the stage, select the arrow that appears, and select **Edit**.

2. In the **Stage properties** dialog box, in the **Event** section, do one of the following:

- Select **This stage is based off a date property on the item**. In the **Time Period** list, select a Time Date field, such as, **Created**, **Modified**, or **Declared Record**. In the box to the right of the **Time Period** list, enter a value. In the right list, select a unit of time, such as, **days**, **months**, or **years**.

- Select **Set by a custom retention formula installed on this server**. (This option is only available when a custom retention formula has been installed.)

3. In the **Action** section, do one of the following:

- In the list, select one of the following actions: **Move to Recycle Bin**, **Permanently Delete**, **Transfer to another location**, **Start a workflow**, **Skip to next stage**, **Declare a record**, **Delete previous drafts**, or **Delete all previous versions**.

> **TIP** You cannot create a retention policy that uses a Start A Workflow action if no workflows are associated with the content type, list, or library, nor can you use the Transfer To Another Location action when the Send To connection has not been configured by your SharePoint server administrator. Additionally, when the In-Place Records Management site collection feature is not activated, you will not be able to use the Declare Record option.

14

Specify an event that activates the stage and an action that should occur if the event condition is met

4. In the **Recurrence** section, select **Repeat this stage's action**. In the **Recurrence period** box, enter a value, and in the list to the right of the box, select a unit of time, such as **days**, **months**, or **years**.

> **TIP** The Repeat This Stage's Action option is available only when the selected ac tion is repeatable. For example, you cannot repeat the Move To Recycle Bin action.

5. Select **OK** to close the Stage Properties dialog box.

6. Repeat the steps in this procedure to create additional retention stages.

> **TIP** Specify a sequence of retention stages to manage and dispose of content. When you specify multiple stages, each stage will occur sequentially in the order they appear on the page.

To configure events to audit for a content type

1. Display the **Edit Policy** page for the content type at the site, list, or library level.

2. In the **Auditing** section, select **Enable Auditing**.

Policy usage reports help identify the content being used and assist with regulatory compliance

3. Select the events you want to audit.

To turn on barcodes for a content type

1. Display the **Edit Policy** page for the content type at the site, list, or library level.

2. In the **Barcodes** section, select **Enable Barcodes**.

Barcodes	
Assigns a barcode to each document or item. Optionally, Microsoft Office applications can require users to insert these barcodes into documents.	☑ Enable Barcodes
	☐ Prompt users to insert a barcode before saving or printing

Turning on barcodes adds a barcode to the properties of the document and displays the barcode in the header area of the document

3. If you want users to insert barcodes into their documents, select **Prompt users to insert a barcode before saving or printing**.

To turn on labels for a content type

> ⚠️ **IMPORTANT** The label policy feature has been deprecated and should not be used in SharePoint Server 2013 or SharePoint 2016. Follow these steps only if you have migrated from previous versions of SharePoint and need to maintain previously configured content types.

1. Display the **Edit Policy** page for the content type at the site, list, or library level.

2. In the **Labels** section, select **Enable labels**.

3. If you want users to add a label to their documents, select **Prompt users to insert a label before saving or printing**.

4. If you want to lock the labels, select **Prevent changes to labels after they are added**.

5. In the **Label** format box, enter the text for the label. You can refer to up to 10 column values, and you can add a line break by entering **/n**.

Labels	
You can add a label to a document to ensure that important information about the document is included when it is printed. To specify the label, type the text you want to use in the "Label format" box. You can use any combination of fixed text or document properties, except calculated or built-in properties such as GUID or CreatedBy. To start a new line, use the \n character sequence.	☑ Enable Labels
	☐ Prompt users to insert a label before saving or printing
	☐ Prevent changes to labels after they are added
	Label format
	Wide World Importers, Copyright 2016
	Examples:
	• Project {ProjectName}\n Managed By: {ProjectManager}
	• Confidential -- {Date}

Use the Labels section to add labels to documents

14

> ⚠️ **IMPORTANT** Do not lock a label when the label refers to a column value if you want the label to be updated when the column value is updated.

6. Select the font, font size, font style, and justification for the label.

7. Select the label's height and width. Both can range from 0.25 through 20 inches.

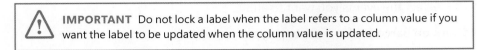

The font size can affect the amount of text displayed on the label

8. Select **Refresh** to preview the label.

To generate a file plan report to a list or library

1. Do one of the following:

    - On the **List Settings** or **Library Settings** page, under **Permissions and Management**, select **Generate file plan report**.

    - On the **Information Management Policy Settings** page, in the **Library Based Retention Schedule** section, select **Generate a File Plan Report for this library**.

Audit user actions

Policies and permission control who can access specific content, what they can do, and how long content is retained; however, you might still need to track user actions on SharePoint content. Knowing which users have performed certain actions is as important as controlling who can perform certain actions; therefore, the auditing feature in SharePoint is just as critical.

You can configure events to audit for the site collection, or you can create an information management policy to specify audit events for a content type.

> **SEE ALSO** For information about creating an information management policy for a content type, see the "To configure events to audit for a content type" procedure in the previous section.

To configure events to audit for a site collection

1. On the **Site Settings** page, under **Site Collection Administration**, select **Site collection audit settings**.

2. On the **Configure Audit Settings** page, in the **Documents and Items** and **List, Libraries, and Sites** sections, select the events you want to audit, and then select **OK**.

To view an audit log report for a site collection

1. Do one of the following to open the View Auditing Reports page:

   - On the **Site Settings** page, under **Site Collection Administration**, select **Audit log reports**.

   - Display the **Compliance Details** dialog box as described earlier in this chapter, and then select **Generate audit log report**.

14

2. Select the report you want to view, to display the Customize Report page.

View Auditing Reports ⓘ

⊞ **Content Activity Reports**

⊞ **Information Management Policy Reports**

⊟ **Security And Site Settings Reports**

Auditing settings
This report shows all events that change the auditing settings of Microsoft SharePoint Foundation.

Security settings
This report shows all events that change the security configuration of Microsoft SharePoint Foundation.

⊞ **Custom Reports**

The nine audit reports are grouped in four categories

3. Enter the URL or browse to the library where you want to store the report, and then select **OK**.

4. On the **Operation completed successfully** page, select **click here to view this report**.

 TIP If the report contains no data, a Sorry, Something Went Wrong page is displayed. Select Go Back To Site to return to the site.

Skills review

In this chapter, you learned how to:

- Manage documents
- Store and manage records
- Protect data in SharePoint

Practice tasks

The practice files for these tasks are located in the SP2016SBS\Ch14 folder.

> ⚠ **IMPORTANT** You must have sufficient permissions to perform the operations involved in each practice task to complete that practice task. For more information, see Appendix A, "SharePoint 2016 user permissions and permission levels."

Manage documents

Go to your SharePoint team site, and then perform the following tasks:

1. Create a records center named **WWI Records Center**, with the description **Use this site as Wide World Importers' records repository** and a URL of **WWI_RecordsCenter**.

2. Activate the document IDs and document sets features for your site collection, if they are not already activated.

3. Turn on document IDs, if they are not already enabled.

4. Go to your SharePoint team site, upload the **WWI_Financials** Excel workbook from the practice file folder to your Documents library, and view the document ID of the file.

   > **TIP** If document IDs were not previously activated or enabled, you might have to come back later to complete this task.

5. Create a site document set content type named **Product Proposals**, with the description **Create a document set for product proposals**, and add the **WWI_ProductSheet** Word document and the **WWI_Presentation** PowerPoint presentation from the practice file folder as default content.

6. Add the **Product Proposals** document set content type to the Documents library, and then create a new **Product Proposals** document set named **2016 Oslo Bedroom Furniture**.

7. Activate the Content Organizer, and create a rule named **Holidays**, to route all Document content types whose file name begins with *Holiday* to your Documents library.

8. In your Drop Off Library, upload the **WWI_HolidayPlanner** and **HolidayPlanner** Excel workbooks from the practice file folder.

 TIP If you upload and submit files individually, they will be automatically processed by the Content Organizer. If you upload more than one file at a time, they are checked out and will not be processed. You will need to edit the properties of the files and check them in before they are processed by the Content Organizer.

The WWI_HolidayPlanner workbook should remain in the Drop Off Library, and the HolidayPlanner file should be moved to your Documents library.

 TIP If you activated any site collection or site features in this practice task, you might want to deactivate them.

Store and manage records

Go to the WWI Records Center you created in the previous set of practice tasks, and then perform the following tasks:

1. Create a document library named **Proposals**.

   TIP If you need a refresher on creating a library, see the "To create a library" procedure in Chapter 3, "Work with content in lists and libraries."

2. In the Proposals library, create a library and folder-based retention, with the description **When proposals are finalized, declare them as records**, so that they are permanently deleted **7** years from the created date.

3. Activate in-place records management.

4. Go to the Documents library in your SharePoint team site, and allow the manual declaration of records.

5. Declare the **WWI_Financials** workbook as a record, and view the compliance details of the file.

Protect data in SharePoint

Go to the top-level site of your site collection, and then perform the following tasks:

1. Activate the site policy site collection feature, if it is not already activated.

2. Create a site policy named **WWI site policy** that closes sites automatically after **1** year and deletes sites **6** months after they have been closed. Set the site collection to be read-only when closed.

3. Delete the WWI site policy, and deactivate the site policy site collection feature, if you activated it in these practice tasks.

Appendix A

SharePoint 2016 user permissions and permission levels

Microsoft SharePoint 2016 includes 33 user permissions that determine specific actions that users can perform on a SharePoint site. Permissions are grouped into permission levels. A permission level is a named collection of permissions that can be assigned to SharePoint users and groups.

Every SharePoint 2016 site provides a few default permission levels. For example, seven default permission levels are available on every team site: View Only, Read, Contribute, Edit, Design, Full Control, and Limited Access. When your site is based on a site template other than the team site template, additional default SharePoint permission levels might be available on your site. For example, three default permission levels are available on every publishing site: Restricted Read, Approve, and Manage Hierarchy. Every community site provides a Moderate permission level.

The following table lists default permission levels along with their corresponding permissions in SharePoint 2016.

Permission level	Description	Permissions included by default
Limited Access	Allows access to shared resources in the website so that users can access an item within the site. Users cannot download files. The Limited Access permission level is designed to be combined with fine-grained permissions to provide users with access to a specific list, document library, item, or document without giving users access to the entire site. Cannot be customized or deleted.	View Application Pages, Browse User Information, Use Remote Interfaces, Use Client Integration Features, Open
View Only	Enables users to view application pages. Users can download files. The View Only permission level is used for the Excel Services Viewers group.	View Application Pages, View Items, View Versions, Create Alerts, Use Self-Service Site Creation, View Pages, Browse User Information, Use Remote Interfaces, Use Client Integration Features, Open
Read	Allows read-only access to the website.	View Application Pages, Browse User Information, Use Remote Interfaces, Use Client Integration Features, Open, View Items, Open Items, View Versions, Create Alerts, Use Self-Service Site Creation, View Pages
Contribute	Allows users to create and edit items in existing lists and document libraries.	View Application Pages, Browse User Information, Use Remote Interfaces, Use Client Integration Features, Open, View Items, Open Items, View Versions, Create Alerts, Use Self-Service Site Creation, View Pages, Add Items, Edit Items, Delete Items, Delete Versions, Browse Directories, Edit Personal User Information, Manage Personal Views, Add/Remove Personal Web Parts, Update Personal Web Parts

Permission level	Description	Permissions included by default
Edit	Enables users to manage lists.	View Application Pages, Browse User Information, Use Remote Interfaces, Use Client Integration Features, Open, View Items, Open Items, View Versions, Create Alerts, Use Self-Service Site Creation, View Pages, Add Items, Edit Items, Delete Items, Delete Versions, Browse Directories, Edit Personal User Information, Manage Personal Views, Add/Remove Personal Web Parts, Update Personal Web Parts, Manage Lists
Design	Allows users to create lists and document libraries, and edit pages in the website.	View Application Pages, Browse User Information, Use Remote Interfaces, Use Client Integration Features, Open, View Items, Open Items, View Versions, Create Alerts, Use Self-Service Site Creation, View Pages, Add Items, Edit Items, Delete Items, Delete Versions, Browse Directories, Edit Personal User Information, Manage Personal Views, Add/Remove Personal Web Parts, Update Personal Web Parts Manage Lists, Override Check Out, Approve Items, Add and Customize Pages, Apply Themes and Borders, Apply Style Sheets
Full Control	Allows full control. Cannot be customized or deleted.	All permissions
Restricted Read	Allows users to view pages and documents. For publishing sites only.	View Items, Open Items, View Pages, Open
Restricted Interfaces for Translation	Allows users to open lists and folders and use remote interfaces. For publishing sites only.	Use Remote Interfaces, Open

A

Permission level	Description	Permissions included by default
Manage Hierarchy	Allows users to create sites; edit pages, list items, and documents; and change site permissions. For publishing sites only.	View Application Pages, Browse User Information, Use Remote Interfaces, Use Client Integration Features, Open, View Items, Open Items, View Versions, Create Alerts, Use Self-Service Site Creation, View Pages, Add Items, Edit Items, Delete Items, Delete Versions, Browse Directories, Edit Personal User Information, Manage Personal Views, Add/Remove Personal Web Parts, Update Personal Web Parts Manage Lists, Override Check Out, Add and Customize Pages, Manage Permissions, Enumerate Permissions, View Web Analytics Data, Create Subsite, Manage Alerts, Manage Web Site
Approve	Allows users to edit and approve pages, list items, and documents. For publishing sites only.	View Application Pages, Browse User Information, Use Remote Interfaces, Use Client Integration Features, Open, View Items, Open Items, View Versions, Create Alerts, Use Self-Service Site Creation, View Pages, Add Items, Edit Items, Delete Items, Delete Versions, Override List Behaviors, Approve Items, Browse Directories, Edit Personal User Information, Manage Personal Views, Add/Remove Personal Web Parts, Update Personal Web Parts
Moderate	Allows users to view, add, update, delete, and moderate list items and documents.	View Application Pages, Browse User Information, Use Remote Interfaces, Use Client Integration Features, Open, View Items, Open Items, View Versions, Override List Behaviors, Manage Lists, Create Alerts, Use Self-Service Site Creation, View Pages, Add Items, Edit Items, Delete Items, Delete Versions, Browse Directories, Edit Personal User Information, Manage Personal Views, Add/Remove Personal Web Parts, Update Personal Web Parts

> **TIP** In addition to using the default permission levels provided by SharePoint, you can create new permission levels that contain specific permissions, and you can change the permissions that are included in the default permission levels, with a few exceptions. Although it is not possible to remove permissions from the Limited Access and Full Control permission levels, your SharePoint administrator can make specific permission levels unavailable for the entire web application by using SharePoint Central Administration. If you are a SharePoint administrator and want to do this, do the following: in SharePoint Central Administration, on the Application Management page, select Manage Web Applications; then select your web application, select the Permission Policy button on the ribbon, and then delete the permission levels that you want to disable.

User permissions in SharePoint 2016 can be grouped into three categories according to their scope: list permissions, site permissions, and personal permissions. The following table lists user permissions in SharePoint 2016 in alphabetical order, detailing their scope, permission dependencies, and the permission levels that the user permission is included in by default.

Permission	Description	Scope	Dependent permissions	Included in these permission levels by default
Add and Customize Pages	Users can add, change, or delete HTML pages or web part pages; edit the website by using a SharePoint Foundation–compatible editor.	Site	View Items, Browse Directories, View Pages, Open	Design, Full Control, Manage Hierarchy
Add Items	Users can adds items to lists, documents to document libraries, and web discussion comments.	List	View Items, View Pages, Open	Contribute, Design, Edit, Full Control, Approve, Moderate, Manage Hierarchy
Add/Remove Personal Web Parts	Users can add or remove personal web parts on a web part page.	Personal Permissions	View Items, View Pages, Open	Contribute, Design, Edit, Full Control, Approve, Moderate, Manage Hierarchy
Apply Style Sheets	Users can apply a style sheet (.css file) to the website.	Site	View Pages, Open	Design, Full Control

A

Permission	Description	Scope	Dependent permissions	Included in these permission levels by default
Apply Themes and Borders	Users can apply a theme or borders to the entire website.	Site	View Pages, Open	Design, Full Control
Approve Items	Users can approve minor versions of list items or documents.	List	Edit Items, View Items, View Pages, Open	Design, Full Control, Approve
Browse Directories	Users can enumerate files and folders in a website by using Microsoft SharePoint Designer and Web DAV interfaces.	Site	View Pages, Open	Contribute, Design, Edit, Full Control, Approve, Moderate, Manage Hierarchy
Browse User Information	Users can view information about users of the website.	Site	Open	All
Create Alerts	Users can create email alerts.	List	View Items, View Pages, Open	Read, Contribute, Design, Edit, Full Control, Approve, Moderate, Manage Hierarchy, View Only
Create Groups	Users can create a group of users that can be used anywhere within the site collection.	Site	View Pages, Browse User Information, Open	Full Control
Create Subsites	Users can create subsites such as Team sites.	Site	View Pages, Browse User Information, Open	Full Control, Manage Hierarchy
Delete Items	Users can delete items from a list, documents from a document library, and web discussion comments in documents.	List	View Items, View Pages, Open	Contribute, Design, Edit, Full Control, Approve, Moderate, Manage Hierarchy

Permission	Description	Scope	Dependent permissions	Included in these permission levels by default
Delete Versions	Users can delete past versions of list items or documents.	List	View Items, View Versions, View Pages, Open	Contribute, Design, Edit, Full Control, Approve, Moderate, Manage Hierarchy
Edit Items	Users can edit items in lists, documents in document libraries, and web discussion comments in documents; and customize web part pages in document libraries.	List	View Items, View Pages, Open	Contribute, Design, Edit, Full Control, Approve, Moderate, Manage Hierarchy
Edit Personal User Information	Users can change their own user information, such as by adding a picture.	Site	Browse User Information, Open	Contribute, Design, Edit, Full Control, Approve, Moderate, Manage Hierarchy
Enumerate Permissions	Users can enumerate permissions in the website, list, folder, document, or list item.	Site	Browse Directories, View Pages, Browse User Information, Open	Full Control
Manage Alerts	Users can manage alerts for all users of the website.	Site	View Items, View Pages, Open	Full Control
Manage Lists	Users can create and delete lists, add or remove columns in a list, and add or remove public views of a list.	List	View Items, View Pages, Open, Manage Personal Views	Design, Edit, Full Control, Moderate, Manage Hierarchy

A

Permission	Description	Scope	Dependent permissions	Included in these permission levels by default
Manage Permissions	Users can create and change permission levels on the website, and assign permissions to users and groups.	Site	View Items, Open Items, View Versions, Browse Directories, View Pages, Enumerate Permissions, Browse User Information, Open	Full Control, Manage Hierarchy
Manage Personal Views	Users can create, change, and delete personal views of lists.	Personal Permissions	View Items, View Pages, Open	Contribute, Design, Edit, Full Control, Approve, Moderate, Manage Hierarchy
Manage Web Site	Users can perform all administration tasks and manage content for the website.	Site	View Items, Add and Customize Pages, Browse Directories, View Pages, Enumerate Permissions, Browse User Information, Open	Full Control, Manage Hierarchy
Open	Users can open a website, list, or folder to access items inside that container.	Site	None	All
Open Items	Users can view the source of documents with server-side file handlers.	List	View Items, View Pages, Open	Read, Contribute, Design, Edit, Full Control, Approve, Moderate, Manage Hierarchy, Restricted Read

Permission	Description	Scope	Dependent permissions	Included in these permission levels by default
Override List Behaviors	Users can discard the checkout of a document that is checked out to another user without saving the current changes. Users can check in a document that is checked out to another user, saving changes made by another user.	List	View Items, View Pages, Open	Design, Full Control, Approve, Moderate, Manage Hierarchy
Update Personal Web Parts	Users can update web parts to display personalized information.	Personal Permissions	View Items, View Pages, Open	Contribute, Design, Edit, Full Control, Approve, Moderate, Manage Hierarchy
Use Client Integration Features	Users can use features that start client applications; without this permission, users must work on documents locally and then upload their changes.	Site	Use Remote Interfaces, Open	Read, Contribute, Design, Edit, Full Control, Approve, Moderate, Manage Hierarchy, Limited Access, View Only
Use Remote Interfaces	Users can use Simple Object Access Protocol (SOAP), Web DAV, or SharePoint Designer interfaces to access the website.	Site	Open	Read, Contribute, Design, Edit, Full Control, Approve, Moderate, Manage Hierarchy, Limited Access, View Only, Restricted Interfaces for Translation

A

Permission	Description	Scope	Dependent permissions	Included in these permission levels by default
Use Self-Service Site Creation	Users can create a website by using Self-Service Site Creation.	Site	View Pages, Browse User Information, Open	Read, Contribute, Design, Edit, Full Control, Approve, Moderate, Manage Hierarchy, View Only
View Application Pages	Users can view forms, views, and application pages; and enumerate lists.	List	Open	Read, Contribute, Design, Edit, Full Control, Approve, Moderate, Manage Hierarchy, Limited Access, View Only
View Items	Users can view items in lists, documents in document libraries, and web discussion comments.	List	View Pages, Open	Read, Contribute, Design, Edit, Full Control, Approve, Moderate, Manage Hierarchy, Restricted Read, View Only
View Pages	Users can view pages in a website.	Site	Open	Read, Contribute, Design, Edit, Full Control, Approve, Moderate, Manage Hierarchy, Restricted Read, View Only
View Versions	Users can view past versions of list items or documents.	List	View Items, Open Items, View Pages, Open	Read, Contribute, Design, Edit, Full Control, Approve, Moderate, Manage Hierarchy
View Web Analytics Data	Users can views reports on website usage.	Site	View Pages, Open	Full Control, Manage Hierarchy

Index

About the authors

Olga Londer is a Cloud Solution Architect at Microsoft. She works on global projects that implement Microsoft cloud technologies for large enterprise customers. Her particular focus is Microsoft Azure and SharePoint products and solutions. She is an author of several books on Microsoft SharePoint and Internet Information Server (IIS), a winner of the British Computer Society IT Trainer award, and a frequent speaker at numerous conferences. For a number of years, Olga was a content lead for pan-European Microsoft technical conferences, such as TechEd Europe. Before joining Microsoft in 2004, Olga was a Microsoft Most Valuable Professional (MVP) in SharePoint and IIS, and worked for QA Ltd, a leading IT training and consulting company in the United Kingdom, where she led many SharePoint enterprise projects for blue-chip clients. Olga is based in London, United Kingdom.

Penelope Coventry, M.Sc., is a 10-year recipient of the Microsoft Most Valuable Professional (MVP) Office Servers and Services award, with the MCSE: SharePoint 2013 and MCITP: SharePoint Administration 2010 certifications. She is an author and consultant based in the United Kingdom, with more than 30 years of industry experience. Penny has authored or co-authored more than 10 SharePoint-related books, including *Exploring Microsoft SharePoint 2013: New Features and Functions*, *Microsoft SharePoint 2013 Inside Out*, *Microsoft SharePoint 2013 Step by Step*, and *Microsoft SharePoint Designer 2010 Step by Step*.

Penny has spoken at a number of conferences, including TechEd North America, and SharePoint and Office 365 conferences, in addition to SharePoint Saturdays and user groups in the United States, Canada, Australia, New Zealand, Germany, Netherlands, Belgium, Hungary, Slovenia, Croatia, Sweden, Norway, and the United Kingdom. She is also a keen supporter of the UK SharePoint User Group #SUGUK community. Penny has worked with SharePoint since 2001, and when she's not writing, she works as the Product Specialist for a number of clients and as a trainer at Combined Knowledge.

Now that you've read the book...

Tell us what you think!

Was it useful?
Did it teach you what you wanted to learn?
Was there room for improvement?

Let us know at https://aka.ms/tellpress

Your feedback goes directly to the staff at Microsoft Press,
and we read every one of your responses. Thanks in advance!

Microsoft